THE HERERO GENOCIDE

War and Genocide

General Editors: Omer Bartov, Brown University; A. Dirk Moses, University of North Carolina at Chapel Hill

In recent years there has been a growing interest in the study of war and genocide, not from a traditional military history perspective, but within the framework of social and cultural history. This series offers a forum for scholarly works that reflect these new approaches.

The Berghahn series War and Genocide *has immeasurably enriched the English-language scholarship available to scholars and students of genocide and, in particular, the Holocaust.* —**Totalitarian Movements and Political Religions**

Recent volumes:

Volume 31
The Herero Genocide: War, Emotion, and Extreme Violence in Colonial Namibia
Matthias Häussler

Volume 30
Voices on War and Genocide: Three Accounts of the World Wars in a Galician Town
Edited by Omer Bartov

Volume 29
A Sad Fiasco: Colonial Concentration Camps in Southern Africa, 1900–1908
Jonas Kreienbaum

Volume 28
The Holocaust in Bohemia and Moravia: Czech Initiatives, German Policies, Jewish Responses
Wolf Gruner

Volume 27
Probing the Limits of Categorization: The Bystander in Holocaust History
Edited by Christina Morina and Krijn Thijs

Volume 26
Let Them Not Return: Sayfo—The Genocide Against the Assyrian, Syriac, and Chaldean Christians in the Ottoman Empire
Edited by David Gaunt, Naures Atto, and Soner O. Barthoma

Volume 25
Daily Life in the Abyss: Genocide Diaries, 1915–1918
Vahé Tachjian

Volume 24
Microhistories of the Holocaust
Edited by Claire Zalc and Tal Bruttmann

Volume 23
The Making of the Greek Genocide: Contested Memories of the Ottoman Greek Catastrophe
Erik Sjöberg

Volume 22
Genocide on Settler Frontiers: When Hunter-Gatherers and Commercial Stock Farmers Clash
Edited by Mohamed Adhikari

For a full volume listing, please see the series page on our website:
http://berghahnbooks.com/series/war-and-genocide

THE HERERO GENOCIDE

War, Emotion, and Extreme Violence in Colonial Namibia

Matthias Häussler

Translated from the German by Elizabeth Janik

berghahn
NEW YORK · OXFORD
www.berghahnbooks.com

Published in 2021 by
Berghahn Books
www.berghahnbooks.com

English-language edition
© 2021, 2024 Berghahn Books
First paperback edition published in 2024

German-language edition
© 2018 Velbrück Wissenschaft, Weilerswist

Originally published in German as
Der Genozid an den Herero

The translation of this work was funded by Geisteswissenschaften International—
Translation Funding for Work in the Humanities and Social Sciences from Germany,
a joint initiative of the Fritz Thyssen Foundation, the German Federal Foreign Office,
the collecting society VG WORT, and the Börsenverein des Deutschen Buchhandels
(German Publishers & Booksellers Association).

All rights reserved. Except for the quotation of short passages
for the purposes of criticism and review, no part of this book
may be reproduced in any form or by any means, electronic or
mechanical, including photocopying, recording, or any information
storage and retrieval system now known or to be invented,
without written permission of the publisher.

Library of Congress Cataloging-in-Publication Data

Names: Häussler, Matthias, author. | Janik, Elizabeth, translator.
Title: The Herero Genocide: War, Emotion, and Extreme Violence in Colonial
   Namibia / Matthias Häussler; translated from the German by Elizabeth Janik.
Other titles: Genozid an den Herero. English | War and Genocide; v. 31.
Description: English-language edition. | New York: Berghahn, 2021. | Series: War
   and Genocide; volume 31 | "Originally published in German as Der Genozid
   an den Herero"—Title page verso. | Includes bibliographical references and
   index.
Identifiers: LCCN 2021004790 (print) | LCCN 2021004791 (ebook) |
   ISBN 9781800730236 (hardback) | ISBN 9781800730243 (ebook)
Subjects: LCSH: Genocide—Namibia—History—20th century. | Namibia—
   History—Herero Revolt, 1904–1907. | Germany—Colonies—Africa—
   History—20th century. | Germany—Foreign relations—Namibia. | Namibia—
   Foreign relations—Germany.
Classification: LCC DT1618 .H3813 2021 (print) | LCC DT1618 (ebook) |
   DDC 968.8102—dc23
LC record available at https://lccn.loc.gov/2021004790
LC ebook record available at https://lccn.loc.gov/2021004791

British Library Cataloguing in Publication Data

A catalogue record for this book is available from the British Library.

ISBN 978–1-80073-023-6 hardback
ISBN 978-1-80539-151-7 paperback
ISBN 978-1-80539-563-8 epub
ISBN 978–1-80073-024-3 web pdf

https://doi.org/10.3167/ 9781800730236

For Isabella and James

Contents

Preface	viii
Acknowledgments	ix
Introduction	1
Chapter 1 Settlers, Herero, and the Spiral of Violence	30
Chapter 2 The Strategic Horizon: Leutwein—Metropole—Trotha	76
Chapter 3 The Campaign	115
Chapter 4 Small Warfare and Brutalization	199
Chapter 5 From the Regime of the Camps to "Native Policy"	240
Conclusion	258
Bibliography	269
Index	291

Preface

The original, German-language version of this book was published in 2018. Positions can change over time, and this is also true of my work on genocide. I am increasingly convinced that a definition of genocide that is limited to the physical destruction of a group's members may be too narrow, particularly with respect to the original intentions of Raphael Lemkin, who coined the term. There is no longer any doubt in my mind that the groups protected by the Convention on the Prevention and Punishment of the Crime of Genocide are social bodies that can be destroyed in ways other the extermination of their members. My original use of the term focused on the (attempted) physical destruction of these groups. This understanding of "genocide" may shine through in some passages. Since this book is a translation of an existing work, I have not undertaken fundamental revisions. This is a useful opportunity, however, to place my remarks in appropriate perspective. A primary goal of this book is to define the exterminatory phase of the campaign against the Herero—its beginning, its logic, and its end—and to distinguish this phase of planned physical destruction from other phases, which had their own, not necessarily less destructive, logics. Then and now, I believe that such differentiation is essential to understanding the process of escalation. I ask the reader not to ascribe too much significance to passages that may appear to equate genocide with physical annihilation.

Matthias Häussler, April 2021

Acknowledgments

I owe my greatest debt of thanks to Trutz von Trotha, who patiently encouraged and supported the completion of this manuscript in every possible way. I regret that he was unable to witness its publication. He was much more to me than only a teacher, mentor, or boss. This book would not exist without him.

I extend special thanks to the Deutsche Forschungsgemeinschaft (DFG) for its generous support of the research project that became the basis for this book. A postdoctoral fellowship from the Seminar für Sozialwissenschaften at the Universität Siegen allowed to me write a first draft of this manuscript. I completed the work as a visiting scholar at the Hamburger Institut für Sozialforschung (HIS), and also as a scholar at the Hamburger Stiftung zur Förderung von Wissenschaft und Kultur (WIKU), for which I am deeply grateful to Jan Philipp Reemtsma.

I am indebted to Thomas Klatetzki for his many helpful suggestions about the direction of this work, although—at least from his perspective—it may have ultimately assumed a more historical character. I thank Aram Mattioli for his efforts and willingness to take on and evaluate a project from another discipline. Such enthusiasm is by no means self-evident in an increasingly bureaucratized scholarly landscape, and its value cannot be underestimated. I owe thanks (once again) to Bernd Greiner, who accepted the role as my second evaluator without a word of complaint. I consider myself fortunate that our paths crossed in Hamburg.

I thank the Trotha family for granting me access to Lothar von Trotha's handwritten war diary, and for approaching my work with great interest, without suspicion or mistrust.

Through my research I have not only met interesting colleagues, but also friends. My many months in Klein Windhoek would have been unthinkable without Christine Hardung, who was working on a related project about the Oorlam-Nama. Irrespective of other privations, my time in Namibia became a truly enjoyable experience that I would never want to have missed. I can hardly bestow a greater compliment.

I met Andreas Stucki at an early stage of my work on colonialism. It should suffice to say that if we had not met, I do not know where I would be today. I presumably would not have come to Hamburg, and so I would not have met Klaas Voss; this alone warrants my gratitude. Andreas Stucki and Klaas Voss have read chapters of this work and offered their expert comments and criticism. Any deficiencies that remain, of course, are my own.

I got to know Jürg Helbling at an early stage of my work on the Herero. I learned a great deal from him, and without his engagement and interest in my work—for which I am very grateful—I may never have come to Lucerne.

Over the course of my research, I met Andreas Eckl and Wolfram Hartmann, who were always encouraging and supported my work in a variety of ways. This is especially meaningful to me, as I have learned so much from their own work.

Unsurprisingly, Roman Bedau was a patient and informative companion on my last trip to Botswana and Namibia.

A project such as this cannot be realized without the support of many colleagues. I received helpful suggestions from Dag Henrichsen at the beginning of my research, and Johann Müller provided detailed information about the archival holdings in Gaborone. Werner Hillebrecht, who was then the director of the National Archives in Windhoek, assisted my day-to-day work at the archives and consistently drew my attention to relevant sources.

I am further grateful to Mihran Dabag and Medardus Brehl for including the German version of this text in the Genozid und Gedächtnis series at the Bochumer Institut für Diaspora- und Genozidforschung, where I also presented and discussed parts of my work. I am also indebted to Marietta Thien and Nino Laufens at Velbrück whose support contributed a great deal to the German edition's success. My further thanks go to Chris Chappell and the entire team at Berghahn Books for their kind assistance, and also to A. Dirk Moses and Omer Bartov for including my book in their War and Genocide series. I would particularly like to thank Elizabeth Janik for lending me her "native" voice and putting my thoughts into delightful scholarly prose.

Finally, I thank the student assistants in Trotha's department—namely, Kora Hoffmann, Anna Meyer zu Schwabedissen, Oliver Hohenschue, Stephan Novak, Ann-Kathrin Schwab, and Melanie Jäger, who made my work easier, and, of course, Anna Samlowitz, who quietly pulled many strings.

I thank my mother for her enduring support, and, above all, I thank my wife, Yeşim, who has long shared the burdens of my work, offered energetic and unconditional support, and, finally, given me a daughter, Giada Elâ. If even Goethe had trouble finding the words to express genuine gratitude, this is certainly true for me.

Introduction

In January 1904, conflict erupted between Germans and Bantu-speaking Herero in central German South-West Africa (SWA), present-day Namibia. The "Herero uprising,"[1] as it became known, touched off numerous wars across the German colony.[2] Once groups of Khoikhoi-speaking Nama and Oorlam in the south also took arms in the second half of the year, South-West Africa descended irretrievably into war.[3] Although the hostilities were formally declared over on 31 March 1907, and the last concentration camps for "prisoners of war" closed on 27 January 1908, neither of these measures ushered in genuine peace.

Colonial wars were "decidedly violent," almost without exception.[4] The colonial powers generally agreed that provisions of international law that were intended to curb violence did not apply to conflicts with supposedly "primitive" societies.[5] In this sense, the title of Lawrence James's 1985 book about the British campaigns in Africa, *The Savage Wars*, is certainly apt. Even so, the wars of "pacification" that Imperial Germany conducted against the Herero, Oorlam, and Nama in SWA between 1904 and 1908 were exceptional in many respects. The Herero people today still remember the war as a devastating and traumatic experience. Combat, flight, internment, and forced labor claimed tens of thousands of victims.[6] German colonists, on the other hand, actually celebrated their cruel treatment of the Herero.[7] The German campaign left behind legacies that are still visible today, more than one hundred years after the end of German colonial rule.[8] The war decimated and weakened the groups that had once dominated the region to such an extent that the Nama and Oorlam in particular still remain on the margins of Namibian society today. The "native policy" of the postwar era, which anticipated some aspects of South African apartheid, added insult to injury.[9]

The "pacification" of SWA ushered in a humanitarian catastrophe. Today's historiographical debates about German South-West Africa focus on the issue of genocide—and rightly so, from a moral and political perspective. But this was not always the case. Humanitarian considerations played a minor, if any, role for most European observers at the time. The racist and Social Darwinist spirit of the era meant that even the extermination of entire peoples could be seen as a "natural," and not particularly upsetting, occurrence. But even setting humanitarian considerations aside, the situation in SWA was catastrophic. The outbreak of war and the apparent lack of alternatives to the brutal subjugation of the Herero sealed the failure of the "peace" policy that Theodor Leutwein had pursued for years.[10] The moniker for Leutwein's policy was certainly a euphemism, but it did show that Imperial Germany had attempted to avoid the military conquest of its colony for as long as possible. The war with the Herero was only the beginning. Upon arriving in the colony, the hastily dispatched German troops proceeded with such severity against their opponent, hardly distinguishing between friend and foe, that even the allied Witbooi-Oorlam rebelled and took up arms against their colonial masters.[11] The conflict continued to expand and became the "most murderous" war that Germany had yet waged, resulting in the death of "every fifth man."[12] The financial burdens were so extreme that the budget debate led to the dissolution of the Reichstag and the so-called "Hottentot elections" of 1907.[13]

Worse, these expenditures produced no real operational success. Despite its utmost efforts, Imperial Germany—a "victory culture" par excellence—was unable to subdue supposedly "primitive" opponents, who sometimes numbered only in the low hundreds.[14] More soldiers came to the colony during the first year of the war than the total number of whites in all years thereafter, until the end of German rule in 1915. In the end, it was raw strategic superiority—the steady influx of manpower and material—that gave the Germans the upper hand to defeat their opponents. Their methods were sometimes undistinguished. They chased the famous Bondelswarts military leader Jacob Morenga into British territory, where he was ultimately killed by Cape Police, and they bought peace with the Oorlam leader Simon Kooper by offering him a pension. Reports from soldiers and other eyewitnesses clearly show that "cruelty and acts of brutality"—supposedly out of character for German soldiers ("because what isn't allowed, can't be")[15]—occurred on a daily basis in SWA.[16]

Despite the vicious fighting, the territory remained "unpacified" for years. Even after the war in the colony was formally declared over on 31 March 1907, the British major Wade (who was assigned to German headquarters as an observer) reported to his superiors that roving Herero continued to pose a threat, although this could not be stated in official reports.[17] Unlimited warfare proved to be expensive for the colony and its future by destroying its resources, especially Herero labor and cattle.[18] Many observers must have questioned whether colonial rule was worth the utter devastation that it wrought. The war that had been set into motion defied any cost-benefit analysis.

The wars of "pacification" upset the Kaiser so greatly that they soon were no longer allowed to be mentioned in his presence.[19] But even beyond the Imperial court, no one seemed to have been satisfied with the outcome of the war. Officers and colonial authorities regarded the military's performance as deficient,[20] while missionaries deplored the excessive violence. Critics of colonialism grew louder, and settlers continued to grouse and complain.[21]

The esteemed Prussian/German war machine fell far short of expectations, although its organization and performance had been regarded as exemplary worldwide. With the utmost effort and sacrifice, it obtained results that satisfied almost no one—indeed, that almost no one foresaw.

There was an astonishing discrepancy between war aims and the means that were employed to achieve them, on the one hand, and the actual outcome of the war, on the other. This discrepancy provides the point of departure for the following study, which—in contrast to prevailing narratives—tells a story of misfires and setbacks, and situates the genocide of the Herero within it. Genocide arose from failures in planning and became the tragic climax in a "campaign of disappointments," as the officer W. E. Montague characterized the British war against the Zulu in 1879.[22] This interpretation of the war and genocide is by no means typical of scholarship on Namibia, but is seen more often in colonial revisionist or apologetic texts—part of an attempt to relativize the wars of "pacification" or to deny the genocide outright.[23] By contrast, I embrace this interpretation as a point of departure for explaining the genocidal escalation.

Three broad themes are central to my investigation of the Herero genocide: *complexity*, which sharpens and refines familiar narratives; *racism*, an ideology that was part of the New Imperialism and essential to the escalation in SWA; and finally, *emotion*. I introduce these themes below, followed by an overview of the book's organization and a discussion of sources.

Complexity

My analysis of colonialism and the wars of "pacification" that were integral to its establishment and entrenchment departs from conventional approaches.[24] Instead, I treat colonial rule as a complex open system that depends upon the interplay of its constituent elements, evolving in unforeseen ways and constantly giving rise to new structures.[25] Open systems must adapt to their environments, as Sidney Dekker explains.[26] Many of these adaptations are not centrally coordinated, but are instead driven by peripheral actors with particular interests and highly limited information. Even seemingly insignificant actions can combine with other, unanticipated factors and set processes into motion with unforeseeable results. This is the essence of complexity. Complex systems are constructs that transcend their individual parts; complexity necessarily characterizes systems, not their components. Individual components cannot comprehend a system in its entirety, and they likewise cannot foresee all of the consequences of their actions. Instead, components act locally, with limited knowledge, mostly governed by the narrower interests of their immediate surroundings. Complexity arises from networks of local relationships and interactions, and these networks can lead to unforeseeable—and sometimes disastrous—consequences. Even innocuous actions can have dire consequences, which is why there can be such disproportion between cause and effect.[27]

My approach is not altogether new to genocide studies. Jacques Sémelin, Michael Mann, Mark Levene, Martin Shaw, and Christian Gerlach have anticipated important aspects of this approach by criticizing the teleological and deterministic tendencies of conventional genocide studies; instead, they understand mass violence as a process that is characterized by contingency.[28] There are, of course, unavoidable pitfalls in dealing with a case that is more than one hundred years old—beginning with the missing records of the South-West African Schutztruppe, or "protection force," which were lost over the course of the two world wars. Thus, an empirically based, detailed analysis of the process of violence is not a simple undertaking. Complexity is a heuristic principle for gauging the gradual escalation of violence in a multifaceted situation. Above all, it means that this study does not limit itself to the search for a single cause or origin, but also considers systemic relations. Wherever possible, I take the entire spectrum of actors, or groups of actors, and their mutual relationships into account. Because complex systems are not coordinated centrally, from the "top down," but are defined by the interactions of their individual components, the focus of my work likewise shifts downward from the "top" to the "bottom."

Before I discuss how colonial rule in German South-West Africa can be understood as a complex system, I will briefly address the characteristic weaknesses of conventional, or "less complex," depictions.

"Genocide" is originally a legal term. Legal authorities seek those who are guilty, and genocide studies support the search. Genocide scholars sometimes appear to be driven less by a desire for knowledge and more by the demands of international law, as they work to build a plausible "case" within the relevant legal norms. Legal summations of this kind tend to follow their own rules, selectively presenting events so that a case corresponds to definitions from the Genocide Convention of 1948, and glossing over other details that do not support this aim.[29] Given the gravity of the crimes in question, it is easy to see how guilty parties are made out to be "monsters" in certain respects.

In the mid-1960s, East German historian Horst Drechsler published *Südwestafrika unter deutscher Kolonialherrschaft*—the first critical, comprehensive portrait of German colonialism in SWA, notwithstanding its Marxist slant. He was the first expert to describe the wars of "pacification" against the Herero and Nama (-Oorlam) as genocide.[30] It is no exaggeration to say that his book, which was translated into multiple languages, shaped a narrative that has remained influential many years later.[31] Drechsler's intent was to expose the particularly aggressive and criminal character of "German imperialism," which he believed was still alive in what was then West Germany.[32] He depicted the driving force of imperialism as an impersonal abstraction, even while ascribing to it the very human capacity of devising criminal strategies—as well as demonic powers to put these strategies into action.[33] Recent studies are more nuanced, and also more personal. They identify Lieutenant General Lothar von Trotha as a key perpetrator; his command marked the beginning of the genocidal phase in the campaign against the Herero.[34] Jeremy Sarkin, by contrast, assigns particular blame to Kaiser Wilhelm II, although his work otherwise resembles Drechsler's in many respects.[35]

Regardless of whom these studies identify as main offenders, a common problem is their emphasis on individual actors, to the neglect of other factors. Worse, these studies distort the actual course of events by imposing a predetermined structure onto their "case."

Before proceeding further, some definitions are in order. According to the Genocide Convention of 1948, genocide is defined, on the one hand, by specific acts that comprise the "physical element" (*actus reus*) of genocide.[36] In addition, genocide involves the "special intent" (*dolus specialis*) "to destroy, in whole or in part, that national, ethnical, racial or religious group, as such."[37] These acts already may be punishable by law, but only *as genocide* if this "special intent" can be proven. Thus, genocidal intent—and being able to prove it—is decisive. Although furnishing legal proof may not be difficult, and in some circumstances this proof is self-evident because of the nature of the acts committed, establishing proof so dominates genocide studies that they frequently overstate their claims. Case studies tend to establish genocidal intent early on, making implementation seem almost inevitable.[38] Historical events are thereby reduced to a sequence of predetermined steps. Drechsler goes so far as to stylize even the most obvious failures of the German war machine as planned successes, making "German imperialism" seem demonic or even omnipotent. In Drechsler's view, the entire German colonial project drove toward a single telos from the very beginning—the extermination of indigenous peoples.[39] More recent scholarship also establishes genocidal intent early on, if not as early as Drechsler, and at least struggles to identify setbacks for the German war machine—which underscores how nonintuitive it can be to tell the history of the campaign as a history of failure. Because the scope of these studies is often modest, they tend to smooth over or compress the course of events, and neglect to differentiate between phases or groups of historical actors. This heightens the impression of a seamless course of events.[40]

A further point to consider is how remarks that seem to reveal Trotha's racist and exterminatory motivations are ordinarily invoked by those who seek to prove genocidal intent.[41] Such remarks can be taken out of their original context and made to fit an ideological profile, which provides the basis for explaining that Trotha's measures actually sought to eliminate the Herero as a group.[42] Because (so the argument goes) Trotha was a "monster" with racist and exterminatory intent, the goal of his violent practices was to exterminate the Herero. In fact, Trotha's letters are full of bloodthirsty, contemptuous remarks—but what exactly does this explain?[43] A closer look often reveals that supposed revelations of Trotha's mindset are highly situation-dependent and tailored to a specific audience. When Trotha addressed certain actors, for example, he may have been trying to compensate for setbacks, or to mask the feelings of powerlessness that they caused. This suggests that such revelations, taken alone, explain very little—and that they must be more deeply explained. It mattered, of course, that the commander-in-chief's intellectual horizons were more deeply colored by Social Darwinism than that of his predecessor, and that he saw indigenous labor as expendable in a settler colony. A commander-in-chief who did not hold similar views might have acted differently in certain situations. But even apart from such considerations, we still have to explain when and how these patterns of thought were activated and translated into action. We would do well to remember that there are always gaps between imagination and intent, intent and planning, and planning and execution. In some circumstances, intentions can be realized only if an appropriate opportunity arises, which in turn depends on an array of factors beyond the control of individual actors. In sum, the "Why?" question about the motivations of perpetrators can be answered only with a detour through the "How?" question—that is, by reconstructing events in a detailed way and differentiating between actors and periods of time.[44] This is the work of this book.[45]

A seamless course of events is hardly plausible because Germans and Herero were at war with one another in a conflict that was evenly matched for some time.[46] This means that we should speak of *interaction*—even in the genocidal phase, which was characterized by an increasingly lopsided balance of power. Interactions develop dynamics of their own that cannot be fully anticipated, transcending the intentions and expectations of all sides. This is especially true of warlike interactions, which are notoriously difficult to predict.[47] Genocides are not one-sided events, but are codetermined by the actions of victims—an observation that has led Martin Shaw to call for an end to one-sided depictions of perpetrators and their intentions, and greater attention to the social dimensions of genocidal violence. This call has gone unheeded, not only by Drechsler.[48] If genocides are to be understood as interactions, then reconstructions that depict only the execution of perpetrators' intentions and plans are necessarily one-sided and insufficient.

Depictions that present a seamless, one-sided flow of events and that focus on main offenders tacitly assume that these events were determined from the top down—as if what was ordered from "above" was carried out "below," and what happened "below" was prescribed from "above."[49] More recent scholarship, generally about other cases, has emphasized how peripheral actors influenced the flow of events and even central decision-making processes.[50] Thus, Jacques Sémelin asserts that extreme violence can be deciphered only when it is observed simultaneously "from above" (the perspective of high-ranking decision-makers) *as well as* "from below" (subaltern perpetrators on site).[51] Members of the latter group are rarely compliant instruments of their superiors, but instead help to determine the momentum and character of the processes in question.[52] We need not dwell on details here. Most significant in this context is that existing scholarship on SWA has remained largely untouched by these developments, continuing to search for (main) offenders. Seeking to prove genocidal intent, these works usually show that the genocide definition has been met *and* surpassed. They overstate their case by disregarding whatever upsets the search for proof, by artificially limiting the field of actors under observation, and by compressing, "rationalizing," and smoothing over events. In short, conventional studies are tailored to a simple, linear system—or more accurately, they tailor the case of SWA to correspond to this system.

To what extent can we speak of colonial rule in SWA as a complex system? When the campaign against the Herero did not go according to plan, leading to outcomes that satisfied no one,[53] one reason was that events were not as determined by "top-down," central control as is usually assumed.[54] The "utopia of statehood"[55] may have informed all modern colonial endeavors to a greater or lesser degree, but most often only as a prescription or a counterfactual ideal. At no time did a strong central authority exist in German South-West Africa. It is true that settlement here was initiated later than elsewhere, coordinated "from above" (that is, by a comparatively authoritarian state),[56] but we should not overstate this distinction. Although the colonial state appeared to be an extension of its metropolitan counterpart, each represented a fundamentally different "order of violence."[57] Within Germany, the state held a monopoly on the use of force, but overseas it was one actor among many in the political arena. In this hybrid system of sovereignty, the state (especially before 1904) mediated between settlers and the autochthonous grandees with whom it held fragile alliances.[58] The settlers cannot be considered "citizens" or "civilians" in a traditional sense because they saw themselves as the vanguard of conquest, or even "race war." The colonial state was a weak state—unable and unwilling to check the privatization of violence by settlers and soldiers. An arrangement of power that I call "despotism by the white colonizing class" coalesced behind its back. The colonial state was not meaningless or irrelevant to the settlers, but—in contrast to the metropolitan authoritarian state—its functions were largely reduced to provisioning, military defense, and regulating colonial society's internal affairs.

Before 1904, uprisings in SWA were local affairs that attracted little attention in the German metropole. The governor, who was also commander of the colonial forces, acted more or less at his own discretion. But after January 1904, when Herero raids cost 123 white lives and sparked public outrage in Germany, Berlin became more and more involved in colonial affairs. This shift brought issues to the fore that had not previously played a role. Thus, securing colonial rule was no longer sufficient; now great power prestige was at stake. The situation grew more complex over the course of the war.

The field of state actors splintered into multiple conflicting groups. A divide opened up between metropole and colony, which was apparent in the differing views of the uprising held by functionaries in SWA and in Germany, as well as in the differing strategies that flowed from these divergent assessments. The long-serving colonial officers known as "old Africans" had previously served mostly as administrators, and this was reflected in their habitus and style of waging war. They felt at least some social responsibility toward the colony and its population[59]—unlike the metropolitan officers who came to South-West Africa only because of the war, and who increasingly shaped the course of events. As experts in the use of force, the latter group distanced themselves from the established colonial officers, seeing themselves as the actual experts in the arena of war. Civil servants, in turn, defined themselves in opposition to the metropolitan officers; their mission was to reestablish a peaceful order after years of military dictatorship and unfettered violence. In short, the "pacification" of South-West Africa was defined by opposing interests—state/private, metropole/colony, and military/civilian.

Extreme violence arose from the tensions between heterogeneous, and sometimes antagonistic, forces. Its escalation should be understood as a gradual process that involved relations between many different historical actors, each of whom were pursuing their own goals and interests—sometimes with a limited perspective and obeying their own logic. These diverse interactions produced new, not entirely predictable constellations that extended beyond the actual intentions of the actors involved. Violence did not have a single author, but many different ones.[60]

The orientation around complex systems frees us from the usual constraints of focusing on main offenders, an approach that neglects too many other considerations. It also redirects our attention to the broader spectrum of actors who shaped the process of violence in one way or another. It is true that Trotha held considerable power and autonomy as the commander-in-chief, and that another leader might have taken the campaign in a different, less devastating direction, especially after initial plans failed. It is a mistake, however, to limit the question of genocide by identifying Trotha as *the* cause. Such an approach neglects, for example, that Trotha was only one candidate for a strategic program that was essentially already in place. Violence and cruelty toward indigenous people had been normalized well before Trotha's arrival in the colony, and they continued to inform daily life there after he left. Although he held special authority and shaped the course of the war like no other single person, he was also one of many actors who enabled the exercise of violence against indigenous people. The orientation around complexity counterbalances the exaggerated "intentionalism" of genocide studies in general, and studies of South-West Africa in particular, which are often teleological or deterministic in their reconstruction of events. Finally, the orientation around complexity heightens our awareness of the limited control that individual actors hold over broader processes.

Racism

The long-serving colonial governor Theodor Leutwein reported back to Berlin that the settlers did not shrink even from murder and manslaughter (*Mord und Totschlag*) because they saw the Herero as an "inferior race."[61] Elsewhere, Leutwein noted that assaults against the Herero went unpunished because judicial authorities were motivated by the same "racial hatred" as perpetrators. His remarks underscore the fundamental importance of racism in colonial society.[62] Racism shaped all social relations in the colony, as we will see in multiple contexts. Here, I would like to emphasize a particular aspect of this racism: normalizing deviance. In his correspondence with superiors in Berlin, Leutwein did not ignore how *Mord und Totschlag* represented—or at least, should have represented—acts of deviance. White subjects were not allowed to do whatever they pleased, yet they escaped prosecution for even the most serious crimes. This points to the normalization of deviance, a process that Sidney Dekker has identified as central to the onset of numerous catastrophes.[63]

Racism provided the foundation for these normalizing processes. Racism was no mere side effect of colonial socialization; rather, it defined relations between colonizers and the colonized in a deep-seated way.[64] The era of German colonialism occurred at the height of what might be called "race-based racism" (*Rassenrassismus*).[65] This presumed that humanity was comprised of different subspecies, or races, which were defined by certain biological and cultural characteristics (some of which were superior to others).[66] These differences provided the basis for establishing a hierarchy of humans, which could be used to justify existing relationships of power and exploitation.[67] Tino Plümecke sees the remarkable expansion of the discourse of race as part of the broad social changes that contributed to European modernity.[68] On the one hand, intercultural contacts multiplied and intensified as globalization accelerated under the banner of colonialism. On the other, modern self-awareness (leading to the postulates of freedom and equality) heightened the need to justify practices of domination overseas. Racism went hand in hand with colonial expansion as a justification for conquest, exploitation, and destruction. Colonial expansion simultaneously strengthened and gave shape to racism.[69] The proponents of "race-based racism" constructed groups of humans ("races") on the basis of supposedly natural differences, arranging them hierarchically so that their own group was at the top, with the rest of humanity underneath. Alongside Social Darwinism, which "naturalized" and de-ethicized politics and history,[70] this racism reached its historical zenith in the era of the New Imperialism. The balance of power shifted in favor of the industrialized colonial powers to such an extent that they were able to divvy up the last remaining "blank spots" on the globe.

Colonial rulers liked to see themselves as servants of a "civilizing mission"—which meant that they accepted, in principle, that indigenous peoples could be civilized, and that the divide separating colonizers from colonized could eventually be overcome.[71] Such pronouncements often had very little to do with actual governance, however, and we should be cautious of taking them too literally. Even the South-West African settler newspapers, which rarely minced words, did not suggest that "natives" could not be Christianized. The newspapers did, however, propose that Christianization might take "centuries,"[72] and that in the meantime Africans ought to be put to work in service to whites. As such, Christian instruction and education for Africans was unnecessary, and possibly even detrimental.[73] This shows that there were ways to exploit Africans ruthlessly without denying them the capacity for "civilization" altogether, and also that the "civilizing mission" was often empty rhetoric, cloaking colonial practices rooted in discrimination and segregation, exploitation, and violence. The high-minded concept of "assimilation," which long informed French colonial policy, was essentially just another instrument of racist discrimination. It constantly placed new demands on colonized peoples in order to keep them at bay.[74] Regardless of what the immediate relationship between colonial masters and colonial subjects looked like, it was always characterized by a fundamental difference that could not be overcome,[75] and this difference was essentially racist.

Racism was ubiquitous, but it did not always lead immediately to extreme violence. Teleological depictions too often draw a continuous line between racism as a negative predisposition toward "others" and racism as a system of extermination, as Pierre-André Taguieff laments.[76] The English, French, Portuguese, and others also claimed African territories in this era, with attitudes that were hardly less racist than the Germans. They also confronted rebellions and put them down brutally—but exterminatory campaigns remained an exception. There is no question that racism gave German settlers and soldiers (the "violent few," as Randall Collins describes them[77]) a motive to humiliate, injure, or kill Africans. Racism also encouraged many officials and bystanders to look away or ignore these transgressions. Racism expressed itself not only in direct actions taken to harm the physical and psychological integrity of colonized people, but also in complementary modes of behavior such as neglect and avoidance—forms of "desocialization" that can be just as injurious as open hostility.[78] Whites were at best indifferent to the fate of indigenous people because of the unbridgeable distance that they kept between themselves and the "natives." Even serious crimes could be tolerated within the shadow of this indifference.

Public discourse in this era shows us that Africans came into view only as *means* (to borrow Kantian terminology), never as *ends in themselves*. This was true even for protagonists who lobbied on the Africans' behalf. Advocates of limited warfare pointed only to the economic damages that the loss of African labor would bring. The "value" of Africans was measured solely by their usefulness to others, not according to any intrinsic humanity. Reichstag delegates who questioned the motivations of indigenous resistance, let alone whether such resistance was justified, drew only scorn and laughter in the assembly.[79] Since almost no one framed their arguments on ethical grounds, a robust opposition to radical military strategies never materialized, even if few people directly advocated for these.

Racism may further help to explain a distinctive aspect of the Herero genocide.[80] This genocide was the first of its kind that was primarily executed by regular army units—that is, by volunteers serving in the home army under the command of professional officers. The "dirty work" was not delegated to a paramilitary force, militia, or similar organization, as was often historically the case.[81] Because the soldiers accepted that Africans were inferior and not fully human, they did not question orders that were diametrically opposed to their oft-touted ethos of "chivalry."

"Privatized violence" perpetrated by the settlers, in particular, plunged the colony into war. State administrators, courts, and the public sanctioned this violence by taking no action against it, obeying the imperative of racial solidarity. The unstated racist consensus meant that belated efforts to stem the violence were half-hearted and ineffectual, and that very soon, soldiers stopped upholding otherwise customary behavioral norms. Racism is an important condition for the escalation of violence, precisely because it lays the groundwork for normalizing deviance.

Emotion

Traditional depictions of the wars of "pacification" in South-West Africa paint a picture of a nearly omnipotent German war machine, which acted in a broadly rational and purposeful way. Such depictions unintentionally mimic the inflated self-image of colonial leaders, who in turn stylized the Africans as unsophisticated creatures of instinct. Needless to say, colonial leaders were human—fallible and susceptible to all kinds of irrational impulses. Their own egos were not as sovereign as they might have hoped.[82] They lost self-control frequently, and their actions were driven by emotions such as fear, shame, and rage. Methodologically speaking, conventional genocide studies with teleological or deterministic schemata tend to adopt a highly rationalist approach. In the present context, however, this approach is insufficient. We must keep in mind that the Herero genocide was a product of war, and that wars evoke—and to a large degree, are shaped by—complex emotions. People react emotionally in exceptional circumstances such as wars, as we can see in Sémelin's "idea of a dynamics of destruction that is liable to change, slow down or speed up."[83] The emotional reactions of people in crisis situations can also heighten the complexity of events, producing feedback effects that are typical of complex systems, and potentially accelerating key developments.

One concern is that a theoretical emphasis on emotion may tread too far into the realm of psychology, beyond the competence of a historical and sociological study. We should keep in mind, however, that emotions are not "private property," but are responses to social reality, as Sighard Neckel has emphasized. And since the origins of emotions are not exclusively individual, they cannot be explained by psychology alone.[84] Indeed, since emotions inform nearly every aspect of human experience and social relations, it is difficult to understand why sociology avoided this field of study for so long.[85]

Emotions represent the relationship between a person's motives and social environment, influencing his or her actions in a motive-serving way.[86] Each person possesses a range of important concerns, including goals and motives, likes and dislikes, and norms and values. Emotions lend meaning to the world by providing motive-relevant appraisals of human encounters and experiences. Thus, emotions constantly evaluate the degree to which internal[87] and external stimuli in the form of objects, persons, and events satisfy individual motives or other relevant concerns.[88] These appraisals trigger "action readiness" for modifying one's relationship to the environment in a motive-serving way, and they lead to a selection of appropriate behaviors.

Emotionality should not necessarily, or even exclusively, be understood as an exceptional condition (being "beside" oneself with emotion). Emotions regulate all of our activities, so we should not regard them as something exceptional, or even pathological. Even so, in *The Emotional Politics of Racism: How Feelings Trump Facts in an Era of Colorblindness*, Paula Ioanide shows us how emotions can override reason and better judgment—which happens again and again.

We will see how colonial socialization was fundamentally shaped by emotions such as fear and mistrust. Using Trutz von Trotha's sociology of colonial rule as a point of departure, we will see how these emotions affected not only the colonizers' external relations to the colonized, but also the internal relations of colonial society, unleashing forces that weakened the colonial state and allowed violence to escalate. Members of colonial society were drawn toward actions that not only failed to advance their interests, but in some respects actually undermined them. The settlement of South-West Africa was formally initiated, planned, and organized by the state, but emotions of colonial society such as fear and mistrust thwarted the state's ambitions and increasingly shaped the course of events. Studying emotions complements the sociological study of governance by encouraging us to look beyond the aspirations of colonial rule—to how it actually functioned, and why.

The Herero campaign developed much differently than German military officials expected, as the usual routines proved ineffective and offered no real guidance. Elsewhere in this book, we will see how the campaign unleashed emotions such as fear, embitterment, and frustration—sources of violence and cruelty that did not depend on orders or plans "from above." These emotions took on a life of their own and, in turn, affected the campaign itself. The emotion of shame was particularly significant for the genocidal escalation of the campaign.[89]

Shame is the social emotion par excellence because it is so closely bound to its particular historical, cultural, and social context.[90] Analyzing shame means delving into the "innermost parts of society" in order to understand its norms, rituals, self-perceptions, and anxieties.[91]

The question of shame is central to the context of colonial rule. To the extent that wars occur within the "colonial situation"—that is, "in the name of a racial (or ethnic) and cultural superiority dogmatically affirmed" by the colonizers[92]—defeat brings humiliation that is practically intolerable for the "superior" power. The example of Italy, which lost its war against Ethiopia at Adwa in 1896, underscores how deeply such humiliation can be felt. Avenging this defeat became an immediate priority of the subsequent Italian fascist regime.[93] For an emerging great power that was still as unsure of itself as Imperial Germany, the very existence of the uprising—and the fact it was not put down immediately—raised uncomfortable questions. The incompetence of Imperial Germany in South-West Africa was on display for all of the other great powers to see. Prussian/German military elites were particularly ill-equipped to deal with shame. Any sign of weakness drew scorn in Wilhelmine society, where a "cult of ruthlessness" prevailed.[94] Shame was bypassed, leading to the "shame-rage mechanism" that was first described by psychologist Helen B. Lewis. Thomas J. Scheff subsequently introduced the concept to sociological discussions of violence.[95] The connection between shame and rage is key to understanding the escalation of genocidal violence in SWA. Emotions increasingly determined the course of the war, and the consequences were disastrous.

Scholars have been reluctant to identify the failures of the German war machine in South-West Africa. Thus, they have rarely investigated the *meaning* of operational failure—including its emotional significance to key historical actors, and what "action readiness" it inspired. Regardless of whether these actors' appraisals were prereflective or unconscious, they took place within a specific political and historical constellation, and they were the product of a specific cultural milieu and its corresponding social expectations. We must understand this social context in order to decipher the actors' emotions and the actions that they evoked.

Organization

I have narrowed the scope of the following investigation in two important ways. First, I focus on the war between the Herero and Germans, leaving the battles in the south largely out of view. These wars were, however, closely related. Because of the fighting against the Bondelswarts in the southernmost part of the colony, troops were absent from the north at the end of 1903, which gave the Herero an immediate incentive to strike. Likewise, the Witbooi-Oorlam's experiences with the Germans in the Herero campaign contributed to their reasons for taking up the fight against the colonial power. Such connections notwithstanding, the wars were different conflicts with different dynamics, and so they deserve to be considered separately.[96] Second, I direct special attention to the year 1904, when the threshold to genocidal violence was crossed.

The narrative follows the progression of violence over time. Each chapter focuses on a particular actor or group of actors. I begin with the settlers, whom I situate within a special "order of violence." The South-West African colonial state was a weak state, which struggled to assert control over the white population throughout its entire existence. Privatized violence overwhelmed the state even in "peacetime," casting a shadow over the entire period of German rule in South-West Africa. Deviance was normalized early on, establishing a precedent that was highly consequential for the later escalation of violence. I show how the violence of the settlers was connected to racism, the "colonial situation," and the effects of this situation on the internal relations of colonial society.[97] I devote particular attention to the emotions of fear and mistrust.

Further, I depict how privatized violence and state inaction ultimately drove the Herero to take arms, as well as how these phenomena influenced the thrust of their attacks. Because the history of the war was told and recorded almost exclusively by Germans, I cannot, unfortunately, present the Herero perspective as thoroughly as that of the Germans. Uneven documentation makes this imbalance unavoidable. In many cases, we can only speculate about the motivations of the Herero. In any event, the Germans deeply resented Herero resistance, and the conflict soon descended into a spiral of violence. The cruelty of colonial society and its desire for revenge shaped at least the first weeks and months of the fighting. The settlers radicalized the direction of the war at both the strategic and tactical levels.

In chapter 2, I investigate the strategic positions that were held by relevant actors at the beginning of the war. On one side, there was the long-serving governor, Theodor Leutwein, who argued on behalf of a traditional, comparatively limited style of fighting. On the other side, there was the metropole, which pushed for unlimited warfare. The metropole sought a war of annihilation—by which I mean a war of political, rather than genocidal, destruction. Disappointed by Leutwein, the metropolitan leaders turned to Trotha as their candidate for waging this war. Trotha's ideas were more radical than those of his predecessor, but their two positions were initially not as far apart as is often assumed.

Chapter 3 examines the campaign, which Leutwein began and Trotha continued. The goal of this campaign—military annihilation—was announced early on, but it seemed attainable only through operations that were difficult to execute in SWA. Trotha assumed the command after Leutwein failed to crush Herero resistance—but operational success eluded Trotha too. Only after the failure of operations, which Trotha long refused to acknowledge, did the campaign "bypass" shame and gradually enter its genocidal phase. The military doctrine of annihilation per se did not lead to escalation; a greater problem was how this doctrine was applied in an unforeseen scenario, which is why it ultimately failed. The initial effects of metropolitan influence and the change in command were ambiguous. The "metropolitanization" of the campaign involved moments of escalating violence, but also moments of restraint. The triumph of the former was by no means inevitable.

In chapter 4, I turn to the brutalization of the troops within the context of the developing war. The field of actors was characterized not only by horizontal, but also vertical, differentiation. Cleavages were evident not only between groups such as settlers, metropolitan officers, and civil servants (who posed a challenge to the military dictatorship); they also ran through the military hierarchy. As in other long wars, the "top" and "bottom" gradually pulled apart. Genocide studies too often focus exclusively on top decision-makers, thereby ascribing comprehensive, causal significance to the decisions of political and military leaders. These studies are distinguished by a hierarchical view "from above." More recent scholarship increasingly emphasizes the influence of peripheral and lower-ranking actors on the course of events, and even on central decision-making processes.[98] I follow this path as well.

Fear and embitterment motivated the soldiers to keep going, even when "combat operations" were reduced to tracking down and slaughtering miserable Herero stragglers—mostly the elderly, women, and children. This brutalization occurred as part of a broader process of normalizing deviance. Fear and embitterment, each in different ways, reflected the disjuncture between strategy and the actual site of operations. The emotions took on special intensity when experienced before an opponent who was seen as inferior. Racism also played a role in this context. Violence "from below" constituted a separate dimension in the process of violence, but it coexisted and interacted with the campaign, which was ordered "from above."

Chapter 5 explores the troubling finding that the violence and cruelty did not end even after Berlin officially revoked the strategy of annihilation. Civil servants were tasked with overseeing the "pacification" of the colony. Responsible for "native policy" and the ideologization of the regime of the camps, they established an order so repressive that Herero society did not recover, but continued to shrink in the remaining years of German rule. Shame continued to play a role, contributing to the radicalization of postwar politics. Civil servants dealt with the failure of Trotha's campaign by continuing the war by other means, thereby laying the groundwork for permanent white rule in SWA.

Sources

My work follows the maxims of the "new" research on violence (see especially Trutz von Trotha, "Einleitung: Zur Soziologie der Gewalt"), and my goal is to provide a thick description (in the manner of Clifford Geertz[99]) of the process of violence. To this end, I have consulted many different sources.

Records from the National Archives of Namibia (NAN) and the Federal Archive Berlin-Lichterfelde (BArch) provide the foundation for this study. These archives hold correspondence between the colonial government and the commander-in-chief of the Schutztruppe in German South-West Africa, in addition to correspondence with authorities in Berlin (particularly the Imperial Colonial Office and Great General Staff). I also consult documents from the colony's district (*Bezirk*) and division (*Distrikt*) offices—including telegrams, orders, reports, assessments, and declarations.

Newspapers published by settlers—above all, the *Deutsch-Südwestafrikanische Zeitung* (*DSWAZ*) and the *Windhuker Nachrichten* (*WN*, called the *Nachrichten des Bezirks-Vereins Windhuk* until 1904)—help to reconstruct the settler "ethos" and the colony's actual political order, as well as the conditions that led to the escalation of violence. These newspapers are available at the National Library in Windhoek. They give voice to the settlers and offer deep insight into colonial society and the tensions and conflicts that defined it. The articles were often written by locals, whose critical tone provides a valuable counterpoint to the official reports that they disputed.

The sociological provenance of this study is evident in chapter 2, which focuses on the settlers. The chapter relies on—and critically engages with—Helmut Bley's *Kolonialherrschaft und Sozialstruktur in Deutsch-Südwestafrika*, which was published in 1968 and remains invaluable. From a different systematic perspective, I formulate my own conclusions about the colony's political order.

The experiences and emotions of historical actors are particularly important to "violence from below," brutalization, and other aspects of this study, and so I devote special attention to ego documents such as diaries and letters.

The personal diaries of military men that were published within their own lifetimes were subject to censorship, and some—like the soldier Max Belwe's 1906 memoir, *Gegen die Herero 1904/1905*—were even enhanced by professional writers. These texts tend to maintain considerable distance from the events they describe, perhaps unintentionally seeking to rationalize events after the fact. They certainly do not give us a sense of "what actually happened" (*wie es eigentlich gewesen ist*), to borrow the words of the young Leopold von Ranke. Rather, these texts present a stylized self-image that addresses special interests and particular audiences in the corresponding language—raising awareness about the "colonial issue," for example, or recognizing the achievements of the troops. These texts contributed to a broader discourse that extended beyond the colonial war. Even so, they contain details about the "face of war" that are not found in official communications, reports, or war diaries.

The same is also true (with some exceptions) for the unpublished personal diaries and letters of soldiers, civil servants, and settlers in the National Archives of Namibia, the Federal Archive in Koblenz, and the German Archive for Diaries in Emmendigen (DTA). These, too, were produced at some distance from the events they describe, in the brief phases of leisure and contemplation that the war sometimes allowed. Even ego documents not originally intended for publication can be shamelessly self-serving—as with the diaries of the long-serving South-West African colonial officer Viktor Franke. But even these texts express disappointments, judgments, and emotions that might have otherwise been suppressed, especially if they involved "comrades," superiors, or the military apparatus. Writers engaged in dialogue with themselves or other confidants to let off steam—even (or especially) about their superiors and the military apparatus. Such writings can teach us a great deal about the frictions in this "small war." Experiences and perceptions are an important dimension of wartime events, particularly with respect to phenomena such as brutalization. While official and semiofficial documents (such as the 1906 report by the Great General Staff's historical department) provide the framework for reconstructing events, ego documents can tell us about feelings, motivations, and morale. They are indispensable for understanding what happened.

This is especially true of Lieutenant General Lothar von Trotha's war diary, which covers the period between the commander-in-chief's appointment in the spring of 1904 and his departure at the end of 1905. Genocide studies, in general, are strongly oriented toward "intent." Since Trotha is rightly viewed as this genocide's defining figure, his notes seem that much more relevant. The South African historian Gerhardus Pool, the Namibian farmer Hinrich Schneider-Waterberg, and the historian Isabel Hull were granted access to this diary, which is otherwise restricted, although they apparently worked only with the typescript (1a; with supplements 2a and 3a), which was posthumously transcribed in 1930 by Lothar von Trotha's second wife and widow, Lucy von Trotha. She supplemented this typescript with additional documents (2a and 3a), the original versions of which apparently no longer exist. The typescript was meant to be published for propagandistic purposes, to disprove the "lie" of colonial guilt. Thus, it is unsurprising that the typescript deviates significantly from the handwritten diary in some places. Particularly bellicose or sanguinary remarks, grievances, and (especially) passages that criticized subordinates and superiors were cut or softened. The differences between the typescript and original diary would be worth a study of their own, especially since these differences are not always immediately apparent. I am grateful to the Trotha family for granting me access to the handwritten war diary for this study.

Holdings in the Botswana National Archives and Records Services (GNARS), Cape Town Archives Repository (KAB), and Public Record Office (PRO) of the National Archive in London have also been exceedingly helpful. These archives contain some of the few contemporary documents that allow the Herero and Nama to speak for themselves. During and after the war, British officers and civil servants who were responsible for the eastern and southern border (with Botswana and the Cape Colony) and outlying areas conducted numerous interviews with refugees and others who fled across the border, in order to learn more about the conditions, morale, and further ambitions of the warring parties. They drafted reports and informed their superiors about the situation along the borders and in German South-West Africa. These records provide an important outside perspective on the war as a whole—and, in particular, on German military efforts and successes. This is especially true of the reports by two British officers, Colonel Trench and Major Wade, who were assigned to the headquarters of the South-West African Schutztruppe as observers. The comparative neglect of such sources is puzzling, particularly since the records of the South-West African Schutztruppe itself has been lost. The holdings in SWA were destroyed with the invasion of South African troops in 1915, while those in Germany apparently fell victim to the bombings in World War II. Without the correspondence that has been preserved in British archives, between South African authorities and the German consul general in Cape Town, we would not know (for example) about the fate of a teamster named James, who was recruited in the Cape Colony and then murdered in South-West Africa. His story helps us understand the routine nature of violence against blacks, as well as the workings (and failures) of German military justice.

To a certain extent, German missionaries also provide an outside perspective on circumstances in the colony. The archives of the United Evangelical Mission in Wuppertal and the Evangelical Lutheran Church in the Republic of Namibia (ELCRN) are rich. Although missionaries were at the forefront of colonial penetration, they consistently, if not always, pursued their own agenda. They sought to missionize "natives" who lived in their midst, and so their primary "clients" were Africans. Insofar as they took their mission and pastoral duties seriously, they could easily run into conflict with settlers and colonial authorities. Shortly after the outbreak of war in 1904, these groups did place some of the blame for escalation in the missionaries' hands. The missionaries saw themselves as Germans, so in the end their loyalty remained with Germany. Nevertheless, in many situations they mediated between the native people and colonizers, and so their own perspective was not always identical with the interests of colonial society. They sought to provide a differentiated view of colonial power relations and the causes and circumstances of the war. Missionary reports and chronicles provide the basis for any detailed depiction of how violence escalated in January 1904, by also taking the indigenous perspective into account. Mission reports further tell us about the deadly conditions of the concentration camps established at the end of 1904.

Perhaps the most controversial source on this topic is the "blue book" that Jeremy Silvester and Jan-Bart Gewald republished in 2003 under the title *Words Cannot Be Found: German Colonial Rule in Namibia: An Annotated Reprint of the 1918 Blue Book*. Apparently conceived by the British during World War I as an instrument of propaganda, the blue book challenged Germans' claims to their colonial possessions. It was unquestionably tendentious and later retracted. Andreas Eckl has clearly outlined the weaknesses of this source.[100] Although its scholarly value is limited, the collected (passages of) interviews with survivors of the war are very moving. I refer to the blue book in this study, but only secondarily, for purposes of illustration, without basing my arguments in the relevant passages entirely on this source.

Attentive readers may notice some similarities between passages in this text and passages in some of my previously published works.[101] My earlier findings and arguments have, of course, contributed to this book, but here they are integrated within an original, more comprehensive argument that differs from my past work in some important respects. Specialists may also note that I do not mention two particularly recent and relevant works by other scholars—Christiane Bürger's *Deutsche Kolonialgeschichte(n): Der Genozid in Namibia und die Geschichtsschreibung der DDR und BRD* and Christian W. Zoellner's *Deutsch-Herero-Krieg 1904: Eine Betrachtung unter dem Aspekt Völkermord*. These were unfortunately published too late to be incorporated here.

Notes

1. This term is misleading in multiple ways. For one, "uprising" implies that the Herero were not a legitimate warring party, despite the dubious legality of the "protection treaties" (*Schutzverträge*) that established German colonial rule. See, for example, Theodor Leutwein, *Elf Jahre Gouverneur in Deutsch-Südwestafrika* (Windhoek, 1997), 222. In this text I use the term "uprising" only for linguistic variation. Moreover, "the Herero" presumes a uniformity that was not necessarily present in polycephalous societies. The circumstances surrounding the firing of the first shots in Okahandja (residence of Samuel Maharero, paramount chief of the Herero) on 12 January 1904 remain murky, as does the escalation of a few local skirmishes into a war that encompassed much of Herero society.
2. Andreas E. Eckl identifies two wars, distinguishing the Germans' war against the Herero from the one against the Nama (-Oorlam). See Eckl, *S'ist ein übles Land hier: Zur Historiographie eines umstrittenen Kolonialkrieges; Tagebuchaufzeichnun-*

gen aus dem Herero-Krieg in Deutsch- Südwestafrika 1904 von Georg Hillebrecht und Franz Ritter von Epp (Cologne, 2005), 16. Since the Nama (-Oorlam) consisted of many independent groups that made their own decisions about war and peace, and—as far I can see—the campaign against them was not waged in a uniform way, it seems appropriate to speak of multiple wars. See Großer Generalstab, *Die Kämpfe der deutschen Truppen in Südwestafrika*, vol. 2 (Berlin, 1907).

3. Andreas Bühler, *Der Namaaufstand gegen die deutsche Kolonialherrschaft in Namibia von 1904–1913* (Frankfurt, 2003); and Walter Nuhn, *Feind überall: Guerillakrieg in Südwest: Der Große Nama-Aufstand 1904–1908* (Bonn, 2000).
4. Dierk Walter, *Organisierte Gewalt in der europäischen Expansion: Gestalt und Logik des Imperialkrieges* (Hamburg, 2014), 151.
5. Dierk Walter, "Imperialkriege: Begriff, Erkenntnisinteresse, Aktualität," in *Imperialkriege von 1500 bis heute: Strukturen—Akteure—Lernprozesse*, ed. Tanja Bührer et al. (Paderborn, 2011), 16–17.
6. Larissa Förster, *Erinnerungslandschaften im kolonialen und postkolonialen Namibia: Wie Deutsche und Herero in Namibia des Kriegs von 1904 gedenken* (Frankfurt, 2010), 132ff.
7. See, for example, Großer Generalstab, *Die Kämpfe der deutschen Truppen in Südwestafrika*, vol. 1 (Berlin, 1906), 218. There is no question that indigenous casualties were substantial—numbering in the tens of thousands for the Herero alone—although we do not have exact figures. To begin, it is unclear how many Herero lived in the colony before the war. The British trader Hewitt estimated a population of 150,000–200,000 at the beginning of 1904. But the missionary Kuhlmann counted only 50,000–60,000 residents, and the missionary Irle proposed an even lower number. See C. H. Rodwell, Acting Imperial Secretary, to the High Commissioner, Johannesburg [?], 9 March 1904, GNARS RC 1/18; and A. Kuhlmann, *Auf Adlers Flügeln* (Barmen, 1911), 85. Furthermore, as Jonas Kreienbaum has recently emphasized, we do not even know the precise numbers of survivors of the German concentration camps. He estimates that "the total number of Herero war prisoners must have easily exceeded twenty thousand." See Jonas Kreienbaum, *A Sad Fiasco: Colonial Concentration Camps in Southern Africa, 1900–1908*, trans. Elizabeth Janik (New York, 2019), 90. The number of Herero who escaped to British-held territory is also unclear, with estimates ranging between 1,000 and 6,000–9,000. See Sarkin, *Germany's Genocide*, 141. The 1911 census counted 15,130 Herero on South-West African territory, although it is important to note that the colonists' knowledge about their subjects was generally quite limited. See Horst Drechsler, *Südwestafrika unter deutscher Kolonialherrschaft: Der Kampf der Herero und Nama gegen den deutschen Imperialismus 1884–1915* (Berlin, 1966), 252.
8. Jeremy Sarkin, *Germany's Genocide of the Herero: Kaiser Wilhelm II, His General, His Settlers, His Soldiers* (Cape Town, 2011), viii.
9. Jürgen Zimmerer, *Deutsche Herrschaft über Afrikaner: Staatlicher Machtanspruch und Wirklichkeit im kolonialen Namibia*, 3rd ed. (Münster, 2004); and Birthe Kundrus, *Moderne Imperialisten: Das Kaiserreich im Spiegel seiner Kolonien* (Cologne, 2003).
10. Leutwein, *Elf Jahre Gouverneur*, 242.
11. As part of an inquiry into the "Witbooi uprising," on 11 November 1904, Leutwein wrote that newly arrived soldiers had warned the Witbooi fighters that it would be "their turn next" after the Herero. Some of the fighters deserted and joined up with Hendrik Witbooi, who declared war on the Germans after learning more about their intentions. (NAN ZBU D.IV.M.1, pp. 3ff.)
12. Rudolf Vierhaus, *Am Hof der Hohenzollern: Aus dem Tagebuch der Baronin Spitzemberg 1865–1914* (Munich, 1979), 221.

13. Matthias Häussler, "'Die Kommandogewalt hat geredet, der Reichstag hat zu schweigen': How the 'Hottentottenwahlen' of 1907 Shaped the Relationship between Parliament and Military Policy in Imperial Germany," *Journal of Namibian Studies* 15 (2014): 7–24; Frank Oliver Sobich, *"Schwarze Bestien, rote Gefahr": Rassismus und Antisemitismus im deutschen Kaiserreich* (Frankfurt, 2006); and George D. Crothers, *The German Elections of 1907*, 2nd ed. (New York, 1968).
14. See, for example, Otto Busch, "Deutschlands Kleinkrieg," Cape Town, 27 January 1906 (no. 14), NAN, A.0529, pp. 6ff.
15. Christian Morgenstern, "Die unmögliche Tatsache," *Alle Galgenlieder* (Zurich, 1981), 164.
16. StBR, 60th session, 17 March 1904, p. 1896B. General Staff officer Maximilian Bayer made similar remarks. See Maximilian Bayer, *Mit dem Hauptquartier in Südwestafrika* (Berlin, 1909), 190–91.
17. See the report from 5 April 1907, KAB GH 35/139: "Correspondence: High Commissioner Re Rising of Natives in G.S.W.A., 1904–1906."
18. "Der Aufstand," *DSWAZ*, 15 December 1904, 1.
19. Vierhaus, *Am Hof der Hohenzollern*, 221.
20. Ludwig von Estorff, *Wanderungen und Kämpfe in Südwestafrika, Ostafrika und Südafrika 1894–1910*, ed. Christoph-Friedrich Kutscher, 2nd ed. (Windhoek, 1979), 117.
21. Sobich, *"Schwarze Bestien, rote Gefahr,"* 227.
22. W. E. Montague, *Campaigning in Zululand: Experiences on Campaign during the Zulu War of 1879 with the 94th Regiment* (LaVergne, 2006).
23. See, for example, Brigitte Lau, "Ungewisse Gewissheiten," in *Der Wahrheit eine Gasse: Anmerkungen zum Kolonialkrieg in Deutsch-Südwestafrika 1904*, ed. H. R. Schneider-Waterberg (Swakopmund, 2006), 141–58; and Karla Poewe, *The Namibian Herero: A History of Their Psychological Disintegration and Survival* (New York, 1985).
24. See Trutz von Trotha, *Koloniale Herrschaft: Zur soziologischen Theorie der Staatsentstehung am Beispiel des Schutzgebietes Togo* (Tübingen, 1994), 32ff.
25. See Klaus Mainzer, *Komplexität* (Munich, 2008), 38ff.
26. Sidney Dekker, *Drift into Failure: From Hunting Broken Components to Understanding Complex Systems* (Farnham, 2011), 87ff.
27. Ibid.
28. See Jacques Sémelin, "Elemente einer Grammatik des Massakers," *Mittelweg 36* 15, no. 6 (2006): 18–40; Jacques Sémelin, *Purify and Destroy: The Political Uses of Massacre and Genocide*, trans. Cynthia Schoch (New York, 2007); Michael Mann, *Die dunkle Seite der Demokratie: Eine Theorie der ethnischen Säuberung* (Hamburg, 2007); Mark Levene, *The Meaning of Genocide* (London, 2005); Martin Shaw, *What is Genocide?* (Cambridge, 2007); Christian Gerlach, "Extremely Violent Societies: An Alternative to the Concept of Genocide," *Journal of Genocide Research* 8, no. 4 (2006): 455–71; and Christian Gerlach, *Extrem gewalttätige Gesellschaften: Massengewalt im 20. Jahrhundert* (Munich, 2011).
29. To assess these works fairly, one must consider the time and circumstances when they were written. Works that coincided with the war's hundredth anniversary appropriately took issue with the Federal Republic of Germany's reluctance to make a clear admission of guilt. Not until 2015 did the first state official, Bundestag president Norbert Lammert, speak of "genocide" (*Völkermord*), thereby ushering in an overdue transformation in the official discourse. Parts of the German and German-Namibian public still dismissed the happenings in SWA as "normal colonial warfare." See Janntje Böhlke-Itzen, "Die bundesdeutsche Diskussion und die Reparationsfrage: Ein ganz normaler Kolonialkrieg?" in *Genozid und Gedenken: Namibisch-*

deutsche Geschichte und Gegenwart, ed. Henning Melber (Frankfurt, 2005), 103–19; Christoph Marx, "Entsorgen und Entseuchen: Zur Diskussionskultur in der derzeitigen namibischen Historiographie—eine Polemik," in *Genozid und Gedenken*, 141–62; and Reinhart Kößler, "Im Schatten des Genozids: Erinnerungspolitik in einer extrem ungleichen Gesellschaft," in *Genozid und Gedenken*, 49–77. Within this context, the social and political significance of these works was unmistakable.

30. Drechsler, *Südwestafrika unter deutscher Kolonialherrschaft*, 15 and 183.
31. Even Drechsler's most questionable theses are repeatedly cited—and thus, to a certain extent, affirmed—without comment. See, for example, David Olusoga and Casper W. Erichsen, *The Kaiser's Holocaust: Germany's Forgotten Genocide* (London, 2010), 145; Dominik J. Schaller, "Kolonialkrieg, Völkermord und Zwangsarbeit in 'Deutsch-Südwestafrika,'" in *Enteignet—Vertrieben—Ermordet: Beiträge zur Genozidforschung*, ed. Dominik J. Schaller (Zurich, 2004), 217, note 156; and Alison Palmer, *Colonial Genocide* (London, 2000), 146. The influence of Drechsler's work extends beyond academic circles. Visitors to Namibia who pose (seemingly) naive questions about the German colonial era may well be asked if they haven't read "the Drechsler."
32. Drechsler, *Südwestafrika unter deutscher Kolonialherrschaft*, 158.
33. Drechsler's image of the perpetrators was wholly monolithic. By contrast, just two years later Helmut Bley distinguished between the interests of the metropole and those of colonial society, emphasizing—at least in principle—that colonialism was a complex phenomenon, involving heterogeneous groups of actors and internal antagonisms. See Helmut Bley, *Kolonialherrschaft und Sozialstruktur in Deutsch-Südwestafrika 1894–1914* (Hamburg, 1968), 15. For the English translation, see Helmut Bley, *South-West Africa under German Rule 1894–1914*, trans. Hugh Ridley (London: Heinemann, 1971).
34. These works point to Lieutenant General Lothar von Trotha's assumption of the military command in May 1904 as the beginning of the genocidal phase. See Wolfgang Benz, "Kolonialpolitik als Genozid: Der 'Herero-Aufstand' in Deutsch-Südwestafrika," in *Ausgrenzung, Vertreibung, Völkermord: Genozid im 20. Jahrhundert*, ed. Wolfgang Benz, 2nd ed. (Munich, 2007), 37; Gesine Krüger, *Kriegsbewältigung und Geschichtsbewusstsein: Realität, Deutung und Verarbeitung des deutschen Kolonialkriegs in Namibia 1904 bis 1907* (Göttingen, 1999), 50; and Schaller, "Kolonialkrieg, Völkermord und Zwangsarbeit," 167. Recent studies that are specifically concerned with genocide focus on the wars between 1904 and 1908. Although these studies' authors address their subjects with greater nuance than Drechsler, their methodological approaches are quite similar. See Joël Kotek, "Le Génocide des Herero, Symptôme d'un Sonderweg Allemand?," *Revue d'histoire de la Shoah* 189 (2008): 177–97; Benz, "Kolonialpolitik als Genozid"; Jan Bart Gewald, "Imperial Germany and the Herero of Southern Africa: Genocide and the Quest of Recompense," in *Genocide, War Crimes and the West: History and Complicity*, ed. Adam Jones (London, 2004), 59–77; Benjamin Madley, "From Africa to Auschwitz: How German South West Africa Incubated Ideas and Methods Adopted and Developed by the Nazis in Eastern Europe," *European History Quarterly* 35, no. 3 (2005): 429–64; and Jon M. Bridgman and Leslie J. Worley, "Genocide of the Hereros," in *Century of Genocide: Eyewitness Accounts and Critical Views*, ed. Samuel Totten et al. (New York, 1997), 3–40. They, too, conclude that the outcomes of the campaign were apparent from the start, and that German warfare entered its genocidal phase early on.
35. See Sarkin, *Germany's Genocide*.
36. This includes the following acts: First, killing members of the group; second, causing serious bodily or mental harm to members of the group; third, deliberately inflicting conditions of life calculated to destroy the group, in whole or in part; fourth, impos-

ing measures to prevent births; and fifth, forcibly transferring children to another group.
37. William A. Schabas, *Genocide in International Law: The Crime of Crimes* (Cambridge, 2000), 214ff.
38. For a critical view, see Levene, *The Meaning of Genocide*, 35ff.
39. Legal scholar Jeremy Sarkin adopts a similar approach, establishing genocidal intent early on. He sees the impetus for genocide in the settlers' hunger for land; acquiring land became a socially sanctioned imperative of Imperial German state policy. Sarkin, *Germany's Genocide of the Herero*, 8.
40. Once again, Sarkin's monograph provides an instructive example. The title *Germany's Genocide of the Herero: Kaiser Wilhelm II, His General, His Settlers, His Soldiers* highlights Sarkin's assumption that the groups in his study acted in concert, orchestrated by the Kaiser from the top down.
41. Jeremy Sarkin traces genocidal intent back to the Kaiser and even explores the monarch's medical history in a chapter titled "The Kaiser's Personality": "The Herero genocide is also clearly linked to the Kaiser's aggressive behaviour and sadistic streak." See Sarkin, *Germany's Genocide of the Herero*, 162.
42. The conventional view eventually confronts a serious problem. The ideological profile that it wants to construct depends on structural logic that, to a greater or lesser extent, must transcend time in order to classify people and their actions. By this reasoning, Trotha's actions that meet the objective criteria of genocide can be broadly characterized as "genocidal" because Trotha *is* a radical racist. How, then, to explain the fact that Trotha initially waged a "conventional" war against the Herero, even though he possessed dictatorial powers after the declaration of martial law, and carte blanche from the Kaiser? Most case studies "solve" the problem by ignoring contradictory evidence and continuing to identify the start of the genocidal phase with Trotha's assumption of command.
43. For a critical take, see Birthe Kundrus, "Entscheidung für den Völkermord? Einleitende Überlegungen zu einem historiographischen Problem," *Mittelweg 36* 15, no. 6 (2006): 7.
44. Trutz von Trotha, "Einleitung: Zur Soziologie der Gewalt," in *Soziologie der Gewalt: Kölner Zeitschrift für Soziologie und Sozialpsychologie*, ed. Trutz von Trotha (Opladen, 1997), 22.
45. Perhaps the most important finding of the (no longer so) "new" research on violence (*neuere Gewaltforschung*) is its emphasis on violence as a *process*. See Trutz von Trotha, "Einleitung"; Trutz von Trotha and Michael Schwab-Trapp, "Logiken der Gewalt," *Mittelweg 36* 5, no. 6 (1996): 56–64; Birgitta Nedelmann, "Dichte Beschreibungen absoluter Macht," *Kölner Zeitschrift für Soziologie und Sozialpsychologie* 46, no. 1 (1994): 130–34; Birgitta Nedelmann, "Schwierigkeiten soziologischer Gewaltanalyse," *Mittelweg 36* 4, no. 3 (1995): 8–17; and Birgitta Nedelmann, "Gewaltsoziologie am Scheideweg: Die Auseinandersetzungen in der gegenwärtigen und Wege der künftigen Gewaltforschung," in *Soziologie der Gewalt: Kölner Zeitschrift für Soziologie und Sozialpsychologie*, ed. Trutz von Trotha (Opladen, 1997), 59–85.
46. Jon M. Bridgman, *The Revolt of the Hereros* (Berkeley, 1981), 104ff. Further, we should not too be too hasty in presuming an asymmetry between victims and perpetrators, thereby underestimating Herero resistance. The conventional view tends to exaggerate the Germans' power over the Herero, constructing a one-sided narrative that is determined by the Germans. Emphasizing Herero agency does not automatically minimize the "extremely repressive character" of German measures. See Jürgen Zimmerer, "Rassenkrieg und Völkermord: Der Kolonialkrieg in Deutsch-Südwestafrika und die Globalgeschichte des Genozids," in *Genozid und Gedenken: Namibisch-deutsche Geschichte und Gegenwart*, ed. Henning Melber (Frankfurt, 2005), 28.

Herero persistence, despite dwindling room to maneuver, may help to explain why the Germans turned to increasingly repressive measures, as this persistence undermined colonial leaders' fantasies of omnipotence and their sense of superiority.

47. Trutz von Trotha, "Formen des Krieges: Zur Typologie kriegerischer Aktionsmacht," in *Ordnungen der Gewalt: Beiträge zu einer politischen Soziologie der Gewalt und des Krieges*, ed. Sighard Neckel and Michael Schwab-Trapp (Opladen, 1999), 72.
48. Shaw, *What is Genocide?*, 81–82.
49. In some cases, forms of violence are simplistically traced back to an intent to annihilate "from above" and situated within an "impressionistic" picture of atrocities in order to heighten their lurid and criminal nature. See, for example, Casper W. Erichsen "Zwangsarbeit im Konzentrationslager auf der Haifischinsel," in *Völkermord in Deutsch-Südwestafrika: Der Kolonialkrieg (1904–1908) in Namibia und seine Folgen*, ed. Jürgen Zimmerer and Joachim Zeller (Berlin: Links, 2004), 80–85; and Casper W. Erichsen, *"The Angel of Death Has Descended Violently among Them": Concentration Camps and Prisoners-of-War in Namibia 1904–1908* (Leiden, 2005). Anything that helps to achieve this effect is thrown into the mix, regardless of the particular actors, circumstances, or distinctive aspects of violence that are involved. In other cases, facts are ignored when they cannot be linked to an order, or to proof of intent "from above," as required by international law. This arbitrarily curtails the process of violence, although—as we will see—violence "from below" is a separate dimension and an integral component of this process.
50. Gerlach, "Extremely Violent Societies," 459.
51. Sémelin, "Elemente einer Grammatik des Massakers," 30–31.
52. Gerhard Paul and Klaus-Michael Mallmann, "Sozialisation, Milieu und Gewalt: Fortschritte und Probleme der neueren Täterforschung," in *Karrieren der Gewalt: Nationalsozialistische Täterbiographien*, ed. Gerhard Paul and Klaus-Michael Mallmann (Darmstadt, 2011), 4.
53. Scholarship on SWA has tended to overestimate the Germans' effective power, while overlooking the extent of their failings. Horst Drechsler, perhaps the harshest critic of "German imperialism," unintentionally reproduced colonial leaders' inflated self-image by depicting them as nearly omnipotent in his 1966 book, *Südwestafrika unter deutscher Kolonialherrschaft*. More recent studies have broken new ground. The very titles of works by Jakob Zollmann (*Koloniale Herrschaft und ihre Grenzen*, or *Colonial Rule and Its Limits*) and Jonas Kreienbaum (*A Sad Fiasco*, about concentration camps in southern Africa) emphasize the discrepancy between aspirations and reality.
54. See, for example, Sarkin, *Germany's Genocide of the Herero*.
55. Trotha, *Koloniale Herrschaft*.
56. Caroline Elkins and Susan Pedersen, "Introduction," in *Settler Colonialism in the Twentieth Century: Projects, Practices, Legacies*, ed. Caroline Elkins and Susan Pedersen (New York, 2005), 7ff.
57. Peter Hanser and Trutz von Trotha, *Ordnungsformen der Gewalt: Reflexionen über die Grenzen von Recht und Staat an einem einsamen Ort* (Cologne, 2002), 315ff.
58. Leutwein, *Elf Jahre Gouverneur in Deutsch-Südwestafrika*, 240.
59. Samuel P. Huntington, *The Soldier and the State: The Theory and Politics of Civil-Military Relations* (Cambridge, 1957), 9.
60. The concept of "multi-causality" (see Gerlach, "Extremely Violent Societies," 465) does not capture this complexity. The number of causes alone is not as significant as how they interact with one another and their effects.
61. Leutwein to the Colonial Department (16 February 1904), NAN ZBU, D.IV.l.2: Herero-Aufstand 1904. Feldzug; Politisches. Vol. 4: October 1904–December 1905, p. 5.
62. Quoted in Bley, *Kolonialherrschaft*, 177.

63. Dekker, *Drift into Failure*.
64. Thomas McCarthy, *Race, Empire, and the Idea of Human Development* (New York, 2009), 24.
65. See, for example, Wolf D. Hund, *Rassismus* (Bielefeld, 2007), 13.
66. Robert Miles, *Racism* (London, 2003), 89. There are as many schemes for classifying human races as authors who seek to create them. One of the earliest, by Carl von Linné, associates somatic traits like skin color with other qualities like laziness—as in the case of "the African." See Plümecke, *Rasse in der Ära der Genetik*, 74. Contemporary research on genetics and evolution shows us that characteristics such as external appearance (the typical basis for constructions of race) reveal little about genetic relationships, as these characteristics developed comparatively late and in response to certain environmental factors.
67. "Race-based racism" was discredited, at the latest, with the demise of the openly racist Nazi regime. Racism itself was by no means defeated, but this variation fell out of favor. Western democracies today discourage hegemonic groups from presenting themselves as superior, or from promoting particularist interests, because this behavior conflicts with liberal ideals. See Yasemin Shooman, ". . . *weil ihre Kultur so ist": Narrative des antimuslimischen Rassismus* (Bielefeld, 2014), 188. Subtler forms of discrimination have emerged, including intellectual categories that exist for precisely this reason. The "new racism" is not grounded in biology or a fixed definition of race; its argument, rather, is cultural. The new racism detects differences between (fictive or actual) human groups, without casting judgment or using these differences to formulate hierarchies. This at least, is the rhetoric. See Pierre-André Taguieff, "Die Metamorphosen des Rassismus und die Krise des Antirassismus," in *Das Eigene und das Fremde: Neuer Rassismus in der Alten Welt*, ed. Ulrich Bielefeld (Hamburg, 1998), 221–59.
68. Tino Plümecke, *Rasse in der Ära der Genetik: Die Ordnung des Menschen in den Lebenswissenschaften* (Bielefeld: Transcript, 2013), 62.
69. See, for example, Plümecke, *Rasse in der Ära der Genetik*, 26; and Christian Geulen, *Geschichte des Rassismus* (Munich, 2007), 41.
70. Hannsjoachim W. Koch, *Der Sozialdarwinismus: Seine Genese und sein Einfluss auf das imperialistische Denken* (Munich, 1973), 56.
71. See George M. Fredrickson, *Racism: A Short History* (Princeton, 2002), 108.
72. "Vortrag des Herrn Erdmann—Haris," *Windhuker Nachrichten*, 15 June 1905, 3, insert.
73. "Aus Südafrika," *DSWAZ*, 7 February 1906, 1, insert.
74. Hund, *Rassismus*, 110.
75. Partha Chatterjee, *The Nation and Its Fragments: Colonial and Postcolonial Histories* (Princeton, 1993), 10ff.
76. Taguieff, "Die Metamorphosen des Rassismus," 223.
77. Randall Collins, *Violence: A Micro-Sociological Theory* (Princeton, 2008), 370–412.
78. Hund, *Rassismus*, 110; and Carl-Friedrich Graumann and Margret Wintermantel, "Diskriminierende Sprechakte: Ein funktionaler Ansatz," in *Verletzende Worte: Die Grammatik sprachlicher Missachtung*, ed. Steffen K. Herrmann et al. (Bielefeld, 2007), 149.
79. See, for example StBR (19 January 1904), 14th session, 363ff.
80. Boris Barth correctly asserts that racism is a necessary condition for genocide. See *Genozid—Völkermord im 20. Jahrhundert: Geschichte, Theorien, Kontroversen* (Munich, 2006), 183. In contrast to the genocide of European Jews or the Tutsi in Rwanda, the Herero were "racialized," desocialized, dehumanized, and excluded from the universe of moral obligation even before the genocidal process began. Discriminating between "white" and "black" was fundamental to colonial socialization.

81. The perpetrators of genocide are usually states. See Helen Fein, *Genocide: A Sociological Perspective* (London, 1993), 12. These regimes may nevertheless use nonstate actors to enact their radical policies. Since state organizations are subject to law and the massacre of women and children is usually considered unjust, state organizations are not easily instrumentalized for criminal plans. For an opposing view, see Stefan Kühl, *Ganz normale Organisationen: Zur Soziologie des Holocaust* (Frankfurt, 2014).
82. See Sigmund Freud, "Eine Schwierigkeit der Psychoanalyse," in *Gesammelte Werke, Bd. XII: Werke aus den Jahren 1917–1920* (Frankfurt, 1999), 11.
83. Sémelin, *Purify and Destroy*, 325.
84. Sighard Neckel, *Status und Scham: Zur symbolischen Reproduktion sozialer Ungleichheit* (Frankfurt, 1991), 15–17.
85. Jonathan H. Turner and Jan E. Stets, *The Sociology of Emotions* (Cambridge, 2005), 1.
86. Manfred Holodynski and Wolfgang Friedlmeier, *Development of Emotions and Emotion Regulation*, trans. Jonathan Harrow (New York, 2006), 12.
87. Emotions also play a significant role in directing attention and memory. The latter is a selective process, based on countless decisions about what is worth retaining (or not). These processes occur at such high speed, and in such quantity, that they cannot be consciously controlled.
88. Holodynski and Friedlmeier, *Emotionen*, 19. In this context, Nico Frijda notes that "appraisals are continuously made, and appraisal is around anyway, because animals and humans are set to make sense of the environment and what happens there." See *The Laws of Emotion*, 112.
89. The sociologist George Steinmetz and the historian Isabel Hull have clearly established that the violence escalated only after original plans of operation failed, and that this turning point represents the key issue that must be explained. See George Steinmetz, *The Devil's Handwriting: Precoloniality and the German Colonial State in Qingdao, Samoa, and Southwest Africa* (Chicago, 2007); Isabel V. Hull, "Military Culture and the Production of 'Final Solutions' in the Colonies: The Example of Wilhelminian Germany," in *The Specter of Genocide: Mass Murder in Historical Perspective*, ed. Robert Gellately and Ben Kiernan (Cambridge, 2003), 141–62; and Isabel V. Hull, *Absolute Destruction: Military Culture and the Practices of War in Imperial Germany* (Ithaca, 2005). It seems to me, however, that neither Hull nor Steinmetz sufficiently recognize the consequence of this failure and what it meant to the Germans. Steinmetz himself concedes that he is not interested in the process of violence itself (*The Devil's Handwriting*, 192). Hull, by contrast, focuses on the role of military organization and routines, so she does not closely examine the crisis brought on by failure.
90. Agnes Heller, *Theorie der Gefühle* (Hamburg, 1980), 111.
91. Neckel proposes that shame can shed more light on a society's moral interior than its formalized norms and ideals. See Neckel, *Status und Scham*, 18.
92. Georges Balandier, "The Colonial Situation: A Theoretical Approach," in *Social Change: The Colonial Situation*, ed. Immanuel Wallerstein (New York, 1966), 54.
93. Nicola Labanca, *Oltremare: Storia dell'espansione coloniale italiana* (Bologna, 2002), 112ff.
94. Norbert Elias, *The Germans: Power Struggles and the Development of Habitus in the Nineteenth and Twentieth Centuries*, trans. Eric Dunning and Stephen Mennell (New York, 1996), 206.
95. See Helen B. Lewis, *Shame and Guilt in Neurosis* (New York, 1971); Helen B. Lewis, "Introduction: Shame—The 'Sleeper' in Psychopathology," in *The Role of Shame in Symptom Formation*, edited by Helen B. Lewis (Hillsdale, 1987), 1–28; Thomas

J. Scheff, *Bloody Revenge: Emotions, Nationalism and War* (Lincoln, 2000); and Thomas J. Scheff and Suzanne M. Retzinger, *Emotions and Violence: Shame and Rage in Destructive Conflicts* (Lincoln, 2001).

96. Eckl, *"S'ist ein übles Land hier,"* 16; and Werner Hillebrecht, "Die Nama und der Krieg im Süden," in *Völkermord in Deutsch-Südwestafrika: Der Kolonialkrieg (1904–1908) in Namibia und seine Folgen*, ed. Jürgen Zimmerer and Joachim Zeller (Berlin, 2004), 126–27.
97. Robert Delavignette, *Les vrais chefs de l'Empire* (Paris, 1939).
98. Gerlach, "Extremely Violent Societies," 459.
99. Clifford Geertz, "Thick Description: Toward an Interpretive Theory of Culture," in *The Interpretation of Cultures* (New York, 1973), 3–30.
100. Jeremy Silvester and Jan-Bart Gewald, eds., *Words Cannot Be Found: German Colonial Rule in Namibia: An Annotated Reprint of the 1918 Blue Book* (Leiden, 2003); and Andreas Eckl, *"S'ist ein übles Land hier."*
101. See especially Matthias Häussler and Trutz von Trotha, "Brutalisierung 'von unten': Kleiner Krieg, Entgrenzung der Gewalt und Genozid im kolonialen Deutsch-Südwestafrika," *Mittelweg 36* 21, no. 3 (2012): 57–89; Matthias Häussler and Trutz von Trotha, "Koloniale Zivilgesellschaft? Von der 'kolonialen Gesellschaft' zur kolonialen Gewaltgemeinschaft in Deutsch-Südwestafrika," in *Zivilgesellschaft und Krieg*, ed. Dierk Spreen and Trutz von Trotha (Berlin, 2012), 293–317; Matthias Häussler, "From Destruction to Extermination: Genocidal Escalation in Germany's War against the Herero, 1904," *Journal of Namibian Studies* 11 (2011): 55–81; Matthias Häussler, "Zur Asymmetrie tribaler und staatlicher Kriegführung in Imperialkriegen: Die Logik der Kriegführung der Herero in vor- und frühkolonialer Zeit," in *Imperialkriege von 1500 bis heute: Strukturen—Akteure—Lernprozesse*, ed. Tanja Bührer et al. (Paderborn, 2011), 177–95; Matthias Häussler, "Grausamkeit und Kolonialismus: Zur Dynamik von Grausamkeit," in *On Cruelty*, ed. Trutz von Trotha and Jakob Rösel (Cologne, 2011), 511–37; Matthias Häussler, "Soldatische Hinterwäldler oder Avantgarde? Über die einsatzbezogenen Erfahrungen der Kaiserlichen Schutztruppe in 'Deutsch-Südwestafrika,'" *Militärgeschichtliche Zeitschrift* 71, no. 2 (2012): 309–27; Matthias Häussler, "Zwischen Vernichtung und Pardon: Die Konzentrationslager in 'Deutsch-Südwestafrika' (1904–08)," *Zeitschrift für Geschichtswissenschaft* 61, no. 7/8 (2013): 601–20; and Matthias Häussler, "'Kultur der Grausamkeit' und die Dynamik 'eradierender Praktiken': Ein Beitrag zur Erforschung extremer Gewalt," *Sociologus* 63 (2013): 147–69.

Chapter 1

Settlers, Herero, and the Spiral of Violence

The settlement of South-West Africa involved the expulsion, expropriation, subjugation, and disenfranchisement of autochthonous groups. It was inherently violent and blurred the boundaries between war and peace, and for this reason the scope of this study is not limited to officially declared hostilities.

"German imperialism," the focus of Horst Drechsler's work, involved many different forces—including the settlers, who receive special attention in this chapter. I begin with the settlers, because they pushed to escalate violence earlier, and more persistently, than any other group. Privatized violence gained the upper hand and eventually dominated colonial politics, while the government itself was "powerless" to intervene.[1] Thus, the settlers should be considered an autonomous motor of colonial expansion. The brutality and anomie of the frontier situation fanned the flames of war, which soon drew in the metropolitan state with its full destructive force. Yet even after the metropole took control of military operations, the settlers continued to influence the course of events. The end of the fighting and the near extermination of entire groups did not pacify the settlers. To the contrary—the war intensified the colony's violent conditions, which continued to inform the postwar order.

The aggression of the settlers provoked the Herero and gave the uprising its particular character. It was no coincidence that the Herero raids of the first days and weeks intentionally targeted settlers. This scandalized the metropolitan public, who knew relatively little about conditions overseas, and helped to foster a climate in which extreme violence was not only conceivable, but acceptable.

Closer investigation of the January 1904 raids shows that the raids were in no way acts of "senseless" violence, even if the settlers tended to portray them as such. Rather, the settlers' angry reactions seem to suggest they themselves knew better. As the Germans, and then the Herero, began to close ranks, the fragile ties between the two groups at last broke apart and no longer kept violence in check. The path to escalation was wide open. The war descended into a spiral of violence and counterviolence, well before Trotha assumed the command in SWA.

The Settlers

The settlers were responsible for starting the war and for inciting ever greater violence. Their racism only intensified as the balance of power shifted in their favor. Fear and mistrust, which were central to the colonial situation, motivated the settlers' aggression, which the colonial state was unable or unwilling to check. The state's half-hearted interventions antagonized the white population and alienated the Herero, who gradually came to understand that they could not count on the protection of the state. Rather than containing violence, government intervention often intensified it.

Double Antagonism:
Between Indigenous People and the Colonial State

Georges Balandier defines the "colonial situation" as "domination imposed by a foreign minority, racially (or ethnically) and culturally different, acting in the name of a racial (or ethnic) and cultural superiority dogmatically affirmed, and imposing itself on an indigenous population constituting a numerical majority but inferior to the dominant group from a material point of view."[2] A fundamental paradox of colonial domination is the foreign minority's fear of the subjugated masses. South-West Africa was no exception. Although the colonizers believed that they were superior to the colonized in every respect, they also understood the power of numbers and the dangers that could arise in a "worst case" scenario. Overseas, this threat was constant, in contrast to their "pacified" societies of origin.[3] In SWA, scattered fortifications were supposed to protect against the internal enemy, the "natives,"[4] but these structures also reminded the settlers that they lived in a kind of permanent state of emergency. Mistrust and fear were underlying conditions of their day-to-day existence. Socialization in the colonial situation had no basis in trust. Interactions with the indigenous people occurred within a context of despotism and threats of violence, which steadily deepened the chasm of misunderstandings that separated both sides.[5]

The antagonism between colonizers and colonized was particularly pronounced in the settler colony of South-West Africa. Contacts—and potential tensions—multiplied between the groups in the colony as a larger white population moved in. The sheer number of contacts was part of the problem, along with the shifting premises under which they occurred. Even the lowliest whites in "colonial society"[6] saw themselves as members of a ruling class. In the eyes of the settlers, all whites were superior to the indigenous people, entitled to "act as masters" in their presence.[7] The Africans clearly distinguished between representatives of the state and private individuals. The government ultimately viewed both settlers and "natives" as subjects, although the settlers were certainly better off. In any case, neither the Africans nor the colonial authorities were prepared to accept each individual settler's claims to "mastery," and this led to tensions.

Settler societies are particularly vulnerable because they include entire families, unlike male-dominated colonial societies. In South-West Africa, families were scattered across wide distances and often lived hours from their nearest neighbors or the closest military station, apparently defenseless against the indigenous people.[8] Settlement involved the transfer of populations, land, and property at the Africans' expense, and the settlers did not expect them to accept this transfer without some resistance.

Unsurprisingly, these circumstances led settlers to call for a complete military takeover of the colony, which placed certain limits on the political pragmatism of the colonial government. Trade, plantation, and mining colonies (which made do without population transfers) could more easily negotiate with local grandees. From the start, however, settlers in SWA bitterly resisted Leutwein's "peace policy,"[9] which allowed autochthonous groups to retain some sovereignty.

Fear and mistrust were part of every colonial situation, but these emotions were particularly evident in settler colonies. Despite their unchallenged political, social, and cultural hegemony, the South-West African settlers saw themselves as "constantly under threat."[10] Just as similar conditions regularly led to hysteria among settlers in South Africa,[11] South-West Africa was infamous for alarming tales that spread like wildfire. These stories whipped the population into a frenzy, although they were usually untrue.[12] Even the most far-fetched rumors flourished because settlers always counted on the worst.

The racist gaze does not see members of the racialized group as individuals, but rather as generic representatives of their kind.[13] This gaze depends on rigid stereotypes, whereby a single "example" is necessarily defined by the typical characteristics of its kind. Stereotyping is a shortcut, which can forestall, override, or negate lived experience. Authentic relationships, which could otherwise alleviate mistrust and fear, are next to impossible under such conditions. Instead, certain narratives emerge and begin to take on a life of their own, reinforcing and dramatizing the negative characteristics of the racialized group.[14] The groups grow further apart, feeding fear and mistrust.[15]

Early on, as Bley persuasively shows, settlers raised their voices against official policies they felt were too "mild," and they continued to do so until the end of German colonial rule.[16] Just days before the outbreak of the January 1904 uprising, an article with the suggestive title "On the Current Situation" appeared in the *Deutsch-Südwestafrikanische Zeitung*. The author, a settler named Schlettwein, reiterated the criticism of Leutwein's supposedly too "mild" and hesitant policies. He complained that the settlers faced a "direct danger" from "armed hordes" of "natives who were beyond inferior," and he made the case for escalation by calling for more troops, espousing radical war aims, and demanding an immediate strike.[17] Schlettwein's words show the painful discrepancy between settlers' feelings of superiority and their actual situation, as well as their discomfort with the passive role that the government had assigned to them. Waiting only to respond, without agency of their own, did not correspond to the settlers' self-image as "masters," and Schlettwein feared that such behavior would appear "weak" in the eyes of the colonized peoples. The settlers felt mistreated and compelled by their government to serve merely as "means to an end," or even as "cultural fertilizer."[18]

The emotions of fear and mistrust gradually became more obsessive. The less that settlers were actually threatened, the more stubbornly they worried about their own security and pushed for radicalization. The ruthless "native policy" of the postwar era was introduced—partially in response to public pressure—only after the remaining members of the defeated groups were languishing in concentration camps and facing eradication. This policy became more extreme over time.[19] Fear and mistrust so pervaded South-West African colonial society that these emotions ultimately became *the* "switch and filter" for the reception of world events.[20] The Russo-Japanese War interested the *Deutsch-Südwestafrikanische Zeitung* only insofar as nonwhites had defeated the "white race" (which is to say, Russia), and because the victory of the "colored peril" threatened to undermine the prestige and dominion of whites in Africa.[21]

Ironically, fear, mistrust, and the tendency to panic saved the lives of many settlers in January 1904. Hypervigilance allowed colonial society to respond promptly to the first rumors of rebellion. By the time that the first shots rang out, many settlers were already hunkered down behind fortifications. Troops were mustered quickly and sent to the locations under attack. However, the settlers' vigilance often escalated the conflict, as Jan-Bart Gewald correctly notes.[22]

The antagonism between settlers and colonized people was closely linked to the antagonism between settlers and the colonial state. The latter was so pronounced that the doctor Ludwig Külz identified dissatisfaction with the government as an essential trait of "Southwesters."[23] There were underlying structural reasons for the settlers' conflict with the state. Tensions erupted whenever they felt patronized or thwarted by government authority, particularly if their pride had been wounded in the presence of the Africans. The state seemed to have consigned them to a condition of powerlessness, which they opposed with all their might. The settler ethos was difficult to reconcile with statehood (*Staatlichkeit*).

In contrast to older settler colonies in America or Oceania, which were distinguished by a high degree of settler autonomy, settlement in South-West Africa was orchestrated by an authoritarian state.[24] Upon landing in South-West Africa, most settlers encountered state authorities who understood their role as an extension of the Imperial German bureaucracy.[25]

We should not, however, overstate the significance of *Staatlichkeit* in the colonial context. In general, colonial rule relied on elements of nonstate and (especially) patrimonial governance. To adopt the terminology of Max Weber, there was no legal rule (*legale Herrschaft*) in a systematic bureaucratic sense. Despotic and intermediary rule prevailed, not only with respect to native, but also white, subjects.[26] The idea of the colonial state was not well realized in many respects, but its representatives nevertheless held fast to this "utopia" undeterred.[27] Frictions and conflicts with the population were inevitable—all the more so as the colonial administration reserved the right to make fundamental decisions in questions of colonial politics.

Within this context, Lorenzo Veracini's observations on settler colonialism and the differences between settlers and migrants are instructive. Both settlers and migrants leave their homelands in order to put down roots elsewhere, but settlers do not intend to join an existing foreign community. Rather, settlers colonize and claim land as their own, seeking to establish a "better" or ideal community, and sometimes rejecting their land of origin.[28]

Unlike "colonial sojourners" such as civil servants, military officers, entrepreneurs, and adventurers, settlers in German South-West Africa came to stay. They invested their money and labor in colonization, even putting their lives on the line in some cases.[29] They sought nothing less than a new homeland overseas, and before long they actually saw themselves as "Africans" or "Southwesters." Veracini describes this process as "indigenization," as establishing a settler society necessarily entails breaking away from a society of origin (and also from those who identify with, or represent, this society).[30] James Belich observes that settler colonies and empires eventually drift apart.[31] Although the dominance of Imperial Germany in South-West Africa was never seriously challenged in thirty years of colonial rule, settlers maintained a separate existence and served as an independent motor of colonial expansion.[32]

One reason that settlers assumed the risks of emigrating to a faraway land was the hope of overcoming the barriers to entrepreneurship and social mobility in Wilhelmine society. Colonists who worked the land emphasized their identity as farmers, not peasants.[33] They saw themselves not as socially and politically subordinate, dependent elements of the old European order—but rather as modern, autonomous actors.[34] The settlers were unwilling to be coddled by state authority. They continued to see themselves as Germans, but not as the lowly subjects that they might have been in their homeland. In the colony, they refused all forms of paternalistic oversight by state authority or the distant metropole.[35] The colonial administration's interventions were a "burdensome restraint" on their free development, while the ties to the "motherland" were a "confining shackle."[36] The settlers called for autonomy and the right to self-governance, pushing blatantly for the democratization of colonial rule.[37] They saw this as their right, as they were primarily responsible for the "work of development" in the colony.[38] From the settlers' perspective, "developing colonial land, adding its treasures and assets to the wealth of the nation, and putting these to use" was not an accomplishment of functionaries and civil servants, but "first and foremost, of colonists."[39] Roads and water systems were often built through private initiative. The people's contributions to infrastructure development were more readily apparent than in Europe. This heightened settlers' self-esteem vis-à-vis state authority[40]—which was evident, for example, in how they raised their voices as "citizens" against the direction of the war effort from Berlin.[41]

It is, however, important to note that these claims often had little to do with reality, which most of the would-be masters perceived as shameful. Helmut Bley uses the term "dependent masters" to accentuate this discrepancy.[42]

"Dependent Masters"

The farmer—according to Brigitta Schmidt-Lauber, the "key figure" of South-West African identity[43]—was particularly averse to state tutelage. Large-scale ranching was central to the colonial economy, since water and pasture were scarce. Outside of the towns, the colony was sparsely populated; farmers lived far apart from one another in relative isolation. They had to know how to take care of themselves, as they were usually left to their own devices.[44] They presided over their land patrimonially, and they were prepared to defend themselves with force—especially when the closest garrisons or police stations were days away on horseback. Captain von Wangenheim told Governor Friedrich von Lindequist that the farmers presided over their property like "small kings," rejecting the influence of any outside authorities.[45] As was typical in most colonies, state power did not extend far beyond the limits of the capital city.[46] Only toward the end of German rule did the state seriously attempt to assert its dominion beyond the towns, particularly with respect to white subjects. In 1913 (that is, just before the colony was effectively lost), several farmers were prosecuted in a series of trials for crimes against indigenous employees,[47] thereby affirming state sovereignty beyond the centers of power.

This is a good place to dispel a common misconception about the settler population. The farmer was hardly typical of South-West African settlers. The settler population was extremely heterogeneous, like South-West African colonial society as whole.[48] On the eve of the Herero uprising, the traveling scholar Georg Hartmann was disappointed to learn that there were just 813 farmers in the population of South-West Africa, only 334 of whom were German nationals.[49] Barely 10 percent of German settlers were in fact farmers. If the farmer was the "key figure" of South-West African identity, it was not because of numerical superiority, but rather the wishful thinking of colonial ideologues.[50]

The settlement of South-West Africa was ideologically charged. German colonialists hoped to preserve the "nation" (*Volk*) by redirecting annual flows of emigrants to destinations such as the United States to their own territory instead.[51] They had high hopes for the colony and high expectations of colonists—but in the end, it was all for naught. Even after thirty years of German rule and hefty government investment, the colony never managed to take in more than fifteen thousand settlers, and most of these were "inferior" elements from the lower classes.[52]

Few settlers brought along the capital that would have been necessary for large-scale cattle farming that was competitive on the world market.

Next to civil servants and military officers, laborers and craftsmen were the largest professional group in colonial society, although they commanded little attention. Tradesmen were not officially counted as part of the population until 1905. Only toward the end of German rule did colonial authorities gradually come to see that the majority of whites depended on the wider economy, not just agricultural production.[53]

In fact, the dependence of the average German settler was even more far-reaching. The majority of settlers were politically as well as economically dependent.[54] The state was weak in many ways, but it was still present. Dependence was a fundamental condition of the South-West African settlers. The idealized image of the economically independent farmer was, at best, counterfactual, pointing to a fundamental tension between the way things "ought" to be and the way they actually were. This tension informed the average German-Namibian biography and encouraged the "particular relations of violence"[55] that combined with other factors to create a special dynamic of cruelty. The settlers' dependence ultimately conflicted with their self-awareness as "masters," and also with the oft-touted prestige of their supposedly superior race.

Many farmers who lived far from the towns first got to know the indigenous groups as autonomous powerholders. After they were assigned a place to settle and do business (farmers who lacked the necessary capital could get their start as traders), they often relied on the goodwill of local chiefs and headmen. Hours or days away from the next garrison, they learned to approach the Africans carefully. Some farmers even considered their relations with local elites to be a privilege and a sign of their own upward mobility.[56]

The majority of settlers who lived in towns had no such cause for moderation. The town was the center of colonial power, and hegemony was experienced differently here.[57] Many indigenous people lived and worked in towns, but they were isolated from their own communities and compelled to serve the whites in dependent, subordinate positions. This shaped white townspeople's image of the colonized Africans and their relative strength, which can explain these whites' amazement at the dogged resistance mounted by the Herero against the German troops in 1904. White townspeople were emboldened to push for escalation because they underestimated the power of autochthonous groups. They were usually still working their way up in the colony, earning wages and trying to raise capital for farming, so they were unconcerned about maintaining good relations with the autochthonous groups. The "dependent masters" in towns pushed for escalation at all costs.[58] The less that settlers resembled the ideal of the independent farmer, the more likely they were to embrace violent solutions. The state had difficulty asserting its authority, even in towns; the white civilian population's willingness to resort to violence posed a serious challenge.

White Despots

The more the "dependent masters" were pulled into the wake of the metropole and feeling out of control, the more presumptuous their demands became. The uprising made the colony a focus of public attention in Imperial Germany. New troops streamed into the colony, so that within one year their ranks had increased by a factor of twenty. No later than Leutwein's departure at the end of 1904, the colonial government had become a military dictatorship that felt responsible only to the Kaiser. Thousands of workers streamed in alongside the troops, and the threat of foreign infiltration worried the settlers deeply.[59] They understood the necessity of admitting new workers, but they were also afraid of undesirable "elements"[60] and no longer felt secure.[61] They saw the war years as a time of alienation, a painful affront to their own autonomy. They did not disguise their reluctance to follow the orders of officers who were new to the colony. One author in the *Deutsch-Südwestafrikanische Zeitung* wrote: "But to assess the local conditions—anyone who has lived in this land for five, ten, twelve years cannot just subordinate his own judgment to the authority of foreign gentlemen, and this is the source of some tension."[62]

Officers became a focus of local resentment; they generally came from loftier social circles than the settlers and often presented themselves as superior. Above all, they insisted upon a clear hierarchy between military and civil authority, as in the metropole. According to the interim settlement commissioner Paul Rohrbach, the officers looked down on the settlers as a "pack" of lowlifes.[63]

Such condescension was frowned upon in SWA. The colonial situation cast its shadow on internal relations within colonial society, too. Aspects of group identity such as nationality, class, and confession[64] could present barriers that were difficult to overcome in the day-to-day interactions of metropolitan society, but these were no longer as important in the colony. In certain respects, settler society was comparatively egalitarian; racial antagonism and skin color shaped colonial life so profoundly that all other aspects of identity were overshadowed.[65] Partha Chatterjee's "rule of difference" establishes the abasement of indigenous peoples as a structural characteristic of modern colonialism.[66] In South-West Africa, this difference became a downright obsession. The settlers never tired of explaining the unique significance of racial antagonism in the colony, and that its intensity could not be compared to any other conflict in the homeland, even class struggle.[67] They suspected that the newly arrived officers from Imperial Germany could not fully grasp the extent of this problem.[68]

An incident from 1905, which occupied the white population of South-West Africa long thereafter, vividly illustrates the tensions between settlers and officers. An officer overheard a white laborer openly criticizing the Kaiser. The officer immediately ordered a "colored" man to fetch a sjambok (a whip made from the hide of a hippopotamus, typically used for corporal punishment) and to flog the malefactor then and there—which he did. The white laborer was subsequently prosecuted for insulting the sovereign and sentenced to two months in prison.

The settlers were outraged that the officer had instructed a "colored" man to beat a white man "out on the street, in broad daylight." The *Deutsch-Südwestafrikanische Zeitung* was dumbfounded: "And this happened while we're in a race war. What else can be said?!"[69] The fact that the court endorsed the officer's actions made matters even worse. The case occupied the local population for months thereafter. On 6 September 1905, the *Deutsch-Südwestafrikanische Zeitung* wrote that the officer ought to be told that his actions represented a "sin . . . against racial solidarity": "Even the most depraved white should not be given up to the sjambok of a black, upon the order of a white. Such incidents inflict far greater damage upon the prestige of the white race than most people in the homeland can only begin to imagine."[70] The anonymous author went on to muse that had the wrongdoer been a soldier in uniform, he almost certainly would have walked off, in order to spare him and his compatriots the humiliation of public punishment. The author concluded, "As soldiers are protected by their uniform, so too must whites be protected by the white color of their skin."[71]

In his report about the war against the Herero, the settler and author Conrad Rust, who was known for his comparatively moderate and reasonable positions,[72] denounced measures taken by General Lothar von Trotha that—as Rust saw it—all too carelessly disregarded racial and political realities on the ground.[73] This included standing at attention before military superiors (a tradition that Trotha had reintroduced) because deferential saluting supposedly demeaned whites in the presence of Africans. This also included disciplining whites in public, and having African rape victims identify their perpetrators by walking the ranks—a supposedly humiliating practice (for the white soldiers!).[74] In short, any measure that might demean a white person in the eyes of a black, or that might harm the "prestige of the white race," was to be curtailed,[75] regardless of justification. "Racial solidarity" took precedence.

The settlers were bothered most, but not only, by the public disparaging of whites. They often took offense at the very idea of being held accountable for their interactions with Africans. In such situations, the settlers essentially demanded the right to do as they pleased. Their spokespersons abhorred all government sanctions and claimed the inalienable right of all whites to personal autonomy (*Willkür*), which was seen as integral to whites' claim to dominance. A true "master," in other words, should not have to submit to any norms. The spokespersons did warn whites not to forget their moral "superiority" over the "natives" by abandoning all behavioral norms. In the same breath, however, they emphasized that all rules were to be followed only for "our sake," and should never become a hindrance.[76] One contributor to the *Deutsch-Südwestafrikanische Zeitung* held that he was in no way advocating for lawlessness, or for abandoning the "natives" to "harsh and severe treatment"—but in the end, only the self-interest of the colonizers mattered, or could be grounds for moderation.[77] Any act of moderation, in other words, ought to be left to the discretion of the individual settler; under no circumstances could the state compel such an act without the settler's consent. Because colonization itself was a "violation" (*Vergewaltigung*), might made right. For the time being, at least, it was illusory to think that the rule of law could be enforced in the colony as in Europe.[78]

The settlers' demands stretched Chatterjee's "rule of difference" to an extreme,[79] leading to despotic rule by the white colonizing class. Their regime was *despotic* because no limits were placed on individual free will (*Willkür*). It was *rule by the white colonizing class* because, in principle, all members of colonial society were supposed to be "masters." This political order entailed the privatization of violence and, conversely, a weakening of the state monopoly on power.

It was First Lieutenant Stuhlmann, an officer who arrived in SWA only in the spring of 1904, who succinctly captured the settlers' expectations. He wrote in his diary: "The colored native must feel the superiority of the white master so strongly that he fears him more than his god. Only then will it remain possible for unprotected whites to dominate the natives, who are numerically far superior."[80] Stuhlmann spoke to a fundamental problem of governance, which had already occupied David Hume in his essay "Of the First Principles of Government": how the few can dominate the many. Stuhlmann's description of "godlike" white masters highlights the asymmetry in the antagonism between masters and subjects in the colonial situation. Such a reputation had to be acquired, and so the "white masters" strove to present themselves as a powerful and punitive force.[81] Of particular interest here is what the "masters" deemed necessary to do, or—better—to refrain from doing, in order to uphold this reputation. All whites, regardless of who they were, could not be allowed to take any action that might "demystify" themselves or their race,[82] or that might otherwise shake the faith of black Africans in the godlike superiority of the whites. Anything that could demean a white person in the eyes of a "native" was to be avoided. This meant that the settlers' supposed right to *Willkür* could not be disputed, and that no norms could impede their interactions with indigenous people. The "rights" that the settlers claimed not only contradicted the state's monopoly on the use of force, but also denied and undermined state interests in the boldest possible way. None of the governors in South-West Africa backed away from the state's claim to dominance, regardless of how settler-friendly they styled themselves—not Leutwein, not the military dictator Trotha, and not the civilian governor Lindequist. Thus, tensions between the legitimate and would-be masters continued after the war. And because the settlers fought not only with words, the violence "from below" persisted as well.

Unfettered Violence

Before the uprising, the orientation of colonial and settlement policy had repeatedly led to fierce disputes between the government and settlers. The *Deutsch-Südwestafrikanische Zeitung* ran the aforementioned article by Schlettwein, which underscored the concerns of so many settlers, just days before the uprising began.[83]

Schlettwein reiterated that the white colonists "could not comprehend certain attitudes and measures taken by the government"—indeed, all they could do was "shake their heads" in response. He was particularly concerned about the government's "weak position" vis-à-vis the indigenous people, which he traced back to the influence of "fanatic friends of the mission" and ignorant "idealists." He blamed "humanitarian stupidity" for threatening to turn relations in the colony upside-down: "Is the real point of German colonization only to bring the blessings of civilization to natives in Africa, and can the private businessman be seen only as means to an end, as cultural fertilizer?" For all of the differences of opinion in the colony, Schlettwein's use of a rhetorical question shows that he did presume general agreement (with the possible exception of "idealists" and "fanatics") about the "end" and "cultural fertilizer" of colonization. Part of the problem, Schlettwein argued, was that the authorities occasionally forgot where priorities lay, and he called upon them to remember "what's what": "Colonization is and remains a hardship, a violation, in the sense that land and property are taken from the indigenous native population." It was unfathomable to him that the government nevertheless acted as if it had to protect the "natives" from white "bloodsuckers," and "to compel uncivilized, brutish people into loyalty and servitude through gifts and kindness." Only "vigorous suppression" and "exemplary punishment" could make an impression on the "colored African."

In Schlettwein's view, the colony should have been subdued long ago, so that "no native would have dared to think about the things that we have experienced, and still experience, in the north and the south." There had been victories, but no "total" victories, which meant that the autochthonous groups had not been permanently defeated, disarmed, and made to serve the colonizers' economic interests. Instead, armed "natives who were beyond inferior" still posed a "direct danger" to the white population. Schlettwein concluded with a call for more troops and radical war aims—that is, for war and more violence.

Schlettwein's article, which appeared shortly before the uprising began, articulated fears that would be realized just a few days later. In retrospect, his words seem prophetic—or perhaps more accurately, they were a self-fulfilling prophecy that the settlers themselves helped come to pass. The settlers argued for the use of force, while the government tried to rein in their lust for plunder and expansion, and to avoid violent conflicts with the autochthonous groups. Newspapers like the *Windhuker Nachrichten* (called *Nachrichten des Bezirks-Vereins Windhuk* until 1904) and the *Deutsch-Südwestafrikanische Zeitung* gave the settlers a platform for articulating their sometimes pointed opposition to official policy and its organs. As I have demonstrated elsewhere, however, these newspapers only appeared to be a vehicle of civil expression.[84] They promoted such expression insofar as they were an outlet for civic engagement; they critiqued and sought to influence official policy, invoking topoi such as democratization and the rule of law. Such principles were, of course, characteristically reserved for the white colonizing class alone; rule of law was to be suspended in interactions with black Africans. However, the settler newspapers' calls for war and violence underscore how little the settler community resembled civil society—especially since the settlers were not content to fight with words, but themselves turned to violence.

The rinderpest epidemic of 1896–97 was an important caesura in the settlement of South-West Africa. The cattle plague claimed a large proportion of autochthonous cattle holdings. Many chiefs were said to have lost more than 90 percent of their herds.[85] This led to a temporary shift in the balance of power. The extraordinary cattle wealth of the Herero had once meant that capital-intensive cattle farming was not very profitable, but the plague changed this. Many Herero lost their livelihoods, and their chiefs and headmen were no longer in a position to support them.[86] They often had no other recourse than working for wages for white employers. This fortuitous turn of events (for whites) encouraged many emigrants to seek their fortunes in SWA. The number of settlers doubled in just a few years.[87] The newcomers' relations with the autochthonous population began to change as well, as numerically and economically emboldened whites increasingly saw themselves as members of a "master race."[88] Leutwein repeatedly advised his superiors in Berlin that "the growing number of whites in the colony has continued to exacerbate relations between whites and the natives."[89]

Colonial conquest is frequently understood as the violent penetration of a foreign lifeworld. This image is apt, as Wolfram Hartmann has persuasively shown that the Germans' acquisition of land in SWA was accompanied at all times by the "highly predatory sexual behavior" of white men. Sexual violence against indigenous women occurred every day and was considered normal.[90] What changed over time was that even members of prominent families were increasingly victimized.[91] This corresponds to the logic of racism, which disregards "fine distinctions" between individuals and treats all members of a group as interchangeable. Why should a settler try to distinguish between "common" Herero and the members of prominent families, when all he sees are "Kaffirs"? (And how could he even do so?) The lives of indigenous people had so little value that anything could be done to them,[92] so it is hardly surprising that, at some point, all boundaries disappeared.

The escalation in violence affected all areas of life.[93] Trutz von Trotha suggests that violence increased as white and black populations moved closer together, and the whites became more concerned with establishing a clear pecking order in the colony.[94] However, this explanation alone is not sufficient.

The racism that increasingly defined all interactions in the colony was the result of what the settlers saw—not always correctly—as an upset to the balance of power. Although the absolute number of German settlers remained vanishingly small compared to the size of the colony itself, the *relative* growth of the German population was substantial around the turn of the century. The Germans' base of power did expand. Because of the rinderpest, they began to live in closer proximity to the indigenous population, as more and more impoverished Herero took jobs with white employers as domestic servants, labors, or herders. Many newcomers no longer got to know the local people as autonomous powerholders,[95] although these circumstances were misleading; the cattle plague was not permanent, and Herero society soon began to recover from its effects.

As a result of this supposed reversal in the balance of power, the settlers' racism became increasingly aggressive and eventually affected all areas of life. Even false assumptions can have real consequences. Because the usurpers increasingly saw themselves as invincible masters, they had only scorn for the supposedly inferior Herero; they eventually abandoned all scruples and treating the Herero however they pleased. This shows how structural power relations are central to racist constructions.[96]

Another factor was at work here. Shifting relations of power in SWA were also related to circumstances that had encouraged the settlers to leave Germany in the first place.[97] The first settlers were fortune seekers who expected upward mobility, but those who left after the turn of the century were fleeing the threat of proletarianization.[98] The fear and heightened sense of competition that these settlers brought with them from Germany undoubtedly affected their interactions with the autochthonous population; itinerant traders, for example, were notorious for their sometimes criminal business practices. Above all, the newcomers' fear of pauperization found an outlet in racism. Max Weber recognized that "ethnic honor is a specific honor of the masses (*Massenehre*), for it is accessible to anybody who belongs to the subjectively believed community of descent."[99] Similar to "poor white trash" in the American South, whom Weber cites as an example, even the most miserable Germans in SWA gained a minimum of "social honor" through the "*déclassement*" of the blacks.

It did not escape the long-serving Governor Leutwein that tensions between the white and autochthonous populations had heightened over the years. In a formal statement about the uprising, Leutwein noted that there had been at least six recent cases where whites had "just shot down" Herero. The whites saw themselves in a "fight against an inferior race," which is why they ultimately resorted to "murder and manslaughter."[100] This is striking evidence that the settlers no longer recoiled from even the most extreme actions. On the eve of the 1904 war, the situation for the Herero was oppressive. Memoirs reveal that beatings and other forms of abuse were ubiquitous and allowed to proliferate unchecked. When questioned by British authorities, Abraham Kaffer later recalled,

> We have never been able to understand the German "Government" . . . because every German officer, sergeant, and soldier, every German policeman and every German farmer seemed to be the "Government." By this we mean that every German farmer seemed to be able to do towards us just what he pleased, and to make his own laws, and he never got punished. The police

and the soldiers might flog us and ill-treat us, the farmers might do as they pleased towards us and our wives, the soldiers might molest and even rape our women and young girls, and no one was punished.[101]

This statement not only underscores the frequency of abuse, but also shows how weak the monopoly on the use of force had become. The settlers believed that the state was too invasive, and that it too often sided with the "natives." For the Africans, however, the state seemed absent, which had to do with the advanced privatization of violence.

Whites were not permitted to treat the indigenous people however they pleased, but in practice they got away with almost everything. The colonial administration did not intervene, in part because its organs often participated in the assaults. Abraham Kaffer testified that Africans were abused and mistreated by police and soldiers. Willem Christian emphasized that blacks often declined to take action against perpetrators because police and soldiers were among the rapists.[102] Failing to act could also lead to complicity. Many of the assaults on record, such as the apparently common practice of "hunting" for indigenous women in the camps and *werfts* (Herero villages), would not have been possible without guards' knowledge and sometimes their active participation.[103]

These events may explain why white settlers repeatedly touted the "closeness" they felt to soldiers and noncommissioned officers in the lower ranks of the Schutztruppe.[104] The troops' misbehavior may have had to do with the fact that many considered settling permanently in the colony after completing their service, and they did not want to alienate their future neighbors.[105] As prospective settlers, they adopted the thought patterns of colonial society.[106] Complicity blurred boundaries between the state and the (white) population at the lowest levels of colonial administration.

The judiciary also did not put a stop to this activity. All legal matters involving whites fell under German jurisdiction. The testimony of Africans had little weight in court, and judges sympathized more or less openly with their fellow Germans. The growing influence of white lay magistrates who could overrule judges' rulings meant that "racial hatred had become rooted in the very framework of justice," as Leutwein later reflected.[107]

In sum, the African population was left to the caprices and self-proclaimed authority of individual settlers, and could not count on protection. In this situation, the Herero ultimately chose to take arms. Samuel Kariko described the circumstances of this momentous decision: "Our people were shot and murdered; our women were ill-treated; and those who did this were not punished. Our chiefs consulted and we decided that war could not be worse than what we were undergoing ... yet we decided on war, as the chiefs said we would be better off even if we were all dead."[108] In a letter to the Oorlam leader Hendrik Witbooi, Samuel Maharero pointed to the "abuses" that drove his decision to take arms against German colonial rule, and he explained that he would rather die than continue to live under such conditions.[109] Violence and cruelty had become so pervasive that the Herero finally sought an "absolute decision."[110]

In a letter dated 6 March 1904, Samuel Maharero reminded Leutwein that "the white people" had begun the war by killing Herero.[111] Privatized violence had apparently assumed a political dimension. Those who had been in the colony long enough understood that the mistreatment and rape of the Herero could become a *casus belli*.[112] The settlers retroactively styled themselves as victims, demanding full compensation from Imperial Germany for the damages that had been incurred by the uprising. The metropolitan public seems to have suspected that the settlers bore at least some responsibility for its outbreak.[113]

Although the settlers had an interest in escalation and pushed for it on their own, their provocations were not necessarily part of a deliberate strategy. They were pleased by the opportunity to "clean house across the land"[114] and to usher in the awaited "new order"[115] of power and property relations, which Leutwein's administration had resisted. And while the settlers generally underestimated the will of the Herero to fight and their capacity for resistance, the risks posed by an uprising once it had begun were difficult to foresee.[116] The actual outbreak seems to have caught the Germans unaware, which undercuts the assumption that the settlers had deliberately pursued this outcome—not least because it implies a solidarity among the settlers that simply did not exist.

Racism developed a dynamic of its own that the government ultimately could not control. As the whites' confidence in their superiority grew, so too did their aggression and contempt toward black Africans. State inaction only encouraged them to push boundaries even further. By allowing the settlers to fend for themselves, the state effectively condoned their behavior. Every offense that went unpunished encouraged bolder acts, until the proverbial last straw broke the camel's back, and catastrophe ensued. It took many small steps to reach this breaking point; there was no single great catalyst (according to what was then considered "normal" in the colony). By the eve of the uprising, the whites seemed to have abandoned all scruples, and the Herero understood that tensions could no longer be eased. The behavior of the whites was so brazen and risky that it is difficult to discern any "rational" planning behind it.[117] More likely, emotions were at work. Fear and mistrust defined colonial society, providing the motive and "action readiness" for violence.

Fear can give way to flight, but the settlers dug in their heels. This had to do with their sense of absolute superiority, and also their specific ethos; they had come to stay, and they were unwilling to yield even one inch to the local residents. Most settlers had invested all of their assets and years of labor in the colonial adventure, which meant that the costs of leaving were simply too high to consider seriously. By ruling out flight, they chose fight instead. Preventive violence was a means of outflanking the Herero, who likewise seemed to be waiting for a favorable moment to strike. Settler violence directly targeted the Herero, but it indirectly took aim at the despised authority of the state. This did not necessarily involve a calculated effort to thwart government policy. Violence restored settlers' sense of agency and affirmed their dominance; they were no longer mere subjects of an authoritarian power.

The spread of similar acts of violence throughout the colony did not necessarily happen by design, although some forms of coordination did exist. Newspapers gave voice to the actors of "uncivil society" who became "entrepreneurs of fear,"[118] warning of the dangers posed by "natives," stirring up white fears, and tirelessly propagating violence. These publications reached many settlers and articulated their concerns.

When the settlers described colonization as a "violation," explaining that under the given circumstances only might could make right, they spoke openly about the lawlessness that defined colonial society's external relations. Although the colonial masters were keen to differentiate between internal and external relations—and the ethics that applied (or not) in each situation—the distinction was much more tenuous than they might have liked. Put another way: the anomie of the frontier situation cast its shadow over colonial society itself. Citing the example of Australian gold miners (who were by no means all failures or misfits in British society), Penny Russell shows how mistrust and violence spread in a climate of anomie and fierce competition, lending colonial society a face that was difficult to square with the colonizers' inflated self-image.[119] "Racial solidarity" was constantly invoked in South-West Africa, precisely because all solidarity was sorely lacking among whites. Once the uprising justified settlers' fears, their mistrust knew no bounds. It was directed against all of the white subgroups whom they suspected of disunity: against the missionaries, who had apparently found common cause with the Herero; against the British, who had apparently provided the rebels with weapons; against the Boers, who had long had their eye on South-West Africa; and against the Imperial German officers who were said to have stabbed the settlers in the back.[120]

The settlers also mistrusted supposedly criminal Italian railroad workers, Jews, and all other outsiders, as well as their own government and the metropole.[121] No one was above suspicion. Colonial society was fragmented, its internal relations fraught with deep mistrust. The litigiousness of Southwesters was notorious in Imperial Germany.[122]

Angelina Godoy writes that collective action "is born not only of solidarity, but also at times of mistrust." Her observations apply not only to Latin America, but also to South-West Africa.[123] The (violent) actions taken to manage fear become the glue that binds scattered individuals into one ethnically determined community. In an atmosphere of mistrust, the "struggle between races" provides the last—perhaps the *only*—communal tie that can unite members of colonial society. The words of Godoy's informer—"What else do we have left?"—could just as easily have come from a settler in SWA. Violence against indigenous people was not only a means to cope with fear, but also to build community.

Herero testimony shows that the privatization of violence and settlers' growing aggression influenced the situation in the colony and how the settlers perceived it, thereby underscoring the role of settlers as an autonomous motor of colonial expansion. Their actions carried growing weight as the state—regardless of its formal authority—became too weak to effectively control its white subjects and check their urges. Leutwein later asserted that the government was "powerless" against the aggression and unprincipled behavior of settlers, who did not shrink even from "murder and manslaughter."[124] The rebels repeatedly told the missionary Kuhlmann (who had lived among the Herero for some time and spoke Otjiherero) about the violence, indignities, and injuries that they had suffered at the hands of the whites, emphasizing that "the governor is a good man; we don't have anything against him. But he answers to the will of the traders and others, and he has to do what they want. It was the traders who dominated before the war."[125]

Traders were the protagonists par excellence of the settlers' autonomous expansion, and the frontier situation was key to this experience. Away from white settlements and the reach of the state, the traders sought contact with the African population, enriching themselves through often deceptive and violent business practices. Many settlers had not yet acquired the necessary capital for farming, so they began their colonial careers as traders. But even beyond such activities, settlers tried nearly everything to undermine the state—not least by co-opting the lower ranks of the military and police.

On 19 January 1904, Oscar Stübel, director of the Foreign Office's Colonial Department, addressed the Reichstag about possible motives for the Herero uprising. He explained that the Herero longed for the time before German occupation, when they had enjoyed "complete freedom, independence, and licentiousness," and that they had always opposed "the political and social order that we ultimately must force them to accept." Stübel had, however, reversed the facts.[126] There was some truth to Leutwein's assertion that the Herero had recognized the authority of the German state, but not the authority of each individual settler.[127] Of course, indigenous groups could not permanently retain parts of their sovereignty and to continue to bear arms without contradicting the state's claim to power. However, it was primarily the *white* population that thwarted this claim and ultimately plunged the colony into chaos. The settlers, more than any other factor, prevented the colonial state from upholding its promise to maintain law and order. As Leutwein describes, the government could not persuasively assert its authority over particular groups and interests. Thus, the Herero ultimately saw no other option than armed uprising.[128]

The state was undoubtedly too weak in many respects to control its white subjects—but it also may not have had the will to exert this control. There were certainly more than enough warnings.[129] The problem was well known,[130] and the structural primacy of executive authority in the colony gave Governor Leutwein plenty of opportunities to intervene.

The other side of Leutwein's policies was his indulgence of the settlers. At least in part for financial reasons, he did not give in to their main demand (to subdue the autochthonous groups), but he may have indulged them in other ways so as not to alienate them altogether. We must keep in mind that South-West Africa was first and foremost a settlement project, which sought to create "a colony populated by whites," as Leutwein himself wrote.[131] In this respect, therefore, Lothar von Trotha's reproach that Leutwein's policies were like a "game of seesaw" is apt.[132]

Conversely, the storm of outrage that Lothar von Trotha unintentionally touched off by (re)introducing certain practices shows us that Leutwein must have already understood and accepted the political imperative of racism. Perhaps Leutwein agreed that minority rule was difficult to uphold without the guarantee of special rights and higher prestige. Perhaps he further agreed that members of colonial society, regardless of the differences and tensions that divided them, were ultimately in the same boat—especially when emergency struck. And perhaps he saw violence "from below" as a distasteful but necessary outlet for fear, which was an emotion that even high-ranking officials surely knew well.

Herero Resistance

The boundaries between the state and colonial society were hazy, and this was especially true in the war's opening phase. Even the "most depraved" member of colonial society presented himself as superior to the "natives" and claimed sovereign rights. The executive organs of government often found common cause with the settlers; the courts did not intervene, and the administration declared itself "powerless."[133] These blurred lines had consequences, as is evident in this exchange from the first days of the uprising, between the missionary Eich and a Herero named Johannes: "I [Eich]: Then you should wage war openly against the soldiers and not kill all innocent people. He [Johannes]: They are all Germans; we don't distinguish between them."[134] Johannes's reply shows that the difference between state officials and private individuals—or better, between "combatants" and "civilians"—had long become meaningless to the Herero. Without reason to distinguish between the two groups, the Herero began to target (supposed) "innocents."

The fight "against German foreign rule itself" meant ending German settlement.[135] Irrespective of the immediate circumstances that may have led to the outbreak of the uprising, leaders such as Samuel Maharero understood that, in contrast to previous conflicts, this war would and could not remain strategically limited. Despite efforts to curb violence at the tactical level, the broader goals that the rebels pursued were actually quite radical. They set their sights on a total victory that would defeat and drive out the Germans, which is why Samuel Maharero also tried to forge alliances with other ethnic groups. Waging war in this way meant killing male German settlers, and plundering and destroying their property—an approach that was not driven by strategic military concerns alone, but also had an emotional component, which we will examine in the pages ahead.

Although the war against the Herero was a product and reflection of the colony's violent conditions, it embittered the Germans deeply. The settler Conrad Rust described the Herero raids: "Feigning friendship and peace, they snuck up like tigers and hyenas and murdered, defiled, plundered, and destroyed in the most frivolous way, pitilessly, without mercy. Yes, the beastliness of these plans for torture is evident, their signature is devilish malevolence! And this is what leads us to call for an eye for an eye, a tooth for a tooth!"[136] Whether the settlers actually saw themselves as innocent, or merely understood the tune they needed to sing—they immediately styled the Herero as "beasts," deliberately ignoring Herero efforts to curb violence and describing Herero acts of war as "murder" and "plunder." Soon the call for vengeance sounded well beyond the borders of the colony. Few eyewitnesses did not express outrage in their memoirs that the raids (especially) targeted civilians. Officers who came to the colony because of the war, and who were unfamiliar with local conditions, were particularly inclined to see the raids as evidence of the supposedly "animal" nature of the Herero. Pervasive racism provided fertile soil for the most far-fetched tall tales. The raids sent the soldiers' imaginations flying, and soon the most unlikely horror stories made the rounds, despite all contrary evidence. When apparently defenseless German civilians were "assaulted, killed, or gruesomely slaughtered," women raped, and children murdered, soldiers no longer saw "mercy" or "compassion" as a viable response.[137]

We still know very little about crucial aspects of the war. Few sources exist, unfortunately, that offer insight into how some or all of the Herero decided to strike, how they coordinated among themselves, or how they planned their course of action. We know little about Herero expectations, or how they evaluated their chances for success. Because we can only speculate about such matters, an exhaustive depiction of the Herero campaign is hardly possible—and it is not my intent here. Rather, the following pages examine aspects of the campaign that were particularly relevant to the process of violence. Here, too, some speculation is inevitable, particularly with respect to the (possible) reasons for the failure of the Herero. The chapter's final section examines colonial society's response to the Herero attacks, and how the war quickly descended into a spiral of violence and counterviolence.

The Herero Take Arms

On 12 January 1904, various Herero groups attacked the German colonial masters. On 25 December 1903, the Second Field Company under Captain Franke had been ordered to subdue the Bondelswarts in the south of the colony, leaving the north temporarily drained of active troops, which provided the immediate impetus for the strikes. I have already discussed the principal causes of the uprising. It is too simplistic to trace the outbreak of the uprising to any one event or measure.[138] A key factor was certainly the profound sense of crisis among the Herero, which intensified with every act of white antagonism. Bley has established that the settler population did not grow substantially in real terms through the end of 1903, and that the land question was not urgent; he rightly argues that the uprising was driven less by "objective" concerns, and more by social and psychological factors.[139] More recently, Jan-Bart Gewald has emphasized the active role of colonial society in escalating this conflict, placing the colonists' often paranoid interpretations and perceptions at the center of his study. Further, he traces the outbreak of the war to the aggressive, erratic behavior of one junior officer, Lieutenant Zürn, who was fatefully stationed in Okahandja, headquarters of the paramount chief of the Herero, Samuel Maharero.[140] Gewald thus asserts that it was the Germans—not the Herero—who began the war, contradicting conventional wisdom that the Herero had planned the uprising long in advance.

If it is true that the uprising was not planned, but more or less situationally dependent, then the uprising of the Herero was, at first, the uprising of the chief of Okahandja, who defended his residence against German attack. The conflict only gradually became a Herero uprising, after Maharero (as paramount chief) successfully persuaded other chiefs to join him.

This interpretation could explain the sometimes substantial delays before individual chiefs joined the fight (see chapter 2), but it seems less plausible in other critical respects. Maharero had already seen for himself what happened to chiefs and other headmen who more or less challenged German rule on their own. It is no exaggeration to say that he owed his own rise to the recklessness of rivals like Nikodemus Kavikunua, who had confronted Imperial Germany alone. Maharero was sensitive to power relations and careful not to risk too much without ensuring that other chiefs would stand by him if the need arose.[141] On the other hand, we should note that an uprising of the paramount chief could have easily had repercussions for all Herero, and so from the outset Maharero was unlikely to make a spontaneous decision on his own—particularly given the importance of consensus in Herero society.[142] The uprising was later associated (not incorrectly) with the extraordinary assemblies held by Herero grandees in 1903, which had aroused white suspicions even then.[143] The details of the uprising may not have been planned in advance, but we can nevertheless assume that it was discussed and generally endorsed among a broader circle of Herero chiefs and headmen.

In this context, another consideration deserves our attention. Although the paramount chief called the other chiefs to arms ("I fight; kill all Germans!"), some hesitated to join him.[144] In some cases, days—if not weeks—passed before action was taken, eliminating the advantage of surprise.[145] Insofar as the Herero ever had a realistic chance against such a strategically superior and determined opponent, their political and social organization placed them at a tactical and strategic disadvantage and likely contributed to their defeat. To be sure, there are examples of acephalous societies (such as Afghanistan) that have successfully defied state opponents, but ultimately the Herero were not among them.

The first attacks caught the colonists completely off guard. The element of surprise may have been the greatest advantage of the Herero, and in some cases they exploited it well.[146] Only one-tenth of German casualties were soldiers; the raids particularly hurt farmers and traders. Women and children—and non-German whites—were usually spared, and even escorted safely to the nearest German settlements. Herero assailants cleverly disguised their malicious intent, making their targets easy prey. Hendrik Witbooi adopted similar tactics when he entered the fight against the Germans nearly nine months later. He ordered house servants, if necessary, to kill their employers as they slept.[147] It has been well established that even individual assaults were planned and executed with the utmost care. Although the assailants overwhelmingly outnumbered their victims, they favored deceptive maneuvers.[148]

The Herero raided stores in order to obtain arms and provisions for future confrontations. However, their plunder paled in comparison to what they might have taken from the garrisons and forts, which were stocked with one year's provisions. Fifty thousand rounds for the Model 1888 rifle, and seventy thousand for the Model 1871, were stored in Omaruru alone—as the Herero apparently knew.[149] Maharero's letters to Hendrik Witbooi and Hermanus van Wyk show that he knew about these strategically important targets, and also that he intended to overrun the towns of Windhuk and Swakopmund.[150] Yet only small military stations were ultimately attacked (four were captured), and no serious efforts were made to storm the forts or towns.[151] The Herero arguably lost the war in its first hours[152] because they failed to establish the necessary conditions for a final victory: destroying or overtaking the infrastructure of the colony, including the towns. Why the Herero neglected to do this, despite knowing better, deserves further explanation.

The explanation I propose has to do with the connection between political and social organization on one hand, and military leadership on the other. Herero society was acephalous; authority beyond the home was not well defined, and leadership was decentralized.[153] There was no strong central authority. A trend toward centralization did emerge in the second half of the nineteenth century,[154] but only small steps were taken. Thus, the ethnologist Frank Vivelo has called Herero leadership "incipient chiefdom."[155] It can be presumed that the Herero had less control over their fighters than German leaders, who hearkened back to a centuries-long process of state-building that went hand in hand with disciplining troops.[156] Boldly stated, this process of disciplining was so advanced that soldiers, if so ordered, were prepared to march in rank and file to their deaths. The nationalization of war allowed soldiers to see giving up their own lives as an honorable, or even desirable, act of heroism. Circumstances were different for the Herero, despite the valor of their fighters. In sum, Herero leaders may have been reluctant to order attacks on fortified positions because they doubted their fighters' willingness to incur heavy losses—or else they feared the consequences for future battles. This could explain why Herero forces bogged themselves down in attacks on strategically unimportant targets, plundering, and destruction. Valuable time was wasted, and the element of surprise was lost.[157]

Tactical problems also affected higher-level strategy and proved no less devastating for the course of the uprising. The hesitation of chiefs and headmen to take up Maharero's call and join him in battle was particularly fateful. By letting days or weeks pass before making up their minds, they missed the chance to place serious pressure on their opponents, the local German population and army. Once again, the decentralized leadership of Herero society became a critical weakness. The institutionalized authority of the chiefs—and particularly the paramount chiefs—was only beginning to coalesce, a process that ended abruptly with the uprising and its suppression.[158] The paramount chief of the Herero had no power over the other chiefs throughout the entire nineteenth century; a hierarchical relationship did not exist. It is questionable whether we should even identify Maharero's call to arms as an "order," as its recipients did not seem to treat it as binding. They decided for themselves whether or not to enter the war, in some cases allowing weeks to pass before they entered the fight. Maharero could do little more than send out emissaries to persuade the undecided, sometimes following up with threats or violence.[159]

More or less accidental factors—and not an order from the paramount chief— might lead a chief to enter the war, as the example of Zacharias Zeraua from Otjimbingwe shows. A combination of circumstances drew Zeraua into the war, although he did not want to fight the Germans (which is why they refrained from executing him when he surrendered at the end of 1904). In general, conflicts escalated quickly in the colonial situation. Even in "peacetime," fear and mistrust were so pervasive that just a small straw was needed to break the proverbial camel's back. Once news of the uprising reached Otjimbingwe, the Germans watched every Herero move with growing suspicion. In this tense situation, the "violent few," who for various reasons sought or tolerated escalation,[160] could easily bend even a reluctant Herero majority to their will. The instigators might have been outsiders, criminals, or anyone who sought to prey on the vulnerable, with no particular interest in the broader situation. Even the smallest incautious act could have grave consequences. In Otjimbingwe, it was the unresolved murder of a white person. As noted in the mission chronicle, "The murder brought all negotiations to an end. According to the Herero way of thinking, Zacharias bore responsibility for what his 'children' had done, and so he had no other choice but to take the side of his people."[161]

Once again, this shows how much easier it is to escalate than de-escalate conflicts. The news that three hundred Herero horsemen from Okahandja had joined the fight, frightening and terrorizing the surrounding areas, spread like wildfire across the colony. The news must have bolstered the confidence of some Herero and heightened their appetite for war, but others seized the opportunity to take what they could.[162] Conrad Rust reported that numerous "marauders" and "plunderers" contributed to the uncertainty of the first days of the uprising.[163] In such circumstances, isolated acts could have political repercussions that decided between war and peace.

Escalation occurred through the logic of "bimodal alienation," an irrational form of conflict management.[164] The first mode of alienation occurs between warring parties, which isolate themselves and cut off all ties to one another. This leads to the second mode of alienation, within the warring parties themselves. External isolation leads to pressure for conformity from within; the group demands the total subordination of its individual members, abhorring deviation. Individuals are alienated from themselves, compelled to give up parts of their own personalities in order to meet expectations of conformity to the group. Both modes of alienation were present in South-West Africa. Just as every black African had become suspect to the whites by the time the uprising began, the Herero likewise sought to end all ties to whites. Anyone who associated with the enemy was considered an enemy, too.[165] The Germans had set the course for these developments early on. Longstanding emergency plans were driven by fear and mistrust. Settlers' private homes were part of the lines of defense, and had often been (re)built for this purpose.[166] Everyone knew what to do in case of emergency. In January 1904, the makeshift fortresses were swiftly expanded and placed on high alert. The "script" was already in place and waiting to be put into action. Events ran their course, sometimes taking the very path that the colonists had hoped to avoid. The white settlers' retreat to fortified positions in preparation for war deeply unsettled the Herero, and in some places this actually sparked the outbreak of hostilities.[167]

The next section of this chapter examines the "communal terror" (*Gemeinschaftsterror*) that spread through colonial society. As we will see, even unpremeditated individual actions and the dynamics of particular situations could affect the course of events no less than the orders of a chief, even a paramount chief. This pattern is by no means unique to

Herero society, but societies with a low degree of centralized leadership are particularly susceptible. For the Herero, the consequences of decentralized leadership became particularly apparent at the strategic level.

Maharero knew well that this war would be different from previous local conflicts. This is why he tried—for the first time—to build a broad coalition of Africans by forging alliances with the Witbooi-Oorlam, the Basters, and the Ovambo in the north.[168] Maharero pursued radical war aims, as we will see in the pages ahead. It is doubtful whether he entertained the possibility of a negotiated peace. He believed that the war was a moment of "absolute decision" for the rebels, and that it would take on an existential dimension. He saw no exit strategy.[169] The goal was to fight and to win; the stakes were all or nothing.

The particulars of the conflict illustrate how radical Herero war aims were. German men were usually killed; farms, houses, and stores were plundered. Anything usable was stolen, and the rest was destroyed. Buildings were razed and burned to the ground; herds, driven away. Contemporary texts abound with the "horrors of devastation": "furniture, books, pictures, letters, everything, everything" was "destroyed to the ground"; beds were torn up, "sofas battered, stuffing ripped out, porcelain shattered to pieces, ovens ripped apart, nothing, nothing, was spared."[170] This was not "senseless violence," as one sometimes hears in such circumstances. The violence was not random, but pursued a clear goal: to destroy the colonists' existence, compelling them to abandon settlement and leave South-West Africa forever.[171] Once the men were killed, property and means of production plundered or destroyed, and houses rendered uninhabitable, families had no basis for survival. The way to Swakopmund was held open for women and children—so they could go back to Germany.[172] The conduct of war was limited, in that women, children, and non-Germans were spared, but the aims of war certainly were not. The Herero targeted German colonial society as a whole and sought to end German rule and settlement.

Such a radical goal could not be achieved unless all groups and their leaders did their part. And herein lay the problem, as the course of the war shows: the chiefs reserved the right to decide for themselves whether or not to enter the war, just as they later held open the options of a separate peace or retreat across the border.

Samuel Maharero made the fateful decision to unite various groups, which had to this point operated successfully in their own territories, at the Waterberg mountain. Elsewhere I have interpreted this decision as an attempt to counteract the dangerous centrifugal forces that were growing stronger, due to wartime setbacks and shortages.[173] The concentration of forces must have given the groups a sense of confidence and strength, as thousands of fighters came together at the foot of the Waterberg. Concentration also gave Maharero more control over the chiefs, so he could halt any attempts to break ranks.[174] This was all the more important, since the great battles in April had produced many casualties without the desired results. These battles, which I will discuss more in the pages ahead, came close to strategic defeat. Although the Herero dealt the Germans heavy casualties and even some defeats, they did not succeed in beating the Germans *decisively*. Given a strategic imbalance that was steadily worsening, they must have understood that this was increasingly unlikely to occur. As their forces dwindled, and they were unable to compensate for the loss of lives and munitions, their opponent continued to receive new material and personnel.

The area around the Waterberg was well chosen in that the Herero had enough water and pasture to last for some time—away from the railroad line and beyond the Germans' immediate reach. However, other evidence suggests that they lacked a clear strategy for this phase of the war. They dallied for weeks at a location that was known to their opponent; they allowed German forces to approach undisturbed and prepare for battle; and, once the fighting began, many fled so abruptly that they had to abandon large numbers of cattle.[175] This suggests, in turn, that the decision to pool forces at the Waterberg may not have been driven by military considerations in the stricter sense.

Beyond this specific issue, the social and political organization of the Herero was clearly disadvantageous for waging war on several different levels. Although the rebels had the advantage of surprise, and their warriors were in many ways superior to German troopers, in the end they were unable to turn the war in their favor. The Germans held the strategic advantage, and they were determined to assert their authority over SWA. Defeating and expelling the Germans was difficult enough, so that even the tiniest frictions on the side of the Herero could have undermined the uprising—and the frictions that did arise were substantial.

Although the uprising did not end as the Herero had hoped, the stakes of the war that they unleashed were all-or-nothing from the start. Their raids sought nothing less than an end to German rule and settlement in SWA, and so the war was particularly acrimonious. On one hand, the uprising posed a threat to the aspiring great power—an affront that German elites could in no way accept. On the other hand, the rebels directed their violence against colonial society itself, which did all it could to retaliate. The settlers' response, which encouraged further Herero violence, can be explained as follows. Acts of destruction and plunder cost the Herero valuable time, and were not merely the result of insufficient soldierly discipline. Rather, these acts represented an "excess" of violence that must be explained on its own. Even when haste was in order, the rebels took time to destroy whatever they could not use themselves. They celebrated the destruction outright, going at it with "love and care," as one officer concluded from the ruins. Overindulgence in alcohol often reinforced the celebratory mood.[176]

Homes, businesses, and colonial infrastructure were a physical representation of the colonizers' power. Now the colonizers were powerless to stop all of this from being razed to the ground. The frailty of their buildings, their power, and their entire existence was paraded before their eyes. Years of painstaking labor invested in construction (bricks were usually self-produced, for example, and other materials imported from far away) were erased in moments by the rebels. The oft-cited desecration of corpses, including those that had already been buried, showed the Germans in no uncertain terms that they would find no peace in this land. Through the act of castration, Herero men symbolically reversed the emasculation that they had experienced when forced to stand by as the colonizers sexually assaulted their wives and daughters.[177] These were not isolated incidents and have been well documented.[178] Herero violence was not an expression of blind rage, as German sources often suggested; the Herero understood how to apply violence in a precise and measured way. They drew selectively from the repertoire of precolonial warfare.[179] They remained concerned about the containment of violence. They sought to negate the colonists' claim to power as dramatically as possible. The Germans got the message, and this profoundly wounded their sense of superiority.

The Revenge of Colonial Society

The uprising hit the settlers like a bolt from the blue. Many settlers in the interior of the colony were lucky to save their own skins. Some watched from forts as their possessions were stolen and their houses went up in smoke. In Grootfontein and elsewhere, they spent months in cramped, improvised dwellings, anxiously wondering about the state of the colony and the fate of family members, neighbors, and friends. Without contact to the outside world, all they could do was wait. For the settlers, the need to hunker down and defend themselves against the supposedly "inferior natives" was "a humiliation and a disgrace." They were no were no longer masters over the colony, or even their own fates.[180]

Colonial society mobilized right away, even in Swakopmund, which was separated from the area of the uprising by the Namib Desert (more than one hundred kilometers wide and difficult to penetrate). The militarization of Swakopmund was so complete that the town seemed "dead," its "commercial affairs nearly brought to a standstill."[181] Viktor Franke wrote that the fort in Windhuk was "stuffed full of armed men and women. Every cripple was in uniform and carried a weapon."[182] Women also bore arms.[183] Conrad Rust remarked that when it "came to defending life and property . . . everyone reached for weapons; everyone is a soldier."[184] The distinction between "combatants" and "noncombatants" was meaningless because everyone was part of the defense. Conversely, this meant that every black African—man or woman—was the enemy.

By order of the district office in Swakopmund, every white person was permitted to carry a weapon and had police authority over the local people; conversely, every "native" was suspect.[185] Soon the Africans were corralled onto two steamships that were anchored in Swakopmund, so that they could be sent to South Africa. The logic of "bimodal alienation" was fully evident. The settlers closed ranks, watching more vigilantly than ever to uphold the boundaries between "white" and "black." They undermined Leutwein's efforts to reach out to the Herero, doing their part to ensure that (diplomatic) relations with the other side were broken off for good.[186] Under the banner of "racial solidarity," they enforced a regime of communal terror that tolerated no dissent. From this point forward, the suspicion of "treason" hovered over everyone and everything.

A desire for revenge took hold of many groups in colonial society, including troops who were already in the colony as the uprising erupted, and those who arrived soon thereafter.[187] The animus was extreme.[188] Missionaries were unsettled by the calls for revenge and the "thirst for Herero blood."[189] Sensing a pogrom-like mood, they worked hard to keep the enraged population from turning to acts of violence.[190] The missionary Elger recalled, "There was all sorts of trouble with agitated people. A high-ranking personality wanted to hang all Herero on site, guilty or not, and he was kept from doing so only because I threatened to report the matter. Nevertheless, many did hang in those days, and for many German women it was a performance that they absolutely had to watch."[191] The desire for revenge was so pronounced that it did not dissipate even after the devastating wars and the deadly regime of the camps. Years after the uprising, settler newspapers continued to run stories about fleeing or insubordinate Herero, or they accused the government of spoiling the "natives." They were unconcerned by the inordinate suffering that the few surviving Herero had endured, or by the Great General Staff's report that the Herero had long since ceased to be "an independent tribe."[192]

No later than the raids of January 1904, the Herero people had come to recognize how vulnerable the whites really were, and that it ought to be easy enough to kill them and seize their possessions. Now that the cat was out of the bag, and—to return to the ideas of First Lieutenant Stuhlmann—that the "transcendence" of the white master, and the invulnerability of everything that belonged to him, was "beyond saving,"[193] how could white superiority be restored? Revenge was the first part of the settlers' response.

By taking revenge, the settlers reasserted their own agency and overcame the sense of humiliation and powerlessness that the rebels had thrust upon them. Revenge restored the fractured relationship between "white masters" and "black beasts." The goal of revenge is for others to suffer; the suffering of perpetrators is brought into line with the suffering of victims. In South-West Africa, however, the desire for revenge was boundless. Colonial society placed no limits on the exercise of violence. Deep-seated racism led the colonists to believe that they should be avenged *many times over*. Even in "peacetime," colonial justice had permitted revenge that was fueled by racial hatred. The *murder* of blacks might go unatoned, but the death of one white person could trigger the execution of multiple blacks.[194] Revenge in colonial society might be summarized by the principle: "For every one of us, ten of you will die."[195] The desire for revenge was so extreme that some settlers demanded that the "natives" be eradicated altogether.[196]

Violence "from below" had always been a side effect of the weak colonial state. As the authorities became more willing to tolerate this violence, it was difficult to stop.

Once alarming news about the conduct of the war in SWA made its way back to Germany, Social Democratic delegates brought the matter before the Reichstag and accused the government of waging a war of extermination against the Herero. The charges were so serious that Oscar Stübel, director of the Foreign Office's Colonial Department, demanded an immediate explanation from Governor Leutwein. Leutwein's reply from 17 May 1904 is astonishing for two different reasons. First, a high-ranking civilian and military official conceded that the Social Democratic party leader August Bebel was "generally" correct.[197] Second, he admitted candidly, "However, after all that has transpired, it is only natural that our soldiers have not proceeded with particular restraint. It is just as natural that no superior has ordered this restraint."[198]

Leutwein confirmed that in the first weeks and months of the war, the Germans took no prisoners and also killed women and children. He disputed only that these actions had been ordered by military leaders. By his telling, it was "our soldiers" who had initiated the unfettered violence. If the governor had already felt "powerless" to stop the settlers' assaults in times of "peace," then this was especially true after the uprising. He was unable to halt the violence on or off the battlefield, including the arbitrary authority of courts-martial that "regularly sentenced cattle thieves and marauders to death."[199] He remarked that even Bebel could not have countered this "popular mood" (*Volksstimmung*).[200] But even as the governor distanced himself from these proceedings, he could not bring himself to condemn them. To the contrary: pointing to the given circumstances ("after all that has transpired"), he expressed sympathy for the soldiers and justified the colonial leaders' reluctance to intervene.

An observer from the British enclave Walvis Bay (near Swakopmund), who communicated regularly with the Germans, reported, "The general feeling among the Germans at present partakes of an unreasoning and vindictive bitterness which is almost as nearly allied to barbarism as the unbridled passions of the Hereros themselves. I have heard, myself, Germans who were in action describing boastfully how their troopers bayonetted Herero women."[201]

The inaction of the government had serious consequences. We know from other contexts that when military leaders no longer insist on upholding the norms of international law and punishing violations, the brutality of a minority is soon accepted by the majority, and the "violent few" begin to set the standards for the conduct of war.[202] This seems to have happened in SWA, with consequences for the war as a whole. The ruthlessness of the Germans incited greater cruelty among the Herero. "The position is most serious and the vindictiveness displayed on both sides is almost without parallel," according to the aforementioned report from Walvis Bay.[203] Once one knew to expect no mercy from the other side, all that remained was a fight to the bitter end. Colonial society's campaign of revenge rapidly descended into a spiral of violence and counterviolence. Long before Lothar von Trotha had assumed the military command, unfettered violence was already rampant in SWA. It was often initiated from below. This violence did not need any orders to be put into motion, and the more it proliferated, the less likely any orders were to contain it.

Members of colonial society—above all, the settlers—had laid the groundwork for this violence. Violence from below had a long history in the colony; it was responsible for stirring up the war. Revenge brought a new dimension to the violence, quietly establishing the informal standards that would define warfare in SWA for the rest of its existence.

The outstanding role of the settlers is underscored by the fact that the number of settlers who took arms in the first weeks of the war (as volunteers or reservists in the Landwehr or Landsturm) far outstripped the number of regular troops—especially since most of the field troops were still tied up with the rebellious Bondelswarts in the south of the colony. The settlers' influence on the war was not only a matter of numbers, but also expertise. Overwhelmed soldiers, who had been rushed to the colony, looked to experienced locals for guidance.

Even after the regular army took control of operations and relieved most of the reservists, staff officers desperately sought settlers for taking on difficult assignments.[204] A report from the Admiralty Staff of the navy noted this:

> Those who were well-versed in African affairs eased the difficulties that the inexperienced European encountered at every turn, and they introduced the newcomer to the idiosyncrasies of African warfare. The horsemen in the department, largely reservists and Landwehr men or volunteers, helped a great deal. Having traversed the land as farmers and traders, they performed a great service as guides, patrols, and leaders of the wagon columns.[205]

These remarks show that the settlers commanded special respect as experts in the colonial forces. This was true not only of those who served in the forces. Newly arrived soldiers came into contact with the white population on transports and marches to the interior of the colony, and sought to engage them in conversation "wherever possible."[206] "The only topic [was] the war," according to the soldier Max Belwe, who claimed to have learned "many peculiar things" during these talks.[207] I have already discussed the touted "closeness" between settlers and soldiers in a previous section of this chapter.[208]

The sight of those who had been injured or left behind often aroused the sympathies of newcomers, who adopted the settlers' values, emotions, and viewpoints as their own. Incoming troops landed in Swakopmund, which is also where refugees from the interior of the colony gathered to wait for passage back to Germany. These images made a deep impression on many observers:

> Watching the ships depart for Germany can now be quite sad. This is where the wounded leave, or those who have recovered from a serious illness but still carry traces of illness in their faces or demeanor. In the boat one sees old acquaintances who had achieved something through hard work and endurance; only a few months ago they believed their lives were secure, and today through no fault of their own they have lost everything, in greater need than ever. But the bleakest sight of all, happening again the day before yesterday ... widows and orphans of farmers who were treacherously murdered. Seeing that, one is overcome with rage all over again.[209]

For weeks and months, the settlers comprised a large part of the forces—at first, as much as two-thirds.[210] Even after they left the forces, they continued to serve as expert advisors and to exert significant influence over the soldiers and the conduct of war. As local experts, their influence was less immediate than before, but in this way they served as multipliers for the emotions and thought patterns of colonial society.

The settler newspapers played an important role in this process. They had long propagated war and violence, and pilloried the "humanitarian stupidity" of government policy.[211] This continued during the war. The rumor that Leutwein sought to negotiate with the Herero unleashed a storm of outrage, and the calls for total victory grew louder. Unrelenting criticism of the governor's policies, which were supposedly too moderate, weakened his position considerably. The settlers did what they could to hasten his dismissal. Ironically, Lothar von Trotha was willing to wage the war they demanded, but—to their chagrin—he proved so reluctant to compromise that the colony was soon on the verge of economic ruin. For the military dictator Trotha, who felt responsible only to the Kaiser, the interests of the settlers and the economic development of the colony were secondary at best—as we will see in greater detail in the pages ahead. The settlers' push for radicalization led to developments that they did not agree with, and that they were no longer able to control. Thus, certain "elements" in colonial society had a far-reaching influence that that the elites of Imperial Germany had not foreseen.

The settlers did not rest easy even after the war was long over. As the few Herero survivors languished in concentration camps, the *Deutsch-Südwestafrikanische Zeitung* called "now at last, [for] a return to a sharper tone" in dealing with the "Herero problem."[212] Even at "peace," the settlers continued to push for a tougher "native policy." The settlers were, and remained, a motor of violence.

Notes

1. Leutwein (16 February 1904), NAN ZBU D.IV.l.2, vol. 4, pp. 5–6.
2. Balandier, "The Colonial Situation," 54.
3. Wilhelm E. Mühlmann, "Der Ernstfall als ständige Erfahrung in den Primitiv-Kulturen: Über die Unwahrscheinlichkeit unserer modernen Existenz," in *Der Ernstfall*, ed. Rüdiger Altmann (Berlin, 1979), 198–211.
4. Kurd Schwabe, *Der Krieg in Deutsch-Südwestafrika 1904–1906* (Berlin, 1907), 156.
5. Trutz von Trotha, *Koloniale Herrschaft*, 440–41; and "Was war Kolonialismus? Zu Soziologie und Geschichte des Kolonialismus und der Kolonialherrschaft," *Saeculum* 55, no. 1 (2004): 63.
6. Delavignette, *Les vrais chefs de l'Empire*.

7. Leutwein to the Colonial Department (17 May 1904), BArch. R1001/2115, p. 64.
8. The military officers who came to SWA because of the uprisings quickly realized that the farmers were isolated and vulnerable to attack. See, for example, Georg Maercker, *Unsere Kriegsführung in Deutsch-Südwestafrika* (Berlin, 1908), 49; and Stuhlmann, Tagebuch, NAN, Private Accessions A.0109, p. 196.
9. Leutwein, *Elf Jahre Gouverneur*, 242.
10. Helmut Bley, "Gewaltverhältnisse in Siedlergesellschaften des südlichen Afrika," in *Siedler-Identität: Neun Fallstudien von der Antike bis zur Gegenwart*, ed. Christof Dipper (Frankfurt, 1995), 141.
11. Jeremy Krikler, "Social Neurosis and Hysterical Pre-Cognition in South Africa: A Case-Study and Reflections," *Journal of Social History* 28, no. 3 (1995): 491–520.
12. Panic-inducing rumors were apparently enough of a problem that Lothar von Trotha made spreading rumors a punishable offense. NAN ZBU D.IV.l.2. Herero-Aufstand 1904. Feldzug; Politisches. Vol. 3 (August 1904–September 1905), p. 110.
13. Graumann and Wintermantel, "Diskriminierende Sprechakte," 151.
14. Albert Memmi, *Rassismus* (Frankfurt, 1987), 170–71.
15. Contemporary reports by travelers, settlers, and soldiers inevitably reproduced the same stereotypes, which suggests that these authors had no relations with the colonized peoples. It appears as if reproducing these codes could and did prove the authors' "knowledgeability."
16. Bley, "Gewaltverhältnisse in Siedlergesellschaften des südlichen Afrika."
17. "Zur augenblicklichen Lage," *DSWAZ*, 5 January 1904, 2.
18. Ibid.
19. Häussler, "'Kultur der Grausamkeit.'"
20. Luc Ciompi and Elke Endert, *Gefühle machen Geschichte: Die Wirkung kollektiver Emotionen—von Hitler bis Obama* (Göttingen, 2011), 24–25.
21. "Die farbige Gefahr," *DSWAZ*, 28 February 1906, 1.
22. Jan-Bart Gewald, *Herero Heroes: A Socio-political History of the Herero of Namibia 1890–1923* (Athens, 1999).
23. Ludwig Külz, *Tropenarzt im afrikanischen Busch*, 3rd ed. (Berlin, 1943), 143.
24. Elkins and Pederson, "Introduction," 7.
25. Bley, *Kolonialherrschaft und Sozialstruktur*, 15.
26. Whites were subject to consular law, with only two instances in the judicial hierarchy. Prosecutors and judges were civil servants, who typically held both executive and judicial authority. See Bley, *Kolonialherrschaft und Sozialstruktur*, 274. There was no separate judicial branch to limit executive power. See Jakob Zollmann, *Koloniale Herrschaft und ihre Grenzen: Die Kolonialpolizei in Deutsch-Südwestafrika 1894–1915* (Göttingen, 2011), 49.
27. See Trutz von Trotha, *Koloniale Herrschaft* and "Was war Kolonialismus?"
28. Lorenzo Veracini, *Settler Colonialism: A Theoretical Overview* (Basingstoke, 2010), 3–4.
29. "Ein Ukas," *Windhuker Nachrichten*, 1 July 1905, 2.
30. Veracini, *Settler Colonialism*, 20ff.
31. James Belich, *Replenishing the Earth: The Settler Revolution and the Rise of the Anglo-World, 1783–1939* (Oxford, 2010), 23.
32. Veracini, *Settler Colonialism*, 6.
33. Brigitta Schmidt-Lauber, *"Die verkehrte Hautfarbe": Ethnizität deutscher Namibier als Alltagspraxis* (Berlin, 1998), 238.
34. However, this "modernity" was always broken, lending Southwester identity its characteristic shape. Scholars tend to see the "individualism" touted by the settlers as central to Southwester identity, although this overlooks an important issue. See, for example, Brigitta Schmidt-Lauber, "Die ehemaligen Kolonialherren: Zum

Selbstverständnis deutscher Namibier," in *Namibia—Deutschland, eine geteilte Geschichte: Widerstand, Gewalt, Erinnerung,* ed. Larissa Förster et al. (Cologne, 2004), 227. "Individualism" should not necessarily be equated with the pursuit of personal freedom—in some respects, in fact, the opposite was true. When settlers emphasized that in the colony they were no longer just a "number" (as they had been in the metropole), they gave voice to a conservative cultural pessimism that opposed the ongoing industrialization and urbanization of the metropole. This pessimism was grounded in a deep-seated fear of proletarianization among the lower middle classes, the social background of a majority of settlers. See, for example, Wahrhold Drascher, *Auslanddeutsche Charakterbilder* (Stuttgart, 1929), 37. Back in the German homeland, "diffuse" relationships between "whole people" in rural communities were rapidly being replaced by more functional relationships between actors in limited roles See Georg Simmel, *Die Großstädte und das Geistesleben* (Frankfurt, [1903] 2006), 12–13; and Hartmut Häußermann and Walter Siebel, *Stadtsoziologie: Eine Einführung* (Frankfurt, 2004), 35–36. The settler colony represented an alternative social model. With respect to the colonial towns of South-West Africa, this meant preserving the social controls that had given way to greater personal freedoms in the European big cities. See Wolfram Hartmann, "Urges in the Colony: Men and Women in Colonial Windhoek, 1890–1905," *Journal of Namibian Studies* 1, no. 1 (2007): 55–56.
35. "Über die Teilnahme der Bevölkerung an der Verwaltung," *DSWAZ,* 7 September 1904): 2–3.
36. Ibid.
37. There were repeated calls for a popular assembly. See the annual report by Conrad Rust in *Nachrichten des Bezirks-Vereins Windhuk,* 17 December 1903, 1. The settlers hoped to establish district councils (as in Swakopmund) and eventually a council for the colonial government, but their hopes were disappointed as the government would not grant the councils more than an advisory function. See, for example, "Über die Teilnahme der Bevölkerung an der Verwaltung," *DSWAZ,* 7 September 1904, 2–3.
38. "Über die Teilnahme der Bevölkerung an der Verwaltung," *DSWAZ,* 7 September 1904, 3.
39. "Zur Entschädigungsfrage," *DSWAZ,* 8 June 1904, 1.
40. One settler remarked that anyone who had lived even a short time in the colony would no longer be able to tolerate the overbearing hand of the state in Imperial Germany. See Ludwig Conradt, *Erinnerungen aus zwanzigjährigem Händler- und Farmerleben in Deutsch-Südwestafrika,* ed. Thomas Keil (Göttingen, 2006), 75.
41. "Ein Ukas," *Windhuker Nachrichten,* 1 July 1905, 2.
42. Bley, *Kolonialherrschaft und Sozialstruktur,* 213ff.
43. Schmidt-Lauber, *"Die verkehrte Hautfarbe,"* 79.
44. This temporarily changed during the colonial wars, when the military took control and nearly fifteen thousand troops arrived in German South-West Africa. This situation inspired a poem by longtime settler, Ludwig Conradt, in *DSWAZ,* 3 May 1905): "The old days are gone / But what bothers me now / We're no longer frank and free here / There's too much governing. / But all the men in town hall / With all their fine things / Can't turn southern Africa / Into Europe." ("Die alten Zeiten sind vorbei, / Doch was mich jetzt geniert, / Man lebt hier nicht mehr frank und frei, / Es wird zuviel regiert. –/ Doch all die hohen Herr'n im Rat / Mit allen schönen Sachen, / Sie werden aus Südafrika / Doch kein Europa machen.")
45. Quoted in Zollmann, *Koloniale Herrschaft und ihre Grenzen,* 275.
46. Trutz von Trotha, "Das 'deutsche Nizza an Afrikas Westküste': Zur politischen Soziologie der kolonialen Hauptstadt am Beispiel Lomés der Jahre 1897–1914," *Sociologus* 49 (1999): 104.

47. Bley, *Kolonialherrschaft und Sozialstruktur*, 295–96.
48. After the defeat of 1915, when South African forces invaded South-West Africa, no less than half of the German population left the colony—civil servants and military officers first of all. (See Brigitta Schmidt-Lauber, "Die ehemaligen Kolonialherren," 228.) Although these professionals comprised a large part of the white population, they had never been counted as such in official statistics.
49. Georg Hartmann, *Die Zukunft Deutsch-Südwestafrikas: Beitrag zur Besiedlungs- und Eingeborenenfrage* (Berlin: Mittler, 1904), 15.
50. The influence of ideology on official population statistics is astonishing enough; it is even more surprising that scholars today continue to reproduce this erroneous picture of the settlers. The ethnologist Brigitta Schmidt-Lauber investigates the "ethnicity of German Namibians" through the example of farmers, whom she identifies as the "key figure" of German South-West African identity. See *"Die verkehrte Hautfarbe,"* 79; and *Die abhängigen Herren: Deutsche Identität in Namibia* (Münster, 1993). She counts extensive land holdings, numerous employees, a university education, and foreign travel as typical features of German Namibian biographies, but all this applied to only a small, almost "aristocratic" class of farmers. When Schmidt-Lauber discusses the "dependent masters," she is referring to their effective dependence on indigenous labor. In any event, she focuses exclusively on a type of settler that was not representative of colonial society under German rule, nor of postcolonial Namibia.
51. Horst Gründer, *Geschichte der deutschen Kolonien*, 5th ed. (Paderborn, 2004), 26ff.
52. Bley, *Kolonialherrschaft und Sozialstruktur*, 144.
53. Ibid., 110.
54. Steinmetz, *The Devil's Handwriting*, 21 and 29ff.
55. Bley, "Gewaltverhältnisse in Siedlergesellschaften des südlichen Afrika."
56. Ibid., 142ff.; and Bley, *Kolonialherrschaft und Sozialstruktur*, 176.
57. Trutz von Trotha, "Das 'deutsche Nizza an Afrikas Westküste,'" 99.
58. In light of this situation, it is interesting to note that the towns were considered to be sites of cultural and civil sophistication. Within just a few years, Windhuk had come to resemble a provincial small town in Germany. The population was not as socially homogenous as in the capitals of other colonies. Sociability was defined by a certain "clannishness" and attention to social hierarchies. Residents used institutions of civil society such as associations and newspapers to exert political pressure, to lobby against paternalism and despotic state authority, and to amplify calls for democratization. See Trutz von Trotha, "Das 'deutsche Nizza an Afrikas Westküste,'" 108; and Margarete von Eckenbrecher, *Was Afrika mir gab und nahm* (Berlin, 1940), 91.
59. This fear was by no means directed only against "colored" workers, who were generally recruited from the Cape Colony. The arrival of Italian railroad workers caused great resentment and immediately met with local resistance. See, for example, "Eingesandt," *DSWAZ*, 15 March 1904, 3. The figure of the "foreigner" was closely associated with the big city. The settlers' mistrust of foreigners reveals their distaste for city life, even though many resided in towns themselves.
60. "Nötige Reformen," *DSWAZ*, 25 October 1905, 1.
61. "Aus Swakopmund," *DSWAZ*, 8 November 1905, 2.
62. "Aus dem Schutzgebiet," *DSWAZ*, 1 March 1905, 1.
63. Rohrbach to Stübel (6 February 1905), Sächsisches Hauptstaatsarchiv Dresden, Nachlass Stübel no. 10, p. 24, as quoted in Zollmann, *Koloniale Herrschaft und ihre Grenzen*, 2011.
64. Upon the creation of a new "white" cemetery in Omaruru in 1906, it was noted that "membership in the superior white race" had created such a close bond among the

white population that the question of confessional difference was no longer relevant. See "Aus dem Schutzgebiet. Aus Omaruru," *DSWAZ*, 12 September 1906, 1.
65. For the dark side of democratic tendencies in settler societies, see Häussler and Trutz von Trotha, "Koloniale Zivilgesellschaft?"
66. Chatterjee, *The Nation and Its Fragments*, 16–34.
67. "Die farbige Gefahr," *DSWAZ*, 28 February 1906, 1.
68. The settlers did not resent military officers as such and in fact appreciated their pragmatism. Rather, the settlers took issue with officers from the homeland whose loyalties lay with the metropole and its military culture, and who insisted on priorities that ran counter to the imperatives of colonial rule (as understood and practiced by longtime residents). Some settlers favored the military officers over the bureaucrats in the civil administration and even invoked the "danger of assessorism." See *DSWAZ*, 5 January 1904, 2. Assessorism, or governance by academically trained bureaucrats, had been "fundamentally discredited" in parts of settler society. See "Aus heimischen Blättern," *DSWAZ*, 13 July 1904, 2.
69. "Aus Swakopmund," *DSWAZ*, 5 July 1905, 1.
70. "Aus Deutschland," *DSWAZ*, 6 September 1905, 2, insert. Conversely, the officers were accused of "spoiling" the "colored" laborers who worked for the troops. See "Aus Windhuk," *DSWAZ*, 21 September 1904, 2. Documents from the Cape Colony attest to how cruelly these workers were actually treated. The settlers, however, apparently believed that this treatment was still too good. An illustrative example is the teamster named James who fell ill during a convoy. Witnesses reported that he was summarily shot by a soldier after lagging behind. In a letter from 21 April 1906, the Foreign Office did not dispute the accusation and confirmed that the soldier had been sentenced on 16 December 1904—to seven weeks in prison. KAB GH 35/157: "Treatment of Natives in G.S.W.A. 1905," "Ill-Treatment of 3 Natives in G.S.W.A. 1905–1906."
71. "Aus Deutschland," *DSWAZ*, 6 September 1905, 2, insert.
72. Bley, *Kolonialherrschaft und Sozialstruktur*, 284.
73. Conrad Rust, *Krieg und Frieden im Hereroland: Aufzeichnungen aus dem Kriegsjahre 1904* (Leipzig, 1905).
74. Rust, *Krieg und Frieden im Hereroland*, 401–4.
75. "Aus Deutschland," *DSWAZ*, 6 September 1905, 2, insert.
76. "Kamerun und Natal," *DSWAZ*, 25 April 1906, 1, insert.
77. A common argument was that workers who were treated poorly were also less productive. By this logic, the employer's self-interest was the only legitimate reason for easing the workers' burden; ethical obligations or other binding norms were not considered. See "Mutterland und Kolonie, II.," *DSWAZ*, 9 May 1906, 1.
78. "Zur augenblicklichen Lage," *DSWAZ*, 5 January 1904, 1.
79. This asymmetry was heightened by the logic of settler colonialism, which involved the appropriation of land and resources—if necessary, by force—at the cost of the autochthonous population. Because settlers came to the colony only to improve their economic status, the otherwise common idealization of colonization as a "civilizing mission" did not play a role here, and settlers were mostly indifferent to the "natives'" wellbeing. See "Zur Eingeborenenfrage, I.," *DSWAZ*, 22 September 1906, 1. Settlers saw the "natives" as resources—that is, exclusively as means, never an ends in themselves. Settlers did not have to be concerned about the indigenous population, especially if this involved acting against their own interests. Doing what was right meant acting in the interest of whites and their expansion. See "Mutterland und Kolonie," *DSWAZ*, 2 May 1906, 1.
80. NAN, Private Accessions A.0109, p. 196.

81. On the formative role of the massacre in (colonial) state-building, see Trutz von Trotha, *Koloniale Herrschaft*, 37ff.
82. Just as "natives" rarely possessed names or individual personalities in the descriptions—and likely the perceptions—of colonial masters, similar thinking applied to whites. All people were, in the first place, representatives of their race. This encouraged a form of kin liability (*Sippenhaft*): anything that was done to one, was done to all, and in turn reflected back on the group.
83. Schlettwein, "Zur augenblicklichen Lage," *DSWAZ*, 5 January 1904, 2.
84. See Häussler and Trotha, "Koloniale Zivilgesellschaft."
85. Drechsler, *Südwestafrika unter deutscher Kolonialherrschaft*, 119.
86. Gewald, *Herero Heroes*, 139.
87. Bley, *Kolonialherrschaft und Sozialstruktur*, 168 and 176–77.
88. Udo Kaulich, *Die Geschichte der ehemaligen Kolonie Deutsch-Südwestafrika (1884–1914): Eine Gesamtdarstellung* (Frankfurt, 2001), 247.
89. Leutwein to the Colonial Department of the Foreign Office (14 March 1904), BArch. R1001/2114, p. 106.
90. Hartmann, "Urges in the Colony," 39, 65, and 67 (note 98).
91. The proliferation of sexual violence was grounds for earlier wars, and it may also have played a role in January 1904. Contemporary accounts strongly suggest that the assaults by German soldiers and settlers were an important reason for the armed rebellion. See Hartmann, "Urges in the Colony," 65.
92. In this context, Wolf D. Hund speaks of the "erasure of all social differences among those who are subjected to racial discrimination": they "are no longer commoners or elites, respectable women or upright men, helpless children or dignified elders, but rather equal representatives of a supposedly natural, unmediated state . . . having prepared their social death, we are able to comprehend and treat them as primitive, uncivilized beings." See *Rassismus*, 122.
93. The number of corporal punishments that were imposed in South-West Africa doubled between 1901–02 and the outbreak of the war in 1904. The numbers decreased thereafter, primarily because contacts between whites and blacks decreased as well. The rate of corporal punishment recovered after the war. See Fritz Ferdinand Müller, *Kolonien unter der Peitsche: Eine Dokumentation* (Berlin, 1962), 112.
94. Trutz von Trotha, "'One for Kaiser': Beobachtungen zur politischen Soziologie der Prügelstrafe am Beispiel des 'Schutzgebietes Togo,'" in *Studien zur Geschichte des deutschen Kolonialismus in Afrika: Festschrift zum 60. Geburtstag von Peter Sebald*, ed. Peter Heine and Ulrich van der Heyden (Pfaffenweiler, 1995), 535.
95. Bley, *Kolonialherrschaft und Sozialstruktur*, 183.
96. Hund, *Rassismus*, 24.
97. Bley, "Gewaltverhältnisse in Siedlergesellschaften," 142.
98. Numerous malcontents and deviants also found their way to the colony. Leutwein observed that many whites had not comported themselves as the "morally higher race" and had misused their power, which he attributed to the negative selection practice of "pushing unsuitable elements out of the homeland and into the colony." See Leutwein to the Colonial Department (17 May 1904), BArch. R1001/2115, p. 64.
99. Max Weber, *Economy and Society: An Outline of Interpretive Sociology*, ed. Guenther Roth and Claus Wittich (Berkeley, 1978), 391.
100. Leutwein to the Colonial Department (16 February 1904), NAN ZBU, D.IV.l.2: Herero-Aufstand 1904. Feldzug; Politisches. Vol. 4: October 1904–December 1905, p. 5.
101. Quoted in Silvester and Gewald, *Words Cannot Be Found*, 159.
102. Silvester and Gewald, *Words Cannot Be Found*, 161.
103. The author of a "top secret" mission report from 19 May 1906 described how "multiple whites" rode to a camp where Herero prisoners were detained. "They captured

three Herero women with the knowledge of the guard and took the women along with them. The next evening, the same hunt was repeated at dark." See Archiv der Vereinten Evangelischen Mission (Wuppertal), RMG 2.660 6/05, p. 28.
104. "Aus dem Schutzgebiet," *DSWAZ*, 1 March 1905, 1.
105. Bley, *Kolonialherrschaft und Sozialstruktur*, 108–9.
106. "Die Zukunft Deutsch-Südwestafrikas: Beitrag zur Besiedlungs- und Eingeborenenfrage," *DSWAZ*, 8 March 1904, 1. Oskar Hintrager recalled that, in 1906 alone, around one thousand active members of the colonial forces announced their intent to remain in the colony after they completed their service. See *Südwestafrika in der deutschen Zeit* (Munich, 1955), 84.
107. Quoted in Bley, *South-West Africa under German Rule*, 140.
108. Quoted in Silvester and Gewald, *Words Cannot Be Found*, 95.
109. Leutwein, *Elf Jahre Gouverneur*, 468.
110. Trutz von Trotha, "Formen des Krieges," 83. The condescension that even junior officers had for Herero notables is astonishing. Lieutenant Zürn is said to have publicly admonished Samuel Maharero with the words *"Halte das Maul, du Schwein!"* (Shut up, you pig!). Zürn boasted that he had struck and chased away "natives" who came to him with complaints. See Gewald, *Herero Heroes*, 149.
111. Quoted in Kuhlmann, *Auf Adlers Flügeln*, 66.
112. Hartmann, "Urges in the Colony," 65.
113. This is why the settlers' claims for compensation were approved only with such hesitation. See "Aus dem Schutzgebiet," *DSWAZ*, 25 May 1904, 1. In the course of debate, settlers did admit that the indigenous population had been mistreated in some cases, although they largely blamed one professional group (traders). See Conrad Rust, "Der deutsche Reichstag und das südwestafrikanische Schmerzenskind," *DSWAZ*, 11 May 1904, 1.
114. "Der Aufstand," *DSWAZ*, 2 February 1904, 2, insert.
115. "Der Aufstand," *DSWAZ*, 19 January 1904, 1.
116. The cost of the "new order" did not initially seem that high. Even experienced officers were surprised by the dimensions that the uprising eventually attained, and by the bravery and doggedness of their opponents. See Estorff, *Wanderungen und Kämpfe*, 100; and Maercker, *Unsere Kriegsführung*, 46. After hearing early reports about an uprising, the officer Conrad von Stülpnagel, who was stationed in Outjo, still did not believe that coordinated Herero action was possible. Moreover, the settlers believed that they could turn to the state and metropole in any emergency. For this reason, the later colonial governor von Schuckmann called the settlers "ill-bred and demanding." See Bley, *South-West Africa under German Rule*, 192. It is hardly surprising that they relied entirely on the government and metropole to cover the costs of a potential uprising.
117. The missionary Jakob Irle reported that "injustices" perpetrated by whites had caused the Herero to lose "all respect" for them, filling the Herero with "bitter hatred." The behavior of the whites was dangerous and "unheard of." See "Noch ein Wort zum Herero-Aufstand," *Der Reichsbote* (22 March 1904), BArch. R1001/2113, p. 87.
118. Bernd Greiner, "Made in U.S.A.: Über politische Ängste und Paranoia," *Mittelweg 36* 24, no. 1/2 (2015): 137–55.
119. Penny Russell, *Savage or Civilised? Manners in Colonial Australia* (Sydney, 2010), 84ff.
120. Häussler and Trotha, "Koloniale Zivilgesellschaft?," 304–5.
121. See, for example, "Eingesandt," *DSWAZ*, 15 March 1904, 3. The *DSWAZ* printed a high-ranking administrator's positive remarks about an anti-Semitic text by Kurd von Strantz (a member of the Pan-German League) without additional commentary.

The review was titled "Disagreeable Citizens" ("Unliebsame Staatsbürger"). See "Eingesandt," *DSWAZ*, 18 August 1906, 2.

122. Schmidt-Lauber, "Die ehemaligen Kolonialherren," 227. The state's monopoly on power had weakened significantly, but it did not disappear. Despite the growing influence of the white colonizing class, the state continued to be responsible for much of the colony's internal affairs. The litigiousness of white settlers shows that they did not rely entirely on themselves, but also looked to the state as a mediating authority. See Bley, *Kolonialherrschaft und Sozialstruktur*, 243. Weakening state power primarily affected the colonists' relations with "natives." Only the former were permitted to resolve their disputes by force. "Native" violence was never tolerated, and always punished severely by the authorities. The murder of a white person was grounds for draconian punishment, often affecting several indigenous persons at once. Whites who killed Africans, by contrast, frequently went unpunished.

123. Angelina Godoy, *Popular Injustice: Violence, Community, and Law in Latin America* (Stanford, 2006), 122.

124. Leutwein (16 February 1904), NAN ZBU D.IV.1.2, vol. 4: pp. 5–6.

125. Kuhlmann, *Auf Adlers Flügeln*, 52–53.

126. StBR (19 January 1904), 14th session, 363a–b.

127. Bley, *Kolonialherrschaft und Sozialstruktur*, 121.

128. Ibid., 115.

129. The officer Ludwig von Estorff accused Leutwein of underestimating colonial tensions, and the missionary Jakob Irle complained that the Herero had been "despondent" between 1898 and 1903, but that Leutwein had not responded to their pleas. See Jakob Irle, *Die Herero: Ein Beitrag zur Landes-, Volks- und Missionskunde* (Gütersloh, 1906), 343.

130. See, for example, Gewald, *Herero Heroes*, 105.

131. Leutwein, *Elf Jahre Gouverneur*, 271.

132. Entry from 1 July 1904, TA 122/15.

133. "Aus Deutschland," *DSWAZ*, 6 September 1905, 2, insert; and Leutwein (16 February 1904), NAN ZBU D.IV.I,2. Vol. 4, pp. 5–6.

134. Diary of Missionary Eich, entry from 15 January 1904, BArch. N/1783/1, p. 6.

135. Franz Erdmann, *Die Ursachen des Herero-Aufstandes und die Entschädigungsansprüche der Siedler: Dargestellt von der Ansiedler-Abordnung* (Berlin, 1904), 10.

136. Conrad Rust, "Der deutsche Reichstag und das südwestafrikanische Schmerzenskind," *DSWAZ*, 11 May 1904, 2–3.

137. These quotations are from Burkhart Freiherr von Erffa, *Reise- und Kriegsbilder von Deutsch-Südwest-Afrika: Aus Briefen des am 9. April bei Onganjira gefallenen Dr. jur. Burkhart Freiherrn von Erffa* (Halle, 1905), 55–56. He continued: "And what did the patrols see! Mutilated remains of corpses everywhere! After murdering the men, the beasts raped the women and then slaughtered them like mutton, always letting one observe the fate of another! Patrols found parts of corpses hanging like dried meat from trees; carved-up breasts, arms, legs. There, too, the Herero *women* had mutilated adolescent boys with knives, allowing them to lie there and bleed to death!" Most "reports" of supposed atrocities were complete fabrications. They were disproven early on, but continued to spread. See Gesine Krüger, "Koloniale Gewalt, Alltagserfahrungen und Überlebensstrategien," in *Namibia—Deutschland, eine geteilte Geschichte: Widerstand, Gewalt, Erinnerung*, ed. Larissa Förster et al. (Cologne, 2004), 92–105.

138. The criminal business practices of traders are often identified as a contributing factor. See, for example, Kuhlmann, *Auf Adlers Flügeln*, 52. These practices intensified after a new credit regulation (actually intended to protect the autochthonous population) took effect on 1 November 1903. See Bley, *Kolonialherrschaft und Sozialstruk-*

tur, 181. Another contributing factor was the land question, which became more urgent after limits to "native" reserves were announced on 8 December 1903.

139. Bley, *Kolonialherrschaft und Sozialstruktur*, 173ff. Bley shows that the government did not aggressively pursue the land question; by 1903, less than 10 percent of eligible tribal land had been sold. The Herero did not face an acute shortage of land. The symbolic effects of railroad construction were more consequential. Independent of actual circumstances, the railroad created a sense of crisis that spilled over into violence.
140. Gewald, *Herero Heroes*, 142 and 191.
141. Maharero apparently did not seek war himself, but had to be pushed in that direction. Contemporary sources had different opinions about the divisions within Herero society; these sources typically identified one warring party as the instigator of the uprising, without offering deeper insight into specific relationships or background information. See, for example, "Der Aufstand," *Deutsch-Südwestafrikanische Zeitung*, 29 June 1904, 1.
142. All important decisions were discussed with a council of elders that possessed veto power, even among chiefs whose leadership was more institutionalized and broadly recognized than that of the paramount chief. Consensus was always sought. See Gordon D. Gibson, "The Social Organization of the Southwestern Bantu" (PhD diss., University of Chicago, 1952), 149; and Dag Henrichsen, *Herrschaft und Identifikation im vorkolonialen Zentralnamibia: Das Herero- und Damaraland im 19. Jahrhundert* (Basel, 2011), 232. Not least because of the independence of local headmen, political decisions did not reflect the will of one central authority. Rather, decisions represented consensus across different levels of power. Groups and individuals were free to cut ties with their respective leaders. See Trutz von Trotha, *Koloniale Herrschaft*, 243; and Gibson, "The Social Organization of the Southwestern Bantu," 129. Dissatisfied headmen could leave and take their followers with them, either joining another chief or striking out on their own. A chef could do little if his followers abandoned him; he did not have the coercive power to bend them to his will. See Frank Robert Vivelo, *The Herero of Western Botswana: Aspects of Change in a Group of Bantu-Speaking Cattle Herders* (St. Paul, 1977), 135.
143. Gerhard Pool, *Samuel Maharero* (Windhoek, 1991), 20.
144. Walter Nuhn, *Sturm über Südwest: Der Hereroaufstand von 1904—ein düsteres Kapitel der deutschen kolonialen Vergangenheit Namibias* (Bonn, 1989), 58.
145. The brevity of this order, which was not explained or justified in any way, suggests that it had already been introduced and settled upon long before.
146. Bridgman, *The Revolt of the Hereros*, 68.
147. Gustav Menzel, *"Widerstand und Gottesfurcht": Hendrik Witbooi—eine Biographie in zeitgenössischen Quellen* (Cologne, 2000), 184–85.
148. See, for example, Rust, *Krieg und Frieden im Hereroland*, 67 and 99.
149. Schwabe, *Der Krieg in Deutsch-Südwestafrika*, 45; Rust, *Krieg und Frieden im Hereroland*, 35; and Kuhlmann, *Auf Adlers Flügeln*, 23.
150. Silvester and Gewald, *Words Cannot Be Found*, 102. All supplies and reinforcements for the north of the colony arrived in Swakopmund. The railroad connected Swakopmund to the interior of the colony, ending at Windhuk, the colonial capital. It took weeks to cover this distance by oxcart, underscoring the importance of the railroad for the colony and its defense—which is why the Herero also attacked the railroad line. See Kuhlmann, *Auf Adlers Flügeln*, 13–14.
151. Leutwein, *Elf Jahre Gouverneur*, 467.
152. They may have lost the war as soon as the Germans successfully entrenched themselves in fortified positions. Long-range breechloaders gave the advantage to the defense. Once the Germans had barricaded themselves in, they were difficult to beat.

The forts were only small islands of power, but they provided a secure foothold for incoming troops, who were soon able to reassert control over the territory.
153. Christian Sigrist, *Regulierte Anarchie: Untersuchungen zum Fehlen und zur Entstehung politischer Herrschaft in segmentären Gesellschaften Afrikas* (Hamburg, 1994), 158ff. and 189ff.
154. Henrichsen, *Herrschaft und Identifikation im vorkolonialen Zentralnamibia*, 241ff.
155. Vivelo, *The Herero of Western Botswana*, 135.
156. Ulrich Bröckling, *Disziplin: Soziologie und Geschichte militärischer Gehorsamsproduktion* (Munich, 1997), 57ff.; and Jens Warburg, *Das Militär und seine Subjekte: Zur Soziologie des Krieges* (Bielefeld, 2009), 110ff.
157. Resignation and even panic spread among the Herero once they realized they had not used the advantage of surprise to defeat the Germans and drive them out of the land. The missionary Kuhlmann, who had visited Samuel Maharero's camp, wrote that "the warlike mood of the local tribe has long since given way to severe disenchantment. The people are overcome with trepidation . . . and they are increasingly aware that the end of the war will bring their destruction . . . They have no more hope for this life." News about the return of Franke's Second Field Company incited panic: "Fleeing wildly, everyone raced to the interior to escape to English Bechuanaland." See Kuhlmann, *Auf Adlers Flügeln*, 34 and 46.
158. Vivelo, *The Herero of Western Botswana*, 135; and Matthias Häussler, "Warum die Herero mit den Deutschen kooperierten: Zur 'Pazifizierung' einer akephalen Gesellschaft," *Mittelweg 36* 24, no. 4 (2015): 86–108.
159. According to Kuhlmann, in February 1904 Maharero dispatched men to "break up" disloyal *werfts*, taking cattle and people, in order to coerce the chiefs to take his side. See Kuhlmann, *Auf Adlers Flügeln*, 46.
160. Randall Collins, *Violence: A Micro-Sociological Theory* (Princeton, 2008).
161. ELCRN, Otjimbingwe chronicle, p. 146.
162. With respect to the three hundred riders, the chronicle from Otjimbingwe stated, "Once the African steppe starts to burn, the wind carries the flames from bush to bush so that no one can stop it. After the acts of murder took place, there was no way back for the Herero. The stormy wind of embitterment carried the fire from place to place, from tribe to tribe. The poor, lonesome farmers and travelers who, suspecting nothing, would be surprised by the fire!" See ELCRN, Otjimbingwe chronicle, p. 132.
163. In *Krieg und Frieden im Hereroland*, Rust presents these actions in the context of martial law, justifying swift punishment for those who were apprehended. He may, however, be correct that much of the plundering was done for personal gain, and that it did not involve the centrally coordinated "requisition" of critical wartime goods. Such distinctions are fluid in a society at war.
164. Scheff, *Bloody Revenge*, 2.
165. Fear and mistrust also motivated the colonial subjects. Soon after the outbreak of the uprising, Maharero was said to have ordered the death of every Herero who henceforth associated with a white person, "because a good number of men were siding with the soldiers." See Kuhlmann, *Auf Adlers Flügeln*, 39.
166. Kurd Schwabe, *Dienst und Kriegführung in den Kolonien und auf überseeischen Expeditionen* (Berlin, 1902), 158ff.
167. Gewald, *Herero Heroes*, 152.
168. Dominik J. Schaller, "Am Rande des Krieges: Das Ovambo-Königreich Ondonga," in *Völkermord in Deutsch-Südwestafrika. Der Kolonialkrieg (1904–1908) in Namibia und seine Folgen*, ed. Jürgen Zimmerer und Joachim Zeller (Berlin, 2004), 138–39.
169. Fleeing was apparently out of the question. Maharero was said to have remarked that there were too many Herero people to move to Bechuanaland, where they would only

be seen as intruders; all that the Herero had was the land of their fathers, so they had to fight for it. See Kuhlmann, *Auf Adlers Flügeln*, 46.
170. Quoted in Walter Moritz, *Aus alten Tagen in Südwest*, vol. 3 (Werther, 1996), 42.
171. Bridgman, *The Revolt of the Hereros*, 69.
172. Near Oviumbo, Herero were said to have called out to a woman settler, "Come out, we want to give you a cow so you and your child can go to Swakopmund." And an elder named Ouanjo wrote to an officer, "Surrender the women to me; I want to send them to Germany." See Rust, *Krieg und Frieden im Hereroland*, 81 and 159. Kuhlmann recounted similar anecdotes. See Kuhlmann, *Auf Adlers Flügeln*, 23.
173. Häussler, "Zur Asymmetrie tribaler und staatlicher Kriegführung in Imperialkriegen," 189, note 68.
174. Kuhlmann reported that after the first successes of the Second Field Company, the eastern Herero planned to flee to British territory, but Maharero stopped them with a clever ploy. See Kuhlmann, *Auf Adlers Flügeln*, 46. Maharero may have ordered the concentration of forces at the end of February in order to prevent individual groups from fleeing. See Pool, *Samuel Maharero*, 220; and Rust, *Krieg und Frieden im Hereroland*, 126.
175. The Herero seemed to weary of fighting. Nuhn points to a request for asylum sent by Maharero to the British resident magistrate at Walvis Bay on 12 June 1904. Before the Battle of Waterberg, other Herero leaders also attempted to negotiate for peace. See Nuhn, *Sturm über Südwest*, 185; and Estorff, *Wanderungen und Kämpfe*, 118.
176. Erich von Salzmann, *Im Kampfe gegen die Herero* (Berlin, 1905), 65; and Rust, *Krieg und Frieden im Hereroland*, 107.
177. Rust, *Krieg und Frieden im Hereroland*, 41.
178. Conrad Rust told of decapitations and "the most dreadful mutilations," including "chopped-off hands," "gouged-out eyes," and even cannibalism. See Rust, *Krieg und Frieden im Hereroland*, 75, 89, 133, and 192; and also G. Auer, *In Südwestafrika gegen die Hereros: Nach den Kriegstagebüchern des Obermatrosen G. Auer* (Berlin, 1911), 61–62 and 81.
179. The notorious "Night of Blood" at Okahandja on 23 September 1880 was preceded by the "Bloodbath of Okahandja" thirty years earlier, when the Oorlam leader Jonker Afrikaner cut off the hands and feet of his opponents, including women and children. The missionary Irle claimed to have seen the victims of this "bloodbath" himself. See Irle, *Die Herero*, 192.
180. "Der 12. Januar," *Windhuker Nachrichten*, 14 January 1905, 1.
181. "Mobilmachung," *DSWAZ*, 19 January 1904, 1.
182. BArch. N/1030, vol. 21, p. 6, 11.
183. This is supported not only by Franke, but also the diary of Helene Gathmann, who wrote that her husband placed a revolver in her hand "and ordered: cover." See Deutsches Tagebucharchiv, Sign. 1704 (17 January 1904), p. 13. Likewise, in his own diary the missionary Eich recalled the words of Else Sonnenberg: "I have to prepare to defend the store, but I don't have a weapon." See BArch. N/1783/1 (14 January 1904), p. 5.
184. Rust, *Krieg und Frieden im Hereroland*, 9.
185. "Bekanntmachung vom 13.1.04," *DSWAZ*, 19 January 1904, 1.
186. At an assembly in Windhuk, the settlers informed Leutwein that "on this point, the government should in no way deceive itself as to the mood of the land; the Hereros must immediately be dealt a crushing defeat, which will stave off any renewed desires for an uprising in the future. Should *the Hereros thereupon* seek negotiations, these could be introduced *only* on the basis of unconditional surrender." See "Aus dem Schutzgebiet: Aus Windhuk," *DSWAZ*, 19 April 1904, 2.

187. The "convergence" between settlers and troops was a well-known problem. The established colonial forces interacted with the settlers on a footing of "complete equality," identifying with them all too closely. See Curt von François, *Kriegführung in Südafrika* (Berlin, 1900), 80–81. In the "land of the enemy" (Schwabe, *Dienst und Kriegführung*, 156), the colonizers sat "in one boat"—a metaphor used by various colonial officers to illustrate living conditions for whites in the colonial situation. The boat metaphor reappears in various texts. See, for example, Hermann von Wissmann, *Afrika: Schilderungen und Rathschläge zur Vorbereitung für den Aufenthalt und den Dienst in den deutschen Schutzgebieten* (Berlin, 1895), 77ff.; and Simplex Africanus, Leutnant Laasch, and Hauptmann Leue, *Mit der Schutztruppe durch Deutsch-Afrika* (Minden, 1905), 52–53.
188. Diary of Helene Gathmann, DTA, Sign. 1704 (17 February 1904), p. 33.
189. Diary of Helene Gathmann, DTA, Sign. 1704 (19 January 1904), p. 19. See also Rust, *Krieg und Frieden im Hereroland*.
190. Missionary Elger to the Rhenish Missionary Society, BArch. R1001/2114, p. 81.
191. NAN A569, p. 27.
192. Großer Generalstab, *Die Kämpfe der deutschen Truppen in Südwestafrika*, vol. 1, 214.
193. Deputy Governor Hans Tecklenburg believed that the uprisings had exposed the vulnerability of the colonial masters, and that "our prestige with the natives, the prestige of the white man is beyond saving." See the report from 15 October 1904, BArch. R1001/1139, p. 233, quoted in Kundrus, *Moderne Imperialisten*, 56.
194. Bley, *Kolonialherrschaft und Sozialstruktur*, 177. Whites could be sentenced for three months to three years for murdering Africans, but Africans invariably received the death penalty for murdering whites. In most cases, more than one black was executed for the murder of a white. See Silvester and Gewald, *Words Cannot Be Found*, 94.
195. Peter Waldmann, "Rache ohne Regeln: Zur Renaissance eines archaischen Gewaltmotivs," in *Terrorismus und Bürgerkrieg: Der Staat in Bedrängnis*, ed. Peter Waldmann (Munich, 2003), 174.
196. Jakob Irle, *Was soll aus den Herero werden?* 2nd ed. (Gütersloh, 1906), 4.
197. BArch. R1001/2115, p. 61.
198. Ibid., p. 62.
199. Ibid., p. 63.
200. Ibid.
201. Office of the Resident Magistrate, Walfish Bay, to the Secretary to the Native Affairs Department, Cape Town (18 May 1904), PRO WO 106/265: "Herero-Rising 1904–7; Bondelzwart Rising 1903," p. 148.
202. Bernd Greiner, *Krieg ohne Fronten: Die USA in Vietnam* (Hamburg, 2007), 123; and Collins, *Violence*.
203. Office of the Resident Magistrate, Walfish Bay, to the Secretary to the Native Affairs Department, Cape Town (18 May 1904), PRO WO 106/265: "Herero-Rising 1904–7; Bondelzwart Rising 1903," p. 148.
204. See, for example, Bayer, *Mit dem Hauptquartier in Südwestafrika*, 64.
205. Admiralstab der Marine Admiralstab der Marine, *Das Marine-Expeditionskorps in Südwest-Afrika während des Herero-Aufstandes* (Berlin, 1905), 17.
206. The British officer W. E. Montague, who arrived to fight the Zulu with his regiment in what is now South Africa in 1879, was unsettled by the settlers' ongoing attempts to stir up the troops. Recounting bloody tales of Zulu atrocities, settlers sought to persuade the soldiers of the urgency of annihilating the Zulu people. See Montague, *Campaigning in Zululand*, 31.

207. Max Belwe, *Gegen die Herero 1904/1905: Tagebuchaufzeichnungen von Max Belwe: Mit einer Übersichtsskizze und achtzehn Abbildungen im Text* (Berlin, 1906), 11.
208. See also "Aus dem Schutzgebiet," *DSWAZ*, 1 March 1905, 1.
209. *DSWAZ*, 3 August 1904.
210. Großer Generalstab, *Die Kämpfe der deutschen Truppen in Südwestafrika*, vol. 1, 15–16.
211. "Zur augenblicklichen Lage," *DSWAZ*, 5 January 1904, 1.
212. "Aus dem Schutzgebiet: Aus Omaruru," *DSWAZ*, 18 August 1906, 1.

Chapter 2

The Strategic Horizon
Leutwein—Metropole—Trotha

The settlers were unable to put the genie back in the bottle that they themselves had uncorked. Events in South-West Africa were pulled into the wake of forces beyond the colony, beyond the control of the settlers, military officers, and civil servants on site. Once reports of the uprising reached Germany and sparked an uproar, Berlin moved quickly to assert control over South-West African affairs. Bit by bit, the colonial governor lost his once considerable autonomy. Significant discrepancies arose between the metropole and colony, between Berlin and Windhuk.

I begin this chapter by examining Leutwein's longstanding colonial policy and his approach to colonial warfare. The governor saw these aspects of leadership as closely intertwined. His strategic vision clearly set him apart from officers like Trotha and aroused the suspicions of the military establishment. Leutwein was, by nature, a proponent of limited warfare.

In the second section of this chapter, I investigate how the metropole influenced the course of the war. Public pressure played a role in shaping the Berlin authorities' attitudes toward the uprising, which contrasted sharply to Leutwein's.[1] The metropole pushed for unlimited warfare and demanded a "political war of annihilation," as I explain in an excursus. Leutwein was unable or unwilling to implement Berlin's strategic imperatives, and so he was ultimately relieved as commander of the South-West African troops. It is important to recognize that Trotha was only one candidate for a strategic program that had already existed for some time.

The third section looks at the principles that informed Trotha's wartime leadership. His appointment was part of the Berlin authorities' efforts to align the war effort more closely to their own expectations, and this included delivering the Herero a crushing defeat. Trotha approached this task with great zeal, which does not mean that he commenced a genocidal campaign of annihilation against the Herero. His command initially remained within "conventional" horizons of warfare, as his reading of the work of Georg Hartmann suggests. The decisive shift toward escalation was more structural than personal, once military perspectives alone came to determine the course of the war.

Leutwein's Limited Warfare

In just under eleven years, Theodor Leutwein decisively shaped the development of the colony in South-West Africa—first as an observer, then as Landeshauptmann, and finally, as governor. Leutwein's early service in the colony set the tone for the rest of his years in office. He was initially sent to relieve the bellicose Curt von François, whose aggressive stance threatened to plunge Imperial Germany into a long and expensive war with the Witbooi.[2] François's "dashing demeanor" was not universally admired.[3] Authorities in Germany were dissatisfied with the fruits of his politics and ultimately recalled him.[4] The Imperial government finally acted upon its claims to dominion over South-West Africa in 1893, but it preferred means that were formally peaceful, and thus also cost-effective.[5] François did not have sufficient resources to conclude the war of annihilation that he had provoked by attacking Hornkranz, the Witboois' main settlement. Most Witbooi fighters escaped the massacre at Hornkranz and commenced a guerrilla war that the colonial forces, less than three hundred men in all, were ill-prepared to handle. Leutwein inherited the unenviable task of ending this war as quickly as possible, without damaging the authority of Imperial Germany.

Leutwein henceforth saw his principal task as expanding and solidifying German rule over South-West Africa, without imposing excessive costs on the Imperial government. This policy of austerity became so second nature to him that he resisted changing course even after the mood in Germany had long since reversed itself.[6] After the uprising erupted in January 1904, Berlin responded to public pressure by forsaking all financial restraint in colonial affairs.[7] For the time being, successes seemed more important than the costs they incurred.

Austerity constrained Leutwein in some ways, but it also offered him considerable autonomy and the opportunity to solidify his personal power. The German public's everyday interest in colonial affairs had traditionally been limited, as was their willingness to expend larger sums for this cause. Drawn-out wars and calls for additional funds brought colonial affairs onto the political agenda, particularly since the Reichstag was responsible for approving the budget. The sudden interest in colonial affairs brought new questions and invited public scrutiny; it also encouraged the metropole to assume a more active role.[8] Before this turn of events, as a frugal governor, Leutwein had largely been able to set his own policies. He worked to ensure that conflicts remained limited or were quickly resolved. This may explain why Leutwein adopted a reassuring tone and downplayed the extent of the uprising in his January 1904 telegrams to Berlin—and also why his judgment and credibility were ultimately questioned. Subsequent intervention by the metropole heightened the intensity and significance of the local conflict so quickly that it slipped completely from the control of the colonial government.[9]

Leutwein's personal rule was a throwback to the premodern era, coexisting uneasily with the bureaucracy in which the colonial administration was formally integrated. Leutwein compared his relationship to the African chiefs with that of the "Holy Roman Emperor to the dukes [*Stammesherzöge*] in the Middle Ages."[10] It was a relationship based on pledges of loyalty between specific individuals. Leutwein understood that the chiefs' allegiance was to him as a person, not to an abstract entity like the state.[11] He was convinced that the Herero uprising had erupted because he had left Windhuk.[12] The officer Ludwig von Estorff, Leutwein's longtime colleague, unambiguously praised his integrity, but even Estorff saw a certain hubris in Leutwein, and accused him of trusting too deeply in the "impression made by his own personality," thereby overlooking the "high degree" of dissatisfaction among the Herero.[13]

Leutwein, like most of the era's purported experts on South-West Africa, believed that indigenous labor was indispensable to the colonial economy. An important policy goal was thus to preserve and develop the colony's indigenous workforce. For Leutwein, enhancing the value of colonial "resources" was one reason to limit warlike violence against the autochthonous population.

The autochthonous population's "right to exist" hung by a thread in the settler colony SWA. The colonizers did not see this right as an end in itself. Rather, the future of the indigenous population depended on their usefulness to the colonial masters.[14] There was broad consensus in colonial circles that the value of indigenous people was limited to their usefulness to others; it was not intrinsic to their humanity. Leutwein, too, adopted this inhumane logic—either out of genuine conviction or as a matter of strategy because he sensed the futility of an ethical argument on behalf of indigenous people. Even so, it is possible that over time Leutwein developed a paternalistic bond with "*his* natives" that shaped his behavior—a bond that was, and remained, utterly incomprehensible to his successor, Lothar von Trotha.[15] We should, in any event, acknowledge two key aspects of his policy: cost sensitivity and the preservation of indigenous labor.

For Leutwein, too, the end goal of colonization in South-West Africa was "the creation of a colony populated by whites."[16] This could be accomplished in two different ways—either by subjugating the black Africans with violence, conquering the territory militarily, and establishing direct rule; or with an indirect guardianship based on negotiated treaties. Leutwein called the former approach "actual rule" (*tatsächliche Herrschaft*), and the latter, "protective rule" (*Schutzherrschaft*).

Military conquest of the colony and the subjugation of autochthonous groups would have been too expensive for Imperial Germany. Leutwein understood that the metropole lacked the political will for this before the 1904 uprising. Thus, he opted for an approach that would supposedly succeed "without severity and without the use of force." Leutwein's "policy of conciliation between the opposite races" sought to reconcile the indigenous people with their fate as helots, "gradually accustoming them to the present conditions."[17] He believed that he could rely completely on the "pressure of civilization," as the Herero would not be able to withstand formally peaceful competition with the whites. He did not believe that the Herero understood how to manage their own resources. Their dependence on European commodities would impoverish them; they would be forced to sell off their land and cattle, and in the end they would be compelled to work in service to the whites.[18] This was the end goal of Leutwein's policy. He bore no illusions about the apparently inevitable fate of the autochthonous peoples: "Independence will ultimately be nothing more than a memory for them. Hand in hand with this policy of peace, the natives could be gradually disarmed in cases of insubordination, and tribal groups dissolved."[19]

The "political death" of the Herero[20]—the necessity of which Leutwein underscored in February and again at a public meeting in Windhuk on 6 September 1904[21]—was a longer-term political goal that had been in place well before the uprising earlier that year. For Leutwein, therefore, colonization already had at least an ethnocidal goal; indigenous people were expected to give up their political independence and characteristic elements of their cultural identity.[22] They were to remain in the colony, but only as subordinate, propertyless workers in a society tailored to European needs. Although Leutwein's settlement policy sought to uphold the coexistence of whites and blacks, it was based on fundamental inequity between the two groups. Who would be the masters of the colony and who would be its servants was an unavoidable question. Leutwein's "peace policy" attempted to answer this question with formally peaceful means. The governor did all he could to avoid subduing the indigenous people with weapons and overtaking the colony by force. Instead, he hoped that the indigenous population would eventually come to accept its subordinate position, allowing itself to be reshaped as a fungible proletariat in service to whites.[23] His peace policy sought to preserve indigenous labor and integrate it within the European colonial economy, while simultaneously avoiding costly military adventures.

In this context, it is important to ask what Leutwein proposed to do if his peace policy failed, or encountered resistance from the colonized peoples. As early as the 1890s, he stated that the German government would either have to give up "colonization among the Herero as hopeless," or order a "struggle of annihilation" (*Vernichtungskampf*) against them. Unsurprisingly, he believed that a "struggle of annihilation" was more likely than giving up the colony.[24] On another occasion, he described how such a battle would have to be waged: "A rigorous colonial policy would doubtless demand killing all prisoners who were fit to bear arms. I would not like to adopt these methods myself, but I would bear no reproach for the person who did so."[25]

Leutwein's remarks reflect the first weeks and months of the Herero war under his command, when no prisoners were taken, and even the lives of women and children were not spared—although the governor later disputed that he had directly ordered these measures. While he may not have adopted "these methods" himself, he also bore "no reproach" for the actors who did. Further, this passage shows that Leutwein clearly understood what would be demanded by a "rigorous colonial policy" in case of an uprising, but also that he was not necessarily prepared to adopt the rigorous measures himself. This may have departed too crassly from the approach that he stood for. In any event, Leutwein was reluctant to change course in 1904, and this resistance sealed his fate.

Even so, we should not whitewash Leutwein's own wartime leadership. He led an 1897 campaign that nearly wiped out the "Afrikaners" (|Aixa|aen), the remaining survivors of the once-powerful Oorlam group, who in the first half of the nineteenth century controlled much of present-day Namibia.[26] The Khauas (Kai|khauan), too, ceased to exist as a political entity after 1896; their members were worn down by combat, detained and forced to labor in concentration camps, or expelled from the land altogether.[27] Concentration camps with their many detainees, primarily women and children, had been a fixture in Windhuk since its colonial-era founding.[28] These examples show once again how colonial wars differed from internal European conflicts. By the start of the twentieth century, European laws of war forbade practices such as killing all men who were fit to bear arms, taking hostages, and compulsory labor, but in the colonies these practices were considered acceptable or even taken for granted. Campaigns against indigenous groups usually pursued radical goals—including disarming and dissolving the groups as independent political entities, expulsion, or even physical extermination. In short, there were hardly any limits on the use of force in the colonies; we should therefore be wary of any talk of "limited warfare." All this notwithstanding, in contrast to a François or Trotha, Leutwein did not seek to bolster his own position of power at any price. He favored comparatively moderate sanctions, such as punishing leaders or appropriating land—although it is clear that unfettered violence was always just a small step away.

Leutwein governed according to the principle of "divide and rule." Thus, in order to gain the trust of the indigenous population and their leaders, Imperial Germany had to be willing to negotiate, even from a position of military superiority, and to refrain from violence whenever possible.[29] Conversely, this meant accepting the chiefs as negotiating partners and allowing them to bring forth certain claims that could not be dismissed out of hand. In a sense, therefore, Leutwein did recognize the autochthonous groups.

This condition was essential to his concept of limited warfare. In an 1899 lecture on the battles in South-West Africa between 1894 and 1896, Leutwein explained why he believed that limited warfare was inevitable in SWA. As we have already seen, the colonial government had only limited means at its disposal. Its armed forces confronted opponents who were evenly matched—or superior—in many respects; mobility is one example.[30] Indigenous fighters were willing to give up their position on the battlefield, or even surrender territory, because they could quickly regroup in another location.[31] They did not see retreat as dishonorable, but often as operative success. Thus, by European standards, "victories" over such opponents were relatively easy to achieve—but not the decisive victories that would compel lasting peace.[32] Vast expanses of land offered ample room for retreat, playing into the opponents' hand and reinforcing their tactics of delay. In these circumstances, the prospects for a decisive victory were slim.

South-West Africa's sparse vegetation placed natural limits on the scope of military operations. The cost of supplying troops anywhere in the colony, but particularly in remote areas far from the railroad lines, was exorbitantly high. Despite considerable expense and months of work on a supply network, Lothar von Trotha managed to bring no more than 1,500 fighters to the Waterberg. Many more troops, meanwhile, were needed to supply these units, which hardly succeeded. It was not merely a question of the financial and personnel costs that the metropole was willing to bear; nature imposed its own limits on all undertakings. Insufficient water and pasture prevented larger numbers of troops from occupying the same stretch of land, and operations might even come to a complete standstill in the dry season. Small troop concentrations in large areas often meant pursuing comparatively modest goals.[33] The Germans could attempt to pursue their opponent and attack when an opportunity arose, but a decisive, devastating strike was hardly possible in such circumstances.

The attacks of 1904 aside, the indigenous opponents had the advantage of not always needing a "victory," and being able to put off decisive action. They were successful as long as they could avoid a final defeat.[34] The colonial masters, meanwhile, feared a long war more than almost anything else. Such a display of weakness would damage their much-touted prestige as colonial masters, emboldening other groups to rise up against them.[35] Further, a long war would disturb or interrupt the colony's economic development for an unforeseeable length of time.[36] As the consequences of a long war were difficult to predict, it was best to avoid such a conflict by setting aside goals that were all too ambitious.[37]

In other words, Leutwein's experience in numerous campaigns was that the technical superiority of the German troops translated only with difficulty, if at all, to the South-West African theater, and that in many respects indigenous forces were (at least) evenly matched with their German counterparts. Under these difficult conditions, demonstrating keen strategic judgment was all the more essential.[38]

In a particularly revealing document from 23 February 1904, the governor refuted various charges that had been leveled against him and defended his actions, including the supposed "negotiations with the insurrectionary Hereros" that had incensed the colonial and metropolitan publics. Leutwein conceded that upon returning to Okahandja he had "immediately" written to Samuel Maharero, paramount chief of the Herero, and his headmen, but he disputed that his actions were negotiations in the literal sense. They were instead a wartime ploy, or "fake negotiations," which sought to uncover information about the opponent, and also their whereabouts, strength, and morale.[39] He later walked back parts of his own correction, however, and even defended the negotiations:

In colonial wars the diplomat and the leader must always stand together. The rebels have to know that there is still an open path for their retreat that doesn't have to lead to death. Otherwise we will drive them to desperation, and the result will be a war without end, with the disadvantage on our side. Then the natives will have nothing more to lose . . . while we suffer every day, as the work of colonization comes to a standstill. So, for example, the Spaniards were "victorious" in Cuba for years, without . . . end, and then they lost the island.

These lines are noteworthy in multiple respects. Even after the uprising, the governor continued to make the case for limited warfare. He believed that soldiers or experts trained only in the exercise of violence were ill-suited for conducting a successful colonial campaign, even when they seemed "victorious" from a narrow military perspective. This is not as contradictory as it might appear. Leutwein recognized that the political dimension of war framed, or should frame, the use of force. Violence is generally situated within a particular context and oriented toward particular interests. Strategic thinking includes cost-benefit analyses, which limit the use of force. Carl von Clausewitz described the "abstract purpose" of war as the utter subjugation of an opponent—eliminating the danger he poses once and for all, and bending him to your will. Thus, destroying his capacity to fight, occupying his territory, and compelling him to obey your will might seem to be the most certain way to achieve this end.[40] But reflecting upon the history of warfare, Clausewitz himself notes that "real war" rarely goes this far. Violence usually remains limited because no party is so vested in the conflict that he is prepared to do whatever it takes to crush an opponent utterly—or, conversely, to fight to the bitter end without giving in, thereby running the danger of incurring an absolute defeat. The use of force is limited not least by the concern that its costs may exceed its potential benefits. Moreover, because warring parties rarely go their utmost limit, they can align their use of force to the resistance that they expect to confront. In other words, they do not have to proceed from the worst possible scenario and apply maximal force; they can adjust their behavior according to the probable degree of resistance that they are likely to encounter.

These considerations troubled Leutwein. He knew that excessive force could be dysfunctional and exact a high price. "With colonization one has to take all possible factors into account, because one should build and not destroy," a settler named Buslow wrote in Leutwein's defense.[41] The governor worked to keep communications open with the opponent; this was the only way to determine the appropriate degree of force for achieving the Germans' war aims without disrupting longer-term colonial political goals. The rebels had, of course, attempted to overthrow German colonial rule, and Leutwein was determined to reassert his country's claim to power—but not at all costs, or with all available means. He initially emphasized economic factors to defend his point of view.

If the colonial power insisted on utterly crushing the rebels and ruling out any concessions, it would drive the opponents to "desperation" and a "struggle for existence." They would have nothing more to lose, and would continue to fight until the bitter end. Imperial Germany had more to lose. Every day that the war dragged on incurred new costs and damages. Parts of the economy lay in ruins. The longer that the uprising and its suppression continued, the more settlers considered leaving the colony, and the fewer new colonists were willing to replace them.[42] The increased troop presence cost untold sums, while the fighting threatened to ruin the colony's wealth in livestock. The price of unfettered violence was high, as the struggle for dominion could wipe out the colony's wealth and resources. From an economic perspective, this threw the sense of the entire colonial endeavor into question.

Leutwein responded to his critics (unfortunately, not identified here by name) who pushed for complete annihilation—that is, for the genocidal escalation of the war: "We still need the Hereros as small cattle breeders and especially as workers." Military leaders could not neglect the fact that indigenous labor was indispensable to the colonial economy. Limits had to be placed on violence, to protect indigenous life wherever possible. Within this context Leutwein even introduced an ethical argument, suggesting that the numbers of rebel fighters showed that the entire people could not have been involved in the uprising. Since some Herero groups had apparently not taken arms, the entire people could not be declared the enemy, and force therefore had to be exercised in a differentiated way.

Leutwein understood that he would not be able to maintain his previous course without disruption. Although the indigenous people had once enjoyed sovereign rights and the opportunity to fend for themselves, the era of indirect rule now seemed irretrievably past. At a minimum, the Herero would have to be disarmed and "contained" in reserves, where they could eke out a meager existence. In contrast to the later practice of collective punishment, Leutwein considered only those Herero who engaged in "plunder" and "murder" as "prisoners of war," with military courts determining their status.

For Leutwein, avoiding long wars had always meant abstaining from radical political goals. He understood the danger of driving opponents "to desperation," thereby provoking "a war without end, with the disadvantage on our side."[43] Particularly in colonial wars, soldiers had to work together with diplomats, who could build opponents a "golden bridge" in order to win their support for a peace settlement.⁴⁴ The colonial government had to remain prepared to make certain concessions, and so it never broke off diplomatic relations with opponents.

Leutwein did not depart radically from this course in 1904. Although he reiterated his disapproval of Herero "misdeeds" in his 23 February letter, agreeing with the Colonial Department that the war could end only with the "unconditional surrender" of the Herero, he did not want to commit to destroying tribal structures for good.⁴⁵ Before the uprising, he had proposed establishing reserves to protect the indigenous societies from the settlers' hunger for land,⁴⁶ but this hardly persuaded his superiors that he would end the campaign as they desired—even though he took pains to present the "containment" of Herero in reserves as a disciplinary sanction.⁴⁷

The subtext of Leutwein's letter—and even more, of his actions—suggests that although he disapproved of Herero resistance, he remained willing to recognize the opponent as an independent warring party (with lesser rights). His demand for a "free hand . . . with respect to diplomatic channels, until the conclusion of negotiations," points in this direction.⁴⁸

After the Herero had so provocatively challenged German dominion in January 1904, Leutwein's stance stirred opposition in the colony and beyond. After this turn of events, at the latest, a policy that was prepared to concede even a lesser degree of independence to the indigenous societies was no longer acceptable. The governor's son, Paul Leutwein, who fought in the war himself, later remarked that his father might have succeeded in bringing around the white colonists to his moderate conditions for peace—but not the homeland.⁴⁹

The Metropolitan War

The metropolitan center gained decision-making power over the course of the war. Foreign powers increasingly determined the direction of the war in SWA, and the governor lost much of his earlier independence.⁵⁰

Leutwein returned to Swakopmund from the southern theater of combat on 11 February 1904. Once on site, he revised his initial assessment of the situation—but authorities in Imperial Germany had already bypassed his declared intentions and decided to send more troops.⁵¹ Moreover, Kaiser Wilhelm II had tasked the chief of the Great General Staff with coordinating operations.⁵²

As news of the uprising spread, a German Colonial League pamphlet from 14 January 1904 accused Leutwein of a "policy of whitewashing, hesitation, and a weak hand."⁵³ Soon a rumor made its way to Berlin that Leutwein wanted to negotiate with the Herero, as he had done in the past. The colonial and metropolitan public took the news as a "slap in face."⁵⁴ "The entire German press concerned with this matter has explained that peace negotiations with the rebels are *impossible*," the *Tägliche Rundschau* newspaper asserted on 9 March 1904, underscoring the position of key Berlin authorities.⁵⁵ Leutwein was directed "to abstain from all bilateral negotiations with Hereros, and to demand unconditional surrender"; under no circumstances could negotiations be allowed to begin without the "approval of His Majesty."⁵⁶ The metropole extended the logic of "bimodal alienation" to the level of strategy.

A few months later, Leutwein was ousted as leader of the South-West African Schutztruppe. I will discuss the circumstances of his dismissal in greater detail below, but certainly his "civilian" habitus played a central role. Influential voices in public, political, and military circles responded to the news of the overseas uprising with remarkable consensus. Reichstag delegates agreed enthusiastically with Oscar Stübel, director of the Colonial Department, as he addressed the German parliament on 17 March 1904: "The honor of Germany calls for the suppression of the uprising, with all available means."⁵⁷ Stübel recognized the importance of prestige for a "great power like Germany" and its military.⁵⁸

The conflict was recontextualized as the center of decision-making shifted from Windhuk to Berlin. From the South-West African point of view, the British were white neighbors who could generally be counted upon as sympathetic and cooperative. But to Imperial Germany, Britain was a hostile great power that precisely noted every weakness in order to take advantage of its rivals. As the regional lens was replaced by a global one, the Herero uprising was seen—and responded to—less as an attack on German settlement in the north of the colony, and more as a challenge to Germany's great power status.

Understanding the uprising as an assault on (national) honor corresponded to the ethos and thought patterns of Wilhelmine Germany's militarized social elites. From their perspective, there was only one appropriate response to the rebels' attacks; the violence that the Germans had suffered had to be avenged with superior counterviolence.

Leutwein was perhaps too level-headed to blindly join those who were clamoring for war, but in the eyes of his peers this circumspection made him an outsider, and thus the wrong man for the job. His repeated objections to unrestricted war aims may well have been justified. Even Trotha, his harshest critic, conceded that Leutwein was "politically quite smart and correct in his assessments,"⁵⁹ and that his arguments were "plausible."[60] However, none of this mattered in the given circumstances. Because the defense of honor was at stake, any objections that pointed toward moderation were dismissed as "petty misgivings,"[61] hardly worthy of an officer of a great power.

The *Tägliche Rundschau* went a step further. In the name of "national honor," it demanded that the rebels be taught a lesson "that they would not forget for generations," and firmly rejected any talk of peace before this occurred.[62] The emphasis on a "lesson of warning" (*Denkzettel*) is highly important, foreshadowing the immoderation and cruelty that would distinguish the further conduct of war in SWA. Although the colonial masters were primarily concerned with restoring "national honor" and "punishing" the rebels, the pursuit of these goals marked a highly consequential transition from the instrumental use of force to autotelic violence.[63] In autotelic violence, the use of force increasingly becomes an end in itself, and other purposes recede from view. Thus, the "lesson of warning" had to be an act of overwhelming power (*Aktionsmacht*), decoupled from concrete strategic goals or any means-end calculations, and existing independently of such provisos. Before entertaining conditions for peace, the "masters" had to demonstrate their superior strength as emphatically as possible.

The aforementioned *Tägliche Rundschau* article criticized Leutwein's supposedly too moderate stance, calling for "the war and its severe justice" to take precedence and ruling out any concessions to the Herero. Only "subduing the rebels by force of arms"—that is, through proof of overwhelming *Aktionsmacht*— could establish the "superiority of the white man." And only on the basis of this evidence would it be possible for "negotiations" to commence.[64]

Leutwein's peace policy had found official favor as long as saving money had been the top priority in colonial affairs. But once the Herero so boldly challenged German rule before the eyes of the world public, such "petty misgivings" (to borrow the words of Lothar von Trotha) were cast aside.[65] Now the defense of honor was at stake—and honor was priceless. After years of penny-pinching, suddenly "hundreds of millions" were being spent in the colony "to maintain prestige," as one observer bitterly noted.[66]

The concept of honor deserves closer attention here. The purpose of Imperial-era duels and other "matters of honor" was not merely to demonstrate bravura, or to outflank one's opponent. Being prepared to place one's life on the line if need be was crucial, as this is what distinguished an "honorable" man.[67] In the present context, the stakes were different—or higher—because the opponent was not seen as equal; thus, the pain inflicted had to be paid back many times over.

In no circumstances could a "man of honor" stand for an affront. A challenge issued by another "man of honor" might be resolved by a duel, but a challenge from a person of lesser status had to be punished in such a way that would drive home the challenger's inferior status. Rules that contained violence applied only to conflicts with equals; other situations called for some degree of violent "excess." This was true with respect to the Herero, supposedly inferior "natives" who had dared to challenge the superiority of the white man, supposing that they could compete with him. In a racially divided society, the uprising was an act of audacity that had to be put down at all costs.

A further influence on the thoughts and actions of top leaders in Berlin was the Wilhelmine obsession with militarism and government authority.[68] German elites' support for an authoritarian state shaped their views on the legitimacy of their opponents. In November 1904, Alfred von Schlieffen, chief of the Great General Staff, described military elites' general attitude toward the campaign against the Herero and its potential conclusion: "With rebels, there can be no peace settlement without unconditional surrender."[69] Because the opponents were seen as "rebels," they had no legitimacy.[70] All "*bilateral* negotiations" were unacceptable,[71] one newspaper explained, because the Herero could not be recognized as a warring party "with equal status."[72] In Schlieffen's view, the Germans could only initiate a "peace settlement" unilaterally—when the opposing side was brought to the point of surrender, without issuing further conditions. The fact that the "rebels" were Africans may not have been decisive for German leaders. A General Staff study, *Der Kampf in insurgierten Städten*, suggested that the same conditions would have applied to workers' uprisings.[73] What mattered was that the opponents had revolted against state authority, and they were not a legitimate warring party according to state-centered norms of international law. This does not mean that the Berlin leaders did not hold racist views—but rather that their "class racism"[74] was just as pronounced as their "race-based racism."

To paraphrase Schlieffen: the opponent had to be dealt a crushing defeat, so the terms of peace (actually measures of atonement) could be dictated to him. Because negotiations were ruled out on principle, there was no alternative to a total victory. The military craving for prestige reinforced this demand.[75] "Ordinary" victories were insufficient; only an illustrious, "total" victory would do.[76]

A total victory would also have laid the groundwork for a fundamental reorganization of power relations in SWA. Leutwein's "protective rule" had allowed the autochthonous groups to retain some of their sovereignty, so the Herero had used their remaining power to dislodge the yoke of German rule. Oskar Stübel, director of the Colonial Department, presented the political and strategic framework of the campaign against the Herero before the Reichstag on 19 January 1904. In his view, there was an "urgent need to do away with the political semi-independence that the natives were granted to this point."[77] In order to abolish the last traces of their independence, the Herero people had to be vanquished completely and rendered incapable of any organized collective resistance. The metropole sought a war that would annihilate the opponent, eliminating the Herero as an independent political entity once and for all.[78]

Leutwein's style of diplomacy was no longer an option. It was a nonstarter for the metropole, which considered the Herero mere "rebels," not a legitimate warring party. The Germans were so convinced of their own superiority that they did not consider using diplomacy even when this might have been useful for deceptive purposes. They believed that they could win by focusing solely on their own actions, without regard for their opponent.

Leutwein still attempted to explain the causes of the uprising to his superiors, thereby defusing some of its tension. His explanation that "the unqualified trading practices of the Germans and their careless brutality was the sole cause of the uprising" seemed "plausible" enough to Trotha—but Trotha did not consider reevaluating his further actions in light of these insights.[79] The reasons the Herero had decided to revolt held no interest for him whatsoever. They had dared to challenge German rule, and this challenge had to be answered.

In Berlin, too, Leutwein's proposals fell on deaf ears. Kaiser Wilhelm flatly rejected his suggestion that "a higher-ranking civil servant on site" might investigate the causes of the uprising. As long as operations were ongoing, the Kaiser believed such an investigation was "premature."[80] A key aspect of strategic judgment is understanding one's opponent, including their motives and objectives. Knowing more about the causes of the uprising could have provided insight into the goals of the Herero and the energy that they were prepared to expend in order to meet them. Further, this could have opened paths to rapprochement and negotiations for peace. These considerations played an important role for Leutwein, but not for his superiors in Berlin. To the contrary: they were so convinced of their own superiority that they practically ignored their opponent. Focusing on German concerns and procedures seemed to be all that was needed for the upcoming campaign.

Organs of public opinion and official policy foregrounded themes such as "national honor" in their discussion of the uprising, thereby encouraging escalation. Seemingly innocuous terms such as *Denkzettel* (literally, a "memorandum") were used to describe the violent "lesson of warning" that the German troops had to impart. In a narrow strategic sense, the directions issued by the Imperial government amounted to what I call a "political war of annihilation" (*politischer Vernichtungskrieg*). Leutwein was unwilling or unable to wage such a war, and so he was ultimately dismissed.

Excursus: What Is a Political War of Annihilation?

Colonial revisionists triumphantly assert that *Vernichtung* had a narrow military meaning around the year 1900; the term implied rendering one's opponents completely defenseless, but by no means their genocidal annihilation.[81] When colonial-era sources mentioned *Vernichtung*, so the revisionist argument goes, the extermination of opponents and their society was not yet intended—in contrast to the eastern campaigns of the National Socialist regime in World War II.

Without denying the "limits of comparison,"[82] it is nevertheless important to recognize that the military use of *Vernichtung* was more ambiguous than the apologists suggest. These authors deny the potential for escalation by dogmatically absolutizing a particular aspect of the term. *Vernichtung* does not necessarily imply the utter devastation of an opponent—but it does not rule out this possibility either. Inconspicuous adverbs such as "completely"[83] often signal extreme dimensions of violence, without stretching or changing the meaning of *Vernichtung* in an unnatural way. *Vernichtung* does not specify the degree of force that is necessary to achieve certain aims, but it covers a wide spectrum that includes extreme forms of violence.

From the very beginning of the war against the Herero, *Vernichtung* could refer to actions that were openly genocidal. In early 1904, Leutwein countered indiscriminate calls for eradicating the Herero by noting that "60,000–70,000 souls cannot be so easily destroyed."[84] Genocidal violence was already a possibility.[85]

The Herero campaign is often described as a *Vernichtungskrieg*[86]—meaning a genocidal war of annihilation that has been closely associated with Lothar von Trotha's command. Even beyond the case of South-West Africa, *Vernichtungskrieg* is reflexively understood as a genocidal war of annihilation.[87] Upon closer investigation, however, this determination seems premature.

Susanne Kuß has correctly established that the annihilation in a *Vernichtungskrieg* is not merely instrumental;[88] it is not the means to a political end, but instead the war's only, all-encompassing goal. A war of annihilation does not have limited goals; its aim is broader. Annihilation is not limited to the opponent's armed forces, but extends to the opponent *as such*. The military historian Karl Linnebach described this type of war as the "most extreme case," demanding "the largest imaginable sacrifice," because it involves at least one warring party seeking to wipe out the other in its existing form.[89] The *Vernichtungskrieg* accentuates "total victory,"[90] approaching Clausewitz's "abstract purpose" of war.

This raises the following question: if the annihilation in a *Vernichtungskrieg* applies to the *opponent as such*, does this automatically mean that the annihilation extends to all or parts of the opponent's society?

This proposition deserves our attention, particularly with respect to the apologist positions that I introduced at the beginning of this section, as it acknowledges the full potential for violence that has *always* accompanied the term *Vernichtung*, which the apologists deny. The military use of *Vernichtung* is distinguished precisely by its fundamental ambiguity or "ambivalence," as stated by Andreas Stucki.[91] *Vernichtung* does not specify the degree of force that is necessary to achieve certain aims, but it does cover a wide spectrum that includes extreme forms of violence. How far this spectrum extends ultimately has to do with the dynamics of the fighting. Thus, the meaning of *Vernichtung* can depend on the opponent's resistance—whether he lays down his weapons in the face of certain defeat, or fights on until the bitter end. The degree of violence varies accordingly; *Vernichtung* can be limited to disarmament and taking prisoners, thereby rendering the opponent defenseless—or it can escalate to physical annihilation.

Both the apologist and critical positions are essentially one-sided; they mark opposite poles on the spectrum of meaning for that slippery term, *Vernichtung*. Even in wars of annihilation, the degree of violence can depend on the dynamics of the fighting (insofar as an "enemy" population was not targeted from the very beginning).[92] A classic "trinitarian war"—which is distinguished by strict separation between government, army, and civilians[93]—is characterized by a different degree of violence than a "people's war" that blurs such distinctions. Conversely, and particularly relevant to the circumstances in South-West Africa, a war of annihilation can occur even when the threshold to genocide is not crossed.

We have already established that a war of annihilation is directed against the *opponent as such*. This does not (automatically) mean destroying the society of the opponent. If the aims of a war are to utterly devastate the opponent by vanquishing his armed forces, occupying his land, and permanently wresting away his independence and sovereignty, we can reasonably call it a war of annihilation—even without other "total" or genocidal features. Even "extreme" wars of annihilation do not mean abandoning all scruples and moving directly to obliterate one's opponent. Linnebach advocated on behalf of the new German military leadership in the interwar era, and he was unwilling to rule out genocidal violence. Yet he emphatically asserted that the foremost goal of a war of annihilation was the "annihilation of the enemy state"—in other words, its political structures—and not the "extermination of the enemy people."[94]

This form of war represents a clear contrast to the "cabinet wars" of the eighteenth century.[95] The Peace of Westphalia ushered in a system of states as independent political entities, a status that was never questioned, even when these states went to war with one another.[96] War was an exercise and affirmation of the sovereignty of princes, independent of a conflict's outcome. The cabinet war was diametrically opposed to the war of annihilation, which involved one warring party denying the right of another to exist (at least in its current form), and seeking its elimination.

Examples of such conflicts include civil wars, and also wars of conquest and subjugation in an imperial context. In both cases, at least one of the warring parties asserts an indivisible claim to power, seeking to defeat the opposing side that rejects this claim.[97]

The historian Martin Zimmermann writes of the "extreme bipolarity" between warring parties in the civil wars of ancient Greece, which left no room for negotiation. Demands for the "complete obliteration of the opponent" could lead to "wars of extermination," although in many cases the victors were satisfied with the expulsion or exile of political opponents or ringleaders.[98]

Colonial or imperial wars often pursued similarly "absolute goals," although they generally emphasized conquest or subjugation, not the extermination of indigenous peoples.[99] Identifying such conflicts as anything less than wars of annihilation risks downplaying their radical goals and their consequences for the defeated peoples. At a minimum, we can describe these wars as *ethnocidal* (drawing upon the terminology of genocide studies). A further risk is misunderstanding the distinctive nature of these wars. Colonial or imperial wars consistently sought to destroy the opponent as an independent political entity—and often much more than that. This makes them wars of annihilation, even if an interest in preserving the conquered societies kept the violence within limits.[100]

In contrast to conventional wisdom about wars of annihilation, and about the case of SWA in particular, we can indeed refer to the war that Berlin demanded (and that Leutwein was not prepared to lead) as one of annihilation, without implying that its aim from the very beginning was to *eradicate* the Herero. Rather, the conflict initially resembled what I call a "political" war of annihilation, which seeks to permanently destroy the opponent as an independent political entity. The continued existence of the Herero as a political entity was not merely uncertain, but was to be eliminated altogether. Negotiations were out of the question because there was nothing more to negotiate; the Germans would accept nothing less than unconditional surrender. Chiefs and headmen were "ringleaders" who could expect execution. The end of their leadership was intended as the end of the entire political, social, and cultural organization of the Herero.

Gesturing to Clausewitz, Hannes Heer proposes that wars of annihilation have their own "grammar" and "logic"; from the outset, therefore, wars of annihilation avoid the political considerations that limit conventional wars.[101] We need not go this far, but it is nevertheless evident that wars of annihilation have considerable potential for escalation.

Clausewitz presumes that rendering the opponent defenseless is only the "abstract purpose" of war—a theoretical extreme that "real" wars rarely, if ever, reach. Throughout history, in fact, "many treaties have been concluded before one of the antagonists could be called powerless—even before the balance of power had been seriously altered."[102] Things are different in a war of annihilation. The warring party who seeks to destroy his opponent essentially pursues just one military goal: victory[103]—which is to say, total victory. Because there is nothing left to negotiate, he will use ever greater force in order to achieve his radical goal. Even if the goal of the other side was defensive and limited,[104] he "compels [his] opponent to follow suit; a reciprocal action is started which must, lead, in theory to extremes."[105] There is no shortage of historical examples to demonstrate how the demand for unconditional surrender can drive an opponent to desperate resistance.[106] When the very existence of one of the parties is at stake, war takes on existential meaning and approaches its "pure" form.

The war in South-West Africa, waged according to directives from Berlin, was the kind of existential battle for the Herero that Leutwein had always sought to avoid. The prospect of unconditional surrender under the command of an intransigent Trotha must have seemed extraordinarily risky, and so after the Battle of Waterberg the Herero took flight in order to save themselves—but they met their downfall instead. The Germans responded to the refusal of the Herero to surrender with ever greater force. The political war of annihilation that Berlin demanded was not initially genocidal, but it was undoubtedly a new stage of escalation, and it pointed the way for more violence to come.

Trotha Takes Command

Trotha was the candidate for a profile that was already well defined by authorities in Berlin. He promised to fulfill their ambitions, particularly those of the Kaiser,[107] who was said to have personally commissioned him "to put down the uprising by all means."[108] The circumstances surrounding Leutwein's dismissal show that Berlin expected the commander-in-chief to deal the Herero a crushing defeat. Trotha was ready and willing.

The conventional view is that Trotha's assumption of the command signaled a clear break with the previous conduct of the war. In fact, there were substantial continuities, as evidenced by the fact that Trotha was only one candidate for a profile and a strategy that had already been developed in Berlin. This does not mean that Trotha obeyed orders passively, or that he merely fulfilled "his duty." To begin, he made sure that the Kaiser agreed that he would not be responsible to any civil authority,[109] and he acquired dictatorial powers through the declaration of martial law. He created space for himself that allowed him to act on his own. Further, his sanguinary pronouncements—such as wanting to drown the uprising in "streams of blood"[110]—point to a tendency for excess (which may have encouraged the Kaiser to give Trotha the command in SWA). Trotha had his own perspective on colonial affairs. In contrast to Leutwein, he did not see indigenous labor as essential to the settler colony, and so he dismissed what had been the most influential argument for curbing wartime violence.[111] Also unlike Leutwein, he repeated Social Darwinist topoi such as the "struggle between races" (*Rassenkampf*),[112] and he saw the extermination of North American "natives" as a positive example.[113]

Trotha's violent fantasies were extreme. As radical as they were, however, they alone do not show that his command was driven by an exterminatory racism from the very beginning. As the racism scholar Robert Miles has established,

> beliefs may not be accompanied by logically appropriate actions, and some actions are inconsistent with beliefs. Actions can produce consequences consistent with motivations and intentions, but they often have unanticipated outcomes. These "inconsistencies" are omnipresent in social life, and give rise to major methodological problems for the determination of "causality."[114]

Fantasies are different from intentions, and intentions are not yet plans. There is often a wide gulf between plans and how they are put into action.[115] Overcoming this divide can depend on opportunity.

Those who would establish genocidal intent based upon Trotha's isolated remarks ignore all of these caveats, identifying exterminatory racism as the "cause" of unfettered violence. However, the unavoidable inconsistencies raised by Miles, and the slippery nature of "causality" in general, challenge the inevitability of events that were affected by all kinds of conditions, allowing the campaign to take the shape that it ultimately did.

Worth emphasizing in this context—as we have already seen—is that the rejection of Leutwein's limited warfare did not *necessarily* signal a shift toward genocidal strategy.[116] But Leutwein was succeeded by an officer with few scruples, who was prepared to go to almost any lengths to fulfill his mission. As we will see, Trotha did not shrink even from the prospect of eradicating an entire people. This kind of "final solution" was not foreordained—but it was also no longer out of the question. Trotha's approving reference to Frederick C. Selous's *Sunshine and Storm in Rhodesia* highlighted a triad of extreme solutions that were analogous to subjugation, expulsion, and extermination—an apt characterization of the course of the subsequent campaign.[117] Extermination may have been "only" one option among many, and not even the first choice, but Trotha considered it an acceptable option for ending the conflict. In this respect, Trotha's appointment signaled at least the potential for ever greater violence.

Within the present context, it is crucial to recognize that Trotha's "Plan A" was not extermination.[118] His diary entry from 22 May 1904 provides some insight into his concrete objectives. Even before landing in SWA, he noted, referring to his chief of staff Martin Chales de Beaulieu, "Beaulieu has given me some essays by Dr. Hartmann . . . about S.W. Africa, climate, land and people, and the war against this uprising, and I think these are excellent. If Leutwein doesn't thwart my plans by initiating new operations first, I will probably act accordingly."[119] The essays, which Trotha did not describe further, most likely included *Die Zukunft Deutsch-Südwestafrikas: Beitrag zur Besiedlungs- und Eingeborenenfrage* (The future of German South-West Africa: A contribution to the settlement and native question), which was first published at the end of 1903, and *Der Krieg in Südafrika und seine Lehren für Deutsch-Südwest-Afrika* (The war in South Africa and its lessons for German South-West Africa). Both essays dealt with the "native question," which Hartmann understood to mean the "superseding of native rule by the white race."[120] Hartmann accused (previous) German colonial policy of failing to recognize, or dramatically underestimating, the significance of this question for colonization.

The excessive austerity of German colonialism was particularly evident compared to British settlement policy in southern Africa, as Hartmann argued in *Die Zukunft Deutsch-Südwestafrikas*. Because of this austerity, not even three thousand German citizens lived in South-West Africa after twenty years of colonization. The government (before 1904) did not fully control the land, which discouraged broader settlement. For these reasons, Hartmann believed that a fundamental reorientation of South-West African colonial policy was essential. He credited Leutwein for fulfilling his mission "with skill and success, to a certain degree," with few resources, while sharply condemning the premises of his leadership. However, relations between blacks and whites had to change. By settling for indirect rule and pursuing a policy of peace, Leutwein treated the indigenous people "improperly" and failed to recognize the conflictual nature of this relationship. Contrary to the beliefs of the colonial government, Hartmann continued, the indigenous people felt no loyalty to the colonial power and only superficially recognized its authority; they secretly longed for a return to the days when they had enjoyed "boundless freedom." If the colony seemed secure, this was only because the indigenous people were afraid of German state power.[121]

Boldly stated, Hartmann seems to have agreed with Machiavelli that it is better for a ruler to be feared than loved by his subjects.[122] Fear provided a more secure foundation for German rule than the (supposed) trust and close personal ties that Leutwein had worked to cultivate for years. Attempts to address the "native question" had thus far relied on "half-measures and insufficient means" instead of solving it "thoroughly, once and for all," and so Hartmann feared that the Germans would come to regret these policies.[123] After the great uprising of 1904, his words must have seemed prophetic to many contemporaries. Hartmann rejected Leutwein's policies as fundamentally flawed, pleading for a *definitive solution* to the question of sovereignty in SWA—without going so far as to seek a *"final solution."* He assumed that Germans would continue to coexist with the indigenous population—with the notable exception of the supposedly "degenerate" Nama-Oorlam—and he put considerable thought into what this coexistence might look like.[124]

It is hard to imagine broader agreement with Hartmann's ideas than Trotha expressed in his own diary; as long as Leutwein did not "thwart" his plans "by initiating new operations" (which did not happen), Trotha wanted to "act accordingly."[125]

We know that Hartmann criticized Leutwein sharply and called for a fundamental transformation in South-West African colonial policy. He rejected Leutwein's peace policy and sought a "thorough solution" to the "native question," including the military conquest of the colony and the violent subjugation of its autochthonous population. Hartmann's call for a definitive solution to the "native question," not a "final solution," suggests that Trotha's initial objectives still adhered to familiar paths of securing colonial rule and "conventional" warfare. Trotha's personal relationship to Leutwein was fraught from the start, and later deteriorated to the point that the governor had to leave the colony.[126] In policy matters, however, the two officers were initially not so far apart that they shared no common ground; their dispute was *not* between openly genocidal and limited warfare. Rather, both sides initially occupied a horizon that Jacques Sémelin associates with "subjugating," rather than "eradicating," processes of destruction. Both sides, in other words, initially remained within the bounds of "conventional" colonial practice and limited warfare; their aim was to conquer and subdue, not to eradicate, their opponents.[127] Within this horizon, however, they occupied opposite poles.

Irrespective of the racist and Social Darwinist jargon that Trotha employed, his conflict with Leutwein touched upon a problem pertaining to the sociology of domination. As we have seen, Leutwein was a proponent of "protective rule" grounded upon (bilateral) treaties. This implied at least partial recognition of the autochthonous groups as independent negotiating partners, allowing them to retain some parts of their sovereignty. They could possess weapons, for example, which meant that they still had some capacity to defend themselves by force. By agreeing to "protection treaties," the chiefs "gave up part of their sovereignty, but they also *retained* a substantial part."[128] In retrospect, Leutwein noted that the chiefs had known full well that the governor, as the Kaiser's emissary, merely exercised a kind suzerainty (*Oberherrschaft*) over them on the basis of "*voluntary* treaties." These voluntary treaties, Leutwein concluded, were "the rocks that could break the governor's power."[129]

Like Hartmann, Trotha believed that Leutwein's peace policy was fundamentally misguided, as it underestimated the intensity of the antagonism between colonial masters and colonized peoples. In this respect, he may have been more clear-sighted than Leutwein, who tended to overlook the dissatisfaction of his colonial subjects.[130] The general saw the colonial situation as unavoidably fraught; the power of persuasion alone could not ease the "struggle between races."[131] A policy based on bilateral agreements and voluntary participation, seeking formally peaceful compromise, was an unacceptable "game of seesaw": "The colonial lands must be conquered," wrote Trotha, "there is no partial solution."[132] Thus, the new commander-in-chief supported the second option that Leutwein had named for organizing colonial rule—not "protective rule" (or "suzerainty"), but "actual rule," which necessarily meant conquering the colony and subjugating the autochthonous societies.[133] He unambiguously rejected Leutwein's governing principle of "divide and rule,"[134] insisting instead upon *undivided* rule. In this respect, he agreed with the settlers much more than Leutwein.[135]

In retrospect, Trotha asserted that the fight for undivided rule had to be settled once and for all, "until the opponent was devastated," and ideally before the actual "work of colonization" began.[136] Only such devastation seemed to offer the opportunity *"to build something new, that promised to last."*[137] The general saw this as the only way to establish stable and secure colonial rule.[138]

Trotha believed that Leutwein had focused too intently on restoring friendly relations with the opponent as quickly as possible. The result was a *"feeling of powerlessness"* that Trotha could not reconcile with the colonial power's claim to superiority. A situation such as Leutwein's could only be temporary, since "in the long run, every government of every nation would have to develop the conviction that, at some point, it would need to use violence to break the inhabitants' self-awareness as masters."[139]

The general thus addressed a fundamental sociological problem that is not unique to the colonial state. As Heinrich Popitz notes, violence is no "mere accident of social relations," but instead represents the basis of every comprehensive social order.[140] Likewise, Trutz von Trotha shows that violence is a precondition for state-building, and that superior, destructive force (*Aktionsmacht*) is essential to establishing a monopoly on power. "Pacification" is a violent process, no different in principle from other forms of "racketeering," as Trutz von Trotha and Charles Tilly assert.[141] Superior, deadly force coerces subjects into an order that they fear. Order arises from chaos that the "ordering" power itself creates.

Even Leutwein recognized the role of violence in implementing claims to power. Violence was integral to his governance, although he often went no further than issuing threats, and passed over favorable opportunities to neutralize his opponents.[142] In order to create a climate of "trust," he took pains to abide by certain rules and to avoid the appearance of acting arbitrarily.[143] Here he differed from Trotha, who feared that the colonized peoples would understand "mildness" only as sign of weakness.[144] Trotha believed that superiority actually had to be proven in order to lay the groundwork for stable colonial rule. If South-West Africa sank into chaos, it could only mean that the German government had not offered this proof.[145]

Although Lothar von Trotha's insistence on the primacy of violence undoubtedly signaled a further stage of escalation, this alone did not implicate him in anything out of the ordinary. His approach still adhered to the "usual" discourse and techniques of colonial rule, which were intended to guide the longer-term coexistence of colonizers and colonized. In any case, there was no suggestion yet of "colonialism without the colonized."[146] Because Leutwein's peace policy was thought to have failed, a new, more aggressive course was a natural response.

This new course of action brought even more bloodshed, as Trotha announced his intent to drown the uprising in "streams of blood."[147] In pointed contrast to his predecessor, who waged war in order to achieve certain narrowly defined goals, Trotha espoused autotelic violence. Even so—as we will see in the following chapter—the power that he sought to demonstrate might still have been confined to a more or less limited act. The change in command ushered in a new stage of escalation, but not the genocidal phase of the campaign.

The general, who tended neither toward remorse nor whitewashing the past, later remarked that the "need to use violence to break the inhabitants' self-awareness as masters" had been at issue in 1904.[148] It does not seem at all far-fetched that an overwhelming victory at the Waterberg would have been a satisfactory—and perhaps even the preferred—outcome for Trotha and his campaign. Ethical considerations would not have played a role, only military prestige. On the eve of the Battle of Waterberg, the arrogant Trotha could never have dreamed that conditions would arise that might eventually make something like a "final solution" necessary. Rather, he counted on dealing the Herero a crushing defeat, so he could punish the "murders and ringleaders" and extend "the very greatest mercy" to the rest.[149] Had Trotha and his troops succeeded in encircling the Herero completely, a large number of them would have been left under his control. Survivors would have surrendered unconditionally, placing their lives in the victor's hands.[150] The general would have been master over life and death, his power absolute.[151] Under these circumstances, he may actually have chosen the path of mercy over vengeance.

In "Politik und Kriegführung," Trotha remarked that the situation caused by outbreak of the uprising in January 1904 demanded "an answer, but one worthy of a great nation. All petty misgivings had to disappear; the law of war took effect and had to be heard until the opponent was prostrated."[152] "National honor" depended upon avenging the violence that had been suffered. For a "great nation" like Germany, the only "worthy response" to an affront was military victory. This meant pushing aside all "petty misgivings," such as Leutwein's political considerations. The "law of war" had to remain in effect until the opponent was devastated. Thus, Trotha described and justified the decoupling of military violence from all immediate ends. All "petty misgivings"—in other words, any economic and political interests beyond the pure military concerns that were the most fundamental elements of strategic thinking—had to be set aside until total military victory had destroyed the opponent. Until then, the course of events would be determined by the "law of war" and its practitioners: military specialists in the use of force.[153]

The devastating consequences of this position became apparent only after operations failed. Had Trotha achieved the victory he desired at the Waterberg, the violence might have been contained. But because these plans were foiled, and the Herero fled without continuing to fight or being compelled to surrender, the "law of war" remained in effect, ensuring that violence would continue to increase until total victory was achieved. Trotha's path led to full escalation.

The Herero had not taken arms to lose everything they had, but by the time they were on the run, at the latest, their losses were so great that many of them might have surrendered in the right situation. But having experienced Trotha's relentless brutality and "iron fist" since the Battle of Waterberg, the Herero had become so bitter and mistrustful that they were no longer receptive even to an "invitation with the promise of mercy."[154] Even after the strategy of annihilation was officially revoked, many were still too afraid to surrender to the Germans. It was surely no coincidence that thousands of distressed Herero did not surrender until Trotha had departed and Friedrich von Lindequist assumed the top position in the colonial government.[155] German intransigence even emboldened some fighters, as a 25 January 1905 memorandum from Williams, the British magistrate in Ngamiland, reveals:[156]

> The German methods of conducting operations against the Hereros during the present war have led the Damaras [Herero] to hold them in considerable contempt—and they openly state with conviction that were they able to obtain a sufficient quantity of arms and ammunition they would still—if properly organized—be able to contend with the German forces in such a manner as to make it necessary on the part of the Imperial German Government to come to such terms with them as would ensure more tolerable treatment in the future.

Antagonism between the warring parties hardened under Trotha's unrelenting command. The general sought a total victory and was unwilling to compromise; he relied only on force. The campaign descended into a spiral of violence and counterviolence, or violence and nonsurrender—what Clausewitz called a "reciprocal action" (*Wechselwirkung*)— bringing the Herero to the verge of extinction and the colony to the verge of ruin.[157] The consequences of Trotha's command were still apparent years later. On 5 April 1907, the British major Wade (who was assigned to German headquarters as an observer) reported to Cape Town that roving Herero continued to pose a threat, although this could not be mentioned in official reports.[158] This meant that parts of the farming economy had still not recovered. Insistence on the strategy of annihilation—to critics, the "terrible product of rigid military doctrine"[159]— devastated the colony's most important resources: its population and wealth in cattle. Settlers complained "that the wealth of the land, our own land, was lost here, [and] that the enemy had been weakened at our expense."[160] Unconcerned about the needs of the colony, the general sought to restore the "majesty of the German name,"[161] even if this devastated the very colony for which the war was being fought. By November 1904, the futility of Trotha's efforts had become apparent, and authorities in Berlin asked how the Herero might be persuaded to surrender.[162] By this point, however, many had already perished.

Isabel Hull has brilliantly depicted how Prussian/German militarism influenced the escalation in SWA.[163] Militarism was already evident in the circumstances surrounding Trotha's appointment. Oversight of operations had been transferred to the Great General Staff (away from political influence) in February 1904, although the colonial forces were otherwise responsible to the Imperial chancellor.[164] This transition marked an important turning point in the process of violence. "Pure military interests" prevailed from this point forward,[165] with politics playing, at best, a subordinate role. Trotha's military dictatorship (from the end of 1904 to the end of 1905) represented the peak of this development, as the military acted independently to address what were actually political questions, about the goals and purpose of the war. All that mattered to Trotha was defeating the rebels, whatever the cost.[166] Only after Bülow's successful intervention with the Kaiser in November 1904 did political concerns regain influence in the South-West African arena— when the task became picking up the pieces of a failed strategy.[167]

Summary

Leutwein was an advocate for limited warfare, a position he did not want to abandon despite the dimensions that the 1904 uprising assumed. He looked for the causes of the revolt, showed consideration for the Herero response, and sought to uphold diplomatic relations. By demonstrating interest and even empathy for the opponent, he challenged the boundaries of an inflexible racism that had become increasingly influential. Even the Herero raids did not change his mind. As in previous years, he did not lose sight of the colony's economic development, and he would not consider war aims that seemed too radical.

Events in the colony were increasingly pulled into the wake of the metropole and its debates, lending the war an ideological charge and dashing Leutwein's hopes for a comparatively pragmatic solution. The escalation that followed was driven by the metropole. Autotelic violence loomed behind the talk of teaching the Herero a "lesson." Berlin demanded nothing less than a political war of annihilation. The goal of the war was to shatter the political and social order of the Herero, removing the last traces of their sovereignty. The Herero were no longer to be considered a legitimate warring party. The logic of "bimodal alienation" extended to military strategy.

Leutwein was dismissed because he was not willing or able to lead the war that was expected of him. The new commander, Lothar von Trotha, did not hesitate to fulfill the expectations of the metropole; Leutwein's comparatively moderate, paternalistic approach toward the indigenous people was foreign to him.[168] Trotha's racism was more highly developed and more radical than Leutwein's—not because it was exterminatory from the start, but because of the sheer, unbridgeable distance that he placed between himself and his opponent. Such distancing, borne of indifference and ignorance, corresponds to notions of collective uniformity and "undifferentiated lethal objectification," which are characteristic of massacres and colonial rule.[169] Trotha's racism disposed him toward extreme solutions, but he was not necessarily committed to them.

Trotha—like other authorities in Imperial Germany—rejected Leutwein's limited warfare, but this did not mean his command sought to eradicate the Herero from the very beginning. There is some evidence that his opposition to Leutwein occurred within the boundaries of what Sémelin calls "subjugating" (as opposed to "eradicating") processes of destruction. Trotha asserted much more vehemently than Leutwein that violence was essential to state-building, and thus not "pathological." This conviction undoubtedly led to greater violence, but not automatically to genocide. The rebels had to be taught a lesson, and not just any victory would do. Rather, their inferiority and the futility of resistance had to be put on display as dramatically as possible. Bloodshed was unavoidable. Thus Trotha noted in his diary, "Every other idea for creating peace here, without streams of blood, is wrong."[170] Because every act of war was stylized into a demonstration of annihilatory *Aktionsmacht*, violence took on a life of its own, and it was no longer restrained by concrete goals.

Various factors associated with the change in command paved the way for further escalation: First, Trotha was willing, "by all means," to implement a strategy that entailed such radical measures as annihilation, killing, disarmament, expropriation, and forced labor. Because his views on settlement politics were colored more strongly by racism and Social Darwinism, he had fewer scruples than Leutwein. Second, the transition in leadership sealed the complete estrangement between Herero and Germans. Trotha's racism reinforced this insurmountable divide. Diplomatic relations—the medium and *conditio sine qua non* for containing violence—came to an end. Finally, the declaration of martial law and the subsequent establishment of military dictatorship meant that military perspectives prevailed, and that specialists in the use of force made decisions on their own. By ruling out compromise and relying only on violence, the Germans engendered such mistrust and embitterment that their opponents were no longer willing to surrender. Trotha's insistence on violence brought the Germans to an impasse with no way out.

Notes

1. The role of the public and especially public advocates of colonialism should not be underestimated, although it is beyond the scope of this study. Compared to more democratic systems, the regime of Wilhelm II may have been particularly susceptible to public opinion. See Wolfgang J. Mommsen, "Der Topos vom unvermeidlichen Krieg: Außenpolitik und öffentliche Meinung im Deutschen Reich im letzten Jahrzehnt vor 1914," in *Bereit zum Krieg: Kriegsmentalität im wilhelminischen Deutschland 1890–1914: Beiträge zur historischen Friedensforschung*, ed. Jost Dülffer and Karl Holl (Göttingen, 1986), 195; and Stig Förster, *Der doppelte Militarismus: Die deutsche Heeresrüstungspolitik zwischen Status-quo-Sicherung und Aggression 1890–1913* (Stuttgart, 1985), 15.
2. See, for example, Franz von Bülow, *Deutsch-Südwestafrika: Drei Jahre im Lande Hendrik Witboois: Schilderungen von Land und Leuten* (Berlin, 1896), 225ff. and 284ff.
3. Irle, *Die Herero*, 215.
4. This was the assessment of missionary Johannes Olpp in his "Beitrag zur Missionsgeschichte des Witbooi-Stammes für das Archiv des Barmer Missionshauses," quoted in Wilhelm J. G. Möhlig, ed., *Die Witbooi in Südwestafrika während des 19. Jahrhunderts: Quellentexte von Johannes Olpp, Hendrik Witbooi jun. und Carl Berger* (Cologne, 2007), 224.
5. Imperial Chancellor von Caprivi's position on securing German dominion in SWA, which he had declared before the Reichstag on 1 March 1893: "We don't want to wage war; we want to become masters of the land without bloodshed, and to solidify our dominion. We have South-West Africa for once; now it is German land and must remain German land." See StBR (1 March 1893), 55th session, 1359c. Leutwein felt loyal to this mission.
6. Many contemporaries held him in contempt for this. Ludwig von Estorff blamed Leutwein for pinching pennies when it came to the troops, and for turning self-sufficiency into a point of honor. See Estorff, *Wanderungen und Kämpfe*, 114.
7. Leutwein's own remarks (from an interview that he gave in Wiesbaden after leaving the colony) show the extent of his commitment to the original mission: "I wanted

to save money for the Imperial government and prevent bloodshed with my mild approach, and I would much rather be accused of encouraging an uprising by being too lenient, than by doing the opposite." See "Aus Deutschland," *DSWAZ*, 8 February 1905, 3.

8. Following the Khaua revolt of 1896, Leutwein admonished Major Müller for his alarmist tone in communications with Berlin. See NAN ZBU D.IV.C.1: Feldzug gegen die Khauas-Hottentotten, p. 187. Although Leutwein could hardly have objected to increasing the strength of the troops, he may not have appreciated the accompanying interference from his superiors in Berlin.
9. Trutz von Trotha, "Genozidaler Pazifizierungskrieg: Soziologische Anmerkungen zum Konzept des Genozids am Beispiel des Kolonialkriegs in Deutsch-Südwestafrika, 1904–1907," *Zeitschrift für Genozidforschung* 4, no. 2 (2003): 52–53.
10. Leutwein, *Elf Jahre Gouverneur*, 240.
11. Wissmann, *Afrika*, 16.
12. Leutwein attempted to persuade Trotha that the uprising would not have occurred had he, Leutwein, not left Windhuk to travel south. His words fell on deaf ears, as the factors that had contributed to the uprising made no difference to Trotha (or to the top Imperial leaders). See Trotha diary, TA 122/15 (22 June 1904).
13. Estorff, *Wanderungen und Kämpfe*, 114.
14. The settlers emphasized that they had come to the colony to improve their own economic wellbeing, not that of the "natives." See "Zur Eingeborenenfrage, I.," *DSWAZ*, 22 September 1906, 1. Consideration for local residents could not be allowed to impede their own interests. The measure of each policy was whether or not it promoted white colonization. See "Mutterland und Kolonie," *DSWAZ*, 2 May 1906, 1.
15. Franke, for example, also felt a connection with "his" chiefs from the Omaruru division. Despite strong patrimonial overtones, the bond did encourage a kind of "reconciliation." See Franke, *Die Tagebücher des Schutztruppenoffiziers Victor Franke: Die Tagebuchaufzeichnungen vom 16.5.1896–27.5.1904*, vol. 1 (Delmenhorst, 2002), 351.
16. Leutwein, *Elf Jahre Gouverneur*, 271.
17. Ibid., 240, 242, and 271.
18. Bley, *Kolonialherrschaft und Sozialstruktur*, 157 and 159.
19. Leutwein, *Elf Jahre Gouverneur*, 242.
20. Leutwein to the Colonial Department (23 February 1904), BArch. R1001/2113, p. 55.
21. "Aus dem Schutzgebiet," *DSWAZ*, 21 September 1904, 2.
22. Colonization involved implementing the model of the European state, accompanied by the dissolution of tribal structures and the introduction of wage labor as the basis of a European-style economy. Leutwein's vision was to reshape the autochthonous population according to the expectations of the colonial masters. Helen Fein defines "ethnocide" as the intentional destruction of a group or culture without the physical eradication of its members. See Fein, *Genocide*, 10.
23. John H. Bodley, citing the work of Augustus Pitt-Rivers, notes that the only difference between direct and indirect rule (Leutwein's "actual" and "protective" rule) in the colonies was that the former reached its goal faster: "In the long run detribalization and deculturation occurred either way." See Bodley, *Victims of Progress* (Mountain View, 1990), 72.
24. Quoted in Drechsler, *Südwestafrika unter deutscher Kolonialherrschaft*, 105.
25. Quoted in Schaller, "Kolonialkrieg, Völkermord und Zwangsarbeit," 210.
26. Leutwein, *Elf Jahre Gouverneur*, 142–43; and Kuno F. R. H. Budack, "Kampf in den Oranjebergen 1897: Der 'Afrikaner-Aufstand' in Deutsch-Südwestafrika," in *Afrikanischer Heimatkalender 1980*, ed. Kirchenbundesrat des Deutschen Kirchenbundes Süd- und Südwestafrikas (Windhoek, 1980). A telegram sent from Major Elliott (Up-

ington) to the police commander in Cape Town on 9 May 1906 indicates that, nearly ten years later, the indigenous population south of the Orange River remained horrified by the brutal behavior of the Germans, who had summarily executed all rebels in their custody. See KAB CO 4567, Correspondence on Campaigns against Natives in German South West Africa 1904–1907.
27. Gewald, *Herero Heroes*, 107–8. Fighters who did not surrender after a certain period of time were declared "fair game," and bounties were offered for chiefs and headmen. See Leutwein, *Elf Jahre Gouverneur*, 114; and Leutwein's dispositions from 10 April 1896, in NAN ZBU D.IV.C.1: Feldzug gegen die Hereros und die Khauas-Hottentotten, vol. 3. These practices were diametrically opposed to European traditions of warfare.
28. Hartmann, "Urges in the Colony," 40.
29. Bley, *Kolonialherrschaft und Sozialstruktur*, 28 and 39.
30. See, for example, Admiralstab der Marine, *Das Marine-Expeditionskorps*, 19.
31. Bayer, *Mit dem Hauptquartier in Südwestafrika*, 45.
32. Theodor Leutwein, *Die Kämpfe der Kaiserlichen Schutztruppe in Deutsch-Südwestafrika in den Jahren 1894–1896, sowie die sich hieraus für uns ergebenden Lehren* (Berlin, 1899), 5 and 29.
33. An "insider" from the Colonial Department who was also a trusted contact of the British military attaché Count Gleichen is said to have remarked: "Fifty old colonial hands are worth 500 inexperienced soldiers. The country is mostly poor, and there is little water. If you send fifty men on fifty good horses, to a place where there is pasture and water for fifty, you will get fifty horses worth of work out of them: but if you send 500 men and horses to the same place, you won't get any work out of them at all, for they will starve and die of thirst." See KAB PMO 199: Correspondence Files Nos. 211/05—286/05, Native Rising in German South West Africa, 1904–1906, file no. 229/05, vol. 2.
34. Leutwein, *Die Kämpfe der Kaiserlichen Schutztruppe*, 28.
35. See Charles Edward Callwell, *Small Wars: Their Principles and Practice* (Lincoln, 1996).
36. Leutwein, *Die Kämpfe der Kaiserlichen Schutztruppe*, 29.
37. Leutwein to the Colonial Department (3 June 1904), R1001/2115, pp. 112–13.
38. See John Stone, *Military Strategy: The Politics and Technique of War* (London, 2013), 4ff.
39. Among the South-West African officers, this was a typical practice that also served reconnaissance purposes. After a brief skirmish en route to the Waterberg in mid-January 1904, the commander of the Fourth Field Company in Outjo, Captain von Kliefoth, wrote to the Herero leaders at the Waterberg and demanded the surrender of headmen and other leaders who were responsible for the attack. If they refused, he wrote, "as we assume," then "the expected response and the report from the messenger will contain valuable insights about the position, strength, and intentions of the rebels." See Conrad von Stülpnagel, *Heiße Tage: Meine Erlebnisse im Kampf gegen die Hereros* (Berlin, 1905), 34.
40. Carl von Clausewitz, *Vom Kriege: Vollständige Ausgabe im Urtext* (Bonn, 1952), 114.
41. F. v. Buslow, "Der Krieg mit den Herero und seine Folgen," BArch. R1001/2115, p. 11.
42. See, for example, Lieutenant von Zülow's "Bericht über die Kriegsereignisse im Hererolande," Okahandja (19 January 1904), R1001/2113, pp. 3–4.
43. Leutwein to the Colonial Department (23 February 1904), BArch. R1001/2113, p. 54.
44. Leutwein, *Die Kämpfe der Kaiserlichen Schutztruppe*, 5.
45. Leutwein wrote, "If it can somehow be achieved, they should no longer have a tribal government." Ibid., p. 54.

46. The reserves had two different functions. On the one hand, they set aside "tribal land" that could not be sold to whites, and so they offered indigenous people some protection from European economic expansion. See Leutwein, *Elf Jahre Gouverneur*, 266ff. The settlers, in particular, saw the reserves as an instrument for protecting the Herero, introduced by the government in response to pressure from the mission. This point of view is evident in Erdmann, *Die Ursachen des Herero-Aufstandes*, 7. On the other hand, however, we should not forget that the reserves were also grounded on the assumption that Europeans and Africans could not live together—even if the latter were integrated within colonial society as workers. See Bley, *Kolonialherrschaft und Sozialstruktur*, 155–56. Thus, reserves also imposed a massive constraint on the indigenous population. See Förster, *Erinnerungslandschaften*, 43.
47. Leutwein to the Colonial Department (23 February 1904), BArch. R1001/2113, p. 54. Leutwein emphasized that even groups or villages that had apparently not participated in the uprising were nonetheless "morally complicit," and that they would have to abide by the measures of disarmament and settlement in reserves. Aside from disarmament, his main policy innovation was bringing all "prisoners of war" before a military court. Those who were found to have participated in "plundering farms, or even the murder of peaceful residents," were "always to be punished with death." Ibid., p. 55. Paul Leutwein remarked that the governor "really could not have been more accommodating" in his conditions for peace, underscoring his willingness to make concessions. See *Kampf und die Onjatiberge: Gouverneur Leutweins letzter Feldzug: Tatsachenbericht aus dem Hererokrieg* (Berlin, 1941), 23.
48. Leutwein to the Colonial Department (23 February 1904), BArch. R1001/2113, p. 55.
49. Leutwein, *Kampf und die Onjatiberge*, 23.
50. Trutz von Trotha, "Genozidaler Pazifizierungskrieg," 52–53.
51. Ibid. According to the Great General Staff's official report from 1906, Leutwein "did not ascribe serious importance to the news about the insurrectionary movement of the Hereros, and also reported to Berlin that there were enough troops in the land to put down the uprising." As Leutwein soon recognized, he been wrong on both counts, and this weakened his position.
52. Großer Generalstab, *Die Kämpfe der deutschen Truppen*, vol. 1, 62. What's more, British sources reveal that the Kaiser had considered sending a general with six thousand men at the beginning of the uprising, which means that he had considered using reinforcements to ease Leutwein from power. See PRO, FO 64/1645, Lascelles to Marquess of Lansdowne K.G., Berlin (30 April 1904), p. 2.
53. BArch. R1001/2111, p. 28.
54. Quoted in the *Tägliche Rundschau* (6 March 1904), BArch. R1001/2112, p. 169. The rumor occupied numerous newspapers. See BArch. R1001/2112, p. 169, 188–89.
55. BArch. R1001/2112, p. 188.
56. Ibid., p. 25.
57. StBR, 60th session, 17 March 1904, p. 1896c.
58. Paul Leutwein, *Kampf und die Onjatiberge*, 24; and Hull, "Military Culture," 146. The German colonial military sought to avoid a "loss of prestige" at all costs, which would require "total retribution." See Ulrike Lindner, *Koloniale Begegnungen: Deutschland und Großbritannien als Imperialmächte in Afrika 1880–1914* (Frankfurt, 2011), 230.
59. Trotha diary, TA 122/15, 1 July 1904.
60. Trotha diary, TA 122/15, 22 June 1904.
61. Lothar von Trotha, "Politik und Kriegführung," *Berliner Neueste Nachrichten*, 3 February 1909, 1.
62. Quoted in the *Tägliche Rundschau*, 6 March 1904, BArch. R1001/2112, p. 169.

63. Jan Philipp Reemtsma, *Vertrauen und Gewalt: Versuch über eine besondere Konstellation der Moderne* (Hamburg, 2008), 116–23.
64. Ibid.
65. Lothar von Trotha, "Politik und Kriegführung," 1.
66. "Aus dem Schutzgebiet," *DSWAZ*, 1 February 1905, 1.
67. Ute Frevert, *Ehrenmänner: Das Duell in der bürgerlichen Gesellschaft* (Munich, 1991), 29. See also Pierre Bourdieu, *Outline of a Theory of Practice*, trans. Richard Nice (Cambridge, 1977), 11.
68. Thomas Nipperdey, Deutsche Geschichte 1866–1918, vol. 2 (Munich, 1992), 288.
69. Schlieffen to Bülow (24 November 1904), BArch. R1001/2089, p. 3.
70. According to the report by the Great General Staff, on 12 January 1904 Herero in the central part of the colony began "to *murder* all whites . . . sometimes with bestial cruelty, to *plunder* the farms, and to *steal* whatever cattle they could" (emphasis added). See Großer Generalstab, *Die Kämpfe der deutschen Truppen*, vol. 1, 24. Eyewitness diaries tend to criminalize the actions of the Herero. Particularly significant in this context is that the Berlin authorities considered the Herero to be German subjects because of the "protection treaties" they had signed with Imperial Germany. Thus, strictly speaking, the conflict was not a war, but rather an "internal" problem or uprising. A *jus ad bellum* for the Herero was disputed, so the claim to a *jus in bello* was also precarious.
71. Colonial Department to Leutwein (20 February 1904), BArch. R1001/2112, p. 25 (emphasis added).
72. Quoted in the *National-Zeitung*, 9 March 1904, BArch. R1001/2112, p. 182.
73. Schlieffen's argument against negotiations—that the colonial war in South-West Africa could end only with the opponent's unconditional surrender—corresponded with the 1906 General Staff study, *Der Kampf in insurgierten Städten*, which foresaw in this situation only one possible outcome: "a fight to the death, or *unconditional surrender*" (emphasis in original). Quoted in Wilhelm Deist, "Voraussetzungen innenpolitischen Handelns des Militärs im Ersten Weltkrieg," in *Militär, Staat und Gesellschaft: Studien zur preußisch-deutschen Militärgeschichte*, ed. Wilhelm Deist (Munich, 1991), 122.
74. Pierre Bourdieu, *Distinction: A Social Critique of the Judgement of Taste*, trans. Richard Nice (Cambridge, 1984), 178.
75. See Hull, *Absolute Destruction*, and "Military Culture and the Production of 'Final Solutions.'"
76. Jehuda L. Wallach, *Das Dogma der Vernichtungsschlacht: Die Lehren von Clausewitz und Schlieffen und ihre Wirkungen in zwei Weltkriegen* (Munich, 1970), 83.
77. StBR, 19 January 1904, p. 364b.
78. This included the reserves, which Leutwein had supported. The idea was apparently to destroy not only tribal structures, but also Herero society and culture—at least to the extent that this interfered with reshaping the Herero as a proletariat in service to whites. Tribes and local groups were to be dissolved. As needed, workers would be resettled near companies or farms. This model of "relocation" was carefully distinguished from reserves, which allowed the indigenous people some independence and were therefore unacceptable. Instead, the indigenous people would have "to stand under the immediate oversight of white authority," so they would never again organize politically. See "Keine Reservate!," *DSWAZ*, 1 November 1905, 1.
79. Trotha diary, TA 122/15, 22 June 1904.
80. Kaiser to the Imperial Chancellor (19 April 1904), R1001/2114, p. 38. Investigating the causes of the uprising was put off until the postwar period, and even then, restricted to narrow military and technical considerations. See Hull, *Absolute Destruction*, 194–95.

81. The work of Karla Poewe has been especially influential on colonial revisionist positions. She writes, "The use of the word 'vernichten' which unknowledgeable people translate as *extermination*, in fact, meant, in the usage of the times, breaking of military, national, or economic resistance." See Poewe, *The Namibian Herero*, 60.
82. Kundrus, "Grenzen der Gleichsetzung." See also Robert Gerwarth and Stephan Malinowski, "Der Holocaust als 'kolonialer Genozid'? Europäische Kolonialgewalt und nationalsozialistischer Vernichtungskrieg," *Geschichte und Gesellschaft* 33 (2007): 439–66; and Michael Hochgeschwender, "Kolonialkriege als Experimentierstätten des Vernichtungskrieges?," in *Formen des Krieges: Von der Antike bis zur Gegenwart*, ed. Dietrich Beyrau et al. (Paderborn, 2007), 269–90.
83. Reporting on a skirmish near Owikokorero, in which a larger German patrol was ambushed by a superior detachment of Herero, Paul Leutwein wrote that the leader of the Herero wanted to "completely annihilate" his opponent. See Leutwein, *Kampf und die Onjatiberge*, 16. Leutwein did not describe this as a monstrosity, but rather as a normal wartime occurrence. The military meaning of "complete annihilation" can go beyond subduing and breaking a body of troops, to the physical destruction of its members. But this is only a possibility.
84. In German: "60.000–70.000 Seelen sich nicht so leicht vernichten lassen." See Leutwein to the Colonial Department (23 February 1904), R1001/2113, p. 55.
85. Military thinking at this time was already preoccupied with total war, although elites still hoped that a short war might keep violence in check. See Stig Forster, "Optionen der Kriegführung im Zeitalter des 'Volkskrieges'—Zu Helmuth von Moltkes militärisch-politischen Überlegungen nach den Erfahrungen der Einigungskriege," in *Militärische Verantwortung in Staat und Gesellschaft: 175 Jahre Generalstabsausbildung in Deutschland*, ed. Detlef Bald (Bonn, 1986), 83–107. A 1902 manual by the Great General Staff considered which restrictions in international agreements would actually be binding in case of war. According to the manual's decidedly "realistic"—or opportunistic—guidelines, the "excessive humanitarian views" of the day failed to grasp the nature and purpose of war. War called for "certain severities," and "often the only true humanity" lay in their "ruthless application." What mattered was the law of the stronger or victorious party, and this ultimately justified any means necessary to achieve final war aims. See Großer Generalstab, *Kriegsbrauch im Landkriege* (Berlin, 1902), 3 and 9. "Military necessity" prevailed over all restrictions. The meaning of *Vernichtung* may have initially been limited, but in a drawn-out war it could surreptitiously expand and overwhelm existing boundaries. As we will see, there were precedents for this development, even in the "cabinet war" era.
86. Jürgen Zimmerer, *Deutsche Herrschaft über Afrikaner*, 38; and Wolfgang U. Eckart, "Medizin und kolonialer Rassenkrieg: Die Niederschlagung des Herero-Nama-Aufstandes im Schutzgebiet Deutsch-Südwestafrika (1904–1907)," in *Kriegsverbrechen im 20. Jahrhundert*, ed. Wolfgang Wette and Gerd Ueberschär (Darmstadt, 2001), 59.
87. Susanne Kuß, "Deutsche Soldaten während des Boxeraufstandes in China: Elemente und Ursprünge des Vernichtungskrieges," in *Das Deutsche Reich und der Boxeraufstand*, ed. Susanne Kuß and Thoralf Klein (Munich, 2002), 165–81.
88. Kuß, "Deutsche Soldaten während des Boxeraufstandes," 165–66.
89. Quoted in Susanne Kuß, "Von der Vernichtungsschlacht zum Vernichtungskrieg: Militärpublizisten in der Zwischenkriegszeit (1920–1939)," in *Der Zweite Weltkrieg und seine Folgen: Ereignisse—Auswirkungen—Reflexionen*, ed. Bernd Martin (Freiburg, 2006), 62.
90. Gerhard Ritter, *Der Schlieffenplan: Kritik eines Mythos* (Munich, 1956), 17.

91. Andreas Stucki, "Die spanische Anti-Guerilla-Kriegführung auf Kuba 1868–1898: Radikalisierung—Entgrenzung—Genozid?" *Zeitschrift für Geschichtswissenschaft* 56, no. 2 (2008): 130.
92. Susanne Kuß, by contrast, argues that the violence in a war of annihilation cannot be explained entirely by the dynamics of events, and that terms like "internal dynamics" and "escalation" are also insufficient. See Kuß, "Deutsche Soldaten während des Boxeraufstandes," 166.
93. Martin van Creveld, *The Transformation of War* (New York, 1991).
94. Quoted in Kuß, "Von der Vernichtungsschlacht zum Vernichtungskrieg," 62.
95. Stig Förster describes the "cabinet war" as the dominant form of warfare between European states in the 1850s and 1860s, characterized by the semidemocratic governments' use of limited means to pursue limited military goals. Cabinet wars "were mostly fought by traditional armies (with the exception of Prussia!); they were limited in time, or at least in space; and they were mostly decided by a few large-scale battles. Once the military action had proved conclusive, the political consequences were worked out in diplomatic negotiations between the governments involved, with the political survival of the losers ever fundamentally being threatened. Even when these wars were waged in the name of the national idea, they remained under the control of cabinets." See Stig Förster, "Facing 'People's War': Moltke the Elder and Germany's Military Options after 1871," *Journal of Strategic Studies* 10, no. 2 (1987): 211; and Stig Förster, "Einleitung des Herausgebers," in *Moltke: Vom Kabinettskrieg zum Volkskrieg: Eine Werkauswahl*, ed. Stig Förster (Bonn, 1992), 3.
96. Herfried Münkler, *Der Wandel des Krieges: Von der Symmetrie zur Asymmetrie* (Weilerswist, 2006), 63.
97. This was true, for example, of the United States Civil War (1861—65). The mere existence of the Confederacy negated the idea of the Union, and a Union victory demanded "annihilation of the Confederacy." See Raymond Aron, *Peace and War: A Theory of International Relations* (New York, 2017), 27.
98. Martin Zimmermann, "Antike Kriege zwischen privaten Kriegsherren und staatlichem Monopol auf Kriegführung," in *Formen des Krieges: Von der Antike bis zur Gegenwart*, ed. Dietrich Beyrau et al. (Paderborn, 2007), 58; and Bernard Eck, "Essai pour une typologie des massacres en Grèce classique," in *Le massacre, objet de l'histoire*, ed. David El Kenz (Paris, 2005), 101. Stephen Morillo makes similar observations about "subcultural" wars in the Middle Ages. See Stephen Morillo, "A General Typology of Transcultural Wars: The Early Middle Ages and Beyond," in *Transcultural Wars from the Middle Ages to the 21st Century*, ed. Hans-Henning Kortüm (Berlin, 2006), 36ff.
99. H. L. Wesseling, "Colonial Wars: An Introduction," in *Imperialism and War: Essays on Colonial Wars in Asia and Africa, 1870–1914*, ed. H. L. Wesseling and J. A. de Moor (Leiden, 1989), 3; and Trutz von Trotha, "Genozidaler Pazifizierungskrieg," 41ff.
100. The historian Dierk Walter has similarly argued that colonial wars belong within the category of "total war." His observation is limited to the mobilization of resources on the side of the colonial powers, but their goals and use of force can certainly be identified as "total." In many colonial wars, the colonial power sought not only to extinguish the political independence of its indigenous opponents, but also their social structures and economic basis for survival. This was accomplished through policies such as the seizure of land, forced resettlement, and the introduction of wage labor. See Dierk Walter, "Warum Kolonialkrieg?," in *Kolonialkriege: Militärische Gewalt im Zeichen des Imperialismus*, ed. Thoralf Klein und Frank Schumacher (Hamburg, 2006), 38.

101. Hannes Heer, "Die Logik des Vernichtungskrieges: Wehrmacht und Partisanenkampf," in *Vernichtungskrieg: Verbrechen der Wehrmacht 1941 bis 1944*, ed. Hannes Heer and Klaus Naumann (Hamburg, 1995), 129–30.
102. Clausewitz, *Vom Kriege*, 114. The English translation is from Carl von Clausewitz, *On War*, ed. and trans. by Michael Howard and Peter Paret (Princeton, 1976), 91.
103. Aron, *Peace and War*, 26.
104. The United States Civil War is one example. The Confederates, unlike their opponents, did not seek to gain control over enemy territory. See Peter Browning, *The Changing Nature of Warfare: The Development of Land Warfare from 1792 to 1945* (Cambridge, 2006), 59.
105. Clausewitz, *Vom Kriege*, 92. The English translation is from Clausewitz, *On War*, 91.
106. Aron, *Peace and War*, 27.
107. Details about Trotha's appointment come from a report by the Bavarian military representative in Berlin, Nikolaus Ritter von Endres. Trotha was apparently the Kaiser's favored candidate, chosen over the opposition of Schlieffen and others. See Susanne Kuß, *Deutsches Militär auf kolonialen Kriegsschauplätzen: Eskalation von Gewalt zu Beginn des 20. Jahrhunderts* (Berlin, 2010), 83, note 1.
108. Trotha to Leutwein (5 November 1904), BArch. R1001/2089, pp. 100–2.
109. Trotha to Hülsen-Haeseler (10 December 1904), copy in TA 315, 2b, p. 72.
110. Trotha to Leutwein (5 November 1904), BArch. R1001/2089, p. 101.
111. "'But S.W.A. is, or should be, precisely that colony where the European himself can work," was his response to Leutwein's plea for a "merciful" campaign. Trotha diary, TA 122/15, 1 July 1904.
112. Many people instinctively associate this term with the "race wars" (*Rassenkriege*) of National Socialist Germany, using it to demonstrate the (supposed) continuities between the Herero campaign and the Nazi wars of destruction. See, for example, Jürgen Zimmerer, "Annihilation in Africa: The 'Race-War' in German Southwest Africa (1904–1908) and its Significance for a Global History of Genocide," *GHI Bulletin* 37 (2005): 52; and Jürgen Zimmerer, "The First Genocide of the Twentieth Century: The German War of Destruction in Southwest Africa (1904–1908) and the Global History of Genocide," in *Lessons and Legacies VIII: From Generation to Generation*, ed. Doris Bergen (Evanston, 2008), 52. Trotha's "struggle between races" is thus presumed to have been a genocidal "race war" or a "final solution." See Eckart, "Medizin und kolonialer Rassenkrieg,"; Reinhart Kößler and Henning Melber, "Der Genozid an den Herero und Nama in Deutsch-Südwestafrika 1904–1908," in *Völkermord und Kriegsverbrechen in der ersten Hälfte des 20. Jahrhunderts*, ed. Irmtrud Wojak (Frankfurt, 2004), 45; and Zimmerer, *Deutsche Herrschaft über Afrikaner*, 55. Trotha's use of the term, however, does not support this presumption beyond all doubt. The meaning and scope of *Rassenkampf* is not well defined. The *Deutsch-Südwestafrikanische Zeitung*, for example, asserted that *Rassenkampf* in no way implied the "physical destruction" of the other side, but "only" meant that "one race would absolutely be victorious, the other absolutely defeated." See "Mutterland und Kolonie, Teil IV," *DSWAZ*, 1 August 1906. The "struggle between races" was a widespread Social Darwinist topos around the turn of the century, part of a thought world that saw history as a natural phenomenon in which the strong prevailed and the weak perished. See Richard Weikart, *From Darwin to Hitler: Evolutionary Ethics, Eugenics, and Racism in Germany* (New York, 2004), 127ff. Ludwig Gumplowicz's book, *Der Rassenkampf*, which first appeared in 1879, promoted an "understanding of history" that presented "humanity as an unfree part of nature," eternally subject to "natural laws" that led it down "predetermined, natural paths." See Ludwig Gumplowicz, *Der Rassenkampf* (Innsbruck, 1928), 5. Moral considerations were removed from history, trivializing the eradication of entire peoples. The concept of "struggle between races" drama-

tized conflict. If struggle is a "natural" manifestation of the (supposed) difference between races, then it must inevitably lead to a final reckoning; otherwise it will continue to flare up and endanger the colony's white population.
113. Trotha diary, TA 122/15, 1 July 1904.
114. Miles, *Racism*, 78–79.
115. Even in the case of the Shoah, where exterminatory racism was almost certainly present, some evidence suggests that the idea of destruction evolved gradually, becoming more concrete over time. According to Norman Naimark, even though Hitler and his associates affirmed their desire to destroy the Jews early on, what this "destruction," or *Vernichtung*, would look like remained unclear for some time. At first, Nazi leaders did not exclusively, or perhaps even primarily, seek the *physical* destruction—that is, the murder— of Jewish men, women, and children. Destruction sometimes meant "destroying the ability of Jews to affect their fate," or ending the presence of Jews in Germany or Europe through forced emigration. See Norman M. Naimark, *Fires of Hatred: Ethnic Cleansing in Twentieth-Century Europe* (Cambridge, 2001), 62. The "annihilation of the Herero" underwent a similar transformation before taking on broader genocidal meaning.
116. See, for example, Kotek, "Le Génocide des Herero," 182.
117. Trotha retrospectively cited the following passage by Selous, a Rhodesian settler: "Therefore Matabeleland is doomed by what seems a law of nature to be ruled by the white man[,] and the black man must go, or conform to the white man's laws[,] or die in resisting them." See Frederick Courteney Selous, *Sunshine and Storm in Rhodesia* (London, 1896), 67; and Lothar von Trotha, "Politik und Kriegführung," 1.
118. As Michael Mann notes, perpetrators or groups of perpetrators rarely *start out* seeking to annihilate groups of victims. More often, annihilation is a "Plan B" or "Plan C" that emerges only as the process of violence unfolds. See Michael Mann, *Die dunkle Seite der Demokratie*, 7–8.
119. Trotha diary, TA 122/15, 22 May 1904.
120. Georg Hartmann, *Der Krieg in Südafrika und seine Lehren für Deutsch-Südwest-Afrika* (Berlin, 1900), 21.
121. Hartmann, *Die Zukunft Deutsch-Südwestafrikas*, 15–21.
122. Niccolò Machiavelli, *The Prince*, ed. and trans. Peter Bondanella and Mark Musa (Oxford, 1998), 56.
123. Hartmann, *Die Zukunft Deutsch-Südwestafrikas*, 21.
124. Ibid., 23. See also Georg Hartmann, "Gedanken über die Eingeborenenfrage in Britisch-Südafrika und Deutsch-Südwestafrika," *Koloniale Rundschau* (1910): 26–43. Equality under the law was out of the question, as the Africans would first need instruction in "truth, justice, reliability, and sense of duty," and this could hardly occur "without violence." See Hartmann, *Die Zukunft Deutsch-Südwestafrikas*, 22. Thus, coexistence demanded subservience from the indigenous people for an unspecified period of time.
125. He was concerned that Leutwein might end the war before he arrived on the scene.
126. See chapter 3, note 327.
127. Sémelin, *Purify and Destroy*. See also Trutz von Trotha, "Genozidaler Pazifizierungskrieg," 41ff.
128. Leutwein, *Elf Jahre Gouverneur*, 238 (emphasis added).
129. Ibid., 240 (emphasis added).
130. Estorff, *Wanderungen und Kämpfe*, 114.
131. Lothar von Trotha, "Politik und Kriegführung," 1.
132. Trotha diary, TA 122/15, 1 July 1904.
133. Leutwein, *Elf Jahre Gouverneur*, 240.
134. Drechsler, *Südwestafrika unter deutscher Kolonialherrschaft*, 137.

135. Trotha's notion of "pacification" initially corresponded with the outlook of the settlers, who called for the armed subjugation of autochthonous groups on the eve of the uprising. His interpretation of the colonial situation as a "struggle between races" gave the settlers a useful rallying point. See, for example, Schlettwein, "Zur augenblicklichen Lage," *DSWAZ*, 5 January 1904. Even so, official policy was not oriented toward the settlers. Trotha represented the metropole, particularly the Kaiser and the military, and it became increasingly clear that he placed their interests before the settlers', as demonstrated by the serious conflicts that beset his tenure in the colony. The settlers' goals were clear, and their approach toward achieving them was comparatively pragmatic. They were prepared to support whatever worked—either the "old Africans'" strategy of attrition, or the metropolitan army's strategy of annihilation. Already on 2 February 1904, the *Deutsch-Südwestafrikanische Zeitung* ("Der Aufstand," 2, insert) recalled Leutwein's military priorities: "It seems to us now that an important task is stopping the fugitive mob from escaping, taking back our cattle, and protecting our borders." After the disastrous battle at the Waterberg, the settlers' criticism of Trotha grew. The Herero fled eastward and threatened to cross into British territory with the herds of cattle that the settlers had wanted to keep for themselves. See "Der Aufstand," *DSWAZ*, 21 September 1904. Suddenly the settlers wanted Leutwein back, although they had contributed to his dismissal. The formal send-off for Leutwein at the end of 1904 may have been intended as a "lesson of warning" for Trotha, who received a much cooler farewell when he departed one year later. See "Gouverneur Leutwein" and "Gouverneur Leutweins Abreise," *DSWAZ*, 7 December 1904; and "Das Interregnum von Trotha—und sein Ende," *Windhuker Nachrichten*, 2 November 1905.
136. At a farewell dinner that was hosted by the colonial administration on 23 June 1906, the departing General von Trotha remarked, "Investing in plowshares before the end of this war is a futile endeavor." See "Aus Deutschland," *DSWAZ*, 28 July 1906, 2.
137. Lothar von Trotha, "Politik und Kriegführung," 1.
138. It seems valid to base these observations on Trotha's retrospective remarks, as he made no secret of the extent of the violence under his command, and he acknowledged that he had been a "cruel leader of war." See "Aus Deutschland," *DSWAZ*, 28 July 1906, 2. He still saw no alternative to his course of action, which had been the only way to bring the war to a "definitive end."
139. Lothar von Trotha, "Politik und Kriegführung," 1 (italics in the original).
140. Heinrich Popitz, *Phänomene der Macht*, 2nd ed. (Tübingen, 1992), 57.
141. Trutz von Trotha, *Koloniale Herrschaft*, 33–40; and Charles Tilly, "War Making and State Making as Organized Crime," in *Bringing the State Back In*, ed. Peter Evans et al. (Cambridge, 1985), 169–91.
142. These threats included theatrical troop movements that Leutwein staged to intimidate opponents. See, for example, Bley, *Kolonialherrschaft und Sozialstruktur*, 29.
143. Bley, *Kolonialherrschaft und Sozialstruktur*, 28. The case of the Khaua leader Andries Lambert is a prominent example. Lambert had refused François's order to hand over the murderer of a German trader, and he sentenced the messenger who had delivered this order to 150 lashes. The Khauas had also attacked a Bechuanaland settlement under German protection, killing many residents and stealing their cattle. Leutwein marched his troops into the Khaua settlement, catching them off guard and capturing their leader, but Leutwein offered to pardon him if he agreed to accept German sovereignty, hand over weapons and munitions, return stolen cattle, and maintain "peaceful and quiet behavior in the future." Lambert accepted these conditions on 17 March 1894, and in return Leutwein agreed to let the trader's murder go unpunished. Once Lambert was released, however, he tried to evade these conditions by fleeing with his entire tribe. His plans were discovered, and the escape

foiled. Court martial proceedings were initiated the next day, and Leutwein charged Lambert with the trader's murder. Lambert pleaded guilty, but his request for clemency was denied. He was sentenced and executed. Leutwein then called together the remainder of the tribe, proclaimed Lambert's successor, and negotiated a treaty of protection. The case drew widespread attention because the conflict was resolved "without fighting." Although the Germans were more powerful, they did not resort to plundering or massacring the Khauas. See Bley, *Kolonialherrschaft und Sozialstruktur*, 24–27.

144. Trotha to Schlieffen (4 October 1904), BArch. R1001/2089, p. 5.
145. Trotha believed that this proof was essential. Early in his command, he worried that the Herero would shun a great battle and surrender instead. This possibility did not sit well with him (TA 122/15, 20 June 1904).
146. Steinmetz, *The Devil's Handwriting*, 202.
147. Trotha to Leutwein (5 November 1904), BArch. R1001/2089, p. 101.
148. Lothar von Trotha, "Politik und Kriegführung," 1.
149. Ibid. Of course, merely abstaining from genocidal annihilation says little about the living conditions that survivors would have faced. By declaring his intent to "place all surrendering Herero in chains" after the end of 1904, Trotha indicated that "mercy" would be accompanied by harsh collective punishment, costing countless human lives—as evident in the camp regime that was intended to replace Trotha's strategy of annihilation. See Bülow to Trotha (13 January 1905), BArch. R1001/2089, p. 116.
150. Schlieffen believed that the desired military success could be achieved only by completely encircling the opponent on four sides. This ideal represented the culmination of Schlieffen's radical notion of annihilation. See Wallach, *Das Dogma der Vernichtungsschlacht*, 76.
151. Popitz, *Phänomene der Macht*, 53.
152. Lothar von Trotha, "Politik und Kriegführung," 1.
153. Trotha's "law of war" resembles martial law (or a "state of emergency"), which he had declared before arriving in South-West Africa, thereby receiving dictatorial powers. See Trotha to Hülsen-Haeseler (10 December 1904), copy in TA 315, 2b, p. 72.
154. "Ein Schritt näher zum Ziel," *Windhuker Nachrichten*, 24 December 1904, 2. On 31 August 1904, Trotha wrote in his diary, "Prisoners supposedly said they wanted to go to Leutwein and make peace, but it wouldn't be possible with the new major with the red pants [Trotha], he fought too roughly" (TA 122/17).
155. Jonas Kreienbaum, "'Vernichtungslager' in Deutsch-Südwestafrika? Zur Funktion der Konzentrationslager im Herero- und Namakrieg (1904–1908)," *Zeitschrift für Geschichtswissenschaft* (2010): 1019.
156. "Native Inhabitants of German South West African Protectorate," GNARS RC 4/18.
157. Paul Rohrbach, *Aus Südwest-Afrikas schweren Tagen: Blätter von Arbeit und Abschied* (Berlin, 1909), 233.
158. KAB GH 35/139: "Correspondence: High Commissioner Re Rising of Natives in G.S.W.A., 1904–1906."
159. Rohrbach, *Aus Südwest-Afrikas schweren Tagen*, 195.
160. "Der Aufstand," *DSWAZ*, 15 December 1904, 1.
161. Rohrbach, *Aus Südwest-Afrikas schweren Tagen*, 160.
162. Schlieffen to Bülow (23 November 1904), BArch. R1001/2089, pp. 3–4.
163. Hull, "Military Culture and the Production of 'Final Solutions,'" and *Absolute Destruction*. Wilhelmine military culture reversed the relationship between politics and war that Clausewitz had defined. Clausewitz presumed that war was subordinate to policy, "for it is policy that created war." Policy was the "guiding intelligence," and war its mere "instrument." Jehuda Wallach has shown how generations of German military officers repeatedly invoked Clausewitz, misreading and ultimately inverting

his ideas, turning policy into a mere appendage of war. Clausewitz understood the danger of an independent military, which brought war closer to its "pure" form. See Clausewitz, *Vom Kriege*, 891 (the English translation is from Clausewitz, *On War*, 607); and Wallach, *Das Dogma der Vernichtungsschlacht*, 28–36.
164. Zimmerer, *Deutsche Herrschaft über Afrikaner*, 36.
165. Leutwein, *Kampf und die Onjatiberge*, 24.
166. Trotha to Leutwein (5 November 1904), BArch. R1001/2089, pp. 100–2.
167. On 24 November 1904, Bülow wrote to the Kaiser about the report he had received the day before from the chief of the Great General Staff, Alfred von Schlieffen. The report included the text of Trotha's infamous proclamation to the Herero from 2 October 1904 (BArch. R1001/2089, p. 8). The Kaiser was persuaded to direct the general to retract the proclamation, and Trotha consequently received this order from the Imperial chancellor.
168. The significance that George Steinmetz ascribes to the ethnographic discourse of the era seems questionable, particularly with respect to Trotha. The commander remarked that he "knows enough tribes in Africa; they all think the same way, yielding only to force" (Trotha to Leutwein, 5 November 1904, BArch. R1001/2089, p. 101). Elsewhere, Trotha wrote that his "precise knowledge of so many central African tribes, Bantu and others" had persuaded him that "the Negro will not bow to any treaty, but only raw force" (Trotha to Schlieffen, 4 October 1904, BArch. R1001/2089, p. 6). His contempt for the Africans was so extreme that it may be better understood as a categorical rejection of ethnographic discourse and nuances. His racist stereotypes were extraordinarily coarse; he deduced Herero intentions and ulterior motives from his "knowledge of so many central African tribes" and "the Negro" in general. His remarks effectively rationalized the risky decision not to engage with the opponent at all.
169. Trutz von Trotha, "Genozidaler Pazifizierungskrieg," 49.
170. Trotha diary, TA 122/17, 16 July 1904.

Chapter 3

The Campaign

At first, Trotha continued what Leutwein had begun. The premises of the campaign were not fundamentally transformed because of the change in command. And yet, less than six months later, Trotha defended a strategy of driving the entire Herero nation into an area where it would "no longer be able to exist" and instead would perish, a strategy that included acts of "crass terrorism and even . . . cruelty."[1]

This chapter, which is divided into three sections, seeks to explain how this escalation occurred. The first section depicts the war effort under Leutwein's command. The character of the war was initially defensive. As news of the uprising reached Germany, the Imperial government sent troops to assist the beleaguered white population and re-establish lines of communication between metropole and colony. The commander-in-chief was expected to seize the initiative and to go on the offensive as soon as the situation had stabilized. Leutwein assumed control of operations in February. Imperial Germany insisted on complete subjugation.[2] The Herero had to be deprived "once and for all" of the opportunity to defy their colonial masters.[3] Germany's political leaders sought a definitive resolution to the "native question" (in the words of Georg Hartmann). Extreme solutions like expulsion or eradication were certainly on the table, but the initial push was for a "conventional" solution. Annihilating the Herero militarily would lay the groundwork for fundamentally restructuring relations of power.[4] However, even a "conventional" solution would undoubtedly have cost a vast number of Herero lives. The first section of the chapter follows Leutwein's attempts to implement a model of annihilation that was dictated by Berlin.

Total victory demanded a single-minded focus on operations (*operative Kriegführung*), and this called for dividing up the troops. The various detachments, each strong enough to hold off the opponent, were to proceed independently, and then in the decisive moment they would come together and attack the opponent from different sides. The Herero would be unable to retreat, and the Germans (of course) would prevail. This manner of waging war had proven successful in Europe, but it posed significant challenges in the South-West African theater—as Leutwein repeatedly warned, to no avail. The results did not satisfy leaders in Berlin, who responded by exchanging the commander, but not the strategy.

The second section in this chapter shows how Trotha continued the campaign that Leutwein had initiated, without altering its objectives. What changed was that the new commander-in-chief, unlike Leutwein, was prepared to implement the metropolitan idea of annihilation without hesitation. The fact that the "majority of the Herero" had retreated to the Waterberg only made things easier.[5] The plan was to stage a "concentrated," "simultaneous attack from multiple sides" in order to deal the Herero a decisive defeat, thereby bringing the campaign to an end with a single, great maneuver.[6]

An excursus within the second section draws upon the ethnology and history of war to show how military battles—even battles of annihilation—are characterized by a fundamental ambivalence between the tendency to *unleash* violence and the tendency to *contain* it. The context of "conservative militarism"—which, as Stig Förster proposes, defined the thought and behavior of Imperial German military elites before World War I—helps to illuminate this ambivalence in the battle of annihilation. The relative anomie of colonial wars notwithstanding, the battle of annihilation at the Waterberg still belongs within the horizon of "conservative militarism," and not (for example) genocidal warfare, as in National Socialist Germany.[7]

Trotha's appointment demonstrated the will of the Imperial government to "metropolitanize" the war and conditions in the colony overall—that is, to bring them more in line with European standards. With respect to power relations, the intervention of the Imperial government was an attempt to rein in privatized violence overseas, which it perceived as illegitimate.

As we will see, Trotha maintained his "conventional" strategy of annihilation for some time. This was followed by an alternative strategy, between the "conventional" and ultimately genocidal strategies of annihilation, that aimed to expel the Herero from the colony. Trotha's campaign was characterized by the succession of these three strategies—Selous's triad of subjugation, expulsion, and death (or extermination).[8]

Trotha's command was characterized by strategic continuity, but also gradual radicalization. This is the subject of the third subsection, "The Pursuit," which seeks to explain the genocidal escalation. The second chapter section concludes with the failure of Trotha's campaign. The third chapter section, "The Dynamics of Escalation," examines what this failure meant for those who were responsible, and how they handled it. The "shame-rage mechanism," which has been described by Helen Lewis, Thomas Scheff, and Suzanne Retzinger, is key to understanding the transgression of boundaries during the campaign.[9]

Resistance and Operations under Leutwein

The Germans' first countermeasures were local. Centrally organized resistance was almost impossible because the Herero also attacked railroad and communication lines. Upon the outbreak of hostilities, moreover, the governor was in the southernmost part of the colony, far from the action. Events sometimes unfolded with such ferocity that the local population could do little more than save themselves.

There had been persistent hints of impending rebellion, such as incidents of cattle theft near Gobabis, and other forms of "native insubordination" in the divisions of Okahandja and Karibib.[10] Rumors of hostilities in other locations often preceded actual violence. Government and military officials were able to take precautionary measures to protect the white population, and in some cases they even delayed the outbreak of violence by engaging with local chiefs.

In Okahandja, the epicenter of the uprising, authorities responded promptly to unusual happenings and news. On 11 January 1904, one day before the uprising began, precautionary reinforcements arrived from Windhuk. They "readied the station for defense, posted guards in the towers, and supported the garrison with men from the Beurlaubtenstand."[11] A civilian official, Bergrat Gustav Duft, presided over the reinforcements, and he immediately initiated talks with the chiefs and headmen to defuse the situation. By the time that the first shots were fired on the morning of 12 January, most settlers had already retreated to safety.

In Omaruru, the staff surgeon Kuhn pushed back the start of the uprising to 17 January, winning valuable time for the defense.[12] Only the residents and personnel at the Waterberg station were caught off guard by the violence on 14 January, although here, too, there had already been hints of unrest.[13]

One hundred and twenty-three whites did lose their lives in the first days of the uprising, but many more were saved because they had received advance warning. Men in the reserves and Landwehr were called up to serve, and settlements were fortified. Windhuk was protected by a new "comprehensive security force" of 230 men—an important reason the rebels avoided a direct attack on the capital.[14] The stations stored twelve months' provisions alongside weapons and munitions, allowing them to keep assailants at bay for some time, even without external assistance.[15]

The first measures taken by the Germans were precautionary and defensive in character. Offensive actions were a challenge, as the forces consisted largely of reservists, Landwehr men, and volunteers.[16] Even so, they typically did more than merely defend their own locations. The disruption in communications cut off those who were holed up in the stations from the outside world. Patrols or squads were sent out to break this isolation and get a sense of the broader situation, in some cases even coming to the aid of others in acute danger.

The only active body of troops in central or northern Namibia at this time was the Fourth Field Company under Captain Kliefoth. It was stationed in Outjo, in the northernmost region of German influence. A smaller detachment of this company was in Grootfontein, under the command of First Lieutenant Volkmann. Leutwein had sent the company to the northern part of the colony, which was only nominally under German control, to keep the Ovambo in check. Herero emissaries rallied the Ovambo chief Nechale to take action against the Germans, but the forces at the Namutoni station successfully repelled his attack. Nechale retreated with heavy losses and refrained from further strikes.[17]

After the first reports of suspicious happenings reached Kliefoth on 12 January, he and his entire company set out the next day in the direction of the Waterberg. Another officer in the company, Conrad von Stülpnagel, remarked that the Waterberg Herero had long been "loose cannons." The company confronted fierce resistance en route and quickly retreated. On 27 January, Kliefoth attempted once again to make contact with other stations, this time heading southwest in the direction of Omaruru. The company became ensnarled in another skirmish, and Kliefoth was seriously wounded. The company retreated yet again.[18] The Fourth Company did not reconnect with other German forces until it met up with a new unit, the West Section, on 21 February.

On 11 January, two patrols from Windhuk attempted to reach Okahandja by following the railroad line. Fierce Herero attacks quickly sent them back to the capital. Swakopmund was located on the coast, to the west of a 150-kilometer-wide belt of desert, and it was never threatened by the uprising. First Lieutenant von Zülow, with police and around sixty men from the Beurlaubtenstand, set off from this coastal town by train on 12 January. They made it to Karibib and then Okahandja, but they could not complete the journey to Windhuk.[19]

On 12 January the gunboat *Habicht*, which was anchored off the coast of Cape Town, received news of the siege on Okahandja. Just six days later, the *Habicht* arrived in Swakopmund. In lieu of the governor, who had not yet returned to the area of the uprising, the boat's commander, Captain Gudewill, temporarily assumed the high command.[20]

For five days, there was no word from Zülow's train. A landing corps of nearly fifty men formed under the leadership of Captain Lieutenant Gygas, the *Habicht*'s first officer. Its mission was to find Zülow and to secure the important Karibib railroad station so the connection to Swakopmund could be preserved. The landing corps focused on the strategically crucial task of restoring and securing the railroad line.[21] The railroad was the colony's lifeline; without it, bringing in reinforcements would have taken weeks or months.

The landing corps departed from Swakopmund on the evening of 18 January. The further the train traveled into the interior, the more evident the effects of the uprising became. The Ababis and Habis stations (located 165 and 179 kilometers away from Swakopmund, respectively) were "completely ravaged."[22]

Construction on the Otavi railroad (intended to connect the copper mines of Tsumeb with Swakopmund) had begun in October 1903, but the uprising brought this work to a standstill. Alongside the white personnel of the Otavi Company, Gudewill sent hundreds of indigenous railway workers to Khan (fifty-seven kilometers from Swakopmund) in order to repair the parts of the railroad line that had been damaged by heavy rainfall.[23] On 22 January, a cattle drover from Okahandja reported that Zülow had returned. Heavy rainfall was the greatest hindrance to the railroad repairs; destruction by human hands was curbed by patrols.[24] A routine transport of 226 men, already underway before the start of the uprising, arrived in Swakopmund on 3 February. Led by First Lieutenant von Winkler, the unit was dispatched to the interior the same day and reached Windhuk after a twenty-six-hour train ride.[25]

By order of the Kaiser, a marine expeditionary corps of around six hundred men was mobilized on 17 January; it reached Swakopmund on 9 February.[26] In addition, around five hundred men were sent to reinforce the Schutztruppe; they left Hamburg in two stages, on 30 January and 2 February.[27] Upon landing in SWA, all of these troops found an intact railroad line, thanks to the efforts of Captain Franke and the Second Field Company, who "transformed the entire situation. The Herero retreated from the railroad."[28]

Franke and his company of around ninety men had been heading southward since 30 December 1903. He got word of the uprising in Gibeon, more than three hundred kilometers from Windhuk, on 14 January. With the aid of a heliograph, he obtained Leutwein's permission to turn around so he could hasten to assist the sites under attack. He reached Windhuk by forced marching on 19 January, and he drove the Herero from the vicinity of the capital. The company reached Okahandja on 27 January, fighting back the assailants and ultimately driving them from the area. On 31 January, Franke continued his advance along the railroad line in the direction of Karibib, where he arrived on 2 February. He reached Omaruru on 4 February. After a long and bloody fight, the Herero retreated and gave up the area around Omaruru, "completely and definitively."[29]

The Herero had not succeeded in capturing any of the centers of German power. The Germans, on the other hand, achieved an important success in Omaruru. They reasserted control over the most endangered stretch of the railroad line, between Karibib and Okahandja, so they could quickly move reinforcements from the coast to the interior. Thus, the "triumphal march of Franke's company" held "crucial significance for the following operations."[30] After Franke's advance, the western part of Hereroland, north of the railroad line, was fully restored to German control. Only the area south of the railroad, in the Khomas mountains, still harbored a group of Herero from Otjimbingwe, led by Zacharias Zeraua.[31]

Franke's advance belongs to the "African-classical era of the fighting,"[32] which the settlers later recalled with "especially buoyant feelings." Franke made good use of the "meager resources" that the colony offered. He acted independently and exploited the speed and local knowledge of his well-trained unit. He repeatedly surprised the Herero and forced them to retreat, even though they outnumbered his men. With these "coups," he achieved a strategically meaningful success.

It is possible that a more "African-classical" war in SWA might have limited the bloodshed. This kind of war could be fought with smaller groups of soldiers, but its goals were much more modest than total victory. This does not mean, however, that the campaign against the Herero could have been quickly resolved. The "old Africans" did not believe that such a resolution was possible, even though they consistently underestimated the resilience of their opponent. After the fighting in April, at the latest, Leutwein predicted that the war would "last another one or two years."[33] In contrast to his successor, who hoped to end the war with a single, massive strike, Leutwein foresaw a longer war of lesser intensity.

The boldness of the "old Africans," which was embodied by Franke's advance, should not be equated with the foolhardy attitude of so many metropolitan officers. The "old Africans" accepted certain limits. They understood the strengths of their opponent and the challenges of the terrain, and they knew how to conserve the energy of their men and horses.[34] They had an eye for the colonial theater that officers from the homeland often did not. The Sea Battalion (Seebataillon) that was commanded by Major von Glasenapp clearly illustrates this distinction, casting a revealing light on the metropolitan officers and the expectations they believed they had to fulfill.

The Marine Infantry enjoyed high prestige[35] and the special favor of the Kaiser.[36] In South-West Africa, it sought to bolster its reputation as a powerful deployment force. As commander of the expeditionary corps, Glasenapp must have felt considerable pressure to succeed.

The expeditionary corps set sail on 21 January, just four days after assembling upon the "most high command" of the Kaiser.[37] Regardless of the Marine Infantry's prestigious reputation,[38] it was in no way comparable to its French counterpart, which had proved itself in numerous battles in Europe and overseas, and also served as a vanguard of French expansion.[39] The German Marine Infantry was also not the simple infantry unit that Walter Nuhn describes.[40] It was a defensive force, first and foremost, ill-suited for operations in the field and especially in the colonies. It might have been able to fulfill its original assignments, such as occupying the capital and securing the railroad line, but these tasks had already been completed by the time it arrived in the colony on 9 February. Anticipating the expectations of the metropole, its commander felt compelled to improvise. Glasenapp immediately took command of all troops in the colony and hastily planned an offensive against the main forces of opposition in the north, although their "present locations and relative strength were still to be determined." In the north, he thought he saw an opportunity to apprehend and beat the opponent, who was (supposedly) still intimidated by Franke's success.[41]

Setting aside the fact that Glasenapp had just arrived in SWA and knew almost nothing about the land or his opponent, an Admiralty Staff report noted that the corps did not have enough horses for expeditions within the colony's interior. The report also acknowledged that the Germans had sharply underestimated the power of Herero resistance. As many as 40 percent of the Marine Infantry men in SWA were recruits who had not yet completed their training; many of the soldiers with more experience had been deemed unfit to serve in the tropics.[42]

The transport to the interior of the colony began on 10 February—although Leutwein, who arrived in Swakopmund the next day, immediately rescinded Glasenapp's orders. Leutwein instead sent Glasenapp to Gobabis, in the eastern part of the colony, to stop a larger group of Herero from crossing into English territory. And so the East Section formed under Glasenapp's leadership on 15 February. In the following weeks, this section suffered the worst setbacks and defeats of the entire campaign.

The section was placed under quarantine and ultimately disbanded because of a typhus epidemic. But mistakes in leadership did play a role in the deadly battles of Owikokorero on 13 March, and Okaharui on 3 April. At Owikokorero, Glasenapp led a patrol into an ambush that killed seven officers and nineteen other soldiers.[43] Lothar von Trotha attributed this error to Glasenapp's ambition and overzealousness. Blinded by the prospect of a "speedy" Pour le Mérite, he drove his small section to ruin rather than wait for reinforcements.[44] The failure at Okaharui, by contrast, was the result of Glasenapp acting alone. He was unaware of the opponent's position and wrongly assumed that the Herero were on the retreat. In fact, they were following the section and merely waiting for the right moment to attack. Glasenapp was repeatedly taken in by his opponent's deceptions, resulting in 32 deaths and 17 injuries in his section.[45]

The East Section ultimately did not fulfill any of its missions. Human lives were not all that was lost. According to Trotha, "the whole war ... could have taken another turn if Glasenapp had proceeded more carefully."[46] Undeterred by their lack of expertise, the newly arrived officers sought to seize the offensive at all costs and obtain quick victories.

Even before he returned to the northern theater of war, Leutwein wrote to his superiors in Berlin that there were "already enough troops" in the colony "to put down the Herero uprising." He presumably thought that the news was exaggerated and hoped that he could still encourage the rebels to lay down their arms.[47] Leutwein misjudged the uprising, heightening doubts about his leadership. His lack of urgency in seizing the offensive was considered another serious problem. Wholly misunderstanding the expectations of his superiors, he wrote to Berlin that "larger military operations in Hereroland" could, "in any case, not begin before the end of April" because African horse sickness was still rampant in the north, and the troops in the south would need to stay put.[48]

Leutwein played down the gravity of the situation and reassured Berlin, presumably hoping to gain time and more room to maneuver. Instead, the opposite occurred. By the time he arrived in Swakopmund on 11 February, the decision to send reinforcements had long since been made by his superiors,[49] and the General Staff took charge of the campaign.[50]

Once Leutwein had surveyed the overall situation, he determined that there were three larger Herero groups to be reckoned with. He believed that one was west of the Waterberg, another was near Otjisongati at the southeastern foot of the Onjati mountains, and the third was near Kehoro in the Gobabis division.[51] Although he revised his original assessment and came to regard the situation as very grave, he drew the same conclusions as before and repeatedly advocated for patience. Assuming that he would need all available forces to put down the uprising, he wanted to wait for reinforcements and horse transports before taking action.

In Berlin, there was little understanding of Leutwein's latest ideas. The General Staff directed him to resume operations at Outjo and Grootfontein in the north "as soon as possible."[52] (These were the two stations where the Fourth Field Company and its detachment were posted; communications with these stations had not yet been restored.) The General Staff may have wanted Leutwein to take action against the main Herero forces in the central and northern part of the colony, as Glasenapp had intended. The governor's order to the troops on 15 February accommodated these directions from Berlin, while also postponing a confrontation with the main Herero forces. And so Glasenapp's East Section, comprised of two hundred newly arrived members of the Schutztruppe and two Marine Infantry companies, was tasked with "cleansing" the Gobabis division of the enemy, closing off the eastern border to "fleeing Herero and their cattle herds," and restoring the connection with Grootfontein. Major von Estorff's West Section, comprised of two Schutztruppe companies and a third Marine Infantry company, was to "cleanse" the Omaruru division and restore the connection with Outjo, where it would then temporarily join forces with the Fourth Field Company. The Main Section, still to be formed in Okahandja, was initially comprised of just one Marine Infantry company. It was to be joined later by reinforcements that were expected at the end of February, as well as by contingents of Witbooi and Baster fighters and a German company (and its mountain battery) set to return from the south. Its mission was to "defeat the enemy" at Otjisongati and the Waterberg.[53]

Delaying a (supposedly) decisive strike against the main Herero forces went hand in hand with strengthening the West and East Sections, which were sent to confront larger groups in the Omaruru and Gobabis divisions. Although Glasenapp had initially wanted to march north with the mass of the troops, now he led stronger forces to the east. There were several reasons for Leutwein's decision. He assessed the main Herero forces' capacity for resistance more realistically than many of his colleagues, and he wanted to wait for reinforcements before striking. He was also willing to put the interests of the colony ahead of the metropole's demands. This was particularly evident in his emphasis on sealing the eastern border. He wanted to stop the Herero and their herds from crossing into British territory, which would have cost the South-West African colonial economy millions.[54] Leutwein's memoirs show that on this point he deferred to public opinion in the colony, not the mood of the metropole.[55] Stopping the loss of the cattle herds was more important to the colonists than a victory against the rebels—the priority of the metropolitan public. Although at this point Leutwein did not believe that most Herero would make their way east, he did think it was possible that Tjetjo's group in the Gobabis division might do so, especially since some "eastern Herero" and Mbanderu had lived in British-occupied territory for years.

The deployment of the East Section was not a success. The section was fortunate that the Herero did not yet try to head east, as it would not have been able to keep them from crossing the border. The members of the East Section did not restore the connection with Grootfontein, nor were they able to assist the Main Section when it awaited their support.

The operations of the West Section met with greater success. It met up with the Fourth Field Company on 21 February.[56] Four days later, it fought an intense, ten-hour battle near Otjihanamaparero, where its members were surprised not only that the Herero could mount an effective defense, but also that they fought valiantly, with tactical cunning.[57] Although the section incurred significant losses, including all officers in the Fourth Field Company,[58] it ultimately took the enemy's positions and sent the Herero on the run. A *decisive* victory remained elusive, in part because pursuing the opponent was impossible once darkness fell. The Omaruru division was successfully "cleansed," but the Herero fled toward the Waterberg and joined other groups—exactly what Leutwein had hoped to avoid.[59]

The Main Section had similar successes south of the railroad line. On 16 February, a unit led by Captain Lieutenant Gygas skirmished with the Otjimbingwe Herero at Liewenberg. After hours of fighting, they succeeded in taking the Herero positions, but this victory, too, was not decisive, and only encouraged the Herero groups to join forces.[60] In early March, Captain Puder and nearly two hundred Main Section reinforcements were sent to attack the Herero who remained south of the railroad line. He could not beat them decisively.[61] He also could not stop them from crossing the railroad line and joining the main Herero forces near Okahandja on the night of March 28. Leutwein had wanted to beat the Herero from Otjimbingwe in a "special campaign," but now the state of the war was "substantially less favorable" than before.[62]

The Berlin authorities' idea of annihilation was increasingly evident in the order that outlined the mission of the Main Section, issued on 11 March 1904. The General Staff report imagined a "concentric attack by the three sections planned for early April" against the Herero under Maharero. The attack also targeted Tjetjo's group, which seemed to be retreating west from the Gobabis division toward the Onjati mountains.[63] The Main Section headed east from Okahandja toward the Onjati mountains. The East Section approached the mountains from the east, and the West Section approached from the north.

The Main Section engaged in two larger skirmishes: the first on 9 April near Ongandjira, and the second on 13 April near Oviumbo. It was ambushed near Ongandjira. Samuel Maharero "and his whole tribe"—as well as Herero from the Waterberg, Omaruru, and Otjimbingwe—lay in wait as the Main Section moved through the area. The General Staff report later estimated their numbers at three thousand fighters in all. This Herero force fought valiantly and with tactical dexterity, but it was ultimately no match for the German artillery, which could unleash its full destructive power on this terrain. And so the Germans reported few casualties (four dead and twelve wounded), while at least eighty Herero fighters were said to have fallen. By the end of the day, the Germans had taken the battle site and forced the Herero to flee, "in complete disarray in some cases." Even so, by the standards of the General Staff, this was not a "truly effective victory." Such a victory was still outstanding, and it would require "insistent pursuit." Leutwein, meanwhile, wrongly presumed that the East Section was in its designated position, where it would have been able to intercept the Herero fleeing east and northeast.[64] The East Section had incurred significant casualties at Okaharui just days before, and typhus made a bad situation worse. Soon the section was no longer functional.

Before pursuing the opponent from Ongandjira, Leutwein wanted first to deal with powerful forces near Oviumbo that might have threatened his section during the pursuit. He waited in vain for the East Section, hoping to restore a connection between the two units.[65]

Leutwein's section, surrounded by thorn bushes, came under heavy fire. He fended off Herero attacks for more than ten hours. Once darkness fell and the fighting subsided, Leutwein made a fateful decision. His troops were nearly out of munitions. He could not hold their position or resume fighting the next morning without help from the East

Section—the "most significant condition for the success of the entire operation," and thus for an "annihilating strike." Unable to count on the section's support, he decided to postpone the attack for several weeks and gave the order to retreat.[66]

Leutwein lost all credibility with his superiors. He had misjudged the situation completely and hesitated to seize the initiative. Whether he was unable or unwilling to follow the strategic guidelines from Berlin, he repeatedly distanced himself from them.[67]

Although the idea of annihilation began to take shape in the operational plans of February and March, a lack of effective cooperation between the different sections meant that no "decisive" victories were achieved. Instead, the sections even reported losses. The East Section, which had never performed well, was placed under quarantine in April and ceased operations thereafter. The results of the battles fought by the Main Section disappointed authorities in Berlin, clinching Leutwein's dismissal as Schutztruppe commander. Some evidence does suggest, however, that Leutwein's accomplishments were more significant than observers in the German capital wanted to acknowledge. Time was not on the side of the Herero, who had *not* won.[68] All of their victories were limited. As Herero numbers, resources, and morale dwindled, the capacity of their opponent grew. Even their extraordinarily dogged, "death-defying" raids did not overwhelm the German sections. As the balance of power increasingly shifted against the Herero, their prospects for victory dimmed.[69] Having achieved no better than a stalemate, the tide finally turned against them. Of course, Leutwein had not succeeded in dealing the Herero a crushing defeat. Even worse, the cautious commander had retreated near Oviumbo. Regardless of the immediate circumstances, Leutwein's order to retreat had broken a taboo; conceding to the Herero wounded the colonial masters' sense of superiority more than almost anything else. Charles E. Callwell, the era's most influential theorist of colonial wars, advised colonial powers to take their time in seizing the initiative—but, he added, once seized, they should not relinquish it, and they should avoid retreat at all costs.[70] Callwell believed that the "natives" would perceive this as weakness, emboldening their resistance. "There is no retreating from natives in southern Africa. Every march is a march forward," Leutwein's predecessor Curt von François wrote.[71] His approach corresponded to the mood in the metropole much more closely than Leutwein's.

Discussion of the retreat near Oviumbo as a "failure" upset Leutwein deeply. In a 25 April 1904 letter to the General Staff, he suggested that the retreat had saved the troops "from catastrophe." However, he also acknowledged that he did not possess the "full . . . trust of the General Staff," and that "fruitful cooperation" would no longer be possible. For this reason, he requested his own "replacement by a high-ranking officer."[72]

The General Staff report later conceded that Leutwein had been forced to make due with "insufficient resources." However, Leutwein was also responsible for the "initially erroneous assessment of the enemy's capacity for resistance, which proved fateful." After the April fighting, there seemed to be no alternative to sending additional reinforcements. This included older staff officers, which would allow Colonel Leutwein to be relieved of the high command and replaced by a general.[73]

The metropole's high expectations posed significant challenges for the military leaders in SWA.[74] In order to crush the opponent, more troops were needed than had ever previously been assembled in the colony. The land produced little, and so the troops had to bring along almost all provisions for both people and animals.[75] The scarcity of water and the threat of infection placed additional limits on the concentration of troops, as the fate of the East Section shows. In order to meet the homeland's stipulations for annihilating the opponent, the individual sections had to proceed independently, but at the decisive moment take coordinated action—another challenge that Leutwein identified in a letter to the Colonial Department.[76] It was possible that the Herero "would divert east toward English territory, or north toward Ovamboland," so "the troop command could not be content with a frontal attack." The available forces had to be distributed in such a way so that the opponent could not easily escape. But if a single section confronted the opponent "without the support of the other sections," victory might not be assured. Dividing the troops into different sections was essential. But when individual troop sections (like the East and West Sections) operated separately, the "uniform direction of operations" that was essential for victory became almost impossible, especially since a "connection between the separately operating columns" was not easily maintained.[77] Wireless telegraphy would have helped, but it was not available to the troops in SWA.[78]

Leutwein applied his "divide and rule" strategy of governance in the military arena, too, sometimes in a figurative sense. He consistently sought to divide the ranks of his opponent. He initially tried to beat the Herero (or compel their surrender) by isolating the various groups—which is why he was so incensed upon hearing that, in advance of the Battle of Waterberg, Trotha had rejected an offer of surrender from the Herero leader Salatiel Kambazembi without consulting him as governor.[79] Leutwein, unlike his successor, would not have turned down this opportunity to weaken Herero solidarity.[80]

This kind of differentiation was inconceivable to Trotha. To begin, his distance from the indigenous groups—whom he identified as *Neger* ("Negros")[81]—was too great to accommodate such nuances. Separate peace agreements with separate conditions would only complicate Trotha's ambition to pave the way for a new order in the colony, eliminating the last traces of indirect "protective rule." The very concept of "struggle between races" ignored the fine differences that had always informed Leutwein's policy.

Trotha's objections contributed to the failure of Leutwein's 30 May 1904 proclamation to the Herero people, which sought to create a more radical kind of division—vertical, not horizontal—than Leutwein's previous efforts.[82] The proclamation offered the "majority of the Herero" an incentive to abandon their headmen and surrender to the Germans instead—a chance for mercy as long as they had not directly participated in "plunder" or "murder." The proclamation aimed to break the solidarity of the opposition by offering the bulk of the Herero people an exit from their "struggle of desperation." Leutwein underestimated the cohesion of the Herero and overestimated the role of the headmen—but as the war dragged on, his approach might have been more fruitful. We can only speculate, however, because Leutwein's proclamation never took effect.

Trotha's Campaign

The Battle of Waterberg

After Leutwein's (supposed) failure, it was now up to Trotha to meet the high expectations of the Imperial government. Although Leutwein himself had offered to resign, after ten years at the helm of the Schutztruppe, he had a hard time ceding responsibility. He wanted to end the campaign quickly and to present his successor with a *fait accompli*, but Trotha intervened and directed him to cease all such efforts.[83] This shattered Leutwein's last hopes for ending the campaign himself, on his own terms.

After assuming the command before his arrival in South-West Africa, Trotha made clear that he did not want to see Leutwein, at the last moment, crowning his own "head with laurels." He did not believe that Leutwein was even capable of a breakthrough victory. Leutwein's latest plan of operations was "the same aimless thing" as previous efforts, which had brought no (satisfactory) results.[84] Trotha's criticism was distinctively technocratic. In a diary entry from 22 July 1904, the new commander revealed how he hoped to overcome this "aimless" leadership: "All in all, Leutwein could not have done anything without the expert build-out of the supply line. He could beat them [the Herero] one more time, yes, and push them in a particular direction, but beating them decisively, never." The problem, as Trotha saw it, was that the advance of a single section might lead to another battle and beating the opponent "one more time"—but never *decisively*. At best, the opponent could be pushed "in a particular direction." In the given circumstances, particularly because provisioning was so precarious, the sections could not pursue the opponent. They could not exploit the victories they had already achieved, turning them into a decisive victory. Trotha believed that a decisive victory would demand a "concentrated approach" by different sections and a "simultaneous attack from multiple sides."[85] His scheme essentially affirmed the main ideas behind Leutwein's operational plans from 11 March, but Trotha pursued these ideas more systematically and pushed them to their limit. Because large numbers of Herero had joined forces at the foot of the Waterberg to await the Germans' next steps, ending the campaign with a single, great maneuver was a real possibility. As evidenced by the 4 August 1904 directive for attacking the Herero, which established the premises for battle, the command planned to encircle the majority of the Herero with concentric troop movements and deal them a crushing blow. In other words, the command sought a battle of annihilation at the foot of the Waterberg.[86]

Trotha's assumption of the command was part of an effort to "metropolitanize" the South-West African campaign—that is, to bring the campaign closer in certain respects to the standards of "great" wars between states.[87] This observation is often overlooked, as most historical accounts tend to emphasize elements (such as the general's racism) that separated this African conflict from "conventional" European wars. The ambiguous nature of Trotha's efforts to metropolitanize the campaign is similarly overlooked. These efforts led to greater violence, but they also pointed toward approaches for containing it. I will examine this ambiguity more closely in the pages ahead.

In Trotha's eyes, the small wars fought by the "old Africans," which were oriented toward local conditions, did not count as "serious warfare."[88] Waging a small war amounted to little more than "stealing cattle or shooting down individuals"; it was part of the "game of seesaw" that was Leutwein's entire colonial policy. Unsurprisingly, as Franz Epp noted in his diary, the high command "ridiculed" the "old Africans" and did not take their ideas seriously.[89] Now that "real" military officers from Imperial Germany had assumed control of operations overseas, the era of pinching pennies seemed gone at last. The general grandiosely announced his intent to drown the uprising "in streams of blood and streams of money."[90]

The metropolitanization of the war was about channeling the campaign toward a grand, decisive battle that would become the war's final act. As described by Paul von Lettow-Vorbeck, one of the general's adjutants, the command staked everything on seizing the opportunity—rare in small wars—to apprehend the Herero assembled at the foot of the Waterberg "en masse, in one large operation."[91] The goal was to end the fighting before it became a guerrilla war; the officers feared little more than "a prolonged guerrilla war in the bush."[92] An opportunity to deal the Herero a crushing defeat and bring to the war to a speedy end seemed to present itself at the Waterberg.

Trotha's and Epp's remarks show how superior the metropolitan officers felt. Long-serving colonial officers were often treated with contempt, their expertise dismissed out of hand.[93] The metropolitan officers had not learned anything—or least, not the correct lessons—from past difficulties implementing strategic guidelines from Berlin. These frictions were primarily blamed on the "old Africans" and their supposed inability to wage "real" wars. The metropolitan officers failed to consider whether or not the expectations from Berlin were realistic, or even possible, in the South-West African arena. "Victory culture" was essential to the identity of Imperial Germany; the state was the product of military victories against Austria and France. Its officers were unwilling to question routines that had led to such important victories on the European continent, least of all for a "small despicable Kaffir war."[94] They barely considered that SWA was a very different theater of war, and that concentrating and moving large bodies of troops here would present serious logistical challenges. They did not recognize that their opponent held certain key advantages.[95]

Preparations for the battle took months, with particular attention to the "expert build-out of the supply line" that Trotha mentioned in his diary. The expansion was supposed to facilitate the supply and movement of larger troop units away from the railroad line, allowing the German forces to respond to all eventualities, and setting the stage for a military showdown.[96] Irrespective of these lengthy preparations, by mid-August Trotha presided over a force of just fifteen hundred armed soldiers, whom he wanted to deploy along a nearly one-hundred-kilometer front.[97] Proceeding against the outermost lines[98] of a numerically superior opponent, with the intent of encirclement, was a bold, if not foolhardy, plan.[99]

The plan failed because the German command could not steer or control the advance of the different sections, and so it could not ensure the cooperation on which the plan ultimately hinged. Communication technologies were insufficient—or the subordinate commanders simply did not use them, but instead acted on their own. Trotha struggled with the same difficulties as Leutwein, who had previously attempted to realize the idea of annihilation on South-West African soil. The general was likewise unable to ensure cooperation between sections and operational success. Failed cooperation left some sections in dire straits, as the German headquarters experienced directly. Waiting in vain for support from Major von der Heyde's section, the command fought for survival at the Hamakari watering holes. Heyde's section was not strong enough to hold its own against the forces it confronted. Unable to stop the Herero from retreating east, his section was overrun and suffered heavy losses.[100]

This failure was more consequential than those before it, because the pressure from the German sections sent large numbers of Herero on the run. They fled toward the Omaheke Desert, where thousands met their deaths.

Horst Drechsler has argued that the course and outcome of the battle were "criminally planned."[101] Drechsler emphasized that the German leadership intended, from the very beginning, to drive the Herero into the arid Omaheke, where they would die of hunger and thirst.[102] This theory raises various problems. Drechsler not only promoted the genocide thesis as the first South-West Africa expert; he also did so in its strongest conceivable and thoroughly teleological form.

Even the General Staff's official narrative had to acknowledge that— because of the failings and unauthorized actions of certain officers[103]— the Battle of Waterberg had not achieved the desired results.[104] Diaries and letters of officers like Werner von Stauffenberg, Victor Franke, and the military doctor Georg Hillebrecht underscore that the operations were far from a success; all three men were appalled that Trotha sent a *victory* message to Berlin after the battle.[105] First Lieutenant Stuhlmann spoke openly of "failure,"[106] and foreign military officers later shared this assessment.[107]

On 12 August, Trotha described the fighting as "successful." This may have reflected his relief at having overcome a sometimes desperate situation just one day before, or he may have realized that the overall situation was not as bad as he had feared.[108] However, the signs of failure were evident enough that Trotha could not have entirely ignored them. The operations succeeded to the extent that the Herero retreated, sometimes "fleeing in a wild panic," as the chief of staff Martin Chales de Beaulieu described,[109] but the Germans did not achieve the *decisive* victory that was their actual goal. On 12 August, Trotha still hoped that pursuing the Herero would compensate for this setback, but it was soon evident that his forces lacked the necessary provisions and other resources for such an undertaking. The commander-in-chief could (or should) have been held responsible for this shortfall and its serious consequences; he had, after all, devoted considerable energy to building out the supply lines in order to address this very contingency. The first pursuit fell apart already on the night of 13 August, due to the utter exhaustion of men and animals. The pursuing forces were "half-dead from thirst" and almost completely "immobilized" upon their return.[110] "They all felt completely beaten, and they were, too," Stauffenberg noted with resignation.[111] After breaking off the pursuit, Trotha remarked: "I'm bowled over. . . . It's no joke. . . . Now we can, or must, start from the beginning, or *it's over*."[112]

The situation following the Battle of Waterberg was much different than planned, and the German officers could not have been satisfied. The opportunity to end the war in one great strike was gone, and Trotha's plan had failed. Most of the Herero had avoided encirclement, and now they were moving farther away from (or remained beyond) the reach of the Schutztruppe. Stauffenberg saw the Herero as the actual victors at the Waterberg.[113] From the German perspective, nothing had been achieved; in fact, after the unsuccessful battle, the situation was less favorable than before. Planning had to "start from the beginning," although the prospects of apprehending the Herero were now more uncertain than ever. The Herero had avoided a decisive battle and took flight in order to save themselves. Now that they were on the run, they were beyond the reach of German power and would not give in easily. No end to the war was in sight; the position, strength, morale, and intent of the opponent were more uncertain than ever.

Trotha's obstinacy and arrogance exacted a heavy toll. Before the battle, those who knew the land best had warned that, under the given conditions, his plan of attack was not feasible. Some officers were astonished by the small number of fighters that the general had assembled at the Waterberg after months of preparation,[114] although outsiders tended to underestimate the climate-related difficulties that hindered the deployment of larger troop units.[115] For this reason, Trotha's battle plan seems especially audacious. Sections of only a few hundred men, posted twenty to forty kilometers apart,[116] were supposed to stop a much stronger and more mobile opponent from escaping. A Belgian officer who reviewed the campaign years later saw the undertaking as hopeless from the start.[117]

The fundamental principle of concentric operations ("march separately, strike together") had been exercised with great success on the European continent by the first chief of the Great General Staff, Helmuth von Moltke. Experienced colonial officers, however, repeatedly noted that this principle did not apply in SWA,[118] and, in fact, that the reverse was more apt ("march together, strike separately").[119] In the dense thorn bushes of central Namibia, even standard precautionary measures such as reconnaissance and securing the surroundings were almost impossible for small units, as they became disoriented and lost their connection to the larger group after only a short distance.[120]

Trotha nevertheless insisted on concentric operations. His approach was so dogmatic that he did not learn even from the bitter experience at the Waterberg, and he clung to his Eurocentric outlook undeterred. Until the end of his command in SWA, he continued to believe that only concentric operations would defeat his opponent.[121] An observer who knew the land well called concentric operations in South-West Africa a "farce," and Trotha a "staunch Prussian officer" who could not see beyond the maxims of European wars between states.[122] "The encirclement of this mass [the Herero], and their annihilating, unconditional defeat by means of one great strike,"[123] may have seemed appropriate by European standards.[124] Simply imposing these standards in the colonial setting, however, actually impeded successful operations. The settlers ruefully contrasted the present phase of "great operations," which rarely led to the desired results, with the earlier "African-classical era," which had been distinguished by small operations led by "old Africans" like Viktor Franke and Theodor Leutwein.[125]

The tendency of the high command to underestimate the opponent proved fatal. Herero fighters knew the terrain, they knew how to track down water and food, and they were far more mobile than their German counterparts.[126] Thus, in the run-up to the Battle of Waterberg, officers who knew the land best did not expect their opponent to wait patiently for encirclement. Bayer recalled that, "in general, the troops worried that the enemy could slip away from us at the last minute."[127] Viktor Franke had nothing but scorn for the metropolitan officers who believed they could quickly finish off the encircled "Herero pie."[128] He called the wartime leadership of the metropolitan officers and their staffs a "great comedy"[129] and a "farce of the worst kind."[130] Things did not turn out as badly for the Germans as Franke had feared,[131] but the majority of the Herero broke through German lines and were stopped only from fleeing northeast.[132]

It is clear that the outcome of the battle (or more accurately, the battle that did not occur) in no way corresponded to the expectations of the high command. This underscores, once again, how greatly Drechsler oversimplified and distorted the course of events, as we can see from various perspectives.

An exaggerated intentionalism permeates Drechsler's entire narrative. Because the United Nations' Genocide Convention magnified the importance of establishing genocidal intent, and Drechsler himself sought to establish the criminal character of "German imperialism," he tended to present events in an "absolute," or overly deterministic, way—so that these not only met, but *surpassed*, the convention's criteria.[133] In this light, even the most obvious failure became a planned success.

"German imperialism" dominates Drechsler's one-sided portrayal of events. Although he sought to give voice to the victims of an inhumane war, they do not play an active role in his narrative. Although the war in its first months was nearly an even contest,[134] Drechsler depicted a stark asymmetry between active perpetrators and passive victims. His approach illuminated the cruelty of German warfare, but he simultaneously underestimated the Herero, who do not appear as the worthy adversaries they actually were. Despite his critical stance, he reproduced the colonizers' inflated self-image in his depiction of a German war machine that singlehandedly determined the course of events.

It is important to recognize that the Herero *chose* to flee, and that they successfully extricated themselves from further skirmishes. Of course, they fled out of fear, to escape the threat that was posed by the Germans. On the one hand, flight implies a loss of autonomy; on the other, it is also an act of self-determination. As various sources suggest,[135] the Herero may have understood their escape from (planned) encirclement as an operational success.[136] And even after the Herero were no longer capable of organized resistance, they did not give in to their pursuers. This underscores the extent to which Drechsler neglected the social dimension of events, which were shaped by interactions between perpetrators and victims.[137]

It is all the more incomprehensible that Drechsler's thesis—that the German leaders had planned the outcome of the battles at the Waterberg—is often repeated uncritically, or even affirmed.[138] Drechsler's legacy has been most influential in a methodological sense. Few recent studies distance themselves significantly from his intentionalist, teleological approach.[139]

Within this context, we should note another variation of the genocide thesis, which similarly identifies an early genocidal turning point in the campaign. This variation acknowledges that the Battle of Waterberg did not turn out as Trotha had planned, but it presumes that the annihilation he had intended already possessed a decidedly genocidal dimension.[140] In this view, the successful flight of the Herero not only thwarted the Germans' plans, but also saved them from certain extermination at the Waterberg.[141]

As we have already seen, the more the metropole involved itself in putting down the uprising, the more influential the idea of annihilation became. It was also clear that the idea of annihilation had a narrower, more "conventional" meaning for much of the campaign. I contend that this was also true of the (planned) battle of annihilation at the Waterberg. The "battle of annihilation" highlights a fundamental ambiguity in the idea of annihilation in Prussian/German military culture at turn of the twentieth century. Within this context, "annihilation" did not automatically entail the extermination of the opponent, but could increase *or* limit the exercise of violence. This ambiguity informed the metropolitanization of the campaign that accompanied Trotha's assumption of the command, and it is the subject of the following excursus.

Excursus: Battles of Annihilation, Conservative Militarism, and Small Wars

We have already examined the concept of the *war* of annihilation, which is important to differentiate from the *battle* of annihilation. The distinction is often blurred, as the concepts are sometimes taken as more or less similar expressions of the idea of annihilation.[142]

Battles of annihilation and wars of annihilation do not occupy the same plane. Battles are elements of war, and wars—particularly in European experience—are typically comprised of a series of battles. The *battle* of annihilation belongs to the arena of tactics and operations; it serves a broader strategy and can be an instrument of many different forms of warfare. The *war* of annihilation, by contrast, has a strategic dimension, or already embodies a particular strategy. In principle, wars of annihilation can be waged without battles of annihilation. Ethnology is full of examples of groups that were wiped out by a series of assaults or ambushes, or many small strikes.[143] Conversely, battles of annihilation do not automatically lead to a war of annihilation. The battle of annihilation was an integral part of German military doctrine before World War I, and it intensified the use of force to a previously unknown degree; however, its essential purpose was *containing* war. Thus, the idea of annihilation was ambiguous or "Janus-faced" (to borrow the language of Norbert Elias).[144]

As a form of combat, the battle is already associated with a threefold limitation on the use of force. First, battles limit of the use of force temporally, by concentrating it into a comparatively short act. Thus, Victor Davis Hanson portrays the battle (the principal form of combat in intracultural wars) as one of the greatest accomplishments of the Greek polis; a swift, unequivocal decision on the battlefield replaced long, bloody, and cost-intensive wars of attrition.[145] Second, battles limit the use of force spatially. Battles were frequently arranged, not least because warring parties first had to find and agree upon a suitable terrain. Armies in the era of linear tactics (and beyond) needed large open spaces to maneuver,[146] which meant that the violence occurred in a space that was removed from everyday "civilian" life.[147] This leads to the third, personnel-related, limit on wartime violence. Because of their spatial separation, battles largely exclude noncombatants. It is no coincidence that the battle is among the most regulated and ritualized elements of war,[148] across cultures and throughout history.[149]

Although the battle has traditionally been the focus of classical military history, empirically it comprises only a small, subordinate component of warfare. Wars have been primarily defined by other forms of combat, which have often escalated the use of force to a much higher degree.[150] Medieval warlords sought to avoid battles wherever they could, although the Middle Ages, more than any other era, is associated with tightly regimented contests between knights. The chances of killing and (especially) being killed in open battle were often evenly distributed, so the outcome of the fighting was uncertain. At all times and places, however, commanders have sought to avoid even fights,[151] favoring scenarios that promise lower risk and higher chances of victory.[152] The battle, as a form of combat, does not necessarily increase the use of force. In the era of linear tactics, guerrilla warfare more often undermined distinctions between combatants and civilians, or "on" and "off" the battlefield.[153] The battle is also not the form of combat that claims the highest proportion of victims; in wars between nonstate actors, for example, the opposite is true. Likewise, we cannot say that a Prussian/German-style strategy of annihilation, primarily based on operational superiority in traditional battles, inherently claimed more victims or caused greater destruction than a strategy of attrition. US military leaders in Vietnam adopted a strategy of attrition that, despite these leaders' intentions, systematically led to civilian casualties.[154] Neither strategic doctrine is inherently more destructive than the other. Under the right conditions, both can lead to an escalation of violence.

If the battle as a form of combat can limit the exercise of violence, is the same true for battles of annihilation? Reemtsma would say no; he presumes that in battles of annihilation "the opposing army should not only be beaten or pushed back, but also killed, to the greatest possible extent." Thus, he considers the battle of annihilation to be a form of the "war of annihilation."[155]

According to Clausewitz, "annihilating" (or "destroying") the opponent's forces means putting them "in such a condition that they can no longer carry on the fight."[156] This can occur in many different ways, including disarmament or taking prisoners. It is interesting that Kurd Schwabe—a colonial officer who repeatedly advocated for extreme violence—considered "taking the enemy troops prisoner" to be an annihilating victory, even in the colonial arena.[157] What happened to the prisoners thereafter was left up to the victors, and thus remained open, but it no longer had anything to do with the battle in the narrower sense.

Historical examples also do not necessarily corroborate Reemtsma's assertion. At the Battle of Cannae (216 BCE), perhaps the best known battle of annihilation in history, the Carthaginians and their allies crushed the inferior Roman legionnaires, almost to the last man. However, more recent examples such as Sedan (1870) and Tannenberg (1914) underscore that tactical annihilation need not include slaughtering the opposing forces "to the greatest possible extent."

Physical annihilation represents the ultimate form of rendering an opponent defenseless, and so it is always present (or at least a possibility) within the concept of annihilation. Whether or not this potential for destruction is realized can depend on the dynamics of the fighting. Variables include the degree of resistance that is offered by inferior adversaries, whether they give up once a tactical victory is out of reach (or only when they can no longer put up an organized and adequate defense), or whether they fight to the bitter end and expect no mercy.

Thus, a battle of annihilation does not necessarily involve the unlimited use of force, nor must such a battle be part of a *war* of annihilation. German military history before the world wars makes this plain, and also demonstrates how the battle of annihilation became the key expression of a doctrine that was associated—not just incidentally—with the containment of war.

After centuries of at least partial success at containment, in the early nineteenth century states began to move closer to the logic of "pure war."[158] Significant changes began in France after its break with the *ancien régime*. The other European powers questioned France's legitimacy, and war became essential to the survival of the revolution and its achievements.[159] This "existential" war directly challenged the international order that had been put into place by the Peace of Westphalia, in which the goals of military conflicts were usually limited, and the continued existence of the warring parties was not in doubt. With its *levée en masse*, revolutionary France mustered armies that far outnumbered any that had existed to this point. French efforts to mobilize the entire population in service to the war or wartime production were likewise unprecedented.

However, it was Napoleon Bonaparte—for Clausewitz, the "God of War"—who moved warfare most decisively toward its "absolute" form.[160] In the words of Hans Delbrück, Bonaparte freed himself from the chains of absolutist warfare, and "from the start he wagered everything on the tactical victory that was to put the enemy army out of action."[161] He sought to beat, even to annihilate, the enemy forces, compelling them to surrender on his terms.[162] In short, Bonaparte revived the idea of annihilation, which had receded into the background in the centuries before him, and he thereby contributed to a significant escalation in the intensity of warfare.

Nevertheless, we should be wary of one-sided or exaggerated generalizations. According to the classicist Victor D. Hanson, Western military history has been broadly defined by its emphasis on the decisive battle—by a preference for comparatively short military conflicts with clear outcomes, distinguished by their particular brutality and extreme bloodshed.[163] Absolutist armies, too, were ultimately assembled to fight battles, although after the Peace of Westphalia commanders increasingly sought to avoid these, resorting to battles only after exhausting all other means, including small war tactics or maneuvering. The more drilling and intense regimentation that was needed to turn generally reluctant soldiers into a functioning army, the more costly and sensitive such an undertaking became—and the more sparingly the solution was applied.[164]

The French Revolution broke with this practice and created new realities—some irreversible—that helped to redefine state wars. The nationalization of war was an essential part of this process. From this point forward, the people were instructed that war was a national concern, relevant to every citizen.[165] This meant that more could be asked of soldiers, and the entire population, than absolute rulers had ever dared. Absolute monarchs made decisions about war and peace, and about private dynastic matters, by consulting a small cabinet of trusted advisors behind closed doors. The people nevertheless felt the consequences of these decisions when compelled to pay taxes or other duties. Apart from these fiscal and material burdens, dynastic rulers worked to keep war at a distance from their subjects.[166] In peacetime, troops were quartered in remote garrisons that were set apart from civil society. Battlefields and the routes to access them were also secluded.[167] An expansive system of military warehousing ensured that contacts between civilians and troops were kept at a minimum.

The nationalization and "existentialization" of war changed these circumstances fundamentally. On the one hand, expectations placed upon "the people" became a matter of life or death, while on the other, political leadership became dependent on public opinion. Absolute rulers presided over small, but very costly, mercenary armies. Because these took so long to train and could not be easily replaced, rulers did what they could to preserve them. A military conflict could quickly reach the point where the weaker party was offered a peace settlement and a golden escape route; the cost of defeat was usually not too high, given the limited goals of these wars.[168] By contrast, since 1792, revolutionary France had relentlessly deployed new forces against the standing armies of the anti-French coalition. Despite heavy losses, the "source [of the French forces]—the human potential of the nation—did not run dry."[169] Now, entire nations could potentially face off against one another. Even a dramatic escalation in casualties became acceptable, and sometimes (as in the Franco-Prussian War of 1870/71) public opinion drove the decision to continue the fight.

In order to hold their own against revolutionary France, the old European regimes were compelled to introduce their own reforms and to exploit their own national human potential, however reluctantly. These regimes were not favorably disposed to the revolution or its goals. The absolutist armies that had resisted reform—in the meantime, no longer organized by private entrepreneurs, but wearing only the uniform of the king—were instrumental to establishing the state's monopoly on the use of force; arming the people threatened to reverse, or at least to endanger, this development. The regimes feared losing order and authority more than any cabinet war.[170] Once Bonaparte was finally defeated, the powers sought to avoid larger conflicts among themselves, succeeding for nearly forty years after the Congress of Vienna, until tensions grew too large. In the meantime, industrialization changed warfare even more dramatically.[171] Military conflict now harbored even greater destructive potential than the Napoleonic Wars.

Within this context, the rise of the Great General Staff and its chief Helmuth von Moltke vividly illustrates the transformation that reinvigorated the concept of "annihilation" in Imperial Germany. The Great General Staff seized its moment to shine during the Austro-Prussian War of 1866. Although the planned annihilation of Austrian forces was ultimately thwarted by some commanders' unauthorized actions, the Great General Staff led the Prussian forces to a speedy and definitive victory. The Great General Staff enjoyed immense prestige. Its victories in the Franco-Prussian War of 1870/71 were key to the enshrinement (and later, ossification) of Moltke's ideas on warfare as official doctrine, since the institution of the Great General Staff instructed the subsequent generations of high commanders.[172]

For all their differences, Moltke can be understood as the direct heir of Napoleon Bonaparte.[173] From the very beginning, Moltke's thoughts on military strategy were permeated by the idea of annihilation, seeking to unite two disparate phenomena. On the one hand, Moltke intensified combat by insisting upon the idea of annihilation, elevating this to a dogma of German warfare.[174] On the other hand, he believed that the intensity of a short campaign, which could be decided in just a few battles, could actually limit wartime violence and prevent hostilities from expanding into a "people's war." In 1866 and 1870/71, Moltke sought to achieve a speedy victory over the enemy's *armed forces*, not to crush the enemy state or its people.[175] The population and economy of both sides were supposed to be affected as little as possible. Moltke was concerned that a war between two great powers, if it expanded into a "people's war," could drag on endlessly and result in heavy casualties. Like other traditional elites in Imperial Germany, he also feared the revolutionary forces at home that such a war could unleash. These elites did not trust the loyalty of the urban proletariat and were reluctant to arm them. Over the opposition of "bourgeois militarists" such as Erich Ludendorff, the prevailing conservative militarists succeeded in limiting the size of the armed forces, despite the formal existence of universal conscription.[176] In sum, by emphasizing the idea of annihilation, which promised to shorten wars substantially, Moltke (as a proponent of conservative militarism) saw an opportunity to eliminate the danger of a "people's war" with all its uncertainties.

The war against Austria in 1866 showed that the idea of annihilation could still be realized within a limited cabinet war. In 1870/71, however, the war against France went differently than Moltke had hoped. The Prussian army quickly dealt France an annihilating blow, but the young French republic would not accept the Germans' exorbitant demands for an armistice.[177] Put another way, the French refused to recognize the military and operational defeat of their regime.[178] Instead, the French minister of war, Léon Gambetta, proclaimed a *guerre à outrance* and unleashed a "people's war." In no time, new armies rose up to fend off the Germans. Units of irregular fighters engaged in acts of terror, and the Germans responded in kind. Despite heavy losses, the French made no moves to surrender. Moltke radicalized his demands only after military victories no longer seemed effective, and the "people's war" was well underway. Once France was finally defeated, Moltke insisted, the terms of the peace had to be so onerous that it would never again pose a military threat. The politician Otto von Bismarck made sure that the Prussian king (and subsequent German Kaiser) rejected this demand.[179]

Alfred von Schlieffen (chief of the Great General Staff between 1891 and 1906, and author of the plan that informed the campaign against

France at the start of World War I) shared Moltke's conservatism. He further radicalized the idea of annihilation, envisioning a contest between two million-strong armies that could be decided in a single great battle. His plan represented an unprecedented intensification of combat, but it was premised on the idea that a perhaps bloody, but quick, decision could shorten the war substantially by preventing it from escalating into a protracted "people's war." Schlieffen's aims corresponded to those of Moltke in 1870, and thus it was an even bolder attempt to square the circle—that is, to wage a short cabinet war with million-strong armies in an industrialized and ideological age.[180] His undertaking was an expression of the changed conditions for conservative militarism, which was, by World War I, long obsolete.[181]

Imperial Germany's "wars of pacification" in SWA occurred in a period of uncontested hegemony for traditional elites and conservative militarism. Schlieffen himself was still chief of the General Staff and responsible for overseas operations. If Trotha, the commander-in-chief on site, planned a great battle of annihilation to end the war against the Herero with a single strike, he did so with the mutual consent of the Kaiser and General Staff, on the basis of conservative militarism as the intellectual frame of reference for the General Staff and its leading commanders. We should not accept Reemtsma's assertion (nor that of Kößler and Melber) that the battle of annihilation—particularly in SWA—was an expression of "total war," which Germany would wage in the full sense only decades later.[182] The tactical and operational emphasis on annihilation in German military doctrine looked very different in the colonial era. For Moltke and Schlieffen, annihilation was not a means to escalate, but rather to contain, war—even though such an undertaking had become illusory by this point in time. In World War II, the battle of annihilation did become an element of the unlimited war of destruction, but at the turn of the century it was still a key expression of limited warfare under the banner of conservative militarism.

In a sense, the battle of annihilation represents the ultimate decisive battle, as it aims to render the opponent incapable of all further resistance. In South-West Africa, the German command sought to bring the war to a speedy conclusion. The contrast between this kind of warfare and the small war tactics of the "old Africans," which Trotha so vehemently rejected, is readily apparent. The long-serving officers' campaigns remained limited in many respects; few intended to compel a final decision. Their approach was diametrically opposed to the "dogma of the battle of annihilation" that Trotha sought to export overseas. Trotha favored a military strategy of annihilation that was oriented toward "great" state wars, while Leutwein's strategy of attrition adopted the methods of small wars. Both forms of warfare could follow "conventional" paths—and did, for some time.

Over centuries, the small war became an established part of warcraft. It was fully developed by the eighteenth century, reappearing without fundamental changes in the centuries thereafter.[183] The small war depended on symmetric constellations that exclusively involved regular armed forces,[184] so it became a subordinate part of warcraft, dominated entirely by the aims of "great" warfare.

The battle was the quintessence of "great" warfare—a temporally and spatially limited, but intense, form of combat between concentrated units of regular soldiers. In the eighteenth century, systematic peacetime drills transformed these units into well-oiled machines. They confronted one another in rigid linear formations that followed strict geometric principles. This highly ritualized form of combat had to be planned in advance, as the forces could be mustered only on an appropriately spacious, open, and even field; natural barriers would have disrupted the moving formations. Military leaders in this era sought to concentrate firepower to heighten its effect, and they maintained control over their troops in combat by upholding an order that was easy to see. Drills neutralized the subjectivity, fear, and anger of individual soldiers as much as possible, so that even under extreme conditions they would execute their function in the military machine.[185]

Lack of flexibility made the large formations vulnerable. Addressing this vulnerability became the task of the small war protagonists—light troops in small mobile units, assembled for this purpose. These troops pursued and disrupted larger units while marching, setting up camp, or moving into battle formation. They avoided direct confrontation and, if necessary, slipped back onto difficult terrain where the larger units could not operate. They shunned open battle, turning instead to tactics such as assaults and ambushes. Reconnaissance and tax collection were among their other tasks.[186]

Although the small war employed its own techniques, it had long been defined by its relationship to "great" warfare—whether as preparation, accompaniment, complement, or even corrective.[187] As a handmaiden to "great" warfare, the small war had little strategic significance on its own.[188]

The status of the small war did not change as long as "wars" were primarily state wars between structurally comparable actors. Once colonial expansion reached its zenith over the course of the nineteenth century, the imperial powers increasingly confronted different opponents, and the small war asserted itself operationally as the primary form of combat. Charles E. Callwell marked this development with his well-regarded study, *Small Wars*, which first appeared in 1896. Callwell presented the small war as a distinct type of warfare, which was characterized by asymmetrical conflict situations in which *one* of the warring parties did not have regular troops.[189] Callwell was interested in scenarios where regular forces confronted irregular units with (supposedly) inferior weaponry, organization, and discipline. The asymmetry between warring parties meant that small wars were not grounded on the same conditions as conventional warfare, which relied exclusively on battles between regular armies.[190] Callwell sought to fill this gap in conventional, state-centered military theory.

Trotha's actions and remarks suggest that he did not fully acknowledge this development, but instead relied on conventional wisdom. Despite his colonial experience in East Africa, he saw small wars as dependent and inferior; only "real" warfare and its battles could be decisive. Even so, his fear of guerrilla warfare suggests that he sensed how small wars could threaten traditional military approaches that relied solely on raw force, although this facet of small war became evident only later in the twentieth century. In the Herero campaign, Trotha's exclusive concern was putting down the uprising with all available means.[191]

Insistence on a battle of destruction intensified the exercise of violence, but also—and not merely incidentally—included tendencies to contain it. Ethical scruples did not play a role. The desire to avoid a long war was far more influential, in part because of the uncertainties that accompanied such a conflict in an age of nationalization. Here, too, we can see that the "dogma of the battle of annihilation" promoted not only unfettered violence, but also the opposite tendency.

It is crucial to ask what happened *after* routines did not succeed, and the expected great victory did not occur. How did the Germans deal with failure, and what consequences did this bring? These questions are key to understanding the genocidal escalation in SWA.

We know that Trotha wanted to crush the Herero decisively, after Leutwein had recoiled from such radical war aims.[192] The new commander broke with the limited, small warfare of the "old Africans," seeking to "metropolitanize" the campaign by bringing it closer to European state war. In one great battle, the Herero were to be dealt an annihilating, decisive defeat. This led to more intense combat, but also limited violence by concentrating it within one short act. Thus, the attempted "metropolitanization" of colonial war was ambivalent.[193]

Trotha's "metropolitanization" efforts tended to contain violence in another respect as well. These efforts were grounded in conservatism and reflected the Wilhelmine obsession with government authority.[194] Leutwein's admission that the colonial government had given up trying to rein in the privatized violence of settlers and soldiers clashed with the authoritarian thinking of political and military elites in Imperial Germany. Leutwein may have strengthened the hand of these elites, who believed that he had lost control.[195] Trotha was unwilling to accept such violence "from below." Not coincidentally, one of his first official acts was an attempt to stem this violence with a proclamation on "provisions for military tribunals etc. during the war in German South-West Africa."[196] These provisions stipulated that only officers could perform summary executions, and only in clear-cut cases; persons merely suspected of wrongdoing were to be tried by court-martial to determine their guilt or innocence. Rank-and-file soldiers, meanwhile, were to refrain from all assaults. This was evidently a measure to limit violence, as it significantly decreased (or was supposed to decrease) the circle of those permitted to exercise it.[197] Further attempts at containment followed. Among them was an order from 25 June 1904, which responded to difficulties in recruiting indigenous labor. Guards were forbidden from mistreating indigenous transport workers, and it was determined that, in the future, only commanders would have the right to punish workers for negligence—not with corporal punishment, but by deducting wages, and good work was to be rewarded with bonuses.[198]

Further, it is noteworthy that Trotha built a stockade for eight thousand prisoners in advance of the planned battle at the foot of the Waterberg in August 1904. This capacity exactly corresponded to the maximum official estimate of Herero fighters. If we accept that the correspondence was not coincidental, then unlimited warfare seems unlikely.[199] In any event, the German command was apparently counting on a large number of prisoners, which speaks for a conventional military interpretation of annihilation in this phase of the war.

Within this context, two passages deserve our particular attention because they appear to contradict, or at least qualify, this understanding of annihilation. Before the Battle of Waterberg, First Lieutenant Stuhlmann wrote in his diary that the troops were instructed that the upcoming encounters would entail "the annihilation of the whole tribe, nothing alive should be spared."[200] A few weeks later, Lieutenant Rudolph von Hardenberg reported in his own diary about a plan to punish the Herero, adding that the punishment was "to kill them."[201] Although these statements are not ambiguous, the source of any such orders or plans is unclear.[202] Stuhlmann and Hardenberg served under Berthold Deimling, who—since he was known for his overzealousness and lack of caution—should certainly be considered a potential author. These diary entries must be taken seriously, despite the uncertainty about the orders they describe. They clearly depict a degree of violence and cruelty that cannot be explained solely by the greater intensity of combat in a battle of annihilation. These passages underscore yet again that the hostilities in South-West Africa were colonial conflicts, not acts of war between European states. They were campaigns against "rebels," outside the reach of international law, and they were punitive expeditions against "illegitimate" adversaries who had to be taught their place in the colonial hierarchy by means of extreme violence. These hostilities had a different frame of reference from European wars[203]—as demonstrated, not least, by the fact that the physical annihilation of entire groups was a viable option. The logic of the *Denkzettel* (or "lesson of warning") not only called for defeating the Herero, but defeating them in such a way that they would never again dare to rise up against their colonial masters; it called, in other words, for a massacre. By demonstrating the deadly threat of colonial rule, imposing collective humiliation and uniformity upon the colonized, and feeding the perpetrators' self-aggrandizement, the massacre was integral to colonial "processes of pacification."[204] It is possible that officers and troops were encouraged to slaughter the opponent ruthlessly. Even so, provisions such as the construction of stockades or prisoner-of-war camps suggest that the command intended, at some point, for the killing to come to an end—and for the war to remain limited, or at least, not to lead directly to the physical extermination of all Herero. This corresponds to the order that Trotha gave after the battle, which at least prohibited the killing of women and children[205]—although by all appearances, and against the German leaders' expectations, the killing did not stop. The command apparently wanted the unfettered, absolute violence—the slaughter of unfortunates who were caught after the failed battle—to remain a genocidal *event*.

In the following sections of this chapter, I will examine how massacres became a regular occurrence and part of a genocidal *strategy*, at some point after the Battle of Waterberg. Too little attention is generally paid to the different stages of escalation. Scholars too often present the triad of Waterberg, pursuit, and proclamation in rapid succession, as if each step naturally arose from the last, leading toward the climax of Trotha's proclamation and its accompanying strategy. As we will see, however, the road to catastrophe was not a straight line.

The Pursuit

A 2003 article by Hendrik Lundtofte gives us a detailed and nuanced depiction of the Herero campaign. Lundtofte's work is instructive, although his timeline for the campaign's radicalization leaves room for dispute. He rightly criticizes the insufficient scholarly attention given to the period of time between the Battle of Waterberg in mid-August and Trotha's infamous proclamation in early October 1904, particularly since these weeks were extremely eventful. A large number of the fleeing Herero presumably lost their lives in these weeks, as Lundtofte contends.[206]

In a pointed departure from conventional interpretations, Lundtofte does not link the genocide directly to the figure of Lothar von Trotha.[207] He correctly asserts that the Battle of Waterberg remained within the bounds of "conventional" warfare, and that at this point the desired annihilation of the opponent had a narrow military definition. In his view, operations to pursue and catch the Herero immediately following the failed battle sought chiefly to compel a decisive victory, and thus were limited in character.[208] Lundtofte argues that violence escalated after this (first) pursuit failed; the hostilities began to resemble "total" warfare and increasingly targeted women and women. He contends that Trotha adopted a qualitatively new, decidedly genocidal strategy in the aftermath of the setbacks on 16 August 1904.[209]

Lundtofte presumes that these setbacks created the conditions that were necessary for the campaign to take a genocidal turn. In other words, Trotha mounted a campaign of extermination against the Herero only after failing to achieve a conventional victory—after the Battle of Waterberg did not turn out as planned, and the subsequent pursuit broke down.

Although Lundtofte's arguments are otherwise sound, there is nothing to support such an early change in strategy; in fact, the opposite is true. Soldiers' diaries indicate that different sections were still planning a concentric approach at the end of August—yet another attempt to encircle the Herero, and apparently the same kind of operation as the battle two weeks earlier.[210]

Trotha's diaries also reveal no fundamental caesura on 16 August or in the weeks thereafter. Until 29 August 1904, there is no indication whatsoever that the operational situation had changed fundamentally for Trotha. Nearly two weeks after Lundtofte's postulated caesura, this is how the commander-in-chief recounted a conversation with Captain Bayer about Leutwein's suggestions for ending the war:

> Palaver with Bayer about Leutwein's view of the situation. He[211] is set on the idea that the war can be ended only by making a pact with the people. He knows just as little as all of the old Africans about the local water situation. *For now I'm staying with my idea, to keep pursuing and beating them where I can,* or [I can] force them onto English territory, and then set up strong protection at the border.[212]

Trotha was determined to stand by his approach, and "to keep pursuing and beating" the Herero as long as he could. However, he had apparently already considered the possibility that the Herero might retreat to English territory, present-day Botswana, instead of reengaging in battle. If the Herero did cross the English border—whether "forced" by the Germans, as Trotha put it, or simply because they escaped—the existing strategy would have been moot. In this case, Trotha suggested he would deal with the changed situation by setting up "strong protection at the border," thereby ensuring that the Herero could not return to German territory. This was the first indication of a new strategy—and it occurred later and in a different way than Lundtofte suggests. At the end of August 1904, Trotha had not yet given up hope that the existing operations might still end in victory.

His diary entry of 6 September 1904 suggests that he still believed the desired operational solution was within reach. Having obtained new intelligence about the whereabouts of the Herero, he concluded, "So it will be possible to catch them [the Herero] again, after all."[213]

On 23 September, Trotha mentioned a meeting with Ludwig von Estorff, commander of one of the sections involved in the pursuit. Estorff himself recalled suggesting to Trotha that opening up negotiations with the Herero could end the war.[214] But Trotha would hear none of it, as his own diary shows: "Big lecture from Estorff about the operation. He wants to negotiate. No, my friend, nothing will come of this. We'll fight as long as we can."[215] Trotha held firm to the same approach. Even on 28 September, he still hoped to lead a decisive strike against the Herero under Samuel Maharero: "We'll scout, and then on 1 Oct. I'll lead the last push to the east against Samuel."[216]

Other sources mention this battle, suggesting that the Germans were counting on a great, dramatic showdown. The soldier Max Belwe recalled how the division chaplain Max Schmidt prepared the troops for what was meant to be the last battle. He presented the impending struggle with dramatic flair, advising the men to be ready for anything and, just in case, to settle their accounts with the Lord.[217] Stuhlmann, too, was counting on a "desperate struggle" against "thousands" of Herero; he believed that their forces were so strong, and the situation so dire, that the German troops could be annihilated.[218]

Once more, however, the Herero frustrated the hopes of the German command. The Herero withdrew just in time, and so the battle never took place. Samuel Maharero's repeated evasions ended the pursuit. By the end of September 1904, the Herero had pushed far enough into the Omaheke that the German troops could not follow them. There were no prospects for another battle. In a report to Schlieffen, Trotha advised that a fundamental change in strategy was now unavoidable: "Insofar as concentric strikes are concerned, the great operations are over. Continuing them is impossible, if we consider water and provisions. Perhaps it could have been done, if the map east of the Otjosondjou-Epata-Epukiro line had not left us completely in the lurch."[219]

Contrary to Lundtofte's depiction, the Germans did not change strategy before the end of September or early October 1904. In principle, the pursuit was based on the same assumptions as the Battle of Waterberg. Trotha had counted entirely on "great operations," which were supposed to culminate in "concentric strikes" that led to the opponent's decisive defeat. Once these operations were no longer possible because the German troops could not follow the (remaining) Herero into the Omaheke, Trotha had to adopt a new strategy. In a diary entry from 1 October, Franz Epp left no doubt that failure of the pursuit represented a fundamental caesura: "The war entered another stage; plan in the works."[220] Although there had been no fundamental change in strategy between mid-August and the end of September, circumstances shifted nonetheless.

The first attempt to pursue the Herero had to be broken off after only a few hours. Trotha had apparently assumed that Deimling had enough provisions for his men and animals to take up the pursuit right away, so the retreating Herero could be engaged in a decisive battle after all. Trotha soon realized, however, that this was not the case.[221] Valuable time was lost and could no longer be made up, despite the troops' utmost efforts. They effectively began the pursuit only on 16 August, and from this point on, they were always a step behind. They could not catch up to the Herero and compel them to fight. The great, decisive battle they had hoped for receded into the distance. The ongoing dry season and the pitiful condition of the troops awakened fears that the Herero were lost for good.[222]

The war, which was originally supposed to be over in "one large operation,"[223] was getting smaller all the time. It was increasingly unlikely that the different sections would reunite for one great battle; they more or less fought on their own, whenever and wherever they encountered their adversaries, who had long since splintered into multiple groups with multiple chiefs. Had a battle in fact taken place on 1 October, the Germans would have confronted only part of the original Herero forces, albeit the part led by Samuel Maharero. Killing or capturing Maharero would have at least had symbolic importance, ending the campaign for the time being. Instead, the campaign fragmented with no more great battles. Once larger operations were halted, in October by the latest, the fighting was left entirely in the hands of smaller detachments and patrols, which "took care of details," as the general tellingly described.[224]

As the pursuit wore on, there were few traditional battles, only smaller skirmishes and rearguard actions. Fighting was otherwise limited to assaults on scattered groups, which were usually slaughtered indiscriminately. Anyone who crossed the path of the Schutztruppe was suspect. San or Damara might have been released,[225] but captured Herero—including women and children—were subject (at best) to interrogation. If they could not point to the whereabouts of chiefs, warriors, or weapons, or if their responses seemed dubious, they were dealt with swiftly.[226] Such behavior was not new to this war, but something had changed; while the strategic premises remained the same, the meaning of "annihilation" quietly shifted.

As operations grow in size and involve more troops, annihilation is more likely to be directed against an abstraction: the organized resistance of the opponent. Annihilation seeks to break down coordinated collective resistance by attacking morale, sowing panic, and unleashing centrifugal forces, until enough of the opposing forces merely want to save their own lives.[227] Fighters are more likely to lay down their weapons if fighting on seems hopeless and futile. In this situation, annihilation does not necessarily result in heavy casualties. This seems to be the kind of outcome that Trotha expected at the Waterberg, which explains preparations such as building prisoner-of-war camps.

The meaning of annihilation becomes more concrete in smaller operations. Once the pursuit began, the Herero campaign was mostly assaults and raids. This form of warfare involved only small numbers of fighters, but led to proportionally very high casualties on the side of the Herero. The Germans rarely spoke of prisoners of war anymore. As the war disintegrated into many small combat actions, as a whole it became more strongly influenced by situational dynamics such as "forward panics"—one of the most dangerous social situations, according to Randall Collins.[228] More importantly, the patrols and other small units that carried out these actions were often no longer equipped to take prisoners, particularly since they, too, were suffering from hunger, thirst, and disease. This is how Trotha justified his infamous proclamation, or "firing order" (*Schießbefehl*), of 2 October 1904. Weeks before, on 13 September, he had already complained in his diary that women and children kept approaching the German guards to ask for water, and so he had "given new orders to drive back everything with force, because amassing a large number of prisoners posed a danger for the provisioning and health of the troops."[229] On 18 September, Lieutenant von Frankenberg acknowledged receipt of this order: "Defecting riffraff are to be turned away because of insufficient provisions; men are to be disarmed, interrogated, and then dealt with according to the laws of war."[230]

In sum, we can say that the narrower the prospects were of apprehending *the* Herero and beating them decisively, the more violence was categorically directed against *every* Herero.

The Proclamation

On 1 October 1904, Lothar von Trotha composed his infamous proclamation to the Herero.[231] Isabel Hull has persuasively shown that much of what the proclamation announced was already common practice by the time it was issued.[232] Nevertheless, we must not overlook how Trotha used the proclamation to articulate a new strategy, which ushered in a new phase of the campaign. To this extent, the proclamation represented a caesura.

To begin, we must establish what the proclamation was *not*. It did not fit seamlessly within the process of violence, and it was not the inevitable climax of Trotha's campaign. Many historical accounts imply just this, spending few sentences on the period between the Battle of Waterberg in mid-August to the proclamation in early October, as if nothing of significance for the rest of the war happened within these few weeks.[233] Joël Kotek even depicts the proclamation as the logical consummation of the hostilities to this point.[234] These accounts overlook the fact that the change in strategy was a reaction to fundamental failure.

The military officers did not necessarily see themselves in a position of strength. They knew the limits of their own power all too well. For these reasons, I am doubtful that Trotha moved to "seal" the western edge of the Omaheke so that he could complete the work of annihilation by doing away with the few remaining survivors of a long beaten opponent.[235] The Germans do not seem to have understood how gravely the Herero had already been affected. As we have seen, they were still counting on a decisive battle against thousands of Herero at the end of September. Trotha's letter to Schlieffen on 4 October shows that he still believed that most of the Herero would hold their own in the Omaheke, or else escape to English territory.[236]

Little had been achieved by early October, when Trotha was compelled to change strategy because his troops could go no further. The Germans had little accurate information about the Herero, who had moved beyond their reach. In the worst case, they were left with an opponent who had not been decisively beaten and was laying low in an inaccessible area, able to return at any time and resume the war. Schlieffen expressed these exact concerns in a letter to Bülow on 23 November, emphasizing that the Herero would pose "a constant threat from Bechuanaland" if the Cape Colony government took no action against them, which is why Schlieffen believed that the Germans had to prepare for an extended war.[237]

Worse, they had lost all control over the situation and could only wait for the Herero; all the Germans could do was react. In order to protect the rear of the colony, troops of sufficient strength had to be sent to remote areas, where they were to stay for an unspecified time. Given the length of the borders and the expanse of the land, overall security remained precarious.

The German officers saw that the proclamation arose from a position of weakness. Despite Trotha's martial (and seemingly omnipotent) rhetoric, he could do little more than issue a threat to stop the Herero from returning to the colony. He sought to achieve with words what he could not do with his troops.[238] Contemporaries like Epp recognized the empty "theatrics" associated with the proclamation and why it was issued.[239] In response to Trotha's report from 4 October 1904, Schlieffen remarked, "We are at present completely unable to inflict any harm upon the Herero. If they do not willfully seek to break through our lines, we cannot take even the smallest action against them. The terrible threats of Trotha's proclamation from 2 October must seem laughable to the Herero."[240] Historical literature usually refers to the proclamation as an order—to annihilate, fire, or engage in genocide.[241] Thus, it is easy to overlook that the text primarily addressed the *Herero* and urged them to act in a certain way; it only secondarily addressed the German troops.[242] This is what was so new.

The proclamation had a genocidal aspect from the start, but it was initially defined by terror. While certainly an extreme case, it promoted measures that Sémelin might describe as "subjugating" processes of destruction.[243] "Subjugating" processes of destruction include killing civilians, but not their systematic annihilation. The primary goal of subjugation is to assert political control over survivors.[244] To be fair, we can hardly say that the goal of German "terrorism" against the Herero— Trotha himself used this term—was to assert political control over Herero survivors, as Trotha himself later suggested.[245] He was uncertain of the strength of the Herero beyond the reach of his troops, and thus he sought to keep them away from "German" territory, now and in the future. The proclamation made clear that the Herero were "no longer German subjects" and would no longer be tolerated "within German borders." The intent of the terror was to uphold the present order, and to drive the Herero out of German-controlled territory once and for all. "Terrorism" was supposed to compel Herero survivors on the other side of the border to bend to Trotha's will, and to give up any thought of returning to the colony. In this extreme case, the "subjugating" processes of destruction aimed for expulsion, rather than political control.[246]

Crucial within the present context is that Trotha (at the time that the proclamation was written, and regardless of whether he was correct or not) believed that a relevant number of Herero were outside the German sphere of influence, and thus could be reached only indirectly, through representative acts of terror. To this extent, we can say that *threat* defined the proclamation *at the time it was written*—which also corresponds with Schlieffen's assessment.[247] If this is true, then Trotha's second strategy was not immediately geared toward extermination, but rather expulsion, thereby completing Selous's triad. References to expulsion in the proclamation are not just "camouflage."[248]

These observations notwithstanding, the proclamation also had an aspect that was strongly genocidal. The addendum ordered the soldiers to kill every Herero man. Even if women and children were excepted from this measure, its systematic execution would have resulted sooner or later in the annihilation of all Herero. The threat that "every Herero, armed or unarmed, with or without cattle, will be shot dead" has categorical implications that are atypical of terrorism, and which more closely correspond to the logic of "eradicating" destruction processes. Acts of terror specifically target the innocent, but they usually affect only a few people who serve as stand-ins for the collective. Trotha, however, ordered the killing of *all* (male) Herero who were unlucky enough to cross paths with the German patrols.

Further, Trotha's proclamation ruled out unconditional surrender, the last remaining exit option that might still have been possible for the Herero.[249] If surrendering had once been exceedingly risky, it now meant certain death, as every Herero person within the borders of the colony had become a target. By eliminating the last exit option, the proclamation marked a turning point in the process of violence by unleashing autotelic violence. All that now mattered was making the opponent disappear. The line between expulsion and extermination was easily crossed.

In case his "conventional" plan of annihilation failed, in August 1904, Trotha already had his eye on a new plan that would force the Herero "onto English territory, and then set up strong protection at the border."[250] This strategy did not take effect until October, but it dated back to a phase of the war when the situation of the Herero was not yet so desperate, and the Germans were unable to assess this situation clearly. A further complication was that Trotha had broken off all diplomatic relations with the Herero (or had had none to begin with), so there were no relations whatsoever with the opponent.[251] He was prone to misinterpret signs and did not want to listen to the advice of the "old Africans,"[252] and apparently no one knew the Omaheke well.[253] Further, the command tended to base decisions on less favorable scenarios for the Germans.

We must not forget that the German officers confronted an opponent who was well-versed in evasive strategy, and willing to interpret a successful retreat as an operational success. In addition, the Herero were accustomed to long and arduous migrations because of their partially nomadic lifestyle. They knew how to scavenge root vegetables and herbs, and also how to locate pasture and watering holes. Unlike their pursuers, they were familiar with old trade routes through the Omaheke.[254]

Trotha may have sincerely believed that the Herero could hold their own in the Omaheke, or that they could otherwise escape to English territory, as he reported to Schlieffen. In any event, he had to admit his own failure, and this could not have been easy, given his tense relationship with Schlieffen.[255] Thus, it is possible that when Trotha issued the proclamation, he did not believe that his measures would achieve more than intimidating the Herero and keeping them from returning to the colony in the future.

This changed in the weeks thereafter, and almost certainly by the time that Trotha's report from 4 October reached Schlieffen and moved him to act. In the intervening weeks, Trotha came to see that the Herero no longer threatened the German troops. They would struggle to survive in the sandveld, and many would be unable to reach English territory. Instead, a large number of those who did not fall to German bullets would likely die from sickness, hunger, or thirst. On 26 October, Trotha wrote to Schlieffen, "The incoming reports [from] Mühlenfels confirm the news of the gradual demise of the Herero nation in the Omaheke."[256] The threshold to genocide was definitively crossed once it became evident that "terrorism" could exterminate the opponent, and that the German measures could have murderous consequences.[257] To borrow a phrase from Dirk Moses,[258] the "genocidal moment" was reached once Trotha grasped the consequences of his actions, affirmed these actions, and decided not to change course.[259]

The Dynamics of Escalation

Isabel Hull proposes that violence escalated gradually during the pursuit.[260] She suggests that the rigid adherence to the standard procedures of Prussian and German military doctrine, and the role of militarism in particular, essentially caused the genocidal escalation. She overlooks, however, that Trotha's approach was by no means uncontroversial among his peers, and that leaders in Berlin came to believe that the situation in SWA had gotten out of hand. Trotha apparently did not take things so far that Schlieffen or Bülow considered relieving him of his command, but the situation created by the proclamation (which they did not learn about until the second half of November) appeared so serious to them that they felt obligated to intervene and change course. Trotha's furious response shows the gravity of this intrusion upon his authority as commander.

Having established the chronology of events, we can now turn to the crucial question raised by George Steinmetz—how to explain the genocidal transformation of a campaign that had long remained limited.[261] We must do more than demonstrate exterminatory racism on the part of Trotha alone. Although the declaration of martial law gave Trotha far-reaching powers upon his arrival in SWA, he long stayed within the bounds of "conventional" warfare. What drove the general to abandon this path, and to turn the screws of violence ever tighter? Despite resistance, why did he adopt a course of action that had little chance of success, that threatened to wear down his own troops, and that led ever more clearly toward the extermination of the remaining Herero?

The escalation of violence can be explained by the failure of original plans, and what this inconceivable failure meant to Trotha. My explanation builds upon the "shame-rage mechanism" that was first described by psychologist Helen B. Lewis, and subsequently brought to sociological discussions of violence by Thomas J. Scheff and Suzanne M. Retzinger.[262] I begin by defining "shame," and then I will elucidate other components of this mechanism.

Shame and Rage

Shame arises from the discrepancy between the ego and the ego ideal.[263] This usually occurs when the self is observed by others, although self-shaming involves seeing oneself through others' eyes.[264] This makes shame an eminently social emotion, if not *the* "social emotion par excellence."[265] Building upon the work of Georg Simmel, Sighard Neckel proposes that the experience—or better, revelation—of incompetence is not an accident that may or may not affect one's sense of self. Rather, the awareness of incompetence shapes self-perception by exposing one's imperfections as a person.[266] This is why shame is often experienced so intensely, as Neckel underscores: "Anyone who is ashamed loathes himself; he is a stranger to himself, and strangeness overwhelms him; he is shamed by and in front of others."[267] At the same time, Neckel's observation illustrates how closely shame is related to what Sigmund Freud calls "social anxiety"—that is, the fear of losing love because of negative attention and the disapproval of others.[268] Scheff and Retzinger suggest that shame can gauge the state of one's social relationships and signal when these are endangered.[269] According to Retzinger, emotions have a signal function that responds to crises, "warning us internally that something is wrong."[270] Shame also possesses a regulative function, which encourages the self to interact with others in a way that upholds important relationships. Shame is not pathological or dysfunctional per se; rather, it is an emotion that enables humans to maintain social relationships.

Even so, it exacts a heavy toll. Shame itself is shameful, which is why it is so often accompanied by an urge to run away and hide, or even to die—but also by an impulse to deny or repress this emotion.[271] As Jean-Paul Sartre has remarked, the self that has been shamed acts as the *object* of others' attention. Overwhelmed and paralyzed by shame, the self remains passive.[272] In the end, shame confronts the self with its structural need for acceptance; the self is compelled to acknowledge that it is not, in fact, self-sufficient. Shame can restore and preserve social relationships, but this does not mean that shame returns these relationships to their original state. Shame can provide a successful response to others' typecasting, by demonstrating that what one is ashamed of does not represent one's innermost self. By being ashamed, however, one acknowledges having erred and thus submits to the judgment of others. This limits the power of the person's subsequent interactions; one can no longer take issue with norms, having previously flouted them. Instead, one is now under observation and compelled to conform.[273] In general, shame is not readily compatible with claims to autonomy and dignity. Cultures that revere these values are inclined to despise or deny shame; Scheff points especially to "modern" societies.[274]

Lewis notes that in her therapeutic practice shame was often denied. She differentiates between two different kinds of "distortion"—on the one hand, open, unidentified shame that is downplayed or misconstrued, although not entirely repressed; and on the other, "bypassed" shame. Bypassing is a special type of defense that prevents the development of shameful feelings and their accompanying pain,[275] and thus it also interferes with resolving or dissipating shame. We might say that bypassed shame is "recursive"; it feeds upon itself and constantly regenerates.[276] Because shame is not acknowledged, its actual causes remain out of sight and cannot be dismantled. Instead, it releases sequences of emotions—including one that was particularly destructive and crucial to the war in South-West Africa. This sequence of emotions can translate bypassed shame into rage and ultimately lead to violence. In general, anger is justifiable. If it does not mix with shame, it can dissipate quickly and remain within accepted limits, enabling necessary adjustments within the relevant social relationships. Together with bypassed shame, however, it can escalate into blind rage, hatred, and resentment. In this case, anger disguises shame and projects the unacknowledged feelings onto the outside world.[277] Rage, hatred, and resentment are not directed against their actual causes, and thus do not constitute adequate coping behaviors, but instead constantly regenerate. The self is caught in a spiral that is difficult to escape, and its subsequent actions take on obsessive and compulsive characteristics.

After the failure at the Waterberg, Trotha became increasingly entangled in a spiral of shame and rage that came to define his actions. This spiral is the mechanism that drove the steady escalation of violence.

Investigating a historic case brings unavoidable limitations. Lewis sat across from her patients; she could observe their expressions and gestures, and note the volume or tone of their remarks. Shame is usually expressed physically—by looking down, avoiding eye contact, or closing eyes. This is particularly true of bypassed shame, as illustrated by the photos that Retzinger incorporates in her analysis.[278] Lewis also posed direct questions. In a historic case, such opportunities are rare. Further, the documents that are available may have been revised many times. Some texts describe emotions that arose in certain situations, but even handwritten diaries and letters were composed after the fact—typically at the end of the day, when the author found a quiet moment to recount his experiences, possibly seeking to make sense of his own actions and reactions. These texts were often typed, and may have been edited or revised many times. They also served as rationalizations of the events they describe. Such limitations are unavoidable, although it should be noted that Scheff and Retzinger have already used the shame-rage mechanism to explore another historic case.[279] Scheff's analysis of the rise and politics of National Socialism (with particular attention to the person of Adolf Hitler) is based on relevant histories and published memoirs, but his conclusions should be taken quite seriously. The sociologists Sabine Haring and Helmut Kuzmics have recently underscored the validity of Scheff's analysis.[280] In contrast to Scheff's studies, my work relies on a significantly broader source base and offers a more thorough reconstruction of the historical context.

Denial

Because the colonial masters also saw the uprising as an attack on the prestige of Imperial Germany, the conflict was highly charged from the very beginning.[281] The mere existence of this large-scale uprising was humiliating, as it challenged German colonial authority before the eyes of the world public.[282] This is why Trotha reacted so angrily to an Englishman's letter that appeared in a colonial newspaper shortly after he arrived in SWA: "England is apparently the only country that understands this [colonization]."[283] As a young great power, Imperial Germany was unsure of itself—and tempted to cover up this uncertainty with brute force. The problem intensified as one setback followed another, and Trotha proved unable to end the campaign as hoped, damaging the military prestige of Germany's "victory culture." As Scheff notes, "prestige" is a code word for the avoidance of shame.[284]

Shame itself was perceived as shameful. Certain cultures and milieus are shame-averse, and this was especially true of elite, or "good," society in Wilhelmine Germany. Its primary integrative element was the ethos of the military aristocracy, which had been reinforced by the circumstances of German unification as a "revolution from above" (Erich Ludendorff).[285] Not coincidentally, the most distinctive hallmark of the Wilhelmine elite was a form of privatized violence with explicitly military and aristocratic origins: the duel. Liberal and humanist traditions gave way to a "cult of ruthlessness" with a distinctively military and aristocratic hue. According to this ideology, which was given philosophical expression by Friedrich Nietzsche, human existence was a constant struggle.[286] Nietzsche's ideology disparaged any admission of weakness (such as shame) as "worthless" and "repulsive." "Honor"[287]—which was, in a sense, overdetermined, referring to both male honor and the honor of officers—allowed no such admission.[288]

Trotha represented the Wilhelmine elite and its ethos like few others. He came from a noble military family, and his father was an officer. He began his own military career in one of the prestigious royal guard regiments.[289] The strategy that he stood for and (especially) refused to change shows how deeply he had internalized the ethos of his class. His insistence on the primacy of violence might be understood as a one-dimensional reification of this ethos—demonstrating strength and absolute superiority without compromise, and suppressing any show of weakness. Leutwein, by contrast, had approached the opponent with a certain measure of empathy and understanding; he hesitated before attacking, and he did not exhibit the expected decisiveness or toughness.

If Wilhelm II sought a commander who was unburdened by scruples or reservations, eager to crush the uprising "by all means," then Trotha was undoubtedly the right man for the job.[290]

The problem was that Trotha fulfilled the Wilhelmine ethos to such a degree that once the campaign did not produce the desired results, the consequences were devastating. The campaign against the Herero confirms the observation that the era's exaggerated, "knightly" militarism, as embodied by Trotha, could not only promote, but also undermine, military achievement.[291] Because of his obsession with strength, Trotha had difficulty admitting that his strategy had failed. He was unable to rethink the premises of his approach and reorganize the campaign. Before the Battle of Waterberg, there had been no shortage of voices to warn about the difficulties of operational warfare in SWA. The more evident it became that the critics were correct, the more Trotha dug in his heels.[292] A change in course would have been an unacceptable admission of fallibility and weakness. The more inevitable that alternative paths such as negotiations appeared, the more categorically Trotha refused them. In December 1904, he again rejected an officer's suggestion to engage in negotiations with the Herero. Troops were needed in the south of the colony, where the Nama (-Oorlam) had taken arms, and the situation of the troops on the western border of the Omaheke had long been unsustainable because of hunger, thirst, and disease. Precisely *because* these objections to Trotha's course of action were well-founded, Trotha saw this as the "worst possible moment for negotiations." He feared that the Herero would say that "the Germans can't finish off the Witbooi and Morenga, and so they're negotiating with us."[293] In a campaign of constant disappointments, a favorable moment for negotiations—in Trotha's view—never materialized.[294]

The escalation of violence did not reveal an exterminatory, racist intent to annihilate that had always been present, and which rose to the fore as the campaign progressed. Rather, escalation derived from Trotha's fear of appearing weak, and it fed upon the shame of repeated failures and the inability to admit this shame. Unfettered violence was a direct expression of the rage that came from bypassed shame. Trotha would not hear of changing course. He responded predictably to every new setback with rage and even more violence. His actions were less a product of rationally considered strategy, and more an expression of emotions like rage and, ultimately, hatred. The longer the war lasted, the more evident this became. The campaign quietly evolved into an end in itself, an exercise in working off aggression.

Various factors contributed to Trotha's predisposition for bypassing shame. To begin, he was a self-assured representative of the Wilhelmine elite. The contrast to Leutwein could not have been sharper. Leutwein did not abide by the emotional script of the era that distinguished an officer and "man of honor." He looked for root causes instead of taking action; he sought contact with the chiefs instead of responding with firepower; and he pled for "merciful warfare"[295] instead of demonstrating superior force. Trotha was utterly confounded that Leutwein, once demoted, could not "find the door."[296] Trotha was cut from a different cloth. He followed a "power script," reacting to negative emotions with anger and rage—particularly when he felt that a show of toughness was in order.[297]

This was compounded by the Germans' assurance that they were "acting in the name of a racial (or ethnic) and cultural superiority dogmatically affirmed."[298] The colonial masters saw the Herero as "savages," who sooner or later would have to succumb. Setbacks were almost inconceivable, even more so because Imperial Germany saw itself as a "victory culture." Such a well-trained army, which had achieved brilliant victories on the European continent against other great powers, would of course make quick work of these "backward" adversaries, in some cases no more than a few hundred men.[299] In this "small despicable Kaffir war," anything less than a total victory seemed unacceptable.[300] Leutwein was familiar with local conditions, and he had a more realistic idea of the opponent's strengths and the uncertainties that lay ahead. Tellingly, he was criticized for weakness and indecision. Trotha's proud ignorance and sense of absolute superiority reflected a kind of racism that was foreign to Leutwein. Trotha came much closer to the self-image of the distant metropole.

Trotha had assumed the command in SWA with the explicit goal of achieving total victory. Convinced of his own superiority, he made grandiose promises and repeated his intent to drown the uprising "in streams of blood and streams of money."[301] The latter did, in fact, flow rapidly into the colony under Trotha's command, even before the first shot was fired at the Waterberg. Preparations for the battle took months. Supply lines were extended at great expense in order to lay the groundwork for Trotha's intended operations. At the same time, he rarely missed an opportunity to show his contempt for the long-serving colonial officers. He made clear that the small wars they preferred did not represent "serious warfare."[302] At command headquarters, the "old Africans" encountered only ridicule.[303] Trotha had gone far out on a limb in all possible respects; he could not turn back without losing face. His own carelessness had artificially narrowed his room to maneuver.

Here we can clearly see the path dependency of events and how this emerged. Although it was increasingly evident that the Germans' chosen path would not lead to the desired goal, it could no longer be easily changed; this would have demanded too high a price—that is, a loss of prestige—for the responsible persons. Trotha preferred to cling to a misguided, murderous course of action rather than admit a mistake and his own fallibility. If the point was to demonstrate to superior strength, then such an admission was out of the question. His grandiose pronouncements bound him even tighter to his chosen course of action; any deviation would mean a loss of face.

"Campaign of Disappointments"

At least according to Trotha's exaggerated expectations, the fighting at the Waterberg ended in colossal failure. The supposedly "inferior natives" thwarted Trotha's plans and evaded encirclement. They outran the German sections and broke free to the east; the Germans succeeded only in stopping those who fled northeast. Stauffenberg recorded his impressions of the battle: "And no one from one section believed they would escape encirclement. They all felt completely beaten, and they were, too, so that the Hereros, the bush fighters, charged ahead with hurrahs and cries of victory, jeering loudly."[304] Some sections found themselves in such dire straits that they feared they would be wiped out entirely. The soldiers not only felt "completely beat," but also mocked by the opponent. Franke noted in his diary, "The conqueror trembled before the conquered. Disgrace upon disgrace!"[305]

In September, Hardenberg noted in his diary that there was "no talk of the punishment that would have been planned, and that they [the Herero] would have earned—namely, killing them. They're still alive, and they still have what's most precious to them, their cattle, except for a small number that were driven away."[306] Not only had the Germans failed to prove their superior might; they instead exposed their own weakness the longer the campaign dragged on with few signs of success. Only a few weeks after Hardenberg's diary entry, the mostly ineffectual pursuit was called off because the German troops could go no further. Trotha next tried "sealing off" the Omaheke, but this created such massive difficulties that the troops feared for their own survival. These circumstances showed yet again that the German colonial masters, despite their utmost efforts, could not even police their own borders.

Trotha ordered the pursuit immediately after the Battle of Waterberg, as the Herero withdrew. However, his chief of staff soon informed him that Deimling, who had been entrusted with the pursuit, had "not a single kernel of oats and no provisions." As was to be expected, Deimling called off the pursuit after only a few hours; his troops barely made it back to their original positions. Trotha noted the following in his diary on 13 August:

> I'm bowled over. And putting this 30 kilom. pursuit into motion, which makes sense only if they, that is, the H. can be caught, after their lead of at least 24 hrs. It's no joke. I thought they had 3 days of oats and rations; then I would have made it 4 days and would have gone to [name illegible]. So it was a straight 48 hrs wasted. Only to report home that we pursued for 30 kil. and could go no further. Ha. He was very piqued; I don't care. Now we can, or must, start from the beginning, or it's over. Now they at least have to be stopped from returning to the area. Encirclement is no longer possible . . . So be it! It looks like it will be too much for me.[307]

The passage is revealing in many respects. Trotha's words ("it's over") show how seriously he took the collapse of the pursuit. He saw that his plans had failed, and that the campaign could no longer continue as before. At the same time, his words offer insight into the emotions that this new setback provoked. The expression "I'm bowled over" (*Ich denke ich falle auf den Rücken*, literally "I think I'm falling on my back") deserves particular attention. *Auf den Rücken fallen* implies a state of shock or utter astonishment. In the present context, the expression indicates that the campaign had taken an unfavorable turn that Trotha had not foreseen, thwarting his plans. He was completely surprised by the development and sought to capture this in his diary. Even so, of all the possible—and perhaps more obvious—expressions he might have chosen, he opted for *auf den Rücken fallen*, which has additional connotations because of its concrete imagery. The words also imply an "implosion of the self"—a reaction characteristic of shame, "in which body functions have gone out of control."[308] *Auf den Rücken fallen* might be an expression of "unidentified" shame (as conceptualized by Helen Lewis), or a code word that registers the feeling of shame while simultaneously masking or deemphasizing it. Because Trotha was ill-equipped to acknowledge shame openly, he registered it with an unobjectionable phrase. He concluded his thoughts on 13 August with the sentence "It looks like it will be too much for me," thereby affirming his sense of being overwhelmed, and underscoring the experience of incompetence, which is the essence of shame.

Shame—or better, the fear of shame—also appears when Trotha anticipated reporting home "that we pursued for 30 kil. and could go no further," but he also spurned such an official acknowledgment of failure with a defiant "ha." What he entrusted to his diary was one thing; what he admitted to his superiors in Berlin was another. His refusal to accept failure, let alone to take responsibility for it, informed the following weeks of the campaign. Trotha pulled himself together quickly and even claimed victory in a telegram to Berlin,[309] which outraged his fellow soldiers. Deeply disturbed by Trotha's shamelessness, Stauffenberg wrote, "So much here is hollow and cowardly and pathetic. If you had only seen the faces of the soldiers when they read Trotha's victory telegram about the Waterberg battles."[310]

Trotha denied shame, a tendency that persisted and permanently defined the campaign. Acknowledging shame can be beneficial; seeing oneself through the eyes of others is an opportunity to rethink one's actions and to correct what "isn't working." Repressed shame, however, can be destructive; it seethes below the surface, combines with rage, and constantly regenerates. The self is unable to develop adequate coping behaviors. The rage that comes from bypassed shame knows no limits, typically affecting innocent victims instead of the actual source of shame. Behavior takes on obsessive and compulsive characteristics.[311]

As we have already seen, the failures did not stop at the Waterberg. Instead, this failure created a situation that could no longer be repaired, and that condemned all future operations to failure. The setbacks mounted, and hopes for a greater decisive battle were thwarted again and again. Although nearly everyone recognized that the pursuit was futile, it was not called off until the troops could go no further. The more desperate his aspirations became, the more stubbornly Trotha clung to them, and the fewer scruples he had in his interactions with the Herero.

The Herero were the primary targets of Trotha's rage, which hit them hardest. In September 1904, after Estorff again recommended peace talks, Trotha informed him that "everything will be shot dead."[312] Trotha's diction corresponded more to the logic of execution than to the logic of battle—an accurate reflection of the character that the campaign had in the meantime assumed. The general had not entirely given up hope for a larger battle, but this hope was illusory. The campaign was already turning into a small, or "degenerate," war, to borrow the terminology of Martin Shaw.[313] Schlieffen was disturbed by the diction that Trotha employed in his official reports. On 30 December 1904, Trotha noted with annoyance that Schlieffen had instructed him that "when Herero shoot back," he should wire "10 Herero fallen, not shot dead." So irritated was Trotha by Schlieffen's "childish" rebuke that he composed a new letter of resignation soon thereafter.[314]

Schlieffen's criticism was directed chiefly against Trotha's use of language, but it pointed to an important change that Schlieffen also eyed warily. Wars in general, and colonial wars in particular, are characterized by escalating violence—and this was especially true of the Herero campaign.[315] The use of force, usually by members of the military, typically includes "shooting opponents dead." However, this does not automatically mean that everything is allowed, or that all forms of killing are the same—not even in a small colonial war that is dominated by escalating violence.

An observation by the historian Jakob Vogel nicely illustrates this idea.[316] As Vogel suggests, the ongoing industrialization of war should have long since rendered the military parade—a holdover from the age of linear tactics—obsolete by the year 1900. Instead, military parades reflected the era's soldierly ideals by highlighting the "domestication and training of soldiers' physical and mental power," and by presenting self-control as a cardinal soldierly virtue. These criteria distinguished ideal, violent masculinity from its "raw" counterpart, which was discouraged. The duel brought this contrast into sharp relief. The private violence of "good society" was highly formalized and ritualistic, and *how* this violence was exercised was by no means incidental. More important than beating a rival was controlling one's emotions in the face of death and not losing composure.[317] Doing whatever it took to win was not permitted. Instead, duelists proved themselves as "men of honor" by maintaining their composure in the moment of greatest physical danger. In short, duels and parades were violent practices, or at least gestured in this direction, but their participants were subject to rules and limitations. "Raw" violence was frowned upon, but self-mastery and emotional control were hallmarks of violent practices that befit a soldier. Unlike duelists, Herero were not considered equal adversaries, nor were they protected by laws of war. Nevertheless, Trotha was still an Imperial general, and the Schutztruppe was still a German army—and so a certain comportment was expected of them, despite allowances for the difficult conditions overseas. Nevertheless, Trotha had discernably crossed boundaries: he was governed by emotion and aggression, and he would do almost anything[318] to bury the uprising for good.[319] His dispute with Schlieffen illuminates these circumstances particularly well.

The pursuit failed, setbacks mounted, and one disgrace followed another. Trotha's futile efforts fed upon themselves, becoming increasingly radical and providing ever more opportunities for shame and rage to explode into violence. These developments reached their sad climax on 2 October 1904. Confronted with the definitive failure of the pursuit, the general ordered his troops to shoot at all Herero from this point forward.

As we have seen, the proclamation and sealing off the Omaheke were measures born of weakness. Trotha attempted to appear powerful and dynamic in order to come to terms with a situation that was deeply unsatisfactory. Staying put on the western border of the Omaheke meant waiting (and, at most, reacting) for an indefinite period of time, as the Germans were not in a position to end the war themselves. The powerlessness was humiliating. "I'm so tired," the general noted in his diary on 30 September, acknowledging yet again how overwhelmed he felt.[320] As it became increasingly evident in the following weeks that the adopted measures might actually eradicate most of the Herero and "clean up" the situation once and for all, Trotha was only too eager to stay the course. The campaign had failed spectacularly, and—despite the Germans' readiness to make sacrifices and set scruples aside—they seemed to have lost control for good, and they feared that during the rainy season the fighting would flare up again. Trotha therefore accepted the final solution, which would erase the traces of failure. Once the measures were announced, he refused to retract them. Only intervention from Berlin eased the pressure of destruction.

Trotha's colleagues also felt his rage, if to a far lesser extent than the Herero. The conflicts were numerous. In particular, Trotha blamed the commander Hermann von der Heyde for the failure at the Waterberg. In his diary, Trotha called Heyde a shithead (*Scheißkerl*),[321] and he toyed with the idea of immediately relieving him of his command and court-martialing him.[322] Trotha repeatedly quarreled with Estorff. A disagreement in November with Mühlenfels, who was responsible for cordoning off the Omaheke, ultimately drove the section commander to resign.[323] Trotha also fell out with his chief of staff, Martin Chales de Beaulieu,[324] who departed in August, ostensibly because of a heart condition. Major Quade left the staff soon thereafter.[325] Trotha's rift with Leutwein is well-known.[326] Trotha also took issue with the colonial press, which sharply criticized his leadership and even accused him of censorship.[327]

When Trotha communicated with his superiors in Berlin, the component of shame became more prominent, while his rage abated considerably, at least with respect to the Kaiser, his "Supreme Commander." At the same time, he obsessed over the smallest nuances of Imperial telegrams, seeking to divine whether the Supreme Commander was satisfied with his performance. He saw contempt and rejection everywhere, perhaps not incorrectly.[328] Ashamed by the failure of his army, the Kaiser also responded with denial. Even when colonial officers came to visit, he would not allow any discussion of the military situation in the colony.[329] The development of operations upset the Kaiser so greatly that these could no longer be mentioned in his presence.[330] After the Kaiser had selected Trotha for the command post and personally sworn him in, their contact stopped. Trotha complained bitterly about this "inconsiderate" treatment; the "complete disregard" for his requests was incommensurate with his position.[331]

Schlieffen, who served as Trotha's intermediary with the Kaiser, became a target of Trotha's rage. Trotha derisively referred to Schlieffen in his diary as the "sad warrior."[332] Trotha was particularly sensitive when reproached by Schlieffen for his "colorless reporting," which he immediately took as criticism of the lack of results in his campaign.[333]

Trotha's conflict with Bülow was especially pointed. The undefined hierarchy between military and civil authorities was a constant source of disagreement. Trotha claimed primacy over Leutwein, who had been relieved of his command over the Schutztruppe, although he continued to serve as the colony's civilian governor until the end of 1904. Trotha did not, however, outrank Bülow, who—as we will see—was of one mind with Schlieffen and ultimately brought the Kaiser around to his position. Trotha demonstratively ignored Bülow's instructions, explaining that he, Trotha, had received the Kaiser's assurance that he was not subordinate to any civil authority, and that he would not budge on this point until hearing otherwise from the Kaiser. His defiance must have annoyed the Kaiser, especially since Bülow clearly could not have intervened without authorization.[334] The conflict reached its climax when Trotha sought to use Bülow's remarks to the Reichstag as a pretense for challenging him to a duel; only the Kaiser's veto stopped him.[335] By this point, the destructiveness and dysfunction of the general's behavior was abundantly clear; a duel would certainly have cast a strange light on the governance of Imperial Germany.

Many of Trotha's conflicts had been brewing for some time. These conflicts had structural causes (like his dispute with Leutwein), but they escalated only after the missed opportunity at the Waterberg. The general invested a great deal of energy in these disputes, which distracted from the actual problems he had been sent to address. The side conflicts solved little, and they only increased over time. After Trotha's departure, the *Windhuker Nachrichten* spoke for many contemporaries, declaring that "no tear" would be shed for him.[336]

The obsessive and compulsive aspects of Trotha's behavior are hard to overlook. Many of his contemporaries were hardly surprised that his single-minded focus on operations ended in failure. Leutwein had tirelessly explained the difficulties that such operations would encounter in SWA.[337] Trotha nevertheless clung to his plans, unswayed by all of the setbacks he was forced to accept. In a few rare moments, the futility of his efforts dawned on him.[338] However, he quickly overcame his doubts and found new resolve to catch and defeat the Herero. From mid-August through the end of the September, the German troops trudged from imaginary battlefield to imaginary battlefield, sometimes encountering "no armed, living Herero" anywhere.[339] The troops had few illusions about the futility of the pursuit. "We won't catch the Herero again, anyhow," Stuhlmann remarked in early September 1904.[340]

The operations not only seemed futile; they also exacted a high price. Rampant typhus thinned the ranks of the soldiers. "One grave after another in endless rows, the lazaretto tents were overcrowded, there was a shortage of real care and provisions," Malzahn noted.[341] Supplying the troops so far away from the railroad line had been "miserable" from the start, as Hardenberg remarked in September, but over time it got worse.[342]

Criticism of Trotha's leadership grew, even in the colony's interior. The Herero had not been beaten, and the territory they had once occupied was not yet "pacified." The *Deutsch-Südwestafrikanische Zeitung* complained that Trotha's campaign was being waged "at our own expense"; expulsion and annihilation destroyed the "property" of the colony: native labor and cattle.[343] Trotha's war—for critics like Paul Rohrbach, the "terrible product of rigid military doctrine"—threatened to ruin the colony completely.[344]

The cruelty and immoderation of Trotha's operations against the Herero became increasingly apparent. Adolf Fischer, who participated in the pursuit, later remarked that anyone who had been involved in these operations understood that "too much had happened here": "The haunted of the sandveld will have lost faith that there is still justice in the world."[345] The soldier Malzahn described the dramatic increase in Herero executions since September and then asserted, "We could not take it any longer in this horrid country."[346] He decided to leave the Schutztruppe. High-ranking officers also raised their voices against the cruelty of the fighting.

Trotha was indifferent to Herero suffering. Defending his approach with the assertion that "the Negro" only "bows to raw force," he underscored yet again the insurmountable distance and lack of understanding that separated the two camps.[347] Trotha's racism had already hardened these divisions and brought the campaign to an impasse; he continued to justify and rationalize his decision to remain on a dead-end path.

The general stubbornly held his course. This had been true for some time, but now that circumstances had changed fundamentally, there was growing reason to change direction. Trotha did not abandon the pursuit until it literally came to a standstill. He could not bring himself to admit that the operations had failed, although this was more or less obvious to everyone else. His diary entries show that he repeatedly found new confidence that he would catch the fleeing opponent.

Needless to say, this battle never came to pass. The last-ditch effort did, however, end the pursuit. Immediately thereafter, Trotha composed the proclamation and cordoned off the western edge of the Omaheke. His actions effectively documented that German power did not even extend to the colony's borders. Trotha's rage was great enough that he could not entirely mask it in the proclamation. Rather than justifying his measures to the Herero, he instead reproached them: "They have murdered and stolen, cut off the ears and noses and other body parts of wounded soldiers, and *now out of cowardice refuse to fight.*"

Sealing off the desert was an essentially passive and static measure, yet it plainly overwhelmed the capabilities of the troops far away from the railroad line. The measure had no foreseeable end, particularly since the "firing order" hardened the fronts and made the status quo difficult to alter. Less than two weeks after the proclamation and cordoning took effect, Stuhlmann noted in his diary, "The most reasonable thing would be to come to an official peace agreement soon."[348]

Sealing off the Omaheke caused a falling-out between Trotha and Mühlenfels, commander of the troops assigned with this task.[349] On 16 November, Trotha wrote in his diary that Mühlenfels had wired that "he has no more provisions; everyone is war-weary,"[350] and that he, Trotha, had renewed the order to continue the war "without deliberation."[351] The grievances only intensified, but Trotha refused to give in, or even to listen to the complaints. Mühlenfels asked to be relieved from his post, as "he could no longer assume responsibility for the troops because of provisions and sickness. Scurvy is taking a toll, and typhus won't stop." In the end, Trotha let Mühlenfels decide whether he would stay or go, but this much was unmistakable: "My orders will stay in effect and basta!"[352] Mühlenfels decided to give up his command, but he withdrew his resignation upon hearing about the intervention from Berlin on 8 December; Trotha was directed to retract the proclamation and pardon any Herero who voluntarily surrendered.[353] On 11 December, Trotha noted in his diary, "After hearing the news that the gang is to be negotiated with, Mühlenfels suddenly wants to stay. Strange!"[354] It is difficult to say whether Mühlenfels's concern for his own soldiers, who barely survived the strains of sealing off the desert, also extended to the Herero. We do know that Mühlenfels did not agree with Trotha's approach, and that he was unwilling to assume responsibility for it.[355] After hearing about the intervention from Berlin, Frankenberg reported that among the officers there was "naturally great joy; Fiedler donated 2 bottles of red wine."[356] There was widespread relief, if not joy, at the retraction of the proclamation and the strategy it represented. Many officers believed that this step was long overdue. For all of the complaints and problems suffered by the officers and troops, it took an order from Berlin to stop this ill-advised, murderous, and even self-destructive course of action.

Summary and Conclusions

The particularities of colonial wars notwithstanding, the campaign against the Herero remained limited for some time, and during this period annihilation retained its "conventional" meaning. Trotha initially sought to accomplish what Leutwein had not; his operations at the foot of the Waterberg, and in the weeks thereafter, sought to annihilate the Herero *militarily*.

Although the escalation in violence was clearly associated with the person of Lothar von Trotha, we cannot say that the change in command per se marked the genocidal turning point of the campaign. Escalation was in no way inevitable; it was the result of failed original plans and Trotha's attempts to deal with this failure. The colonial masters were so sure of their own superiority that they had not considered this contingency. What the military officers saw as failure (although their opponent was, in fact, devastated) was all the more intolerable because they saw themselves as part of a "victory culture." Trotha had no trouble issuing grandiose pronouncements, which made abandoning his original goals that much more difficult. Measured by the expectations that he had set for himself, the situation after the fighting at the Waterberg was downright shameful—but shame was an admission of weakness that he was not prepared to make. Instead, he wired reports of victory back to Germany and nursed the illusion that more great battles would follow. As the chances for victory receded, bypassed shame joined subliminally with rage and erupted in violence. The consequences were devastating. As the pursuit wore on and exposed the limits of German power, the situation became increasingly precarious. The general clung ever more stubbornly to his maximum goals, believing that compromises made from a position of weakness would only result in "false peace." His intransigence grew. After "conventional" annihilation failed, Trotha turned to permanent expulsion. Yet even the most dedicated "terrorism" could not uphold a blockade that exceeded the long-term capacity of the troops. As we will see, Schlieffen endorsed the idea of expulsion, but he also recognized that Trotha "did not have the power to enforce it."[357] This powerlessness, witnessed by metropolitan peers, produced shame and rage. Once it began to appear as if "terrorism" might actually eradicate the remaining Herero in the Omaheke, Trotha would no longer change course.[358]

Although official strategy remained unchanged for some time, the weeks of the pursuit ushered in significant changes underneath the surface. "One large operation"[359] fell apart, degenerating into a small war that soon spared no one. Trotha's diction reflected this change. As the futility of his actions became more and more evident, his language grew increasingly bloodthirsty and coarse.

At first, Trotha's racism was expressed primarily in an insurmountable divide between Germans and Herero. To the extent that this sealed the alienation between the two warring parties, its effects on the war were devastating. Trotha prohibited otherwise typical diplomatic communications and completely ignored the Herero. Upon assuming the command, he felt too strong to compromise with the opponent. A few months later, he felt too weak to do so. One way or another, his rejection of communication and dialogue with the Herero showed the distance between himself and Leutwein.

There was something more, however, that distinguished Trotha's behavior from that of his predecessor from the very beginning—a desire to hurt and punish, as seen in his insistence on the primacy of violence and teaching the Herero a lesson. His excesses were, at first, still domesticated militarily. An overwhelming "conventional" victory that put down the uprising and restored German honor would have been enough to satisfy Trotha. Without this victory, however, Trotha increasingly distanced himself from the official military codes that had once restrained him, and his rage and aggression went unchecked. Adopting the language of execution, he demonstrated how little the campaign had come to resemble "battle" in the traditional sense.

Trotha's diction radicalized alongside his course of action, which depended upon a constellation that was no longer determined by the Germans alone. The triad of subjugation, expulsion, and extermination describes both the progression of Trotha's strategy and a crescendo of racial distancing. At first, Trotha simply *ignored* the Herero, denying them the right to act or be treated as a legitimate warring party. Thus, even a speedy victory would not have restored the conditions before the war. Rather, Trotha's desire to imprison the captured Herero suggests that their subjugation would have led to active desocialization and deculturization, or "social murder."[360] Under these circumstances, many Herero would have escaped with their lives—but little else. Expulsion, the second strategy, sought to make the Herero disappear; "terrorism" was supposed to compel them to leave "German" territory forever. This led seamlessly to the third strategy: extermination. "Terrorism" ultimately meant that all Herero unlucky enough to cross paths with German units would be killed, while the rest would be left to suffer and die on the other side of the German border. In the end, this is how Trotha sought to make the Herero disappear for good. The crescendo of racial distancing was distinguished by an increasingly radical desire to do harm; extermination was its climax.

Trotha was not merely reluctant to change course once he understood the devastating consequences that his actions would have for the Herero. By this point, he *wanted* their extermination and pursued it with all his might, as their continued existence on the other side of the border was testament to his failure. The disappearance of the Herero would effectively negate the previous setbacks of the campaign.

Like all narratives of the war, this one, too, risks rationalizing and instrumentalizing violence and cruelty. The will to annihilate was primarily an expression of emotions like rage and hatred, and so the associated coping behaviors were less directed toward achieving external goals, and more toward venting these emotions. Since rage and hatred derived from *bypassed* shame, the role of conscious decision-making was relatively small. We should not be swayed by Trotha's own rationalizations for his actions. Means-end calculations did not lead to him to exterminate the Herero; rather, he raised such considerations only after the fact in order to justify his actions. The shame-rage mechanism can explain how originally "conventional" operations turned into a genocidal campaign of annihilation—regardless of whether the start of the genocidal phase is pinpointed before or after the proclamation.

As far as I can see, the Herero genocide is the only one of its kind that was largely executed by a state organization, a regular army. To this extent, the genocide may be broadly considered a state crime. However, the genocidal escalation of violence was less a product of the state organization and its routines—the "cult of militarism," as Isabel Hull suggests. Rather, the escalation had more to do with the person of the commander-in-chief and his milieu.[361] Trotha's ability to act for so long as he saw fit, without outside political interference, was a result of the particular relationship between military and civil authorities in Prussian and German military culture. However, this culture merely provided the framework for military leadership, which could have been exercised in very different ways. Regardless of the greater responsibility and pressure to act that accompanied the post of commander-in-chief, it is difficult to imagine that violence would have reached the same dimensions under a Leutwein or Estorff. The fact that Trotha was not relieved of his command, even after authorities in Berlin agreed that he had gone too far, is just as difficult to understand as his behavior itself. He apparently did not go far enough that his behavior was considered "abnormal," or that he had to be dismissed. For all of his idiosyncrasies, I contend that Trotha was still a recognizable agent of a particular ethos and milieu, and that his superiors acknowledged this status.[362] This may initially seem surprising, insofar as the commander-in-chief's actions were determined by a traditional, class-oriented logic that, in some respects, ran counter to the expectations of a commanding general in a modern state army. My contention is that the extreme emotional energy that informed Trotha's command and his disagreements with others had less to do with colonial politics, and more with his sense of responsibility to the ethos of his class, which increasingly saw itself as under threat.

Class-oriented logic does not necessarily correspond with the interests of the state; defending one's "honor" usually leads to unsanctioned violence.[363] This was also true of the Wilhelmine elite, although the right, or duty, to take matters into one's own hands was limited to precisely defined situations and was expected to follow strict rules. In general, only elite social peers were considered *satisfaktionsfähig*—literally, "able to demand and give satisfaction in a duel"; the exercise of violence was highly ritualized.[364] There is an inarguable rationality to defending one's honor and not tolerating an affront, as Pierre Bourdieu shows through the example of Kabyle society; anyone who abides by this maxim acquires a corresponding reputation, which intimidates potential aggressors and protects against future challenges.[365] This applies, however, only to a certain type of society. Societies without central authority provide the social space for "honor." Social actors must be willing to resort to violence in order to promote justice, and they alone are responsible for protecting their possessions and other society members from hostile assaults. The German upper classes around the year 1900 were no longer in this situation. To the contrary—their "affairs of honor" breached the established state monopoly of the exercise of violence, as numerous contemporary critics tirelessly repeated. Sovereigns had long sought to prohibit these feuds in order to keep the peace.[366]

Statehood in Imperial Germany was highly developed in many respects, but it concealed and tolerated elements of an earlier, premodern era.[367] Dueling was originally a privilege of the military aristocracy. Dueling underscored these elites' outstanding political role by placing them above the law in certain circumstances.[368] Wilhelm I and his grandson Wilhelm II were especially attentive to military interests, and they protected and cultivated this "simultaneity of the nonsimultaneous" (*Gleichzeitigkeit des Ungleichzeitigen*).[369] The institution of the duel continued uninterrupted until the end of the Imperial era, and it even expanded into wider, bourgeois circles. As Niklas Luhmann has noted, the prevalence of dueling shows that "order had already been overstepped"; in many circumstances, "the means became the end," and duels were "sought, provoked, or compelled out of proportion to the offense." Since dueling had already lost its structural significance, there was a growing tendency to celebrate this elite interaction as an end in itself.[370] "Affairs of honor" provided a symbolic surrogate for the privileged status of the aristocracy that was now under threat. In light of the powerful social changes that were transforming Wilhelmine society, the longer-term status of traditional elites was no longer assured.

Trotha was a typical representative of the old order, and he defended it doggedly. The circumstances of his appointment as commander-in-chief are telling. Nikolaus Ritter von Endres, the Bavarian military representative in Berlin, reported that Trotha was a personal favorite of the Kaiser—although his appointment was rejected by the chief of the General Staff, the Imperial chancellor, the minister of war, and the director of the Colonial Department.[371] Despite their resistance, Wilhelm decided in Trotha's favor. Why did he make this decision on his own? With some sarcasm, Bülow later described Trotha as a "dashing guardsman" (*schneidiger Gardeinfanterist*).[372] According to Estorff, Trotha was "a fine, handsome soldier, and his self-assured demeanor gave the impression that he could do many things. He was, however, a man of superficiality and pretense."[373] Trotha seems to have possessed what was then called "dash" (*Schneid*), a key military and aristocratic criterion for human potential.[374] Wilhelm II was apparently receptive to the "masculine eroticism" that Trotha embodied.[375] Trotha's martial rhetoric likewise showed "dash." Since the Kaiser sought an officer who was committed enough to put down the uprising "by all means," Trotha must have seemed like the right man for the job.

The Kaiser entrusted Trotha with this important command, even though he did not fit the usual model of a commanding general. Unlike Leutwein or Estorff, Trotha had never attended the War Academy,[376] and he had no General Staff experience. Members of the General Staff were trained specialists (an essentially bourgeois ideal), but Trotha was more of a warhorse; he gained his experience in the field as a petty officer during the wars of unification. Most of Trotha's peers had attended a cadet academy, where young men were schooled early in "camaraderie": the "virtue of taking part and fitting in."[377] But, stated in terms that are familiar to us today, Trotha was an alpha male, not a team player. This may have been what Hermann von Wissmann meant when he later called Trotha a "bad comrade."[378] Trotha embodied an ultra-masculine ideal that had gradually outlived its relevance in modern society.[379] This ideal was especially evident in Trotha's relentless emphasis on strength, particularly in difficult situations, and also in his desire for independence, which he had insisted upon before accepting the command from the Kaiser. The same steeliness that won him the favor of the Kaiser drove him to fight "his" war (to the bitter end) according to his own principles. He refused to defer to others, particularly civil authority.

Bülow and Schlieffen were Trotha's peers. His ethos could not have been foreign to them, but their reservations and scruples made the general suspicious and resentful. Unlike Trotha, they were used to handling political and military power in a differentiated way. Bülow, for example, never lost sight of how Germany's wars affected foreign policy, and he demanded a minimum of "compliance" from the commander-in-chief.[380] Schlieffen, an officer himself, was willing to weigh means and ends against one another and ultimately pled for changing course.[381] Trotha was unwilling to compromise because he saw only *one* way to win the war. Paradoxically, the further away from his goal that his chosen path led, the less likely he was to change course.

The victories that Trotha expected did not come, and he found himself fighting a losing battle. He did not accept his fate, but reared against it. There were substantive reasons for his conflict with Bülow, but Trotha ostentatiously rejected "formal rationality" as a means of resolution. Instead, he turned to the duel—the old "trial by battle," where the stronger party had a chance to force his will on a (physically) weaker opponent.[382] The Kaiser, however, prohibited the duel and settled the conflict without it. The Kaiser restricted the logic that informed Trotha's actions, but he did not declare it invalid. As we will see in the pages ahead, the general was not recalled, nor did he receive orders for a radical change in course that would have made him lose face. Authorities in Berlin may have felt that Trotha had gone too far, but his behavior apparently remained within the realm of what was still considered normal and tolerable. Trotha's behavior was the product of an ethos that was antiquated in some respects, but still enjoyed a certain fundamental esteem. For all of the setbacks and difficulties that Trotha underwent, he was allowed to retain his command until the end of 1905. His colleagues' objections were apparently not strong enough to merit a dishonorable dismissal.

George Steinmetz has rightly emphasized that Trotha's turn to genocidal strategy was "overdetermined," and that it possessed a social dimension.[383] The considerable emotional energy that Trotha invested in defending his course of action, and the numerous conflicts that his defense engendered, had less to do with South-West Africa, and more with Trotha as a person. He fought less to retain overseas possessions than to defend his lifeworld, which he rightly saw as threatened—but he failed in this respect, too.

Notes

1. Trotha to Leutwein (5 November 1904), BArch. R1001/2089, pp. 100–1.
2. Leutwein to the Great General Staff (9 [?] March 1904), BArch. R1001/2112, p. 179.
3. "Der Aufstand," *DSWAZ*, 19 January 1904, 1.
4. Eradication was not considered seriously at first, but it was an option. Leutwein dismissed the voices of those who wanted to see the Herero "completely annihilated from now on" as "ill-advised." See Leutwein to the Colonial Department (23 February 1904), BArch. R1001/2113, p. 90. Discussions about the fate of the Witbooi fighters in October 1904 revealed no fundamental opposition to expulsion or deportation. Leutwein proposed the idea of deportation himself. On 11 October 1904, immediately after establishing that the Witbooi had declared war, Leutwein informed his commanders by telegram that they were to disarm the Witbooi combatants who had fought with the Germans and were still in the field, so that they could be deported to Cameroon as soon as possible. See NAN ZBU D.IV.M.2, vol. 1: Ausbruch der Witbooi-Unruhen.
5. Leutwein to the Imperial Chancellor (25 May 1904), BArch. R1001/2114, p. 223.
6. Trotha to the Great General Staff (copy to the Imperial Chancellor) (25 June 1904), BArch. R1001/2115, p. 78.
7. Because the plan of attack failed, the great battle broke into many smaller skirmishes, including around the Hamakari watering holes several kilometers south of the Waterberg. Herero-speaking Namibians, in particular, do not see the Waterberg as a key symbol of the war of 1904. See Förster, *Erinnerungslandschaften*, 125. I refer to the "Battle of Waterberg" only for the sake of linguistic simplicity.
8. Selous, *Sunshine and Storm*, 67; Lothar von Trotha, "Politik und Kriegführung," 1.
9. Lewis, *Shame and Guilt in Neurosis*; and Scheff and Retzinger, *Emotions and Violence*.
10. Großer Generalstab, *Die Kämpfe der deutschen Truppen*, vol. 1, 23.
11. Ibid., 25. The Beurlaubtenstand was comprised of furloughed reservists and Landwehr men.
12. Großer Generalstab, *Die Kämpfe der deutschen Truppen*, vol. 1, 26–27.
13. Else Sonnenberg, *Wie es am Waterberg zuging: Ein Originalbericht von 1904 zur Geschichte des Herero-Aufstandes in Deutsch-Südwestafrika* (Wendeburg, 2004), 61ff.
14. Großer Generalstab, *Die Kämpfe der deutschen Truppen*, vol. 1, 26.
15. Schwabe, *Der Krieg in Deutsch-Südwestafrika*, 45.
16. Ibid., 120.
17. Großer Generalstab, *Die Kämpfe der deutschen Truppen*, vol. 1, 28.
18. Stülpnagel, *Heiße Tage*, 9 and 31.
19. Ibid., 30–31.
20. Admiralstab der Marine, *Die Tätigkeit des Landungskorps S.M.S. "Habicht" während des Herero-Aufstandes Januar/Februar 1904* (Berlin, 1905), 1–2.
21. Ibid., 7.
22. Ibid., 3 and 6.
23. Ibid., 7. Gudewill decided that the six hundred workers posed a "direct danger to Swakopmund" and corralled them onto steamships. Half were deemed inessential for the railroad repairs, so they were sent to Cape Town to labor in mines.
24. Ibid., 10–11.
25. Großer Generalstab, *Die Kämpfe der deutschen Truppen*, vol. 1, 60.
26. The reasoning behind this decision was that the corps could be assembled and sent overseas faster than yet-to-be-organized volunteer units of the Schutztruppe.
27. Ibid., 59–60.

28. Admiralstab der Marine, *Die Tätigkeit des Landungskorps S.M.S. "Habicht,"* 11.
29. Großer Generalstab, *Die Kämpfe der deutschen Truppen*, vol. 1, 35ff., 47, and 56.
30. Ibid., 57.
31. Nuhn, *Sturm über Südwest*, 95.
32. "Aus Swakopmund," *DSWAZ*, 10 January 1906, 1.
33. Franke, *Tagebücher*, 373.
34. Häussler, "Soldatische Hinterwäldler oder Avantgarde?," 322ff.
35. The Marine Infantry consisted exclusively of volunteers who committed to three (rather than the usual two) years of service, which contributed to its elite status. Its members were considered as loyal and highly motivated as those in the renowned Guards Corps. Marine Infantry commanders could operate independently with their battalions—an authority otherwise reserved for colonels. See Eckard Michels, *"Der Held von Deutsch-Ostafrika": Paul von Lettow-Vorbeck: Ein preußischer Offizier* (Paderborn, 2008), 105.
36. The Kaiser gave a speech honoring the accomplishments of (just) the Marine Infantry at the battle near Otjihanamaparero on 25 February 1904, although they had fought alongside other Schutztruppe units and under the leadership of local officers. The Kaiser stated, "The Marine Infantry has thus added a new leaf to the old ones in the wreath of glory that it has acquired in recent years. As a sign of my special appreciation for the Marine Infantry, after the conclusion of the campaign I will bestow streamers [*Fahnenbänder*] with the name of the battle. As a further sign of my appreciation, I am asking his Royal Highness, the Grand Duke of Hesse, to accept a Marine Infantry commission à la suite." See "Vermischtes," *DSWAZ*, 12 April 1904, 2.
37. Admiralstab der Marine, *Das Marine-Expeditionskorps in Südwest-Afrika*, 1.
38. Michels, *"Der Held von Deutsch-Ostafrika,"* 105.
39. Alexander Sydney Kanya-Forstner, *The Conquest of the Western Sudan: A Study in French Military Imperialism* (London, 1969), 13.
40. Nuhn, *Sturm über Südwest*, 105.
41. Admiralstab der Marine, *Das Marine-Expeditionskorps in Südwest-Afrika*, 1–6.
42. Ibid., 2.
43. Großer Generalstab, *Die Kämpfe der deutschen Truppen*, vol. 1, 68.
44. Trotha diary, TA 122/17, 13 July 1904. Next to the Order of the Black Eagle, the Pour le Mérite was Prussia's highest military honor.
45. Großer Generalstab, *Die Kämpfe der deutschen Truppen*, vol. 1, 116.
46. Trotha diary, TA 122/17, 13 July 1904.
47. Leutwein was convinced that the uprising would not have occurred had he not left Windhuk and traveled south. See Trotha diary, TA 122/15, 22 June 1904. Even an "old African" like Ludwig von Estorff, who, like Leutwein, had been in South-West Africa (with some interruptions) since 1894, lauded the governor's integrity while also acknowledging his hubris. Leutwein had trusted too deeply in the "impression made by his own personality," while overlooking the "high degree" of dissatisfaction among the Herero; he believed that he could resolve all of the tensions himself. See Estorff, *Wanderungen und Kämpfe*, 114. Leutwein probably assumed that, upon his return, he could quickly stifle the uprising.
48. Leutwein to the Colonial Department (28 January 1904), BArch. R1001/2112, p. 156.
49. The naval expeditionary corps had already reached Swakopmund on 9 February. The corps were accompanied by a sixty-man section of railroad troops. In addition, the Kaiser had ordered five hundred Schutztruppe reinforcements. These transports departed on 30 January and 2 February. See Großer Generalstab, *Die Kämpfe der deutschen Truppen*, vol. 1, 59.

50. A point of further concern was Leutwein's letter to Samuel Maharero and his headmen, which he sent after returning from the south. Leutwein was immediately prohibited from engaging in negotiations, which had previously been integral to his conduct of diplomacy and warfare.
51. Großer Generalstab, *Die Kämpfe der deutschen Truppen*, vol. 1, 62.
52. Ibid.
53. Ibid., 62–63.
54. Leutwein to the Colonial Department (19 March 1904), BArch. R1001/2114, p. 158.
55. Leutwein, *Elf Jahre Gouverneur*, 501.
56. Großer Generalstab, *Die Kämpfe der deutschen Truppen*, vol. 1, 71.
57. Franke, *Tagebücher*, 351; and Nuhn, *Sturm über Südwest*, 131.
58. Großer Generalstab, *Die Kämpfe der deutschen Truppen*, vol. 1, 76.
59. Nuhn, *Sturm über Südwest*, 132.
60. Ibid., 118.
61. Großer Generalstab, *Die Kämpfe der deutschen Truppen*, vol. 1, 85ff.
62. Leutwein, *Elf Jahre Gouverneur*, 511.
63. Großer Generalstab, *Die Kämpfe der deutschen Truppen*, vol. 1, 90ff.
64. Ibid., 102–3.
65. Ibid., 103.
66. Ibid., 109.
67. Leutwein could not fully identify with the course of action that Berlin expected him to adopt, as his formulation of a request for reinforcements shows: "For the complete defeat, *as is expected*, 800 troopers and 2 cavalry batteries 96 still needed." See Leutwein to the General Staff (9 March 1904), BArch. R1001/2112, p. 179 (emphasis added).
68. For a contrasting assessment, see Bridgman, *The Revolt of the Hereros*, 105.
69. Schwabe, *Der Krieg in Deutsch-Südwestafrika*, 215.
70. Callwell, *Small Wars*, 195.
71. François, *Kriegführung in Südafrika*, 41.
72. Leutwein to the General Staff (25 April 1904), BArch. R1001/2114, pp. 52–53. Leutwein may still have hoped to receive an expression of confidence from the General Staff. When this was not forthcoming, and his superiors instead named a successor, Leutwein was slow to relinquish power. The Berlin authorities seem to have believed that Leutwein would give up his position as governor, and even leave the colony altogether, once he was dismissed as commander-in-chief. Instead, Leutwein assured the Imperial chancellor, "I will not announce my intent to return to Germany once Herr von Trotha has arrived." Instead, he intended to stand by Trotha's side, "insofar as this is desired by him." See Leutwein to the Imperial Chancellor (12 May 1904), BArch. R1001/2114, p. 146. Leutwein's presence became a source of tension that intensified over the following months. After a major dispute, Trotha all but asked Leutwein to leave the colony, but Leutwein kept delaying his departure. On 17 November 1904, Trotha reported on yet another meeting with Leutwein (TA 122/16): "He [Leutwein] comes at 11, in black coat and top hat, and . . . depicts . . . the danger in the south as very great for Keetmanshoop, and he fears the worst there. Then he repeats that he has, of course, remained unconditionally subordinate to me, and then he offers to remain here as the leader in the south; in short, he can't find the door. Every day, he wants to stay at least 14 days more. Good, if that's what he wants, I'll travel more; but a longer stay is out of the question. *C'est trop tard madame!*"
73. Großer Generalstab, *Die Kämpfe der deutschen Truppen*, vol. 1, 127 and 133.
74. After Captain Puder discovered another group of around one thousand Herero fighters in the Otjimbingwe district, Leutwein requested eight hundred further reinforcements, which seemed necessary for "complete subjugation, as is expected." See Leutwein to the General Staff (9 March 1904), BArch. R1001/2112, p. 179.

75. Admiralstab der Marine, *Das Marine-Expeditionskorps in Südwest-Afrika*, 18.
76. Leutwein to the Colonial Department (19 January 1904), BArch. R1001/2114, pp. 158–59.
77. For military leaders used to independence, the expanded operations demanded new "discipline" and subordination to a central command. Franz Epp, who served under the "old African" Ludwig von Estorff, noted in his diary on 11 May 1904, "V. Estorff would like to wage *orlog* [war] on his own, as far away as possible from headquarters; that he can't be reached is just his way." See Eckl, *"S'ist ein übles Land hier,"* 245. Leutwein seems to have accepted Estorff's independence, despite the changing expectations of the central command. Epp wrote, "Major v. Estorff does not seem to have a particular assignment, he is able to act as circumstances demand." Leutwein's telegrams to Berlin show that he left Estorff room to maneuver, but also that he expected Estorff to follow orders. Leutwein wired the Imperial chancellor and Great General Staff on 22 March 1904: "Estorff has been ordered to cooperate with the Main Section. He knows that it will not be ready for battle until early April and will act accordingly" (BArch. R1001/2113, p. 34). On 22 May 1904, Leutwein informed the Schutztruppe command in Berlin that "Estorff has strict instructions to wait and cooperate with the Main Section, but also to stay in contact with the enemy as far as possible and to work together with Volkmann" (BArch. R1001/2114, p. 209).
78. Leutwein to the Colonial Department (19 March 1904), BArch. R1001/2114, pp. 158–59.
79. On 13 July 1904, Trotha noted in his diary, "Telegram from Estorff at 8, the prisoners say Salatiel does not want to participate anymore, he's ordered his people to sit tight at the Waterberg and refused to fight for Samuel. This won't help him at all—caught together, hanged together (*mit gefangen, mit gehangen*)."
80. This was a flashpoint in the disputes between Leutwein and Trotha, which take up an entire file in the Federal Archive ("Aufstände in Deutsch-Südwestafrika 1904.— Differenzen zwischen Generalleutnant Lothar v. Trotha und Gouverneur Theodor Gotthilf Leutwein über das Verhältnis von militärischen und politischen Maßnahmen," BArch. R1001/2089).
81. See, for example, Trotha to Schlieffen (4 October 1904), BArch. R1001/2089, p. 6.
82. The text reads, "Proclamation to the Herero people. Hereros! After you have risen against your master and protector, the German Kaiser, and shot at soldiers, you know to expect nothing other than a fight to the death. But *you* could stop before this, by coming over to me, turning in your weapons and ammunition, and awaiting your assigned punishment. However, it is well known to me that many of you bear no guilt for all of the evil things that have happened. And these can come to me safely; I can spare their lives. However, I can show no mercy to those who have murdered white people and plundered their homes. These will be brought before a court and must accept the price of their guilt. But the rest of you who are not laden with such guilt, be smart, and do not bind your fate any longer to those who are guilty. Leave them and save your lives! This I say to you, as the representative of your supreme master, the German Kaiser. Okahandja, 30 May 1904. Signed Leutwein, Imperial Governor" (BArch. R1001/2015, p. 111, emphasis in original). On 22 June 1904, Trotha noted in his diary (TA 122/15), "Another meeting with Leutwein. He's arguing for merciful combat, so a proclamation could be issued to the mob before the start of the offensive, securing a pardon for those who already want to defect. The proclamation was written by the Obladen pastor and rather dull. I'm against it." See Andreas Eckl, Matthias Häussler, and Jekura Kavari, "Oomambo wandje komuhoko wOvaherero: Lothar von Trotha's 'Words to the Ovaherero People,'" *Journal of Namibian Studies* 23 (2018): 125–33. This article was reprinted in English translation as "Oomambo wandje komuhoko wOvaherero: Lothar von Trotha's 'Words to the Ovaherero Peo-

ple,'" in *Nuanced Considerations: Recent Voices in Namibian-German Colonial History*, ed. Wolfram Hartmann (Windhoek, 2019), 109–16.

83. On 16 June 1904, the general scornfully remarked in his diary (TA 122/15), "He [Leutwein] is said to have been very upset about my first telegram 'I order,' wanting to depart without delay. But he would still like to remain governor. Aside from this, he seems not to know what he wants."

84. On 11 June 1904, the day of his arrival in the colony, Trotha noted in his diary (TA 122/15), "Glasenapp brought us news from Leutwein. The day before yesterday he headed out from Okahandja, advancing toward the Hereros on the Omurambo-u-Omatako in a strongly fortified position in the bush. He wants to pull in Estorff. So again, it's the same aimless thing. Why now, when I've set foot in the colony. If he wanted to crown his head with laurels, why not 14 days earlier? Happily, he could still receive my order by telegraph to stop right away. I don't put up with such things. I also immediately wired this decision back home." On 12 June, he wired the Great General Staff that when he had arrived in Swakopmund, Leutwein was advancing toward the Waterberg with all of his forces, and that he, Trotha, had ordered him not to seek a decisive battle (R1001/2115, p. 21).

85. Trotha to the Great General Staff (copy to the Imperial Chancellor) (25 June 1904), BArch. R1001/2115, p. 78.

86. The directive stated, "2. I [Trotha] will attack the enemy . . . with all sections simultaneously, in order to annihilate him." Quoted in Großer Generalstab, *Die Kämpfe der deutschen Truppen*, vol. 1, 157.

87. "Metropolitanization" informed Trotha's colonial service from the very beginning. Friedrich von Schele, governor and commander of the Schutztruppe in German East Africa between 1892/93 and 1895, mistrusted long-serving colonial officers; after years of relative independence, they lacked "tight control and discipline." Schele believed that local networks undermined the authority of bureaucratic hierarchies in the homeland. For this reason, he did not appoint a Schutztruppe officer to the position of deputy commander, but rather pushed for a high-ranking army officer, Lieutenant Colonel Lothar von Trotha. By abolishing the Afrikanische Anciennität (the automatic seniority of officers who had served in the colony, introduced by Hermann von Wissmann), Schele sought to break the esprit de corps of the Schutztruppe officers, integrating them more closely into the officer corps of the home army. See Tanja Bührer, *Die Kaiserliche Schutztruppe für Deutsch-Ostafrika: Koloniale Sicherheitspolitik und transkulturelle Kriegführung 1885 bis 1918* (Munich, 2011), 172.

88. Trotha diary, TA 122/17, 20 July 1904.

89. Eckl, *"S'ist ein übles Land hier,"* 279. Stuhlmann made similar remarks. See NAN, Private Accessions, A.0109, p. 74.

90. This phrase turns up frequently. See, for example, Trotha to Leutwein (5 November 1904), BArch. R1001/2089, p. 101.

91. Paul von Lettow-Vorbeck, *Mein Leben* (Biberach, 1957), 77.

92. Bayer, *Mit dem Hauptquartier in Südwestafrika*, 134.

93. Häussler, "Soldatische Hinterwäldler oder Avantgarde?," 309ff.

94. Gertrud Marchand-Volz, ed., *Werner Freiherr Schenck v. Stauffenberg: Von München nach Deutsch-Südwestafrika* (Göttingen, 1998), 137.

95. Trotha often referred to the Herero contemptuously as a "gang" or "mob" (*Bande*), which underscores his view that they were not equal adversaries. See, for example, Trotha diary, TA 122/15, 16 June 1904.

96. Trotha diary, TA 122/17, 22 July 1904.

97. Bayer, *Mit dem Hauptquartier in Südwestafrika*, 139. By comparison, divisions of nearly twenty thousand men controlled front lines that were between three-and-

a-half and five-and-a-half kilometers long in World War I. See Anthony Ashworth, *Trench Warfare 1914–1918: The Live and Let Live System* (Basingstoke, 2000), 9.
98. According to Clausewitz, operating on outermost lines was always disadvantageous, except under special conditions such as "psychological or physical superiority." See Clausewitz, *Vom Kriege*, 679 (Clausewitz, *On War*, 346). These conditions did not seem to be present at the Waterberg, which made the battle plan especially daring.
99. The General Staff report explained that the initial plan was not to "unite all forces for *one* great strike," but rather to engage in a "series of individual skirmishes." Each section would push the opponent "into the guns of another section, which then would have to complete the victory." The opponent would dig into a "strongly fortified position," and "the concentric advance would ultimately unite the forces." See Großer Generalstab, *Die Kämpfe der deutschen Truppen*, vol. 1, 137.
100. After the battles, Frankenberg reported that a "great depression" set in at the section camp. Heyde thought that he had lost all of his officers, so he celebrated each one who returned. See Frankenberg diary, NAN, AACRLS.070, p. 100 (11 August 1904).
101. Drechsler, *Südwestafrika unter deutscher Kolonialherrschaft*, 183.
102. This variation of the genocide thesis sometimes relies on fictional texts such as Gustav Frenssen's novel *Peter Moors Fahrt nach Südwest*, which transformed Trotha's campaign into a triumphant victory. See Benz, "Kolonialpolitik als Genozid," 30. The General Staff report of 1906 provided an official version of events, but it was also a self-portrait. It tended to downplay loss of control, incompetence, and failure, presenting the operations as an overall success. See Eckl, *"S'ist ein übles Land hier,"* 18. This is the context for the oft-cited passage that Trotha "completed the work of annihilation" by "sealing off" the Omaheke. See Großer Generalstab, *Die Kämpfe der deutschen Truppen*, vol. 1, 214. Such passages are repeatedly cited to prove genocidal intent. See, for example, Tilman Dedering, "The German-Herero War of 1904: Revisionism of Genocide or Imaginary Historiography?" *Journal of Southern African Studies* 19, no. 1 (1993): 83–84. In other respects, Dedering's criticism of Brigitte Lau's "Uncertain Certainties" is apt.
103. The General Staff report remarked that the course of the fighting at the Waterberg was quite different from "what had been intended by the high command," emphasizing that Deimling's unauthorized advance had foiled the "great decisive struggle" that the command had hoped for. See also Isabel Hull's outstanding depiction of these events (Hull, *Absolute Destruction*, 33–43).
104. Großer Generalstab, *Die Kämpfe der deutschen Truppen*, vol. 1, 178ff. Deimling commanded the section that was supposed to advance toward Hamakari from the northwest. He did not take his assigned position, but instead pushed ahead on his own. He contributed significantly to the panic that led the Herero to withdraw east. Heyde's section never reached its assigned position near Hamakari, and he unilaterally decided to change direction twice. Trotha angrily called him a shithead (*Scheißkerl*) (Trotha diary, TA 122/17, 12 August 1904). In some situations, however, the officers' unauthorized actions were not the most critical factor. One section reported to headquarters that its planned advance from the southeast was impossible in the given timeframe: "From our position to the opponent, we have a march of 55 km. We can hardly accomplish this at one time. But the attack can only succeed if it is a surprise. We intend to decamp in the afternoon, so that we reach the opponent's position by daybreak" (Anonymous, "Kriegstagebuch," NAN, Sammlung Lemmer, L1032, 26 July 1904). The German command did not accept these objections, and indeed, the section struggled to advance amid the sandy thorn bushes and ultimately gave out from pure exhaustion. On 6 August 1904, Trotha noted in his diary (TA 122/17) that Heyde had expressed his fear "of being overrun by fleeing Herero. He is not that

strong." In fact, the section was overrun. Heyde's section did not fulfill its mission, but this was nearly impossible to fulfill in the given circumstances, with the German command all too hastily overriding any objections that were raised.

105. Marchand-Volz, *Werner Freiherr Schenck v. Stauffenberg*, 144; Eckl, *"S'ist ein übles Land hier,"* 181; and BArch. Nl. 30/3a, 12 August 1904, p. 362.
106. NAN, Private Accessions, A. 0109, 25 August 1904, p. 54. On 17 August, Epp noted in his diary that "the strike did not succeed." See Eckl, *"S'ist ein übles Land hier,"* 269.
107. See, for example, A. Kerremans, *Quelques observations sur la stratégie des Allemands dans leur guerre contre les Hereros* (Paris, 1913), 54.
108. On 11 August 1904, Trotha noted in his diary (TA 122/17), "The most difficult moment was when I recognized that Heyde might not arrive and that we would still have to fight to reach the watering hole [near Hamakari] by nightfall. Leading the squadrons out of the bush under heavy fire was a terrible moment. For some time I believed that this section and the command were lost . . . . The night was awful."
109. Großer Generalstab, *Die Kämpfe der deutschen Truppen*, vol. 1, 189–90.
110. NAN, Private Accessions, A.151, no. 2, I, p. 47 (13 and 14 August 1904).
111. Marchand-Volz, *Werner Freiherr Schenck v. Stauffenberg*, 144.
112. Trotha diary, TA 122/17, 13 August 1904, emphasis added.
113. Marchand-Volz, *Werner Freiherr Schenck v. Stauffenberg*, 144.
114. See, for example, Kerremans, *Quelques observations sur la stratégie des Allemands*, 45.
115. The Germans apparently had no way around the unfavorable conditions. A high-ranking official from the Colonial Department who had spent several years in SWA told the British military attaché Count Gleichen, "The more troops that are sent out, the more transport they want and the more men die. Fifty old colonial hands are worth 500 inexperienced soldiers. The country is mostly poor, and there is little water. If you send fifty men on fifty good horses, to a place where there is pasture and water for fifty, you will get fifty horses worth of work out of them: but if you send 500 men and horses to the same place, you won't get any work out of them at all, for they will starve and die of thirst." See KAB PMO 199: Correspondence Files Nos. 211/05—286/05, Native Rising in German South West Africa, 1904–1906, file no. 229/05, vol. 2.
116. Bayer, *Mit dem Hauptquartier in Südwestafrika*, 139.
117. Kerremans, *Quelques observations sur la stratégie des Allemands*, 56.
118. In a telegram to the Great General Staff, Trotha pointed out one more reason for his plan of operations: "Provisioning, water, and health concerns make the unified advance of all forces . . . impossible." The troops had to proceed separately so that an adequate number could reach the enemy, although a unified advance would have been advisable in other respects. See Trotha to the Great General Staff (copy to the Imperial chancellor) (25 June 1904), BArch. R1001/2115, p. 78.
119. Schwabe, *Dienst und Kriegführung*, 89. An annihilating, decisive victory demanded separate operations, but Leutwein had alerted the Colonial Department early on that this would be difficult; the sections could not stay in touch with one another, so a uniform command was hardly possible. See Leutwein to the Colonial Department (19 March 1904), BArch. R1001/2114, pp. 158–59. As Nuhn correctly observes, the sections lost all contact with one another as soon as they left their bases. They "disappeared into a void for weeks, swallowed up by the bush." See Nuhn, *Sturm über Südwest*, 132.
120. Maercker, *Unsere Kriegsführung in Deutsch-Südwestafrika*, 44.
121. This attitude was evident in Trotha's memorandum to the South-West African officers from June 1905. The memorandum was relayed—with criticism—by the British military observer Lt.-Col. Trench. See PRO, WO 106/268, pp. 214–20.

122. Gleichen's contact described the consequences of clinging to the metropolitan routines of state wars in a colonial setting: "You scatter the enemy, you can't surround him in that country, and then you pursue on weak, half-starved horses: with the natural result that your patrols and reconnoitering parties get ambushed and cut up, depression and mistrust sets in, and you have done more harm than good." See KAB PMO 199: Correspondence Files Nos. 211/05—286/05, Native Rising in German South West Africa, 1904–1906, File no. 229/05, vol. no. 2.
123. "Der Aufstand," *DSWAZ*, 21 September 1904, 1.
124. In a letter to the Colonial Department dated 3 June 1904, Leutwein discussed expectations for the South-West African operations, which he believed were doomed to fail: "Our public opinion is blind to the actual conditions. On the one hand, the public is convinced that the Herero will one day raise the white flag, but on the other, they believe that we can 'encircle' the mass of the people and compel them to surrender. The Herero will not do the former, and with respect to the latter, the power of our troops is too weak to confront a populace of 60,000 souls, beginning with the question of how to sustain our troops. This is true even if the people [the Herero] begin to break apart, as already seems to be the case. The individual groups are still too large for the action that is planned" (R1001/2115, p. 113).
125. "Aus Swakopmund," *DSWAZ*, 10 January 1906, 1.
126. The Admiralty staff report later asserted, "The Herero were ahead of the newly arrived German troops in many ways. The white man cannot approach their mobility in the bush, their stamina in enduring hardships, and their speed covering long distances. In marksmanship and taking cover, the newcomer can only learn from them. On foot, they cannot be caught in the bush or on open terrain; they climb, crawl, and creep with the utmost agility; they cover great distances on foot as messengers or runners, with striking speed and endurance." See Admiralstab der Marine, *Das Marine-Expeditionskorps in Südwest-Afrika*, 19.
127. Bayer, *Mit dem Hauptquartier in Südwestafrika*, 130.
128. BArch. Nl. 30/3a, 12 August 1904, p. 362.
129. BArch. Nl. 30/3a, 26 July 1904, p. 350.
130. BArch. Nl. 30/3a, 16 August, p. 363.
131. On 6 August 1904, after Franke had read the directives for the battle, he noted in his diary that the "whole setup" of the attack left a "proper and sensible impression." However, he also remarked that the troops lacked "the utmost essentials," and he feared that the enemy, when attacked by the full German forces, would be "protected by the unusually dense bush and able to escape through the gaps with strong commandos, attacking our weak rear lines and annihilating, or at least plundering, them." See BArch. Nl. 30/3a, pp. 357–58.
132. Estorff and his section fought the last real skirmish against the Herero on 15 August, near Epata.
133. Shaw, *What is Genocide?*, 84.
134. Bridgman, *The Revolt of the Hereros*, 104.
135. See Annemarie Heywood, ed., *Warriors, Leaders, Sages, and Outcasts in the Namibian Past: Narratives Collected from Herero Sources for the Michael Scott Oral Record Project (MSQRP) 1985-6* (Windhoek, 1992), 143; Andreas Kukuri, *Herero-Texte*, ed. and trans. Ernst Dammann (Berlin, 1983), 125; and Stefanie Michels, *Schwarze deutsche Kolonialsoldaten: Mehrdeutige Repräsentationsräume und früher Kosmopolitismus in Afrika* (Bielefeld, 2009), 112.
136. As Larissa Förster has recently shown, Herero narratives recall the outcome of the battles on 11 August 1904 as "undecided, sometimes even as a victory." See Förster, *Erinnerungslandschaften*, 130.

On 15 August 1904, Trotha noted in his diary (TA 122/17) that a patrol "saw Herero victory dances on the night of 11–12 [August]. *Bon!* Do not let this spread!" He clearly believed that the report could be correct. Epp, too, recounted how the Herero near Hamakari "danced through the night and made jokes" after the battle. See Eckl, *"S'ist ein übles Land hier,"* 291.

137. Shaw, *What is Genocide?*, 81–82.
138. See, for example, Schaller, "Kolonialkrieg, Völkermord und Zwangsarbeit," 217; and Olusoga and Erichsen, *The Kaiser's Holocaust*, 142 and 145.
139. Jürgen Zimmerer argues that setbacks and local and situational factors did not contribute significantly to the escalation of violence, but that, independent of these factors, Trotha sought the genocidal annihilation of the Herero from the outset. See Zimmerer, "Annihilation in Africa," 52–53.
140. Alison Palmer interprets the 4 August 1904 directives "for the attack on the Hereros" as evidence of Trotha's genocidal intent. See Palmer, *Colonial Genocide*, 185.
141. See, for example, Benz, "Kolonialpolitik als Genozid"; and Eckart, "Medizin und kolonialer Rassenkrieg."
142. Kuß, "Von der Vernichtungsschlacht zum Vernichtungskrieg"; and Jan Philipp Reemtsma, "Die Idee des Vernichtungskrieges: Clausewitz—Ludendorff—Hitler," in *Vernichtungskrieg: Verbrechen der Wehrmacht 1941 bis 1944*, ed. Hannes Heer und Klaus Naumann (Hamburg, 1995).
143. See, for example, Lawrence H. Keeley, *War before Civilization: The Myth of the Peaceful Savage* (New York, 1996), 44.
144. Elias, *The Germans*, 175.
145. Victor Davis Hanson, *The Western Way of War: Infantry Battle in Classical Greece* (Berkeley, 1989).
146. Warburg, *Das Militär und seine Subjekte*, 171.
147. Johannes Kunisch, *Der kleine Krieg: Studien zum Heerwesen des Absolutismus* (Wiesbaden, 1973), 2.
148. Ritualization is not specific to "primitive warfare." All battles are fundamentally based on mutual understanding, hence the notion of "accepting" or "answering" a call to battle. "Primitive" battles merely formalize an aspect that is inherent to this form of combat. See Keeley, *War Before Civilization*, 60–61; Mühlmann, *Krieg und Frieden*, 117; and Callwell, *Small Wars*, 104. Keeley investigates certain nonfunctional characteristics of "primitive" warfare, such as the makeup and clothing of "primitive" fighters, and compares them with their counterparts in European military culture. He concludes that, in some respects, modern battles are even more ritualized and dysfunctional. See Keeley, *War before Civilization*, 61.
149. Wilhelm E. Mühlmann, *Krieg und Frieden: Ein Leitfaden der politischen Ethnologie mit Berücksichtigung des völkerkundlichen und geschichtlichen Stoffes* (Heidelberg, 1940), 49. We should not overlook the fact that ritualized fighting can escalate into a costly and bloody "true fight" at any time. See Jürg Helbling, *Tribale Kriege: Konflikte in Gesellschaften ohne Zentralgewalt* (Frankfurt, 2006), 59. This underscores that even "primitive" wars are categorically different from sporting events and games. Rather, these conflicts are *deathly serious*. See Harry Holbert Turney-High, *Primitive War: Its Practice and Concepts* (Columbia, [1949] 1991), 49 and 134.
150. Werner Hahlweg emphasizes that the history of European state wars encompasses both the regular troops of large wars, and the mobile, often irregular units of small wars. See *Guerilla: Krieg ohne Fronten* (Stuttgart, 1968), 26.
151. The fourth-century military theoretician Vegetius argued that battles should be avoided wherever possible, because their outcomes are uncertain; Kortüm shows that his ideas remained influential throughout the Middle Ages. Unlike later eras, battles in the Middle Ages were particularly risky for their commanders, who were likely to

be executed by the victors in case of defeat. The celebrated warrior King Richard the Lionheart fought only three battles in his lifetime, similar to William the Conqueror and Henry II of England. See Hans-Henning Kortüm, *Kriege und Krieger, 500–1500* (Stuttgart, 2010), 170–71.

152. "Primitive" fighters likewise have a tactical preference for asymmetric constellations of combat. This is true of both sides, within the limits of their available means. Battles tend to play a subordinate role in "primitive" wars. Battles are characterized by relatively even start conditions, so chances and risks are distributed relatively equally among opponents. The risks are substantial, particularly in groups that are small in number, while the chances to hurt and weaken the opponent may be no greater than in other forms of combat, such as assaults and ambushes. Keeley notes that hand-to-hand fighting is especially risky in battles because, in order to reach their opponent, fighters must enter the "killing zone" and open themselves up to increasingly dangerous enemy fire. This calls for great coercive authority on the part of military leaders, and strict discipline on the part of fighters—both of which are not always present in "primitive" societies. For this reason, "primitive" war must limit itself to the essentials of warfare—"killing enemies with a minimum of risk." See Keeley, *War before Civilization*, 46 and 175.

153. The example of Colonel von der Trenck, who commanded an infamous (irregular) corps of pandours in the War of Austrian Succession (1740–48) vividly illustrates how the blurring of lines between combatants and civilians—or between "on" and "off" the battlefield—can break down distinctions between the legitimate use of force by a state army, on the one hand, and "privatized," criminal violence, on the other. Despite considerable wartime success, Trenck was put on trial after the war's end. His unit had to be held responsible for excesses that threatened to damage the state's legitimacy. Trenck was punished, and the irregular fighters (the main participants of the guerrilla war) were integrated within the regular army and placed under tighter control. See Martin Rink, "Die Verwandlung: Die Figur des Partisanen vom freien Kriegsunternehmer zum Freiheitshelden," in *Rückkehr der Condottieri? Krieg und Militär zwischen staatlichem Monopol und Privatisierung: Von der Antike bis zur Gegenwart*, ed. Stig Förster (Paderborn, 2010), 155–56.

154. See Greiner, *Krieg ohne Fronten*, 2007.

155. Reemtsma, "Die Idee des Vernichtungskrieges," 377.

156. Clausewitz, *Vom Kriege*, 113. The English translation is from Clausewitz, *On War*, 90.

157. Schwabe, *Dienst und Kriegführung*, 89.

158. Münkler, *Der Wandel des Krieges*, 27–74.

159. This is apart from the *technical* innovations of the Napoleonic wars (dating back, in part, to the prerevolutionary era) that gave the French army an advantage over its adversaries. See William McNeill, *The Pursuit of Power: Technology, Armed Force, and Society since A.D. 1000* (Chicago, 1982), 196; and Larry H. Addington, *The Patterns of War since the Eighteenth Century* (London, 1984), 17–18.

160. Clausewitz, *Vom Kriege*, 857.

161. Hans Delbrück, *Geschichte der Kriegskunst*, vol. 2 (Berlin, [1920] 2006), 551–52. The English translation is from Hans Delbrück, *History of the Art of War*, vol. 4, trans. Walter J. Renfroe, Jr. (Westport, 1985), 421.

162. Napoleon always sought to push "his whole force onto one wing or into one flank of the enemy . . . to envelop him, to drive him away from his base, and in this way to destroy him as completely as possible." See Delbrück, *Geschichte der Kriegskunst*, 570. The English translation is from Delbrück, *History of the Art of War*, 433.

163. Hanson, *The Western Way of War*, 9–18.

164. Kunisch, *Der kleine Krieg*, 2.

165. See, for example, Joël Kotek and Pierre Rigoulot, *Das Jahrhundert der Lager: Gefangenschaft, Zwangsarbeit, Vernichtung* (Berlin, 2001), 26.
166. Münkler, *Der Wandel des Krieges*, 53; and McNeill, *The Pursuit of Power*, 189.
167. Kunisch, *Der kleine Krieg*, 2.
168. Gert Buchheit, *Vernichtungs- oder Ermattungsstrategie? Vom strategischen Charakter der Kriege* (Berlin, 1942), 76.
169. Rainer Wohlfeil, "Der Volkskrieg im Zeitalter Napoleons," in *Napoleon und Europa*, ed. Heinz-Otto Sieburg (Cologne, 1971), 319.
170. Warburg, *Das Militär und seine Subjekte*, 115ff.; and Wohlfeil, "Der Volkskrieg im Zeitalter Napoleons," 327–28.
171. Förster, "Optionen der Kriegführung," 85–86.
172. Förster, "Einleitung," 15.
173. See, for example, Browning, *The Changing Nature of Warfare*, 93–94.
174. Moltke emphasized, "Victory . . . alone breaks the enemy's will and forces him to submit to our will. Neither the occupation of a certain piece of terrain nor the capture of a fortified place, but only the destruction of the hostile fighting force will be decisive as a rule. It is therefore the *most important object of all operations*. The English translation is from Helmuth von Moltke, *Moltke on the Art of War: Selected Writings*, ed. and trans. Daniel J. Hughes and Harry Bell (New York, 1993), 128–29 (emphasis added). See also Dieter Langewiesche and Nikolaus Buschmann, "'Dem Vertilgungskriege Grenzen setzen': Kriegstypen des 19. Jahrhunderts und der deutsch-französische Krieg 1870/71: Gehegter Krieg—Volks- und Nationalkrieg—Revolutionskrieg—Dschihad," in *Formen des Krieges: Von der Antike bis zur Gegenwart*, ed. Dietrich Beyrau et al. (Paderborn, 2007), 171. Schlieffen was also known to be dissatisfied with "ordinary victories" that did not demonstrate annihilating force. See Wallach, *Das Dogma der Vernichtungsschlacht*, 83.
175. Förster, "Optionen der Kriegführung," 88–89.
176. Förster, *Der doppelte Militarismus*, 9.
177. Förster, "Einleitung," 22.
178. Princes and their advisors more easily conceded defeat on the battlefield than a "nation of many voices," which was reluctant to give up land; territorial integrity has always been a core aspect of national identity. See Langewiesche and Buschmann, "'Dem Vertilgungskriege Grenzen setzen,'" 164.
179. Förster, "Einleitung," 25–26. The general Philip H. Sheridan observed the hostilities firsthand, and he was surprised at how conventional the fighting seemed compared to Ulysses S. Grant's campaign of annihilation in the US Civil War. Sheridan was said to have remarked that the Germans knew better than any other army how to beat their enemy, but they did not understand how to truly annihilate their opponent. The advance of the German troops seemed more like a "vast picnic than like actual war." See Langewiesche and Buschmann, "'Dem Vertilgungskriege Grenzen setzen,'" 178–79. The war's fundamentally conventional character is further evident in the conditions for prisoners of war that were still upheld during the campaign. See Katja Mitze, "'Seit der babylonischen Gefangenschaft hat die Welt nichts derart erlebt': Französische Kriegsgefangene und Franctireurs im Deutsch-Französischen Krieg 1870/71," in *In der Hand des Feindes: Kriegsgefangenschaft von der Antike bis zum Zweiten Weltkrieg*, ed. Rüdiger Overmans (Cologne, 1999), 243.
180. See also Manfred Messerschmidt, "Völkerrecht und 'Kriegsnotwendigkeit' in der deutschen militärischen Tradition seit den Einigungskriegen," *German Studies Review* 6, no. 2 (1983): 243.
181. Förster, *Der doppelte Militarismus*, 163.
182. Reemtsma, "Die Idee des Vernichtungskrieges," 390; and Kößler and Melber, "Der Genozid an den Herero und Nama," 46–47.

183. Hahlweg, *Guerilla*, 28–31.
184. In this historical context, a distinction is sometimes made between regular and irregular troops, but this was a technical military distinction, not a legal one; all actors were soldiers. See Carl Schmitt, *Theorie des Partisanen: Zwischenbemerkung zum Begriff des Politischen* (Berlin, 1962).
185. Warburg, *Das Militär und seine Subjekte*, 116–18.
186. Beatrice Heuser, "Small Wars in the Age of Clausewitz: The Watershed between Partisan War and People's War," *Journal of Strategic Studies* 33, no. 1 (2010): 142.
187. Warburg, *Das Militär und seine Subjekte*, 170; Münkler, *Der Wandel des Krieges*, 71; and Hahlweg, *Guerilla*, 26.
188. King Friedrich II captured Prague in 1757, but he had to give up the city because light Austrian troops unsettled the surrounding areas.
189. Callwell's definition of the small war: "Practically it may be said to include all campaigns other than those where both the opposing sides consist of regular troops." See Callwell, *Small Wars*, 21.
190. Ibid., 22.
191. According to Ian Beckett, it was not until World War II that guerrilla warfare began to develop a logic of its own, which now characterizes most warlike conflicts today. In the nineteenth century, countering insurgents with regular armies had not yet been closely considered and was not much different from simple (counter)terrorism. See Ian Beckett, *Modern Insurgencies and Counter-Insurgencies: Guerrillas and Their Opponents since 1750* (London, 2001), 21 and 26. Trotha's wartime leadership confirms Beckett's observations.
192. Leutwein seemed to think that an annihilating strike was impossible in SWA. Trotha remarked in his diary on 16 June 1904 (TA 122/15) that "Leutwein is said to laugh at the idea that the mob at the Waterberg could be encircled in such a way as to annihilate them."
193. This ambivalence is apparent in the remarks of Oscar Stübel, director of the Colonial Department in the Foreign Office, as he sought to persuade members of the Bundesrat to approve the funds that Leutwein had requested. In one breath Stübel cited "upholding Imperial Germany's reputation" by proving its superior power, *and* "avoiding protracted fighting and unnecessary bloodshed" as arguments for approving the funds that would enable a "speedy" and "complete" defeat of the uprising. See Stübel to the members of the Bundesrat (12 March 1904), BArch. R1001/2113, p. 36.
194. Nipperdey, *Deutsche Geschichte*, 288.
195. Leutwein to the Colonial Department (17 May 1904), BArch. R1001/2115, p. 63.
196. Trotha's "provisions for military tribunals etc. during the war in German South-West Africa," announced on 11 June 1904 (NAN BKE 220), corresponded to the tenor of the Great General Staff's *Kriegsbrauch im Landkriege* from 1902. Trotha's motivations were hardly altruistic; instead, he sought to restore the state monopoly of the use of violence.
197. Jürgen Zimmerer draws the opposite conclusion, contending that Trotha's proclamation turned massacre and terror "into a planned instrument of German warfare." At this point, at the latest, steps were taken toward a "war of annihilation and genocide." See Jürgen Zimmerer, "Das Deutsche Reich und der Genozid: Überlegungen zum historischen Ort des Völkermordes an den Herero und Nama," in *Namibia—Deutschland, eine geteilte Geschichte: Widerstand, Gewalt, Erinnerung*, ed. Larissa Förster et al. (Cologne, 2004), 109.
198. KAB GH 35/157: "Treatment of Natives in G.S.W.A. 1905," "Ill-Treatment of 3 Natives in G.S.W.A. 1905–1906."
199. Hull, "Military Culture and the Production of 'Final Solutions,'" 148.

200. NAN, Private Accessions, A.0109, p. 49.
201. See NAN, Private Accessions, A.151, no. 2, II, p. 6 (2 September 1904).
202. See Hull, "Military Culture and the Production of 'Final Solutions,'" 154.
203. Sönke Neitzel and Harald Welzer, *Soldaten: Protokolle vom Kämpfen, Töten und Sterben* (Frankfurt, 2011).
204. Trutz von Trotha, *Koloniale Herrschaft*, 42.
205. Drawing upon a report by Trotha's former chief of staff, Chales de Beaulieu, Schlieffen wrote to Bülow that Trotha had "especially" forbidden the killing of women and children "after the battle near Waterberg, where numerous women and children were found in pontoks [huts], and there was a danger of overstepping boundaries." See Chief of the Great General Staff to the Imperial Chancellor, Berlin (16 December 1904), BArch. R1001/2089. p. 107; and Hull, *Absolute Destruction*, 49.
206. Hendrik Lundtofte, "'I believe that the nation as such must be annihilated . . .': The Radicalization of the German Suppression of the Herero Rising in 1904," in *Genocide: Cases, Comparisons and Contemporary Debates*, ed. Stephen B. Jensen (Copenhagen, 2003), 34.
207. See, for example, Benz, "Kolonialpolitik als Genozid," 37; Zimmerer, "Rassenkrieg und Völkermord," 29–30; Eckart, "Medizin und kolonialer Rassenkrieg"; and Krüger, *Kriegsbewältigung und Geschichtsbewusstsein*, 51.
208. In *Absolute Destruction*, Isabel Hull correctly points out that it was standard military procedure to pursue an opponent who had broken free of encirclement. Pursuit was supposed to make for up for the failure in battle, so the opponent could still be caught and beaten decisively.
209. Lundtofte, "'I believe that the nation as such,'" 30–36.
210. On 13 August, Trotha feared that encirclement would "no longer be possible" (TA 122/17). He correctly anticipated that this would be difficult, although he subsequently regained confidence. And so, on 21 August, Viktor Franke noted in his diary that Deimling had introduced a new "plan for encirclement" (BArch. NL Viktor Franke, Nl. 30/3a, p. 369). On 25 August, Stuhlmann heard that concentric operations were planned against the Herero (NAN, Private Accessions, A.0109, p. 54). Likewise, Epp reported a plan for encirclement (*Kesseltreiben*) on 23 August. See Eckl, "*S'ist ein übles Land hier,*" 274. These remarks clearly show that German strategy had not changed fundamentally by the end of August.
211. This almost certainly refers to Leutwein, since Bayer (the other potential "he") was not an "old African."
212. Trotha diary, TA 122/17, 29 August 1904.
213. In his diary entry from 6 September, Epp noted with resignation, "It seems that the annihilation maneuver has failed for the 2nd time." See Eckl, "*S'ist ein übles Land hier.*" The entry is especially illuminating because it underscores the continuity in operations.
214. Estorff, *Wanderungen und Kämpfe*, 117.
215. Trotha diary, TA 122/17, 23 September 1904.
216. Trotha diary, TA 122/17, 28 September 1904.
217. Belwe, *Gegen die Herero 1904/1905*, 115.
218. Stuhlmann, NAN, Private Accessions, A.109, pp. 62 and 64. On 25 September, Epp commented on the same battle in his diary (echoing his own remarks from 23 September): "Once again, the hope is for a decisive strike." See Eckl, "*S'ist ein übles Land hier,*" 281–82.
219. Report from Trotha to Schlieffen (4 October 1904), copy in TA 315, 2a, Anlage 18/1. Trotha's telegram to the Great General Staff on 1 October 1904 reported "no shortage of pasture" and the discovery of "fresh watering holes" in the sandveld, contrary to previous assumptions, but also that "operating with larger sections" would be

"impossible" here (NAN ZBU D.IV.L.2: Herero-Aufstand 1904. Feldzug; Politisches, pp. 82–83).
220. Eckl, *"S'ist ein übles Land hier,"* 284.
221. On 13 August 1904, Trotha noted in his diary that he had received word that the pursuing troops had "not a single kernel of oats and no provisions." He wrote, "I'm bowled over. And putting this 30 kilom. pursuit into motion, which makes sense only if they, that is, the H. can be caught, after their lead of at least 24 hrs. It's no joke. I thought they had 3 days of oats and rations" (TA 122/17).
222. NAN, Private Accessions, A.109, p. 79.
223. Lettow-Vorbeck, *Mein Leben*, 77.
224. Trotha to Schlieffen (4 October 1904), BArch. R1001/2089, p. 5.
225. On 13 September, Trotha remarked in his diary, "A Kaffir family was brought here in the evening and chased away again" (TA 122/17).
226. The officer von Frankenberg mentioned in passing how a woman who had fallen into the hands of the Germans was "shot as a spy, liar, etc., together with her child," after a short interrogation (von Frankenberg diary, NAN, AACRLS.070, p. 128). Trotha noted on 12 August (well after his thoughts had shifted toward pursuing the Herero), "A Herero woman was captured in the werfts taken yesterday. She claimed that all headmen were on the way to the Omurambo. When I announced that she would be hanged, she said it wasn't true" (TA 122/17).
227. See Randall Collins, "A Dynamic of Battle Victory and Defeat," *Cliodynamics* 1 (2010): 9ff.
228. Collins, *Violence*, 129.
229. Trotha diary, TA 122/17, 13 September 1904.
230. Frankenberg, NAN, AACRLS.070, p. 116.
231. The text of the "call to the Herero people" reads as follows: "I, the great general of the German soldiers, send this letter to the Herero people. The Hereros are no longer German subjects. They have murdered and stolen, cut off the ears and noses and other body parts of wounded soldiers, and now out of cowardice refuse to fight. I say to the people: Anyone who delivers one of the captains to one of my stations as a prisoner will receive 1,000 marks; whoever brings Samuel Maharero will receive 5,000 marks. The Herero people must leave the land. If they do not do so, I will force them with the Groot Rohr [cannon]. Within German borders every Herero, armed or unarmed, with or without cattle, will be shot dead. I will no longer take in women and children, I will drive them back to their people or have them shot at. These are my words to the Herero people. The great general of the powerful German Kaiser." After the proclamation was read aloud, an explanation was added for the German troops: "This proclamation is to be read to the troops at roll call, with the addition that the troop that catches one of the captains will also receive the corresponding award, and shooting at women and children is to be understood as firing over their heads, so as to force them to run away. I certainly assume that this proclamation will lead to taking no more male prisoners, but will not degenerate into atrocities against women and children. They will run away if shots are fired twice above their heads. The troops will remain conscious of the good reputation of the German soldier. The commander v. Trotha, Lieutenant General."
232. Hull, *Absolute Destruction*, 57.
233. See, for example, Zimmerer, *Deutsche Herrschaft über Afrikaner*, 38–39; and Gewald, "Imperial Germany and the Herero of Southern Africa," 70ff.
234. Kotek, "Le Génocide des Herero," 181.
235. See, for example, Bridgman and Worley, "Genocide of the Hereros," 17.
236. BArch. R1001/2089, pp. 5–6.
237. Ibid., p. 4.

238. The *Deutsch-Südwestafrikanische Zeitung* exposed Trotha's strategy as an attempt to make "a virtue of necessity." See "Der Aufstand," *DSWAZ*, 14 December 1904, 2.
239. Eckl, *"S'ist ein übles Land hier,"* 284.
240. Chief of the Great General Staff to the Imperial Chancellor, Berlin (16 December 1904), BArch. R1001/2089, p. 108.
241. Zimmerer, "Rassenkrieg und Völkermord," 31; and Schaller, "Kolonialkrieg, Völkermord und Zwangsarbeit."
242. Eckl, *"S'ist ein übles Land hier,"* 35. The proclamation was also a directive to the German troops, as Trotha's addendum shows; he gave the troops specific tasks in the additional order.
243. Isabel Hull emphasizes the process of violence much more than other authors, but she does not go far enough. She presumes that the meaning of the proclamation was immediately genocidal. Thus, her assertion that the proclamation sanctioned long-established practices shifts the start of the genocidal phase even earlier, to September 1904. See Hull, *Absolute Destruction*, 57. The immediate circumstances that informed the proclamation suggest that it was initially closer to terrorism. Hull omits this intermediate step.
244. Sémelin, *Purify and Destroy*, 327–28.
245. Marchand-Volz, *Werner Freiherr Schenck v. Stauffenberg*, 211; and Lothar von Trotha, "Politik und Kriegführung," 1.
246. In parenthesis, we should note that expulsion, or the means by which it is achieved, fulfills part of the *legal* definition of a crime against humanity, and thus also genocide. See Barth, *Genozid*, 13. Another important consideration is whether a commanding general such as Trotha even possessed the right to expatriate "subjects" of the regime, including "natives."
247. Chief of the Great General Staff to the Imperial Chancellor, Berlin (16 December 1904), BArch. R1001/2089, p. 108.
248. Zimmerer, "Annihilation in Africa," 32.
249. Within this context, the following diary entry by Trotha is instructive: "I think that they [the Herero] will come before long with proposals for peace. If only I can still find a way to shoot down the white flag. They must be annihilated. But maybe things will still turn out another way" (Trotha diary, TA 122/15, 20 June 1904). The entry points, yet again, to the ruthlessness of the general, who would have preferred to shoot the surrendering Herero. But the entry also shows that this was not possible, and that Trotha first would have had to find a pretense to do so. Under certain conditions, Trotha might have found himself compelled to accept their surrender. Thus, the path was not entirely blocked (although it was risky, as the entry shows). Another example underscores this. In line with Trotha's expectations, Major von Estorff directed the war-weary Herero leader Salatiel Kambazembi to stop sending messengers, unless the message was "Salatiel surrenders." Negotiations were out of the question, but apparently not unconditional surrender (Copy of a message from 18 July 1904, BArch. R1001/2089, p. 134).
250. The German troops occupied or controlled all of the known watering holes in a great arc that extended from Otjituuo southwest to the Waterberg, along the Omuramba Omatako, and then eastward along the Eiseb and Epukiro rivers.
251. Franz Epp was one of the newcomers. In contrast to officers like Estorff, he believed Trotha's new strategy was "entirely appropriate," as the Herero were "not yet finished." See Eckl, *"S'ist ein übles Land hier,"* 289.
252. Estorff had suggested to Trotha in September that the Herero were on the verge of extinction, but he and the other "old Africans" at headquarters were "ridiculed," as numerous eyewitnesses affirmed. See Estorff, *Wanderungen und Kämpfe*, 117; and Eckl, *"S'ist ein übles Land hier,"* 294.

253. As the chaplain P. A. Ziegenfuß noted, even the "old Africans" knew nothing about the Omaheke. They were surprised by the conditions they encountered: "The sandveld that was generally thought to have no, or at least little, water turned out . . . to have very generous, good springs, and even larger watering holes; having fled with a large number of cattle, the enemy occupied and claimed these with the utmost tenacity." See "Aus meinen Kriegserlebnissen: Vortrag, gehalten von P.A. Ziegenfuß," *Windhuker Nachrichten*, 1 June 1905, 1, insert. Another report asserted, "From past experience, we should expect that when the dispersed enemy is left alone, allowed to recover and round up cattle during the rainy season so that he can later resume hostilities, even on a smaller scale, then he really has nothing more to lose." See "Der Aufstand," *DSWAZ*, 14 December 1904, 1.
254. See Karl-John Lindholm, *Wells of Experience: A Pastoral Land-Use History of Omaheke, Namibia* (Uppsala, 2006).
255. A report from the Bavarian military representative in Berlin, Nikolaus Ritter von Endres, suggests that Schlieffen opposed Trotha's appointment. See Kuß, *Deutsches Militär auf kolonialen Kriegsschauplätzen*, 83 (note 1). Schlieffen seems to have deliberately sent a section leader from the Great General Staff, Martin Chales de Beaulieu, to serve as Trotha's chief of staff, who then reported to him and exchanged information behind Trotha's back. This became a point of contention with Trotha, and may have led to Beaulieu's eventual departure from the colony under another pretense. See Trotha diary, TA 122/17, 22 July 1904; and NL Viktor Franke, BArch. Nl. 30/3a, 1 and 13 September 1904. As we will see, tensions with Schlieffen continued to mount.
256. Trotha to Schlieffen (26 October 1904), copy in TA 315, 2a, Anlage 20/1f.
257. According to the Great General Staff, the consequences of the German approach did not become apparent until the start of the rainy season. Arid conditions meant that the troops could not push ahead to the eastern border of the colony and confirm the "success" of operations until November 1904 at the earliest. See Großer Generalstab, *Die Kämpfe der deutschen Truppen*, vol. 1, 218.
258. A. Dirk Moses, "Genocide and Settler Society in Australian History," in *Genocide and Settler Society: Frontier Violence and Stolen Indigenous Children in Australian History*, ed. A. Dirk Moses (New York, 2004), 3–48.
259. In pointed contrast to the conventional and legal understanding of intentionality, Helen Fein (drawing upon the work of Robert Merton) has developed a concept of purposeful action that includes not just the directly intended consequences of one's actions, but also those consequences that are merely foreseeable. See Fein, *Genocide: A Sociological Perspective*, 19. Thus, even with the aforementioned reservations, we can still speak of genocide with respect to the events in SWA.
260. Hull, *Absolute Destruction*, 45ff.
261. Steinmetz, *The Devil's Handwriting*, 180.
262. See Lewis, *Shame and Guilt in Neurosis*; Lewis, "Introduction"; Scheff, *Bloody Revenge*; and Scheff and Retzinger, *Emotions and Violence*.
263. Gerhart Piers and Milton B. Singer, *Shame and Guilt: A Psychoanalytic and a Cultural Study* (New York, 1971), 70; and Lewis, *Shame and Guilt in Neurosis*, 40ff.
264. Jack Katz, *How Emotions Work* (Chicago, 1999), 148.
265. Heller, *Theorie der Gefühle*, 111.
266. Georg Simmel, "Zur Psychologie der Scham," in *Georg Simmel: Schriften zur Soziologie: Eine Auswahl*, ed. Heinz-Jürgen Dahme and Otthein Rammstedt, 2nd ed. (Frankfurt, [1901] 1995), 142–43; and Neckel, *Status und Scham*, 85.
267. Neckel, *Status und Scham*, 25.
268. Sigmund Freud, "Über das Unbehagen in der Kultur," in *Gesammelte Werke*, vol. 14 (Frankfurt, 1999), 484.

269. Scheff and Retzinger, *Emotions and Violence*, 5.
270. Suzanne M. Retzinger, "Resentment and Laughter: Video Studies of the Shame-Rage Spiral," in *The Role of Shame in Symptom Formation*, ed. Helen B. Lewis (Hillsdale, 1987), 155. Just as fear signals threat to the physical self, shame signals threat to the social self. See Scheff, *Bloody Revenge*, 51.
271. Leon Wurmser, *Die Maske der Scham: Die Psychoanalyse von Schameffekten und Schamkonflikten*, 5th ed. (Eschborn, 2007), 82; and Lewis, *Shame and Guilt in Neurosis*, 37–38.
272. Lewis, *Shame and Guilt in Neurosis*, 41 and 198.
273. Neckel, *Status und Scham*, 99–100 and 106.
274. Scheff, *Bloody Revenge*, 43.
275. Lewis, *Shame and Guilt in Neurosis*, 38.
276. Scheff, *Bloody Revenge*, 61.
277. Ibid., 113.
278. Retzinger, "Resentment and Laughter."
279. Scheff, *Bloody Revenge*; and Scheff and Retzinger, *Emotions and Violence*.
280. Helmut Kuzmics and Sabine A. Haring, *Emotion, Habitus und Erster Weltkrieg: Soziologische Studien zum militärischen Untergang der Habsburger Monarchie* (Göttingen, 2013), 34.
281. This was even more evident during the Reichstag election of 1907, the so-called "Hottentot election." "Only German honor is at stake" was a common refrain among nationalists (StaBiB, RTW 1903–1912, no. 76: "Kameraden des Deutschen Kriegerbundes!"), who tended to view themselves and Imperial Germany through the eyes of rivals, as is typical with shame and fear of shame: "The whole world is watching us now" (StaBiB, RTW 1903–1912, no. 74: "Für die Kämpfer in Südwestafrika!"). Unless Germany "gladly" risked everything to defend its honor, earning respect through violence and fear, "our enemies" would be emboldened to strike (StaBiB, RTW 1903–1912, no. 67: "Das ist Wahrheit!," p. 3). From this perspective, the battles in SWA had a significance far beyond the interests of power in Africa. The young great power had been put to the test under the eyes of its European rivals; mastering this test with a show of absolute strength seemed essential to its continued existence.
282. This fact was also shameful from a comparatively moderate, paternalistic perspective. If the indigenous "charges" were deprived of autonomy and the colonial masters acted in their best interests, indigenous rebellion raised uncomfortable questions, directly challenging the colonial masters' ability to satisfy this claim. When an uprising—as in SWA—caught the colonial masters unaware, revealing how little they actually knew about the needs and privations of their "charges," it unflinchingly exposed the vast discrepancy between the colonizers' inflated ego ideal and their actual selves. One strategy of denial was stylizing the indigenous people as duplicitous "beasts," cruel "savages," or enemies of civilization. The resistance of these stereotypes to contrary evidence points to their significance for the colonizers, since the rebels could have come to an agreement with the German state, just as they did not behave as "beasts" during the war. The familiar thought patterns bolstered the colonizers' self-image, but vilified their enemies. The gulf that separated the parties was so wide that it seemed unbridgeable.
283. Trotha diary, TA 122/15, 1 July 1904.
284. Scheff, *Bloody Revenge*, 96.
285. I rely here on Norbert Elias's analysis in *The Germans*. Elias shows the extent to which the late nineteenth-century German bourgeoisie forgot its liberal and humanitarian traditions. The bourgeoisie had failed in its efforts to achieve national unity—and democratization—in 1848/49. Instead, traditional elites (princes and military officers, who were chiefly aristocrats) unified Germany over the course of three wars

(1864–71). The bourgeoisie, in turn, oriented itself toward the warrior ethos of the military aristocracy, which became the model for the upper class. The military was an "important motor of internal nation building, under conservative and authoritarian auspices." See Ute Frevert, "Das jakobinische Modell: Allgemeine Wehrpflicht und Nationsbildung in Preußen-Deutschland," *Militär und Gesellschaft im 19. und 20. Jahrhundert*, ed. Ute Frevert (Stuttgart, 1997), 45. The duel became the characteristic institution of "good society." Integration and socialization of the upper class took place at cadet academies and military schools, and also in dueling fraternities. In short, the bourgeoisie absorbed an initially unfamiliar canon and came to resemble the military aristocracy.

286. Elias, *The Germans*, 115–16; 181, and 206.
287. Honor can be understood as a "symbolically generated ability to interact." See Niklas Luhmann, *Gesellschaftsstruktur und Semantik: Studien zur Wissenssoziologie der modernen Gesellschaft*, vol. 1. (Frankfurt, 2010), 96. Honor is "*symbolically* generated" because it derives from the opinion of others, and thus is also "the embodiment of violability" (*das schlechthin Verletzliche*). See Georg Wilhelm Friedrich Hegel, *Ästhetik*, ed. Friedrich Bassenge, vol. 1. (Berlin, 1985), 538. The possession (or not) of honor determines who "counts" within a social group, signaling submission to the norms of the group and the individual's ability to interact within it. Honor is always particular, representing a specific group or collective. See Weber, *Wirtschaft und Gesellschaft*, 534; and Georg Simmel, *Soziologie: Untersuchungen über die Formen der Vergesellschaftung*, ed. Otthein Rammstedt (Frankfurt, 1992), 486. For an opposite view, see Ludgera Vogt, *Zur Logik der Ehre in der Gegenwartsgesellschaft: Differenzierung, Macht, Integration* (Frankfurt, 1997).
288. Bourgeois honor transposed the honor of the officer to civilian life. Military conceptions of honor shaped male gender identity and the social expectations that accompanied it. The Imperial German military served as a "school of masculinity," producing and disseminating the era's "hegemonic images of masculinity." See Ute Frevert, "Das Militär als 'Schule der Männlichkeit': Erwartungen, Angebote, Erfahrungen im 19. Jahrhundert," in *Militär und Gesellschaft im 19. und 20. Jahrhundert*, ed. Ute Frevert (Stuttgart, 1997), 146ff.; and "Das Militär als Schule der Männlichkeiten," in *Männlichkeiten und Moderne: Geschlecht in den Wissenskulturen um 1900*, ed. Ulrike Brunotte and Rainer Herrn (Bielefeld, 2008), 58. Sabina Brändli shows how civilian conceptions of gender identity entered military discourse, influenced the military ideal, and then returned to civilian discourse with a heightened military emphasis. In civilian life, too, masculinity was "measured primarily according to military virtues." See Sabina Brändli, "Von 'schneidigen Offizieren' und 'Militärcrinolinen': Aspekte symbolischer Männlichkeit am Beispiel preussischer und schweizerischer Uniformen des 19. Jahrhunderts," in *Militär und Gesellschaft im 19. und 20. Jahrhundert*, ed. Ute Frevert (Stuttgart, 1997), 203.
289. This prestige was evident, not least, in the particularly high proportion of nobility in the officer corps. See Franz Carl Endres, "Soziologische Struktur und ihr entsprechende Ideologien des deutschen Offizierskorps vor dem Weltkriege," *Archiv für Sozialwissenschaft und Sozialpolitik* 58 (1927): 282–316.
290. This strategy fit seamlessly with Trotha's racist ideas. When he wrote that he knew "enough tribes in Africa; they all think the same way, yielding only to force," this did not show—as he believed—his knowledge of African peoples, but rather his utter lack of relationship to them. Because Trotha rejected all dialogue, only violence remained; its message could not be missed. See Trotha to Leutwein (5 November 1904), BArch. R1001/2089, p. 101.
291. Endres, "Soziologische Struktur," 294.
292. Trotha diary, TA 122/17, 23 September 1904.

293. Trotha to Hülsen-Haeseler (10 December 1904), copy in TA 315, 2a, Anlage 33/2.
294. Montague, *Campaigning in Zululand*, 114.
295. Trotha diary, TA 122/15, 22 June 1904.
296. Trotha diary, TA 122/16, 17 November 1904.
297. Keith Oatley, *Emotions: A Brief History* (Malden, 2004), 107.
298. Balandier, "The Colonial Situation," 54.
299. See, for example, Otto Busch, "Deutschlands Kleinkrieg," Cape Town, 27 January 1906 (no. 14), NAN, A.0529, pp. 6ff.
300. Marchand-Volz, *Werner Freiherr Schenck v. Stauffenberg*, 137.
301. Trotha to Leutwein (5 November 1904), BArch. R1001/2089, p. 101.
302. Trotha diary, TA 122/17, 20 July 1904.
303. Eckl, *"S'ist ein übles Land hier,"* 279.
304. Marchand-Volz, *Werner Freiherr Schenck v. Stauffenberg*, 144.
305. BArch. Nl. 30/3a, 12 August 1904, p. 362.
306. See NAN, Private Accessions, A.151, no. 2, II, p. 6 (2 September 1904).
307. Trotha diary, TA 122/17, 13 August 1904.
308. Lewis, *Shame and Guilt in Neurosis*, 37.
309. Trotha to Bülow (16 August 1904), BArch. R1001/2115, p. 172.
310. Marchand-Volz, *Werner Freiherr Schenck v. Stauffenberg*, 144.
311. Scheff, *Bloody Revenge*, 50.
312. Trotha diary, TA 122/17, 23 September 1904.
313. Shaw, *What is Genocide?*, 111.
314. Trotha diary, TA 122/16, 30 December 1904.
315. Trutz von Trotha, "Formen des Krieges," 72–73.
316. Jakob Vogel, "Stramme Gardisten, temperamentvolle Tirailleurs und anmutige Damen: Geschlechterbilder im deutschen und französischen Kult der 'Nation in Waffen,'" in *Militär und Gesellschaft im 19. und 20. Jahrhundert*, ed. Ute Frevert (Stuttgart, 1997), 249–50.
317. Frevert, *Ehrenmänner*, 193–95 and 213.
318. This does not mean that Trotha had *no* limits, as the following episode demonstrates. In November 1904, it was discovered that Captain Joachim von Heydebreck, an "old African," had sought to open negotiations with a group of Herero, but that First Lieutenant von Beesten had "[lain] in wait . . . and shot down the people," as Trotha noted on 21 November. Gewald argues that Beesten acted in line with Trotha's direction, and that he was merely following the order to annihilate (Gewald, *Herero Heroes*, 182). However, this is not quite correct. The general did say that he wanted to wring Heydebreck's neck because "against my explicit order, he told the Herero they could come and surrender"—because, in other words, Heydebreck had acted against the order to annihilate. But Trotha emphasized that he wanted to wring "both" necks—Beesten's too. By treacherously shooting down the Herero who had naively trusted Heydebreck, Beesten had committed "a 1st-degree nasty trick" (TA 122/16, 21 November 1904). Trotha sought court-martial proceedings against both officers, which shows that even he believed that not all conduct was permissible.
319. From the start, Trotha had interpreted the uprising as a "struggle between races"—a life-or-death contest to be settled once and for all, no matter what, even if the colonized peoples perished in the process. This extreme outlook provided one more rationalization for Trotha's behavior, discouraging self-criticism and any changes in course.
320. Trotha diary, TA 122/17, 30 September 1904.
321. Trotha diary, TA 122/17, 12 August 1904.
322. Heyde did make mistakes, but there is some evidence that they were not the reason for the Waterberg debacle. Estorff, for one, later absolved Heyde of all responsibility.

See Siegfried Godendorff, "Späte Rechtfertigung zur Vorgehensweise der Abteilung von der Heyde bei den Gefechten am Waterberg durch den damaligen Abteilungsführer und späteren Generalleutnant a.D. Hermann von der Heyde," *Befunde und Berichte zur Deutschen Kolonialgeschichte* 6, no. 11 (2006): 49–56. Heyde had pointed out weaknesses in Trotha's plans early on. Trotha noted in his diary that Heyde was afraid "of being overrun by fleeing Herero"—which, in the end, is exactly what happened. In a sense, Trotha acknowledged Heyde's reservations, affirming, "He is not that strong." Even so, Trotha did not change plans (TA 122/17, 6 August 1904). It seems likely that Trotha sought a scapegoat more than anything else.

323. Trotha diary, TA 122/17, 23 September 1904. The circumstances with Mühlenfels will be covered more thoroughly in the pages ahead.
324. Trotha noted, "At 11 Beaulieu explained to me that he was no longer able to continue here. His heart was so weak that the doctor felt he had to depart right away. *Bon!* I'll be glad when he's gone.... I don't believe that he's sick, but I don't care" (TA 122/17, 24 August 1904). Previous diary entries point to fierce disagreements (for example: TA 122/17, 13 August 1904).
325. Trotha himself described a "fierce . . . disagreement with Quade. Always polite, always smooth, General Staff training. Only brutal means will help here. Just like with Leutwein—I wrote to him today that working together will no longer be possible" (TA 122/16, 2 November 1904).
326. The dispute grew to such proportions that in Berlin there was even a dedicated "Leutwein/Trotha secret file" (BArch. R1001/2089, p. 46). The very first entry in Trotha's war diary foreshadows the subsequent conflict: "A direct subordinate relationship for the colonial government is not indicated [in the imperial order that appointed Trotha commander of the Schutztruppe in SWA]. I will take up the decision to introduce this in my first order" (TA 122/15, 20 May 1904). On 25 October 1904, Trotha noted in his diary, "In addition, Leutw[ein] wrote to me that he reported to [the] F[oreign] O[ffice] that he had not been consulted about the offers of surrender, the existence of which he should surely be familiar with, and therefore he could no longer participate or such. I immediately wired the General Staff that this report from Leutw[ein] was a lie; now there is no other way, either him or me" (TA 122/16). Trotha intentionally sought to humiliate Leutwein in this dispute. On 10 November 1904, he wrote that he had wired Leutwein the following: "I forbid you to send telegrams from the theater of war back home." He then added, "I'm curious if he'll now march off" (TA 122/16). On 11 November 1904, Trotha noted with relief, "This evening a telegram from Bülow arrived; [it says] that I won, for the time being I'm *omnis potens*, and that Lindequist will be governor" (TA 122/16).
327. Conrad Rust complained in the *Windhuker Nachrichten* about a directive from Trotha that was intended to punish the newspaper for its criticism of the military authorities, withdrawing its access to official communications. According to Rust, the directive was "a product of conditions that have created a kind of warfare and also politics that—in the view of knowledgeable Africans—is not entirely without reproach. It is a characteristic result of *dictatorial power* directed against the freedom of expression." See "Ein Ukas," *Windhuker Nachrichten*, 1 July 1905, 1–2.
328. On 17 August 1904, Trotha mentioned in his diary, "Many telegrams, some very old. One from the Kaiser. It concludes: 'Extend my Imperial thanks to your officers and enlisted men.' Not a word for me. *Bon!*" (TA 122/17).
329. Vierhaus, *Am Hof der Hohenzollern*, 221.
330. Stuhlmann diary, NAN, Private Accessions, A.0109, p. 271.
331. On 8 November 1904, Trotha complained in his diary, "Still no answer from Berlin. It is utterly incomprehensible. Do they want to start a conflict! If they want to spare L[eutwein], they should just recall me, as I expressly requested. I'll spit on their

whole pie (*Ich huste ihnen was auf die ganze Pastete*). I'm giving up the final years of my life to be treated thoughtlessly here."

332. He called Schlieffen the "sad warrior" (TA 122/18, 20 January 1905). In response to a telegram from the General Staff on 4 January 1905, which indicated a possible Herero presence near Namutoni, Trotha remarked, "Splendid! News of the enemy from Berlin! Who's the ass here?!" (TA 315, Anlage 2a, p. 48). A few days later, he noted in his diary, "This afternoon, a telegram from Alfred [Schlieffen]. According to reliable reports, a big gang is in Kaokofeld. Alfred Alfred! Head to a cloister or take a cold shower (*Geh in ein Kloster oder ein Kaltwasserbad*). That's downright childish. News of the enemy from Berlin. *Risum teneatis amici!*" (TA 122/16, 10 January 1905).

333. On 18 November 1904, Trotha noted, "Today a letter from Beaulieu to Quade, which says that Schlieffen criticized only the colorless reporting. But he has his press boys (*Pressebengels*) for that. He can write what he wants to. I only report facts. I can't report heroic deeds that no one performed. What kind of notions are those. I'm not running a press office here. Besides, I don't want to. That's only Schl[ieffen]'s way of speaking to hide his embarrassment that he's done nothing to protect me from criticism" (TA 122/16).

334. On 10 December 1904—the day after receiving the order to pardon those Herero who surrendered voluntarily—Trotha appealed to Hülsen-Haeseler. Trotha complained that he had, "in the clearest and most poignant way," sought assurance "from any side" that "His Majesty, the Kaiser and King, is in agreement with continuing the war as I intend to," but he had received no response. No one would defend him, although in the meantime he was also being attacked sharply by the press. In Strasbourg, before Trotha's departure, the Kaiser had promised that he would have nothing to do with the Imperial chancellor—but now he had received an order from Bülow that he was to oversee the colonial government. Trotha requested an order from Schlieffen, but Bülow informed him that the chancellor, not the General Staff, was responsible for the order. Trotha wanted the chancellor to clarify who was in charge of political affairs while the not-yet departed Leutwein was still in the colony, and whether he (Trotha) would directly receive the relevant military and political reports. Trotha received no response to either request. "This is too much," he remarked, insisting that he could not submit to an authority that the Kaiser had explicitly told him not to without a definitive, supreme order. He also demanded the Kaiser's affirmation of his policies. The "complete disregard" for his requests, not even a negative response, was incommensurate with his standing (2a, Anlage 33/1).

The quintessence of Trotha's letter was his request that the Kaiser formally confirm his appointment as colonial governor. In a telegram dated 3 February 1905, the Kaiser did confirm that he had empowered the chancellor to assign this responsibility to Trotha (Wilhelm to Trotha, 3 February 1905, 2a, Anlage 53).

335. The bone of contention was a passage from Bülow's speech before the Reichstag on 5 December 1904: "We are neither so cruel, nor so foolish, as to believe that the only chance for restoring orderly conditions is to shoot down the half-starved and dehydrated Herero bands that are now streaming out of the deserts of the sandveld" (StBR, 105th session, 5 December 1904, p. 3376a). On 15 January 1905, Trotha wrote to Count Hülsen-Haeseler, chief of the military cabinet, that he saw the words "so foolish" as a "personal insult"; ignoring this would be "inconsistent with the concepts of honor" associated with "my class and my person," which is why he sought to "settle" the matter. He explained that, as a matter of personal dignity, he was unable to recognize the "sacrosanctity of the Reichstag speaker" (2a, Anlage 51/1). On 23 February 1905, Hülsen-Haeseler responded that the Kaiser saw no "personal insult" in Bülow's remarks, and thus no cause for "personal action" (2a, Anlage 57). Trotha

left it at that, but asked that the Kaiser be told that he might request to be relieved from his command, as soon as the Kaiser saw fit (Reply from 12 April 1905, ibid.).
336. "Das Interregnum von Trotha—und sein Ende, *Windhuker Nachrichten*, 2 November 1905.
337. Leutwein to the Colonial Department (19 March 1904), BArch. R R1001/2114, pp. 158–59.
338. See the sentences from Trotha's diary entry on 13 August 1904, p. xx.
339. Bernd Kroemer, *Für Kaiser und Reich: Kriegstage in China und Südwestafrika* (Windhoek, 2009), 97.
340. NAN, Private Accessions, A.0109, p. 65.
341. Malzahn diary, NAN, Private Accessions, A.510, p. 26.
342. NAN, Private Accessions, A.151, no. 2, II, pp. 12–13 (15–29 [?] September 1904).
343. "Der Aufstand," *DSWAZ*, 14 December 1904, 2.
344. Rohrbach, *Aus Südwest-Afrikas schweren Tagen*, 195 and 233.
345. Adolf Fischer, *Menschen und Tiere in Deutsch-Südwest* (Stuttgart, 1914), 94–95.
346. NAN, Private Accessions, A.510, p. 26.
347. Trotha to Schlieffen (4 October 1904), BArch. R1001/2089, p. 6.
348. NAN, Private Accessions, A.0109, p. 86 (16 October 1904).
349. Großer Generalstab, *Die Kämpfe der deutschen Truppen*, vol. 1, 213.
350. TA 122/16, 16 November 1904.
351. TA 122/16, 17 November 1904.
352. TA 122/16, 7 December 1904.
353. TA 122/16, 8 December 1904.
354. TA 122/16, 11 December 1904.
355. Trotha mentioned another difference of opinion on 23 December. Mühlenfels reported that Zacharias from Otjimbingwe had offered to surrender. "He fears that if not accepted, everything will fall apart," but Trotha insisted on "unconditional surrender" and "transport in chains" (TA 122/16, 23 December 1904).
356. Frankenberg diary, NAN, AACRLS.070, p. 123 (10 December 1904).
357. Schlieffen's report from 23 November 1904, BArch. R1001/2089, p. 5.
358. In pointed contrast to the conventional and legal understanding of intentionality, genocide scholar Helen Fein (drawing upon the work of Robert Merton) has developed a concept of purposeful action that includes not just the directly intended consequences of one's actions, but also those consequences that are merely foreseeable. See Fein, *Genocide: A Sociological Perspective*, 19. Thus, we can still speak of genocide with respect to the events in SWA.
359. Lettow-Vorbeck, *Mein Leben*, 77.
360. Hund, *Rassismus*, 84ff.
361. In *Absolute Destruction*, Hull situates the case of SWA within a broader historic context: the militarism of Wilhelmine Germany. The unification of Germany by means of war brought the military unparalleled prestige, so military and national interests were practically synonymous. The Great General Staff's remarkable operational victories of 1866 and 1870 fostered a kind of tunnel vision. This was evidenced not only by the fixation on certain operational doctrine, the "dogma of the battle of annihilation" (Jehuda Wallach), but also in the one-sided emphasis of tactics and operations, at the cost of strategy, diplomacy, and politics. As Hull emphasizes (*Absolute Destruction*, 182), few military apparatuses in this era were willing or able to fundamentally question their routines and underlying premises. It was all the more important, therefore, that the apparatus had a robust counterweight in nonmilitary institutions, which could limit its sometimes extreme impulses in sensitive situations. The political culture of Imperial Germany (including organs of official policy *and* civil society)

was decidedly militaristic, and did not provide a robust counterweight. Political institutions tended to favor military solutions, which could quickly degenerate into a spiral of violence if speedy victory was not achieved. Even repeated failures did not necessarily move those in authority to rethink their approach or consider alternative action; rather, they responded with a steady increase in violence, which is not surprising given their deference to the schemata of military officers, who were specialists in violence. Hull has unquestionably identified important conditions for the escalation of violence in SWA, but her thesis is not entirely satisfying. She proposes that the routines of metropolitan military culture (and militarized political culture) continued in South-West Africa—or, conversely, that events overseas adopted the well-worn patterns of homeland routines. Upon a closer look, this assumption seems questionable, especially since so many things clearly went wrong. A commanding general who boasted that he would "shoot dead" a fleeing opponent, who took it upon himself to expatriate an entire people, and who considered challenging the Imperial chancellor to a duel over a minor issue was exceptional—even in an era of ascendant militarism. Trotha did not go so far that the authorities in Berlin considered removing him from his post, but he ultimately did lose the Kaiser's favor. His peers may still have considered his behavior to be "normal"—but by no means self-evident or without alternative. This is a blind spot in Hull's argument, which focuses on military organization. Specific actors and their motivations "underneath" the routines—in other words, meso-level aggregates—do not receive sufficient attention. Hull's narrative does not explain why Trotha unleashed ever greater violence and ruled out alternatives, even as most of his peers recognized and openly discussed the futility and cruelty of his actions.

362. This could explain another peculiarity. As we have seen, Deimling contributed no less than Heyde to the failure of the Battle of Waterberg (insofar as the battle plan itself was not at fault) by defying his actual orders. He impetuously stormed ahead and scared the Herero into taking flight and overrunning Heyde's section. As far as I can see, however, no court-martial was initiated—or apparently even considered—against Deimling. While Trotha overtly detested Heyde, he hardly criticized Deimling. Both commanders, Deimling and Heyde, had defied Trotha's orders, but only the latter had to answer for his unauthorized actions, while Deimling continued to receive important assignments. He later was even appointed to lead the South-West African Schutztruppe. Depending on the particular circumstances, unauthorized actions and even mistakes were forgiven. When Deimling pressed ahead too eagerly (in the jargon of the times, he was "spirited" or "forceful"), his actions—despite his mistakes—corresponded to expectations for a high-ranking officer. Intentionally or not, Heyde missed out on fighting because of his unauthorized actions. Consigned to a passive role, all he could do was try to save himself as he was overrun by the fleeing opponent. Although poor planning by the high command placed Heyde and his section in this situation, he appeared incompetent and hesitant (at least in Trotha's eyes) and made a convenient scapegoat.

Underscoring the role of the commanding general need not reduce what transpired to a matter of individual psychology. Rather, Trotha was a typical representative of a particular milieu—"good" Prussian/German society, with its specific notions of honor. Honor regulates human behavior within a society by placing limits on the individuation of its members. Honor always refers to a particular group; an honorable person submits to the norms of this group and demonstrates the appropriate conformity in behavior. Thus, honor always suppresses "illegitimate individuality." See Weber, *Wirtschaft und Gesellschaft*, 534; Simmel, *Soziologie*, 486; and Neckel, *Status und Scham*, 65.

363. The honor of a person or family generally depends on whether they "count" in their social group—whether other members maintain relationships with them, do business

with them, or extend credit to them. Honor reveals who and what matters in the group.
364. Elias, *The Germans*, 51.
365. Bourdieu, *Outline of a Theory of Practice*, 16–22.
366. Frevert, *Ehrenmänner*, 233ff.; and Karl Demeter, *Das deutsche Offizierkorps in Gesellschaft und Staat, 1650–1945* (Frankfurt, 1962), 113.
367. The sovereignty of the monarch derived largely from the army, which defended not only against external, but also internal, enemies. See Hull, *Absolute Destruction*, 103. Franz Carl Endres correctly notes that the German army of 1914 and before was primarily a "dynastic instrument," not a "people's army," even if it was identified as such. See Endres, "Soziologische Struktur," 283. Political leaders feared that the urban proletarian milieu was politically unreliable, and so universal conscription was never fully realized. See Förster, *Der doppelte Militarismus*, 21.
368. The privilege of dueling placed its practitioners above the law, reducing the coercive apparatus of the state to an instrument that held "the unruly masses" in check. The duelers' credo seemed to be "We are the lords of the state. We live according to our own rules, which we impose upon ourselves. The laws of the state do not apply to us." See Elias, *The Germans*, 52.
369. Within this context, Ute Frevert speaks of a "double standard." After intermittent attempts to curb "affairs of honor," Wilhelm I made clear that he would tolerate no officer who was unprepared to defend his own honor, thereby reinforcing the pressure to duel. His grandson Wilhelm II likewise took no concerted action against "affairs of honor," but rather demanded "dynamic action." See Frevert, *Ehrenmänner*, 110ff.
370. Luhmann, *Gesellschaftsstruktur und Semantik*, 96–97.
371. Kuß, *Deutsches Militär auf kolonialen Kriegsschauplätzen*, 83.
372. Bernhard von Bülow, *Denkwürdigkeiten*, ed. Franz Stockhammern, vol. 2 (Berlin, 1930), 21.
373. Estorff, *Wanderungen und Kämpfe*, 117.
374. Elias, *The Germans*, 84.
375. Nicolaus Sombart, "Männerbund und Politische Kultur in Deutschland," in *Männergeschichte—Geschlechtergeschichte: Männlichkeit im Wandel der Moderne*, ed. Thomas Kühne (Frankfurt, 1996), 147–48.
376. The War Academy was founded in Berlin in 1859; its purpose was to train an elite officer corps. By the 1880s, War Academy graduates dominated the Great General Staff. The character of the academy was distinctively bourgeois, as admission depended entirely on anonymous testing. As a military and technical professional school, it molded officers into "military technocrats." See Michels, *"Der Held von Deutsch-Ostafrika,"* 52–53.
377. Thomas Kühne, *Kameradschaft: Die Soldaten des nationalsozialistischen Krieges und das 20. Jahrhundert* (Göttingen, 2006), 84.
378. Estorff, *Wanderungen und Kämpfe*, 117.
379. Frevert, *Ehrenmänner*, 216.
380. Bülow, *Denkwürdigkeiten*, 21.
381. Trotha saw this only as "giving in," which he considered unacceptable. Such a distinction between personal and professional identity may have been inconceivable to him.
382. Endres, "Soziologische Struktur," 306; and Elias, *The Germans*, 51–52.
383. Steinmetz, *The Devil's Handwriting*, 202. George Steinmetz sees the "symbolic class conflict" between Trotha and Leutwein as one of the conditions that led to genocidal escalation. Trotha possessed the specific cultural capital of the nobility, "specialization in the arts of domination and violence," while Leutwein represented the culti-

vation of the educated bourgeoisie. Setting aside the fact that Steinmetz's analysis of the conflict is not always accurate (he identifies Berthold Deimling, for example, as a member of the nobility, although Deimling had not yet received this distinction), the crucial lines of conflict may have been different. Trotha challenged Bülow, not Leutwein, to the duel—and his aversion to Schlieffen was no less pronounced. These conflicts became so intense precisely because they reflected differences in opinion among noble elites, with Trotha defending the military and aristocratic ethos in its purest form against all deviations.

Chapter 4

Small Warfare and Brutalization

> War changes you, changes you. Strips you, strips you of all your beliefs, your religion, takes your dignity away, you become an animal. I know the animals don't—the animal in the sense of being evil. You know, it's unbelievable what humans can do to each other.
>
> —US veteran of the Vietnam War[1]

The whites' interactions with blacks in South-West Africa were defined by despotism, violence, and cruelty, even before the outbreak of war. The uprisings radicalized these violent conditions, which continued after the hostilities ended. As Bley has shown, war did not normalize the situation in SWA; instead, the opposite occurred.[2] All wars are characterized by a reduction in norms and sanctions; even killing is no longer prohibited—and the prohibition of killing, more than any other, is a sign that there are limits to how others may be treated.[3] The war against the Herero, which was never a local or limited conflict, increased white fantasies of power. The settlers' violent acts and claims to autonomy had long frustrated the colonial government and eventually contributed to the Herero taking arms—but the problem got worse during the war.

This chapter examines the brutalization of the troops in the Herero campaign. "Brutalization" was a process of coarsening. It occurred when members of the troops felt less and less bound to soldierly or legal norms, and they turned to illegitimate violence instead. Violence "from below" was an independent dimension of the violence that informed relations between whites and blacks, and it continued well beyond the genocidal phase of the campaign. Borrowing from Gerlach's multicausal understanding of "extremely violent societies," brutalization can be understood as a cause, but also as an effect, of other processes.[4] Brutalization was closely related to the changing conditions of a campaign that posed unanticipated challenges, and that generally did not go according to plan. Brutalization also contributed to the escalation of violence, as the Germans' refusal to pardon their opponent incited even more bitter resistance. This chapter presumes mutual interaction, rather than one-sided cause and effect.

Scholars of war and genocide have long struggled with the problem of violence from below. By focusing primarily on the history of great battles and the "world-historical heroes" who led them, earlier generations of historians arbitrarily narrowed their focus and distorted their subject, neglecting much of what happens at war. Works like John Keegan's *The Face of Battle* (1978) left these limitations behind and demonstrated that the view "from below"—that is, the perspective of combat troops and lower-ranking officers—represents a distinct dimension of warfare that deserves our attention.

The question of genocide, especially the "top-down" scheme that informs conventional genocide studies, has dominated scholarly interpretations of the war in SWA. The question of brutalization, by contrast, emphasizes forms of violence that cannot be traced back to orders "from above"—and that often defy these orders. Accentuating violence from below does not contradict the genocide thesis per se. In some cases, in fact, this emphasis can help to explain how "ordinary men" (Christopher Browning) became instruments of genocidal warfare, thereby complementing the conventional "top-down" perspective. This chapter seeks to explain why the soldiers carried out orders that transgressed usual boundaries and contradicted "chivalrous" soldierly values—and why they even surpassed these orders again and again. Many of the soldiers' actions were not militarily essential, and in fact brought them additional risk.[5]

My observations in this chapter are directed against certain variations of the genocide thesis and their modus operandi. Scholars have repeatedly attempted to support the genocide thesis by pointing to individual atrocities without considering their closer context, but this context sometimes contributed significantly to the escalation of violence. Individual acts cannot always be traced back to corresponding orders "from above," let alone to a broader strategy. Many of the reported atrocities had a different motivation and were committed *against* the orders of superiors. Thus, violence from below must be understood as a distinct dimension of the process of violence.

Small units shaped the course of the war, and even average soldiers enjoyed considerable latitude for decision-making. In the colonial situation, even the lowest-status whites claimed special rights and typically felt above the law.[6] In such a scenario, we should not view the soldiers merely as passive recipients of orders, or as "willing executioners." Small warfare in SWA depended entirely on the initiative of individual soldiers and their willingness to fight. We must, therefore, consider their emotional motivations.

In SWA, as in small wars in general, many aspects of rigidly hierarchical institutions such as the military easily lost their original significance. Thus, members of the colonial Schutztruppen liked to call themselves "mercenaries" (*Landsknechte*), and these forces were first organized like private armies.[7] After the initial wave of enthusiasm for the war in SWA had subsided, by the end of May or early June 1904, German authorities already had to recruit reservists because there were not enough active volunteers. The brutality that was described in soldiers' letters made colonial service less appealing, and the accompanying hardships and perils drew greater attention. The Schutztruppe evolved into a troop of adventurers and ex-convicts,[8] as had occurred in China during the Boxer Rebellion.[9] The blatant "lack of discipline among these new, young soldiers" enraged long-serving officers like Viktor Franke, whose "enthusiasm for a colonial career" dropped off sharply.[10] But even new arrivals like First Lieutenant Stuhlmann shared Franke's assessment of the incoming soldiers; Stuhlmann believed that the incoming reinforcements did not want to abide by military constraints.[11]

Many contemporaries noted that soldiers were changed by the war in SWA, and not for the better. Military leaders were repeatedly compelled to take action against the proliferation of violence from below, particularly the shooting of women and children.[12] The clergy in the colony registered these changes with growing concern, and they even initiated "soldiers' evenings" to counteract this development. Their description of these evenings is instructive:

> That is a good—and perhaps the best—sign that the German soldier's drive for self-discipline and staying above water is strong, despite the temptations and dangers that constantly confront him here, and that he is striving to make his way through the swamp and decay, holding firm above the bar of looming perversion with as little harm as possible.[13]

The clergy sought damage control. They were pleased that the soldiers had not yet entirely lost the "drive for self-discipline and staying above water," but were "striving" to make it through their deployment "with as little harm as possible." The clergy were presumably overwhelmed with the problems of the soldiers, although the vague choice of words does not reveal what had so alarmed them. We can assume, however, that some of the soldiers' problems were related to what is now known as post-traumatic stress disorder. As we will see, the conditions for this were clearly present in SWA.

One challenge was that the public had not properly recognized the problem and sometimes dismissed it. Responding to reports of German war crimes (including some against women and children), Oskar Stübel, the director of the Colonial Department, explained to the Reichstag that the "German character is not inclined to cruelty and acts of brutality." Many Reichstag delegates, and the public at large, were satisfied with this response.[14] The fact that commanders felt obliged to appeal to the "discipline" or "breeding" of the troops suggests that soldierly norms were by no means self-evident. Calls for discipline usually involved "getting tough" with the soldiers and subjecting them to worse humiliation and degradation than their everyday routines already prescribed—a "solution" that only perpetuated the problem, as military psychiatrist Jonathan Shay describes.[15]

The consequences of long wars had worried Imperial German military elites since the tenure of Helmuth von Moltke. The officers were primarily concerned with the scenario of an unlimited "people's war" on the European continent, particularly the popular radicalization and centrifugal social forces that such a war might unleash.[16] They hardly considered, however, what might happen to soldiers in prolonged combat situations (particularly those resembling small wars). It was generally believed that "good character" was enough to "stay clean" and hold firm against outside pressures.[17] This was an illusion that would be thoroughly debunked over the course of the twentieth century, but the problem was never addressed in SWA. At least some documented German atrocities can be connected to the brutalization of the troops.

The observations in this chapter affirm that the genocide in SWA was a process that evolved over time. Drawing upon the ideas and actions of rank-and-file soldiers, I illustrate how violence escalated "from below." In its early stages—and in some respects, thereafter—the war was defined by colonial society; settlers promoted their own form of violence from below that was characterized by revenge. This chapter's focus, however, is the later part of the war, which was increasingly defined by metropolitan actors—the officers, staffs, and soldiers of the regular home army. The Battle of Waterberg was an important caesura in the course of the war. I distinguish here between two different phases, each of which correspond to a dominant form of experience among the German soldiers, related to the escalation of violence and the brutalization of war. The phase that preceded the Battle of Waterberg was defined by raids and assaults, and by the German soldiers' heightened fear of injury or death. The phase after the (failed) battle included the pursuit and measures to seal off the Omaheke, which brought deep embitterment and frustration.

Fear and embitterment (or frustration) are common to the experience of regular armies in small wars, and in fact shift back and forth all the time. On the one hand, soldiers feel helpless and vulnerable because of the "telluric character" of the opposing irregular forces and the advantages this character provides.[18] On the other, soldiers become frustrated that their opponent rarely engages in the kind of battle that regular armies are trained to fight. I propose that each of the phases in the South-West African campaign was dominated by one of these experiences, although the contrast was not a privative opposition.

These experiences assumed such intensity in SWA because they so deeply wounded the white soldiers' feelings of superiority. The feeling of helplessness was especially painful because the soldiers believed they were dealing with "inferior natives" or "Kaffirs." Racism was at the heart of the processes of brutalization described in this chapter, and it lent them special momentum.

Before I turn to the dynamics of brutalization, I will show how small wars tend to be characterized by uncertainty and disorder.

Small Warfare

Like violence in general, war exposes human vulnerability by disrupting chains of events, situationalizing reality, and making behavior less predictable.[19] In his classic study *Small Wars*, which first appeared in 1896, Charles E. Callwell underscored that small wars were characterized by much greater uncertainty than so-called "conventional" wars.[20] The small war veteran and writer Tim O'Brien has depicted the radical break with the routines of conventional warfare; his regular training in the US army did not prepare him for the scenario he encountered in Vietnam, where everything he had learned seemed obsolete: "There is no clarity. Everything swirls. The old rules are no longer binding, the old truths no longer true."[21] In a small war, whatever certainties that exist in conventional warfare disappear, along with the boundaries and categories that define them.

This uncertainty, and the dynamics it fostered, were also key to the Herero campaign. From the beginning, the "old Africans" understood that the conflict would be fought as a small war. Although the first months of fighting included some larger engagements, as a whole the war was defined by long periods "without obvious 'results' or 'great events.'"[22] Its chief protagonists were small detachments and patrols, which occasionally engaged in smaller skirmishes. We should not be taken in by the reluctance of military leaders in Imperial Germany to acknowledge the fundamental character of the campaign. Thus, in this chapter I examine the mismatched relationship between the South-West African theater of war on the one hand, and the strategy prescribed by authorities in Berlin on the other.

Contemporary scholars of war employ a number of competing (and sometimes synonymous) terms that more or less refer to what has come to be known in military theory, in numerous languages, as small war. These terms include "new," "wild," "neo-Hobbesian," "asymmetric," "irregular war," "low-intensity conflict," "civil war," "guerrilla war," and "partisan war."[23] All refer to combat techniques that were fully developed, and described by military theorists, by the eighteenth century. Fighters continued to adopt these techniques in the centuries thereafter, without fundamental changes.[24]

But first, a few words about "great" warfare. "Great" or "conventional" wars are more or less symmetrical, fought by structurally similar adversaries with similar means. These wars typically involve large battles and large bodies of troops, and they uphold a "trinitarian" distinction between government, army, and civilians that restricts the exercise of violence.[25] Historically, these conflicts have usually been state wars. Not coincidentally, international laws of war developed in tandem with the modern state system.[26]

There are at least three fundamental kinds of certainty in conventional warfare. First, it is more or less clear who should be considered the "enemy," and under which conditions. Second, because the warring parties are structurally similar, how to overpower the enemy, and which goals must be met in order to end the war, are also relatively certain. And finally, because each of the warring parties adhere to the same principles, their actions are also somewhat predictable. Clausewitz had these certainties in mind when he noted the tactical significance of the moment of surprise, a rarity in conventional warfare: "Preparations for war usually take months. Concentrating troops at their main assembly points generally requires the installation of supply dumps and depots, as well as considerable troop movements, whose purpose can be guessed soon enough."[27] Clausewitz wanted to illustrate how large troop bodies can hardly move without drawing attention; their preparations and plans for war are quickly transparent. Since other warring parties face the same challenges, they can easily interpret their opponents' moves.

These certainties disappear in small wars. When the doctrine of small warfare first emerged, it played a subordinate role in wars between states. Even so, small warfare was more than mere "accompaniment" or "preparation" for decisions on the battlefield; it might be better described as a "complement" or "corrective"—an autonomous, irreducible part of warfare with its own techniques.[28] Small warfare sought to make combat asymmetrical, exploiting the limitations of great state wars.[29]

The inflexibility of the great line formations made them vulnerable, allowing light units, the protagonists of small warfare, to show off their strengths. Light units generally avoided larger engagements, and they evaded stronger adversaries by retreating to difficult terrain. Dispersed fighters fired individually, not in salvo, and so they cultivated their individual weapons skills. Small warfare demanded the self-initiative that drills drove out of regular linesmen.[30] Light units continuously pursued and unsettled the opponent. They undermined distinctions between "on" and "off" the battlefield by attacking from the rear, and they spurned open combat in favor of assaults and ambushes. They disrupted their opponent's lines of communication and disturbed larger armies while marching, setting up camp, or entering battle formation. Light units were also tasked with collecting taxes and information from local populations,[31] and so they undermined the strict distinction between combatants and civilians.[32]

Light units brought an element of unpredictability and uncertainty to wartime events that were otherwise heavily ritualized, proceeding according to rules that were essentially fixed. There was something inherently lawless about small wars' deviation from "actual" combat. Unsurprisingly, the first specialized units in the eighteenth century—such as the "Croatian" pandours who fought for Austria—were recruited from societies on the European periphery that were not part of European military tradition. Although small warfare techniques contradicted those of large state armies, small warfare remained dependent on its "great" counterpart for some time. Only in exceptional cases did small warfare attain strategic significance in its own right.[33] This changed no later than the great colonial expansion of the nineteenth century, which was accompanied by conflicts with autochthonous societies that were politically, socially, and culturally disparate from their European counterparts. No longer a pendant of great warfare, the small war came into its own and even became the exclusive form of combat in some scenarios. Asymmetric warfare was the rule in the colonial periphery, even though—as the war in SWA emphatically shows—military officers did not always readily accept or adjust to this new reality. For General von Trotha and much of the Imperial German military and political establishment, small warfare (as practiced exclusively by the Schutztruppe in SWA until the 1904 uprising) was not "serious warfare."[34] Trotha's futile efforts to conduct a war of great battles only underscored that small wars could not be fought according to the familiar routines of European state warfare. "Asymmetry" meant that the European powers often confronted structurally different opponents with none of the usual targets that standing armies were used to attacking, and no capital cities or commercial centers to seize. Strategic goals were unclear, as were the criteria to win. This was the "uncertainty" of small warfare that Callwell described.[35]

This asymmetry gave the colonial powers a pretext to ignore the norms that usually limited the exercise of violence in European state wars. In conflicts with substate or nonstate opponents, Imperial Germany, like the other colonial powers, did not feel bound by the restrictions of international law, which applied only to signatory states.[36] Even a "moderate" officer like Leutwein presumed that a general uprising against German colonial rule would "doubtless demand killing all prisoners who were fit to bear arms."[37]

A state that does not enforce or feel bound to the norms of international law affects how soldiers in "conventional," state-organized armies understand their own role. In this respect, it is unsurprising that members of the Schutztruppe called themselves "mercenaries" and also behaved as such.[38] When the officer von Frankenberg mentioned in passing how a woman who had fallen into the hands of the Germans was "shot as a spy, liar, etc., together with her child" after a short interrogation,[39] this was an expression of the brutalization of the troops in small warfare scenarios, which could be confusing and unclear. Conventional, more or less stable distinctions between "on" and "off" the battlefield broke down; the enemy was always out of reach, and yet seemed to lurk everywhere. Uncertainty turned into fear, accompanying the soldiers' every move.[40] Fear of the enemy, injury, and death is fundamental to warfare—but it is heightened in small wars, as the very identity of adversaries is unclear, as well as when and where they might strike. Were the adversaries "colored" servants and transport workers? Or the San family who happened to cross paths with the troops?

After the outbreak of war, stories of atrocities supposedly perpetrated by Herero women against German soldiers made the rounds in SWA.[41] Such stories, which are typical in small war scenarios, reflect the uncertainty and fear that can overcome troops in an unclear situation.[42]

Shocking tales involving women and children showed that no one could be trusted in a small war, and that the enemy could hide behind even the most innocuous facade.⁴³

For Callwell, a primary challenge of small warfare was fighting against a natural environment that was unfamiliar, even hostile, to Europeans.⁴⁴ Some authors who have studied similar conflicts go one step further, depicting uncertainty so great that not only humans, but also animate and inanimate nature, become a source of fear. Jonathan Shay asserts that "in such warfare nothing is what it seems; all certainties liquefy; stable truths turn into their opposites."⁴⁵ Nothing is as it seems: the civilian bystander is revealed to be the enemy; peacefully grazing cattle become a deadly trap; the open path is an ambush; and death lurks behind every bush. From one minute to the next, the most innocuous object can become a weapon that threatens the victim with annihilation.

As central distinctions between "on" and "off" the battlefield, or between combatants and civilians, become obsolete, the question of victims' guilt or innocence assumes a lesser role. Without armies or capital cities to be conquered, small wars rarely come to a "conventional" end. Small wars have an affinity for extreme, even total, solutions. Not coincidentally, compulsory resettlement and deportation to concentration camps occurred within the context of small wars in Cuba, the Philippines, and South Africa.⁴⁶ The war against the Herero affected "innocent" lives as a matter of course. The violence continued, and was even institutionalized, after Trotha's strategy of extermination was officially replaced, and surviving "prisoners of war" were herded into concentration camps and subjected to collective punishment. As one officer complained, the regime of the camps was conceived and directed against a "defeated, abject opponent"—without distinction for women, children, or the elderly.⁴⁷ Deputy Governor Hans Tecklenburg summed up the approach when he explained that there were no innocent prisoners, only those who were "less guilty."⁴⁸ To this extent, the regime of the camps was the continuation of small war by other means.

The German Military in South-West Africa

The Herero—and later, the Nama and Oorlam—posed a significant challenge to German military leaders. They were frugal and highly mobile, and they used their superior knowledge of the terrain to avoid larger skirmishes with the German troops, whom they lured into ambushes.⁴⁹ They adopted evasive strategies and considered a well-executed retreat or escape to be a success, if not a victory.[50] Tactical successes in the European sense (such as taking the opponents' positions or forcing them from the battlefield) usually accomplished little, as this tended to build, not weaken, their morale.[51] Small warfare overwhelmed the German military, precisely because it seemed less demanding. German military doctrine and strategy were oriented toward the large concentric battles that had established the reputation of the Great General Staff and made victory culture essential to German identity. These successes diminished Imperial German leaders' willingness to rethink their military orientation and strategy in a different context, particularly that of a "small despicable Kaffir war."[52] German military leaders—and Lothar von Trotha, in particular—had a Eurocentric view of war, even though Trotha and others did have past experience in China and East Africa.

Their orientation corresponded to weaponry that was intended for conflicts between structurally similar actors, on battlefields that had been selected for this purpose. In the South-West African theater of war, the rebels chose terrain that prevented the German troops from taking full advantage of their superior weaponry. It soon became apparent that German artillery was rarely decisive in battle,[53] but instead posed a significant burden by lengthening German columns, slowing their movements, and making them vulnerable to attack.[54] Mobility was key, but it was impeded by heavy weaponry that had been designed for scenarios unlike South-West African conditions. In the run-up to the Battle of Waterberg, von Brünneck complained that it was impossible to situate a cannon appropriately.[55] Superior firepower could be decisive in larger, European-style battles, but not necessarily in SWA.

German military doctrine traditionally sought the annihilation of the opponent.[56] By contrast, military officers who were familiar with South-West African conditions pleaded for a strategy of attrition. These officers wanted small, mobile units to pursue the opponents as doggedly as possible, wearing them down to the point that losses of humans and cattle would compel them to accept the Germans' terms for peace.[57] Trotha, however, wanted only annihilation. Clinging to a goal that was illusory in the given circumstances, he prolonged the war at the cost of significant casualties on both sides. Plans for the Battle of Waterberg left a "proper and sensible impression" on the officer Viktor Franke, although he also noted that these plans did not seem to match the conditions on site; encirclement would be difficult with the available troops, and the opponent would not wait patiently.[58] Trotha's chief of staff, Martin Chales de Beaulieu, admitted that the directives for the subsequent pursuit had been "drawn up, more or less, only for Berlin."[59] The misguided strategy—oriented toward Berlin, not local conditions—brought few tangible successes. It demanded ever greater sacrifices from the troops and incited resentment against the German commanders and General Staff—the "big talkers" (*große Blechbude*), as Franke sarcastically called them.[60] Stauffenberg complained in a letter, "If certain factors in Germany hadn't always pushed for quick actions and 'victories,' we would have taken things slowly, and—naturally, over time—we would have strangled the Herero at the Waterberg, as we are doing now; this is what I and many old Africans believe. That would have cost not even a fraction of the blood [that was spilled]."[61]

Misguided military doctrine and inappropriate weaponry went hand in hand with deficiencies in training, equipment, and organization.

Conditions of warfare in SWA called for mounted infantry, although this did not correspond to conventional divisions in the home army.[62] Unlike the infantry or cavalry alone, mounted infantry brought together elements of both kinds of military service. Conventional infantry had no experience with horses. This in itself posed a challenge, as insufficient pasture and water in SWA quickly led to horses dying "like flies."[63] Most of the horses had to be purchased on different continents and imported to the colony in order to meet the sudden increase in demand. A large number were deemed "inferior,"[64] and by no means ready for service upon arrival.[65] The imported horses were usually fed with oats, but sufficient quantities could not be brought along on longer operations in the South-West African interior. The horses had to get used to grazing, and particularly to the local pasture.[66] The hasty troop buildup meant that little attention had had been paid to caring for the horses, which was clearly beyond the capabilities of the average infantryman. Most of these "equestrians" were brought to the colony just as hastily as the animals and could hardly stay on their saddles. The twenty new riders assigned to First Lieutenant Epp included seventeen infantrymen who "had never sat on a horse."[67] They had to acclimate the horses to the new and difficult conditions, and the fighting power of the troops depended on their success.

Cavalrymen were schooled in riding and working with horses, but without the infantry training that was essential for a mounted infantryman. Infantry were trained for battle; they knew how to form firing lines, how to conduct an orderly advance, and how to fight a rearguard action. They learned how to use the terrain and seek cover, and also how to shoot on their own. Regular cavalry training was limited to riding and caring for the animals, and practicing special formations that were not used in SWA.[68] Cavalrymen in SWA were thus expected to train daily for combat "in the bush."[69]

The fighting power of the mounted infantry largely depended on their horses' wellbeing. Only reasonably healthy horses could provide their units with the mobility and speed that was necessary to keep up with a highly mobile opponent across vast distances. Experienced South-West African officers like Viktor Franke always had their eye on the condition of their horses, and they emphasized appropriate care when training their companies.[70] The infantry could accomplish little without horses that carried them reliably to the enemy. The cavalry may have understood this better, but they were at a disadvantage in firefights against enemies with better shooting skills.[71] The Admiralty Staff of the navy could not fail to notice that "in marksmanship and taking cover, the newcomer can only learn" from the Herero.[72]

No branch of the home army sent soldiers who were immediately fit for combat in South-West Africa. The soldiers often struggled with their weapons and horses.[73] The problem only got worse as the pressure for rapid mobilization increased; the number of troops grew by a factor of twenty in just a year and a half. There was little time for training or getting to know the new environment.

Compared to the long-serving colonial troops and Herero fighters,[74] the new recruits from Germany were seriously compromised by their lack of self-sufficiency—as even Stuhlmann, a newcomer to the colony, noticed right away.[75] Elite leaders' deep mistrust of the urban lower classes meant that troops were not only ill-prepared for small warfare—but also for great warfare, which had been transformed by tremendous developments in weapons technology.[76] A 1906 training manual (*Exerzierreglement*) emphasized mission-type tactics (*Auftragstaktik*), but even after 1906 the training that soldiers actually received did not change significantly. Recent developments in weapons technology meant that soldiers fought in lines so thin that they could no longer be supervised directly by officers, and so they had to become much more self-sufficient. They had to learn how to use the terrain to seek cover by themselves. No longer firing on command or in salvo, they had to seek out their own targets and manage their own cartridge supply.

This kind of self-sufficiency was essential in SWA. Small units had to cover large areas, while optimally exploiting the range and power of their breechloaders. A comprehensive command was not always possible at the company level.[77] This was particularly true in combat situations. "Even in their own troop, few [soldiers] saw beyond their neighbors to the right and left," as one officer described his experience in SWA.[78] Individual soldiers confronted further challenges. Horseback patrols embarked on reconnaissance missions on confusing terrain, without the usual points of orientation. Riders had to be able to orient themselves;

losing their way could have devastating consequences.[79] "Every patrol is a ride of death," Stuhlmann remarked.[80]

The soldiers were ill-prepared by their training in Imperial Germany. Social considerations were decisive for the country's elites. Recruits for the new mass army increasingly came from an urban proletarian milieu that was considered unreliable, so soldiers were strictly supervised by officers, even in combat. The destructive force of artillery and machine guns made close troop concentrations inadvisable, but soldiers continued to be stationed closely together, so they would remain under supervision.[81] Rank-and-file soldiers were accustomed to direct oversight, and they lacked self-sufficiency.[82]

This led to a related problem. The evolution of weapons technologies and the fundamental transformation of the modern battlefield meant that introducing and implementing mission-type tactics, which demanded a comparatively high degree of autonomy, was long overdue. The turn-of-the-century *Exerzierreglement* did explicitly incorporate mission-type tactics, but "discipline" still tended to mean upholding a visible order—in the sense of behavioral conformity or linear tactics that were long obsolete. Discipline did not necessarily extend to the mindset of individual soldiers, who were not encouraged to acquire or interiorize soldierly norms on their own. Habitualized self-control did not replace external control, which became particularly evident whenever the soldiers were left unsupervised. Stuhlmann noted that they did not fulfill their responsibilities unless they believed they were being watched.[83] This may not have mattered in the barracks yard, but even rank-and-file soldiers had to make life-or-death decisions in small war scenarios. The settler press invoked the moral "superiority" of whites and urged them to behave in a corresponding manner.[84] In the end, however, military leaders did not see soldiers' behavior as a serious enough problem to demand intervention; this small war was not a modern "counter-insurgency," but an example of violent repression.[85] Legitimacy has assumed an increasingly prominent role in modern counter-insurgencies. *How* an opponent is defeated matters as much as the victory itself; superiority is supposed to be reflected in the behavior of one's own combatants—although this aspiration is rarely realized. In SWA, however, the Germans were concerned only with putting down the uprising, whatever the cost. The essential problem of modern counter-insurgency had not yet been recognized as a strategic concern, and the German state did not worry about losing legitimacy because of its hardline approach.[86]

The quality of the reinforcements suffered because of how they were mobilized.[87] Volunteers from armies of the individual German states were recruited to serve in the new contingents, resulting in a colorful mixture from all different regions and branches of service. First Lieutenant Epp complained:

> All this is in the field: Old Schutztruppe, new Schutztruppe, most never on horseback, drafted reservists and Landwehr men from the colony, Landsturm men, former Schutztruppe soldiers who reside here, marines from the *Habicht*, Boers as oxcart drivers, bastards from Rehobott [*sic*], Witbooi Hottentots as auxiliary troops, a few Klippkaffers as native soldiers.[88]

Typical sources of identification and *esprit de corps*—namely, a sense of allegiance to fellow countrymen, or a shared branch of service—were missing in these circumstances.[89] There was no longstanding tradition that might have fostered a sense of unity among the newly formed units. Epp observed that "men are always being sent, but no organized units."[90]

The soldiers' training was complicated by their origins in the different branches of service; members of the artillery, infantry, and cavalry were placed together in new units without a common standard of training. Officers sometimes did not get to know their own soldiers until they were together in the colony. The fighting power of the new units was inevitably weaker than that of the older ones.[91] The German officers and the opponent were aware of this deficiency. The Nama and Oorlam mostly avoided the long-serving units, but they showed not the "least respect" for the new ones.[92] Kurd Schwabe concurred, noting that the difference between old and new troops was "clearly apparent" in battle.[93] Stuhlmann emphasized that a "core of the good old Schutztruppler" was advantageous because they encouraged other soldiers to follow their example.[94]

Germany's military leadership bore responsibility for all of these deficits that affected troop morale. Jonathan Shay notes that an army is a "social construction defined by shared expectations and values," which are embodied in formal regulations as well as traditions passed down over time. "All together, these form a moral world that most of the participants most of the time regard as legitimate, 'natural,' and personally binding. The moral power of any army is so great that it can motivate men to get up out of a trench and step into enemy machine-gun fire."[95] If the integrity of this order is (or seems to be) damaged, the performance of the troops will suffer.

The Herero forces likewise constituted a "moral world," although under different circumstances. Warriors typically fight in groups that formed in "civilian" life and that remain together even in wartime. Because these groups are comparatively self-reliant and less specialized than a modern army, their members do not experience the same degree of alienation as participants in an abstract, anonymous apparatus.

The modern soldier's dependence on a military apparatus resembles a small child's dependence on his parents.[96] This has certain advantages (a combat troop, for example, does not usually have to worry about procuring food or munitions), but also disadvantages in adverse conditions. The more one depends on an apparatus, the more reasons one has to mistrust it. Soldiers are keenly aware of this dependence, alert to any signs that their trust might be misplaced.[97] Should these signs increase, the performance of the entire organization can suffer. Just as an intact "moral world" can move soldiers to overcome their fear of death, a violation of this world (a feeling that one has left been in the lurch, or sent to slaughter by one's superiors) can lead to trauma and brutalization that ultimately endangers the troop's ability to function.[98] Scholars have thoroughly documented and investigated these phenomena in the experience of the US armed forces in Vietnam. American soldiers increasingly defied legal and soldierly norms, murdered disliked superiors,[99] and even engaged in open mutiny.[100] Because Schutztruppe documents were lost or destroyed in the subsequent world wars, an exhaustive investigation of the war in SWA is no longer possible. However, comparable conditions and individual anecdotes suggest that members of the South-West African Schutztruppe were similarly traumatized.[101] The consequences of overt mismanagement and poor decision-making were borne by the troops,[102] dampening the "accustomed enthusiasm" for their "supreme warlord," the Kaiser.[103]

When combat troops feel that the apparatus has abandoned them, a sense of group identity can coalesce, excluding others behind the front lines and back home; Tony Ashworth has identified this effect among soldiers in the trenches of World War I.[104] Distinctions between "high" and "low" begin to break down, and norms and orders are no longer binding. This is especially true when the apparatus seems to fail again and again, so that upholding its rules begins to appear more deadly than not. In total institutions like combat forces, forms of "secondary adjustment" (Erving Goffmann) emerge, as Shay describes in another context: "At the deepest level, survival in war trains or selects men for the skills to ignore, deflect, pervert, or circumvent orders, rules, and standard operating procedures. . . . The soldier quickly grasps that following rules can get him and the people close to him killed."[105]

Structural causes unrelated to the failure of humans who keep the apparatus running can also enflame the troops' resentment. In *Seven Pillars of Wisdom*, T. E. Lawrence compared regular armies to plants.[106] The comparison is apt, as armies, too, are firmly rooted; the most far-flung outpost is utterly dependent on supply lines for food, munitions, information, and commands. Armies rely on provisioning and warehousing systems; in a sense, their supply lines are the umbilical cord that keeps individual units alive. Thus, larger troop movements rarely go unnoticed and are always somewhat predictable—in contrast to the movements of most adversaries in small war scenarios. The standardization of military procedures means that the movements of large armies are easier to predict. As we have already seen, Clausewitz believed that the moment of surprise played only a subordinate role in great wars.[107] In asymmetric conflicts, the inflexibility and predictability of large armies become a weakness. Unlike their opponents, large armies are usually easy to see and especially vulnerable to attack.

In general, Western governments and militaries have had a hard time departing from traditional military doctrine that is geared toward state wars; Imperial German elites were not unique in this respect. In his 1991 study *The Transformation of War*, Martin van Creveld complains that Western armies today are still oriented toward large wars, although low-intensity conflicts have long since displaced classic state wars as the dominant form of warfare. In SWA, the institutional difficulties of adjusting to new realities extended to the realm of strategy and cost soldiers' lives. The fact that state armies were designed for scenarios unlike those in SWA repeatedly raised the question of trust and put the military apparatus to the test.

Fear

When the new troops arrived in SWA, they were ill-prepared for local conditions. They had to adjust to the unfamiliar climate and learn their craft as mounted infantry within a very short period of time. They usually mobilized soon after landing. On foreign terrain, the new troops faced an opponent who was superior "in every way." Almost everything was unfamiliar.[108] The landscape was full of perils and favored the opponent's style of fighting.

The campaign against the Herero brought the Schutztruppe to areas that were overgrown with tall, sometimes "impenetrable," bushes, which created numerous problems.[109] The officer Georg Maercker, who had significant experience in East Africa, explained that reconnaissance and securing the surroundings were often impossible in these conditions. The terrain was so confusing that detachments inevitably lost contact with their column.[110] Franz Epp remarked that in the "usually dense thornbushes of the savanna, the side patrols simply can't make it," and he concluded that "the only protection against surprise attack is movement and being ready for combat."[111] Once the opponent was within sight, it was usually too late. The Herero were sometimes able to kill multiple German soldiers every day, without the Germans managing to take down even one enemy fighter in return.[112] Maercker noted that close-range skirmishes that seemed to materialize out of nowhere were typical of the fighting against the Herero.[113] The advantage of superior weaponry, artillery, machine guns, and even long-range breechloaders was lost in the bush; all of this firepower could not be unfurled at short range or as quickly as the assaults sometimes arose.[114]

A noncommissioned officer named Malzahn illustrated the dangers of fighting in the bush. Soldiers suddenly came under fire from all sides, the command fell apart, and everyone fought for their lives. Since the battle at Oviumbo on 13 April 1904, where the Herero fought doggedly but did not prevail, Malzahn admitted to having "terrible respect" for the densely vegetated terrain. A later incident demonstrated that his fears were well-grounded:

> We hadn't been in the miserable brambles for long, and fateful danger rushed toward us. The infantry was surrounded by blacks, just as we were. Sneering faces crept out of the bushes. It was impossible to set up the cannons. So we unlimbered on the path, shooting left, right, or backwards, wherever it was needed most. The losses of hinnies and horses were dire. No commands broke through; everyone was fighting to save his own skin. It was a colorful mess. . . . I had already given up everything.[115]

The Schutztruppe's adversaries remained hidden as long as possible, allowing the German sections to ride directly toward their secure positions and then opening fire.[116] They often set traps for the Germans.[117] Ambushes could occur at any time. The soldiers found no rest, even in their fortified camps at night. The Herero were constantly reported to be lurking "in the immediate vicinity of camp."[118] Knoke recounted how fear of the opponent had transformed his camp into a fortress of wagons; soldiers had to be alert at all times, keeping a carbine in hand "day and night."[119] Nighttime gunfire kept them from sleeping.[120] "Barking dogs" were enough to startle a fearful sentry and wake the entire camp.[121] Even without gunfire, sleep did not come easily. "With these signs that the predator is near, it's eerie to bivouac at night in the wholly impenetrable bush," the officer Christian Ahrens reported. "In the 3 nights of my last horseback patrol, I was the responsible leader and didn't sleep a wink."[122] A soldier named Belwe found the "eternal watchfulness" upsetting: "Keeping watch by night and working by day exhausts even the strongest [among us]."[123]

Knoke described how the constant threat from the opponent kept soldiers mobilized at all times; they found no physical rest over long periods of time. They literally could not sleep. They dozed off when circumstances allowed, but deep, regenerative sleep was out of the question. Ignoring nearby sounds or movements was simply too dangerous.[124] Recent work in military psychiatry has shown that unrelenting tension, as experienced by the German troops in SWA, can produce dysfunction, which includes or leads to brutalization.

Assaults could arise suddenly, as another example from Malzahn shows. He described what happened as he and his section crossed a plain covered with tall grass and thornbushes:

> We had been on this plain for about an hour, and we were in high spirits, when murderous, rapid fire suddenly erupted on both sides. We got off the horses and shot haphazardly into the bushes. We couldn't see any of the black devils, only their gunshots brought terrible devastation. . . . Once we found our way into combat formation and moved ahead, we found our advance guard scattered and drenched in blood, lying next to their loyal horses. This all happened in the blink of an eye. The Hereros had disappeared.[125]

Assaults like this one occurred "in the blink of an eye." As quickly as the assailants appeared, they disappeared again without a trace. Even as they opened "murderous, rapid fire" and caused "terrible devastation," they remained invisible. Malzahn and his comrades could only shoot blindly into their surroundings. "It's like going into the damned bush blindfolded," Epp complained.[126] Even the experienced South-West African officer Viktor Franke wrote that "nothing can be done about the 'living' bush."[127] Kurd Schwabe recalled that the skirmishes in the "bush" were "dreadful"; the Herero moved so quietly and effortlessly in nature that "they could not be seen at all."[128] After the battle near Oviumbo in April 1904, a sergeant reported to Captain Bayer, "The black demons can't be seen. I've been lying in position since early this morning, I saw bushes and trees and baked in the sun; the bullets zipped past me the whole day, but I didn't catch sight of one Herero."[129] Likewise, Brünneck wrote that he had not seen "one Herero" in the various April battles, although the opponents were often so close by that he could hear them talking to one another.[130]

Such experiences provided the basis for dehumanizing caricatures of the opponent. The Herero were ascribed almost superhuman qualities. Sometimes they were demonized outright, as "black beasts" or "devils" (*Satanskerle*), although most often they were depicted as animals. Malzahn reported about a Herero whose leg was ripped off by a grenade; he nevertheless survived for two days, and—tellingly—attacked Malzahn's troop from a "jackal's lair."[131] First Lieutenant Ahrens described the Herero as *raubtierartig*—literally, "like a predatory animal."[132] Depictions of the Herero fighters' superiority on difficult terrain tended to emphasize their animal-like affinity with their natural surroundings. As James Belich notes, this made their talents "remarkable, but not awe-inspiring."[133] Thus, the Germans developed strategies to explain the setbacks they encountered without having to question their own (supposed) superiority.[134]

Experiences like Malzahn's could lead to the conclusion that conventional means and methods were not enough to defeat the opponent. Even a grenade was not enough to deter a Herero fighter. Serious injuries did not lessen his will to fight, or the danger that he posed—or so the soldiers believed. In response, they turned all too often to measures that were proscribed by international law. Pardoning an opponent who continued to fight without any prospects for tactical success, and who showed no mercy himself, was out of the question.[135] A marine named Auer admitted that the Germans "chloroformed"—in other words, killed—seriously injured Herero fighters, in order to render them "harmless" once and for all.[136] Given the supposed invulnerability of the Herero, the Germans did not feel that they could rely on the power of conventional weapons. Officers advocated for larger caliber weapons because the usual munitions were supposedly not harmful enough. First Lieutenant Stuhlmann criticized conventional full metal jacket bullets, because these did not incapacitate the "natives."[137] Soldiers filed down their projectiles and repurposed them as dum-dum bullets—an act that was at least tolerated by their superiors, the provisions of the Hague Convention notwithstanding.[138]

Dehumanization and exaggeration were expressions of the fear that plagued the soldiers day and night. The newly arrived soldiers were particularly fearful of the opponent. They had been sent hastily and without proper training to a theater of war that was overwhelming and foreign in every way. An unclear threat scenario and a lack of knowledge about the enemy heightened their anxiety, and they feared being fired upon "at every moment."[139]

Panics in the German camps were an outlet for this tension and fear. Frankenberg described the reckless and overhasty use of firearms at night. On a single night in early March 1904, shots rang out three times for reasons that were not entirely clear. By the time that roll call was held between two and three o'clock in the morning, the entire camp was wide awake. In this case, no one was injured,[140] but Stuhlmann reported another incident that did not go as smoothly, underscoring how panics had become a serious problem. He described a "mighty ruckus" on the night of 10 July 1904:

> A drunk soldier entered a Kaffir tent, and he was given a proper hiding. When he came out, he called "help, guard," upsetting the camp so much that a real panic ensued. When around 20 men from the newly arrived transports (who of course smelled enemies everywhere) ran to the tent together, highly excited, someone called out, "That's a black man creeping over there!" They fired like crazy in all directions, only 3 to 4 paces apart from one another. A few men were wounded, in addition to a dead white and a dead black. It's a miracle that nothing worse happened.[141]

The fear and tension were so intense that a single trigger could set off a chain of overreactions. The violence spiraled out of control, and nothing or no one could slow it down. The spread of similar panics has been well documented in other campaigns, including the advance of the German troops in Belgium and France in 1914. Despite the different circumstances, German soldiers in World War I also felt threatened by an invisible enemy (the franc-tireur) and a hostile population. Here, too, rumors of atrocities that were supposedly perpetrated by women spread quickly.[142] The confusion of the overall situation heightened soldiers' fear and the intensity of their reactions. Although the franc-tireur of 1914 was largely a myth, the fear and its consequences were real. Devastating and deadly panics ensued. The numerous atrocities against Belgian civilians are well documented.[143]

The panics continued on the battlefield. In April 1904, Franke reported, "The new men from Germany, including artillery, fire like maniacs after every shot, so the clamor and clangor never ends. Even so, the shots fly continuously into our ranks."[144] The troops opened fire so wildly, for the smallest reasons, that they ran out of munitions after only a short time.[145] Salvos were fired so hastily that they had little effect. Nevertheless, Stuhlmann's description of the panic at the German camp underscores that even (and especially) the incompetent use of force, particularly firearms, can be extremely dangerous—and not only for the intended target.

Confident and self-assured, the soldiers had set off for faraway South-West Africa in order to "wipe the slate clean." As the proud representatives of a supposedly higher race—not to mention a "victory culture"—the German "experts" in the art of war felt superior in every way. However, the conditions that they actually encountered in SWA turned their unrealistic expectations upside down. They soon discovered that they were not only inferior to the "savages," but entirely at their mercy in many situations. Like other soldiers in small wars, they experienced extreme powerlessness.

The movements of the German troops could be seen and heard across long distances. At the Battle of Okaharui in early 1904, the German column was two-and-a-half kilometers long and extremely sluggish with its twenty-two oxcarts.[146] The wagon train was supposed to escort and supply the troops, but the troops essentially became cover for the wagons, and their freedom of movement suffered enormously.[147] The opponent always knew where the German troops were located, and in what numbers. "The H[erero] are constantly aware of our movements," Epp affirmed with resignation.[148] In the meantime, the Herero knew to stay hidden so that they could strike at a favorable moment. At the battle of Ongandjira, it was only indigenous scouts fighting on the side of the Germans who discovered the Herero ambush just in time. The German soldiers understood that they could not flee in an emergency, since this often meant certain death. If they were not taken down by enemy fire, nature would do the rest. After only a short time in the colony, Stuhlmann was well aware of the danger: "Many gravestones read: 'Rider . . . died of thirst'—a specter that haunts all who . . . lose their way."[149] The soldiers could do little more than wait for the opponent to strike, deflecting the small-scale assaults wherever possible. They often had no other alternative, as pursuing the assailants through increasingly dense foliage was out of the question.[150] "Pursuing the opponent would be entirely pointless . . . he'll never stand for a fight," Stülpnagel remarked.[151]

The advancing troops' fear could combine with rage, culminating in an intense need for revenge. Retreating or fleeing was out of the question—not only because of the immediate circumstances, but because of the soldiers' entire training and the self-image it conveyed. Aggression was the only coping behavior that remained, as the following two examples illustrate. In January, Captain Kliefoth's company advanced toward the Waterberg in order to investigate rumors of rebellion. One of the officers in the company, Conrad von Stülpnagel, described an incident that occurred after a Herero assault (with "damned little that could be seen in the thick bush and tall grass"):

> Even before, the men [the soldiers in the company] could hardly be restrained; furious about the assault, they pushed ahead without considering the broader situation. When they heard what had happened, they were overcome; you saw in it their faces, you heard it in their sharp remarks, a deep, sustained rage and the determination that these black wretches should feel what it means to have cowardly ambushed the peacefully marching troops.[152]

Because pursuing the opponent was hopeless, the company returned to its garrison with unfinished business, feeling low. The second report came from Captain Bayer:

> A blind rage gradually overcame us all! We had already been lying for an hour in the hot sand; at most, we had seen one or two of the vile black fellows who shot at us from many sides. We couldn't storm ahead, as we were prone to heading in a wrong direction and firing at ourselves. These miserable thornbushes held us captive on all sides, strangled us, robbed us of light and air . . . one could only lie there in anger and frustration and wait.[153]

The two reports vividly illustrate how rage, anger, and frustration overcame the soldiers. Further, the two accounts mention expressions and gestures of displeasure, and physical signs of rage, such as the struggle to breathe ("strangled us," "robbed us of air"). In the first example, the primary trigger was the opponent's behavior, which was perceived as unfair—the "cowardly ambush," and the (actual or supposed) violation of what was "right." In the second example, the behavior of the opponent—these "vile black fellows"—was also considered unfair, but the emphasis was on the soldiers' helplessness and powerlessness, which was particularly shameful in the colonial context. The Germans cowered in the "hot sand," hardly able to defend themselves; they could "only lie there," powerless and "captive on all sides." Bayer's account is emblematic of the entire war in the bush. It shows the army's vulnerability as it muddled through enemy terrain under the watchful eyes of an "invisible" opponent, unable to do much more than wait to be fired upon, defending itself wherever possible. The prospects for a "fair" battle—a battle that would showcase *German* strengths—were impossibly low.[154]

Fear joined with shame and transformed into rage. Because there was rarely an opportunity to redirect rage toward a "fair" battle, or against its actual cause, it accumulated and erupted in uncontrolled fury once the soldiers caught up with the opponent (or whomever they believed to be the opponent at that moment). The new troops, in particular, tended to fire at everyone who was or seemed to be black. Leutwein complained that many of the Germans' own auxiliary troops, cattle watchmen, and wagon and ox drivers were injured in this way.[155] He did not dispute that German soldiers had committed atrocities against women and children, a reproach confirmed by other sources.[156] Indeed, no prisoners were taken at this time. The hardline approach did not need to be ordered "from above"; the soldiers were sufficiently motivated on their own. "Fear can then lead to terrible atrocities," Michel Wieviorka writes.[157] Moreover, the authorities were all too indulgent of whites and rarely insisted that legal and soldierly norms be upheld. Deviance had long since become the norm in SWA.

In many respects, the defeat at Owikokorero exemplified this phase of the campaign and the mechanism that led to the further escalation of violence. At first, the Germans were overconfident, with all too optimistic expectations that were soon disappointed. Failure and the loss of control triggered shame and rage, which resulted in (even) more violence. Count Gleichen's prognosis proved correct: "The feeling between the races is so bitter that further atrocities, perhaps on both sides, seem probable."[158]

The troops longed for a chance to get back at the opponent, and the Battle of Waterberg seemed to be this chance. During the months of preparation, they impatiently asked when it would *"finally* get started."[159] Although the Battle of Waterberg was not decisive, it did enable greater violence "from below." Soldiers indiscriminately shot those who fled or were left behind, including women and children.[160] The violence was extreme enough that military leaders, who had riled up the soldiers just days before, now felt compelled to prohibit the slaughter of women and children.[161]

Embitterment

The Battle of Waterberg was an important turning point in the war. "Conventional" annihilation evolved gradually into comprehensive genocidal annihilation only after the battle did not turn out as planned. After the military decision that Trotha and most of the soldiers had awaited did not occur—not at the Waterberg, nor in the weeks thereafter—they ultimately had to acknowledge that it was no longer possible. Diaries and letters reveal how gravely these setbacks affected the morale of the troops. The campaign entered a new phase, which corresponded to the changed mood of the soldiers. Fear gave way to embitterment and frustration.

Before the disappointment at the Waterberg, and perhaps even at the beginning of the pursuit, German efforts focused overwhelmingly on a larger battle that would produce a military decision with a clear end. The soldiers looked ahead to the campaign's violent climax, perhaps with anxious expectation, but also with confidence that the campaign would soon come to an end. By the pursuit at the latest, it was clear that there would be no final decision; the pursuit continued to cost the lives of fleeing Herero, but it was an operational failure. The troops had to get used to the idea that they were now in a small war of attrition, with no end in sight.

Before the failed battle, the Herero had seemed to lurk everywhere, and they had repeatedly engaged in larger skirmishes. Now they all but disappeared, pulling farther and farther away from the advancing German troops. From this point on, the Herero forces splintered into ever smaller groups and avoided direct engagement. By September at the latest, the Herero could no longer mount a coordinated resistance and were merely trying to escape with their lives. The German troops nevertheless pushed ahead, enduring significant hardships and casualties, as the command still hoped to make up for the setback at the Waterberg. Men and resources were sacrificed for operational goals that had become almost impossible to achieve.

An incident that occurred at a German camp on 16 August 1904 exemplifies this phase of the campaign and its brutalization. The noncommissioned officer Knoke reported, "A Herero woman was given provisions and then set free. But the men are very bitter. The woman had barely left camp when two shots rang out. A sign that these cost her life."[162] The incident seems to have involved an act of violence from below. There had been no order to shoot the woman; the responsible officers had given her provisions and set her free.[163] The shooting seems to have occurred more or less openly; the shots must have been audible for some distance. It is hard to imagine that the act could have been hidden from anyone in the camp, yet Knoke does not mention any sanctions against the shooter, who openly disregarded orders and murdered an innocent woman. All this suggests that the campaign had acquired its own frame of reference, in which the arbitrary shooting of defenseless civilians had come to seem acceptable, even normal.[164] Knoke did not seem shocked, or even surprised, by what transpired in the camp; he did not condemn the shooting, and even expressed some understanding of it. By tolerating such acts, superiors contributed to the normalization of extreme violence. Officers may have wanted to avoid anything that could upset the troops further—as Leutwein, too, had given in to the settlers' desire for vengeance at the beginning of the campaign.

The act of violence that Knoke described does not seem related to any formal hostilities. Nothing suggests that the perpetrator had reason to feel threatened, or that he was responding to danger. The acts showed none of the frenzied brutality that characterizes violence motivated by fear. Rather, the murder seems to have been perpetrated "in cold blood," although not without emotion, as it was driven by deep embitterment and frustration.

Scholars have not always appreciated that the Battle of Waterberg in no way met the expectations of the German military, so they have not considered how gravely this setback affected the mood of the troops.

Franke commented sarcastically on the supposed triumph at the Waterberg: "When we wanted to approach his proud Excellence [General von Trotha], we had to pass by abatis and soldiers' trenches. The conqueror trembled before the conquered. Disgrace upon disgrace!"[165] Trotha admitted that for a short time, even he had believed that the German command would be lost.[166] This did not stop him from sending victory messages back home—to his officers' dismay. "Another victory like that, and we're lost," Hardenberg remarked in his diary.[167] The soldiers not only felt "beaten," but also ridiculed by the "hurrahs and cries of victory" and the "loud jeering" of the opponent.[168]

Immediately following the battle, Trotha ordered the pursuit of the fleeing Herero. The pursuit did not begin until 13 August because troops, animals, and resources were utterly exhausted—and it was called off just hours later, at two o'clock in the morning on 14 August, for exactly the same reasons. Having accomplished nothing, the riders—now mostly on foot—had to turn back. According to Knoke, 14 August was "the most exhausting day we ever had."[169] With luck, the troops made it back to their original positions, "half-dead from thirst" and almost completely "immobilized." The demoralizing retreat was no march of victory. The stench of death and decay hung in the air: "Horse and oxen cadavers everywhere," Hardenberg noted.[170] On 15 August, the horses in Hamakari were left to starve in misery because there was "nothing" for them. Hardenberg complained that the troops had received "no bread for days"; poor provisions soon made them sick.[171]

The military leadership had not anticipated the setback at the Waterberg, and the operations that they hastily initiated on 16 August lacked a clear vision.[172] It soon became evident that the enemy was on the run, too scattered to mount an organized resistance.[173] Nevertheless, until the end of September, the Germans still intended to catch up with "the Herero" and beat them decisively. The combat troops saw the futility of these efforts, but they paid the price for their leaders' insistence.

Immediately after the battle, the men and animals were in a pitiful state. There was not enough food or water, and the pasture was exhausted.[174] The pursuit occurred too late to offer a realistic chance of catching up with the Herero, and too soon to give the troops time to recuperate, or even to supply them with essentials. On 13 August, Viktor Franke remarked in his diary, "The leaders warn, I warn: We're ruining the half-ruined material all the way, without a glimmer of hope for success."[175] Franke would prove correct. The forced marching that characterized subsequent operations wore down the troops even more. Not only the horses died "like flies."[176] Men and animals alike suffered from hunger, thirst, exhaustion, sickness, and death. In contrast to the

Herero, the German troops depended entirely on reinforcements, but the demand was impossible to meet in remote areas far from the railroad line. The troops lived "from hand to mouth" throughout the entire pursuit, and they had to make due with dwindling rations.[177] Hunger and thirst proved to be "the most vicious enemies."[178]

Sickness spread among the soldiers "to a horrifying degree."[179] Typhus alone claimed more and more lives.[180] The soldiers who were still alive resembled "wandering corpses," Malzahn reported.[181] Of the soldiers who were sent to the field in July, Stuhlmann noted, barely one-third remained just a few months later.[182]

Again and again, the fighting troops had to accept that their efforts and privations had been in vain—at least to the extent that these did not lead to further great battles; casualties among the fleeing Herero were devastating. The military leadership stylized every German advance as the prelude to a decisive battle, but no real progress was made.[183] "The hunt was fruitless again," Epp affirmed after the last great skirmish on 30 September 1904. From this point on, there were no more actual battles; the Germans fired their artillery at dust clouds that receded ever further in the distance. Trotha could hardly describe one of the last "battles" in the Omaheke without lapsing into sarcasm:

> Much dust visible at a great distance, moving NE. The artillery arrives, fires first at the dust clouds, and then scatters the bush. At 11, action on a broad front against the watering hole. No enemy in sight; also no one killed by the 20 cannon shots.... From a scenic perspective, the battle was very beautiful; from a military perspective, 0.[184]

At a distance of more than six thousand meters, the fusillade's actual effect was instilling fear.[185] "We won't catch the Herero again, anyhow," the artillery officer Stuhlmann predicted in early September 1904.[186] When the Herero campaign ended for Ahrens at the end of October 1904 (after serving under Deimling during the pursuit, he was sent to the southern theater of war), he looked back soberly on his experience: "The horses are finished, mostly dead, the survivors are ruined"; the whole time he had not seen one "armed, living Herero."[187]

Military leaders' insistence on clinging to a misguided strategy hurt the morale of the troops, who must have felt that commanders "at the top" were recklessly gambling with their health and lives. As Stuhlmann lamented, the accomplishments of the pursuit were in no way proportional "to the men who had marched to the point of collapse and the many fallen draft animals."[188] The losses on the other side raised little concern.

Troops in the field had little regard for commanders at headquarters. The former often had to make due with a fraction of their rations, rationing "every grain of rice,"[189] while the "sated, Mosel wine–drinking" commanders wanted for nothing.[190] Worse, the top commanders seemed concerned only about the expectations of the homeland and the symbolic victories it craved—although these victories were effectively meaningless and only cost more lives.[191] Commanders who served in the field also were not beyond reproach. Berthold Deimling (who later achieved dubious renown as the "Butcher of Ypres" in World War I) bore some responsibility for the failure at the Waterberg because of his unauthorized actions. He nevertheless retained his command and continued to sacrifice his troops "recklessly" to feed his personal ambition—a cautionary example of the misbegotten circumstances in SWA.[192] Rank-and-file soldiers came to believe that their leaders' solidarity and loyalty was directed less toward them, and more toward authorities back home.

The troops had numerous grounds for complaint. Maps were "wholly insufficient";[193] it was "scandalous" how little land had been surveyed, and how little was known about "vast stretches" of the colony.[194] The supply chain, moreover, was "miserable."[195] The sick and wounded received substandard care.[196] According to Epp, the poor conditions demonstrated either "boundless indifference" or "incomprehension" on the part of higher authorities.[197] In any event, the troops felt shabbily treated,[198] reinforcing their impression that their accomplishments had received "nothing close to adequate recognition" back in Germany.[199] Their mistrust of authority continued to grow, fostering new animosities and even "fierce cravings for revenge" against the rear command with its "fat storehouses," and against the military staffs.[200]

Hunger, thirst, death, and the futility of all these privations created a climate of embitterment and frustration. This climate fostered a new and distinctive form of brutalization, which came to characterize the pursuit and the cordoning measures that followed.

As amply demonstrated, troops quickly lose trust in their leaders if they come to believe that their lives are being recklessly sacrificed for the sake of ill-conceived plans.[201] Casualties are unavoidable in war, but Edward Shils and Morris Janowitz have shown that troops will tolerate casualties as long as these remain within certain bounds and seem objectively justified. Further, troop morale depends on officers' willingness to prioritize the wellbeing of their troops—that is, their responsibility to the ranks "below"—over orders "from above."[202] If this is not the case, the effects can be devastating, as Paul Savage and Richard Gabriel have demonstrated with respect to the US forces in Vietnam.[203] The well-documented example of small warfare in Vietnam shows how the erosion of trust in leadership not only weakens troops' fighting power, but also weakens their adherence to soldierly norms.

On 8 October 1904, the young lieutenant Stauffenberg wrote to his mother from the Omaheke Desert, describing warfare that defied "all rules and norms that cultures and religions have put in place." After weeks of futile pursuit, and only days after Trotha's proclamation, Stauffenberg expressed his disappointment and embitterment freely, complaining in no uncertain terms about the failings of the military apparatus in SWA. He directed his anger against the top commanders, against the "whole supply system," against the "lack of experience overall, the wrong people in essential positions, and especially the misguided frugality," and also against the failed strategy. He rebuked the entire military apparatus, injustice, and incompetence, and he blamed "hollow," "cowardly," and "pathetic" authorities for their indifference and recklessness. These leaders had sacrificed their own soldiers for a strategy that was geared solely toward the (unrealistic) demands of the metropole. Stauffenberg's embitterment and distance from the military leadership could not have been greater; he would have readily accepted further setbacks in order to expose the failure in leadership.[204]

Stauffenberg was not blind to the suffering of the Herero. He wrote, "And in the middle of it all, a deadly shortage of water has the entire Herero people on the move, thousands of languishing cattle and languishing persons. We can't go further, that's true, but if necessary we can stay where we are. But the Hereros can't stay and can't go further, as far we can tell."[205] The desperation of the Herero was so great, Stauffenberg remarked, that a few continued to approach the German positions—although they had to know what awaited them. For all of his complaints about the German leaders and their strategy, he expressed no sympathy for the actual victims. He continued:

> But this is how we crush and annihilate a struggling people, as an unfeeling instrument of torture with iron determination. At least this is what I believe, and this much is certain unless some black-skinned god gives the black people water or an escape. The small rainy season hasn't brought water so far, and by the time of the great one, the skeletons could be just right for anatomy. Over there, you might become sentimental; you certainly feel some personal sympathy. It's different here.—I feel sorry for the cattle; one would like to save and help [them]. The downfall of the Herero is like the man in a tragedy, and as involved as one is, one feels uninvolved; the small despicable Kaffir war is a piece of history. The Herero who annihilated the bushman—this wealthy, imperious, bellicose Herero—will himself be exterminated, and so, time and again, the struggle between races will, and must, sweep away all rules and norms that cultures and religions have put in place.[206]

As strongly as Stauffenberg condemned the military leadership, he in no way identified with the Herero, the actual victims of the Germans' failed strategy. He was deeply frustrated, and he named the sources of his frustration, but he did not direct his aggression against them. He must have felt powerless against the military leadership, and, as an officer, he naturally abhorred any act of "mutiny." Instead, he directed his aggression against the Herero, a less powerful surrogate. Stauffenberg blamed the Herero for prolonging the war because they continued to stand by their leaders, rather than turning them in—an example of displaced aggression.[207]

In contrast to the trench warfare of 1914–18, relations between military leaders and troops in the field were strained, but did not break altogether. In SWA, the chasm between troops and opponent was simply too wide.[208] From the outset, racism had hindered any identification with the opponent. Stauffenberg would have presumably been more empathetic to suffering Europeans. Surprisingly, his attitude toward the Herero only seemed to harden as their desperation grew. He not only was unable to identify with the Herero, but also expressed scorn and contempt for their miserable condition. Stauffenberg embodied the "ruthlessness" that Nietzsche had described: "All that proceeds from weakness" is bad and contemptible; "the weak and ill-constituted shall perish . . . . And one shall help them to do so"; sympathy was misguided, sentimental humanitarianism.[209] The more wretched the "languishing" and "desperate" Herero became, the more they seemed to merit Stauffenberg's contempt, and even their own deaths. This attitude explains his identification with the murderous, misguided strategy of despised commanders ("But this is how we crush and annihilate a struggling people"), and his willingness to execute this strategy with "iron determination." "Unfeeling," "uninvolved," and without "personal sympathy," he administered the "tragic" fate of a people whose downfall was assured. A hardline stance against the "weak" meant keeping them at a distance, and so the Germans were able to close their own ranks by affirming their mutual superiority.

This may explain why the embittered, frustrated troops did not lapse into apathy. Embitterment, frustration, and contempt for the "weak" motivated the troops to keep going, and even to escalate their use of force.[210] They demonstrated remarkable initiative in pursuing and annihilating the opponent. Even after the high command decreed a change in course, some of the officers who led the patrols that tracked down and slaughtered the Herero continued undeterred. Count von Schleinitz, for example, ignored the orders that revoked the strategy of extermination, and he killed a large number of captured Herero.[211] Soldiers and "men of honor" were not supposed to give in. In a sense, the "campaign of disappointments" (as W. E. Montague had described the engagement against the Zulu in 1879) only heightened the Germans' determination.[212] The chaplain P. A. Ziegenfuß, who participated in the pursuit, described the mood of the troops at this time: "We were carried by the hope that soon we would have the enemy on his back once again; there was celebration every time we could settle scores with the Hereros out in the field!"[213] The condition of the Herero who were apprehended—"powerless and isolated," all-too "easy prey" for their pursuers[214]—did not dampen the troops' euphoria. Women were primary targets of the violence,[215] which by now had little to do with "battle"—as evidenced not least by the disproportionate Herero casualties.[216] Diary entries and official reports from this period recount numerous raids in which men, women, and children were indiscriminately "shot away" (*über den Haufen geschossen*)—that is, murdered outright.[217] At comparatively little risk to themselves, soldiers hunted down the scared, largely defenseless Herero survivors who were hiding or on the run. Without haste or noticeable fear, the pursuers tracked down and stalked the Herero, often approaching a settlement with only a handful of men. They "proceeded with weapons ready to fire,"[218] "shot down part of the inhabitants,"[219] and "in no time the werft was cleansed."[220] The soldiers created imaginary battlefields in order to reclaim their feeling of power.[221] In September of the following year, the Germans combed through the (former) Hereroland, "cleansing" forty settlements and taking 750 prisoners; compared to a "larger number" of Herero casualties, only one noncommissioned officer was killed, and two riders were wounded.[222] Such undertakings were celebrated as victories because they gave their actors a feeling of power. Artillery fire at faraway dust clouds, as well as "theatrical hangings" of the few apprehended Herero[223] and burning down abandoned villages (both documented in photos), sent a message to the enemy, to the remaining autochthonous groups, and to the Germans themselves: the campaign was far from over, and the Germans would prevail, whatever the cost.[224]

The idea of "struggle between races" allowed Stauffenberg to rationalize an unlimited war of annihilation as a recurring, even immutable constant of history, even as he also, quite accurately, characterized this warfare as defying "all rules and norms that cultures and religions have put in place."[225]

This chapter has reconstructed the motivations that allowed soldiers to implement a strategy that most saw as illusory and misguided. These soldiers repeatedly exceeded and even defied orders, killing women, children, the elderly, the sick, and the weak on their own initiative. This "excess" underscores that the soldiers were an independent motor of extermination.

Many of the soldiers' experiences in this campaign were devastating, and particularly shameful in a colonial context, as they wounded the white masters' feelings of absolute superiority. Fear, embitterment, and frustration led to rage and the need for revenge, culminating in extreme violence. Leadership that strictly upheld norms and sanctioned deviance might have kept this violence in check, but a shared racism that was accepted as self-evident made this impossible from the start. Small warfare disoriented and overwhelmed the Germans, and the situation spiraled out of control. These dynamics remained in place even after the wars ended and the few surviving Herero languished in German camps.

Notes

1. Jonathan Shay, *Achilles in Vietnam: Combat Trauma and the Undoing of Character* (New York, 1994), 33.
2. Bley, *Kolonialherrschaft und Sozialstruktur*, 214.
3. Trutz von Trotha, "Formen des Krieges," 72.
4. Gerlach, "Extremely Violent Societies," 468.
5. The "bold pursuit" undertaken by Captain Klein at the end of October 1904 pushed the "outer limits of human capacity" and devastated the entire section. Official accounts may have transformed this into an act of heroism precisely because it was militarily senseless. Numerous soldiers, including Klein himself, contracted typhus and died; twenty-five horses and twenty-one donkeys perished. See Großer Generalstab, *Die Kämpfe der deutschen Truppen*, vol. 1, 208ff.
6. Accounts of soldiers acting against orders have been documented in diaries and memoirs. See NAN, Private Accessions, A.538; and Günther A. Pape, *Lorang: Ich, die Seefahrt, der Krieg am Waterberg, meine Farm in Südwestafrika* (Göttingen, 2003.).
7. H. F. von Behr, *Kriegsbilder aus dem Araberaufstand in Deutsch-Ostafrika* (Leipzig, 1891); and Bührer, *Die Kaiserliche Schutztruppe für Deutsch-Ostafrika*, 35–86.
8. "Aus Deutschland," *DSWAZ*, 15 June 1904, 2. The settler newspaper drew upon a corresponding report in the *Berliner Börsen-Zeitung*.
9. Dietlind Wünsche, *Feldpostbriefe aus China: Wahrnehmungs- und Deutungsmuster deutscher Soldaten zur Zeit des Boxeraufstandes 1900/1901* (Berlin, 2008), 188. During the Boxer Rebellion in China, a German officer reported that "among many parts of the troops, discipline is . . . totally rotten"; serious crimes like murder, rape, and plundering were daily occurrences. The offending soldiers were often reservists ("without exception, adventurers of the worst kind"). By September 1901 at the latest, hardly any volunteers from active service could be recruited to serve in China. See Wünsche, *Feldpostbriefe aus China*, 189 and 218.
10. BArch. NL Viktor Franke, Nl. 30/3a, p. 364.
11. NAN, Private Accessions, A.0109, p. 201.
12. Hull, *Absolute Violence*, 49ff.
13. "Soldaten-Abende," *Windhuker Nachrichten*, 15 August 1905, 2.

14. StBR, 60th session, 17 March 1904, p. 1896B. General Staff officer Maximilian Bayer made similar remarks. See Maximilian Bayer, *Mit dem Hauptquartier in Südwestafrika* (Berlin, 1909), 190–91.
15. Shay, *Achilles in Vietnam*, 202.
16. Förster, "Optionen der Kriegführung," 101.
17. Shay, *Achilles in Vietnam*, 31.
18. Schmitt, *Theorie des Partisanen*.
19. Häussler and Trotha, "Brutalisierung 'von unten,'" 66.
20. Callwell, *Small Wars*, 51–52.
21. Tim O'Brien, *The Things They Carried* (New York, 1998), 82.
22. Quoted in Martin van Creveld, *Fighting Power: German and U.S. Army Performance, 1939–1945* (Westport, 1982), 91.
23. Walter Laqueur, *Guerrilla Warfare: A Historical and Critical Study*, 7th ed. (New Brunswick, 2009); Münkler, *Der Wandel des Krieges*; Herfried Münkler, "Was ist neu an den neuen Kriegen?—Eine Erwiderung auf die Kritiker," in *Den Krieg überdenken: Kriegsbegriffe und Kriegstheorien in der Kontroverse*, ed. Anna Geis (Baden-Baden, 2006), 133–50; Herfried Münkler, *Die neuen Kriege* (Reinbek, 2005); Herfried Münkler, *Über den Krieg: Stationen der Kriegsgeschichte im Spiegel ihrer theoretischen Reflexion* (Weilerswist, 2002); Wolfgang Sofsky, *Zeiten des Schreckens: Amok, Terror, Krieg* (Frankfurt, 2002); Waldmann, "Rache ohne Regeln"; Mary Kaldor, *New and Old Wars: Organized Violence in a Global Era* (Oxford, 1998); Christopher Daase, *Kleine Kriege—Große Wirkung: Wie unkonventionelle Kriegführung die internationale Politik verändert* (Baden-Baden, 1999); Trutz von Trotha, "Formen des Krieges"; and Creveld, *The Transformation of War*.
24. Hahlweg, *Guerilla*, 28–31.
25. Martin van Creveld, *The Transformation of War* (New York, 1991).
26. See Münkler, *Der Wandel des Krieges*.
27. Clausewitz, *Vom Kriege*, 278. The English translation is from Clausewitz, *On War*, 198.
28. Münkler, *Der Wandel des Krieges*, 71; and Warburg, *Das Militär und seine Subjekte*, 170.
29. For a more thorough discussion of small warfare, see the excursus in chapter 3.
30. Heuser, "Small Wars in the Age of Clausewitz," 143–44; Hahlweg, *Guerilla*, 30; and Warburg, *Das Militär und seine Subjekte*, 183.
31. Heuser, "Small Wars in the Age of Clausewitz," 142.
32. See chapter 3, note 154, on the example of Colonel von der Trenck.
33. King Friedrich II captured Prague in 1757, but he had to give up the city because light Austrian troops unsettled the surrounding areas.
34. Trotha diary, TA 122/17, 20 July 1904.
35. Callwell, *Small Wars*, 34ff.
36. See Großer Generalstab, *Kriegsbrauch im Landkriege*.
37. Quoted in Schaller, "Kolonialkrieg, Völkermord und Zwangsarbeit," 201. See also H. L. Wesseling, "Colonial Wars and Armed Peace, 1870–1914," *Itinerario* 2 (1981): 62; Wesseling, "Colonial Wars," 3–4; and Erwin A. Schmidl, "Kolonialkriege: Zwischen großem Krieg und kleinem Frieden," in *Formen des Krieges: Vom Mittelalter zum "Low Intensity Conflict*," ed. Manfried Rauchensteiner et al. (Graz, 1991), 124.
38. This was related to the "Africanization" of military leaders who had described and justified the brutalization of fighting in East Africa. More than ten years before his deployment in SWA, Maercker wrote that Africa was "cruel from the ground up." He argued that Europeans had to adjust to (supposedly) local practices of warfare in order to stand their ground. See Georg Maercker, *Unsere Schutztruppe in Ostafrika* (Berlin, 1893), 201.

39. Frankenberg diary, NAN, AACRLS.070, p. 128.
40. Troops in these scenarios found no rest, even at night. This was true, for example, of British troops in the Zulu campaign of 1879 (although their opponent did engage in larger skirmishes). Whether or not enemy scouts were the actual instigators of the nightly panics in the camps, Montague reported that the soldiers hard grown increasingly bitter and apprehensive. See Montague, *Campaigning in Zululand*, 46, 72–73, 88, and 104. Tim O'Brien described the situation well: "No safe ground: enemies everywhere. No front or rear. At night he had trouble sleeping—a skittish feeling—always on guard, hearing strange noises in the dark, imagining a grenade rolling into his foxhole or the tickle of a knife against his ear." See O'Brien, *The Things They Carried*, 63.
41. See, for example, Krüger, "Koloniale Gewalt."
42. Fear of women in combat is a topos that reappears throughout modern German military history, often in association with small wars, or "people's wars," where distinctions between civilians and combatants blurred. *Pétroleuses* were said to pour boiling tar or oil on German soldiers in the battles of the Paris Commune. During the occupation of France and Belgium in 1914, there were stories of girls who fought, tortured, and killed with particular "treachery" and "barbarism." See Horne and Kramer, *German Atrocities*, 107–10. Dangerous *Flintenweiber* joined the Soviet irregulars who fought the Freikorps in the Baltic states. See Matthias Sprenger, *Landsknechte auf dem Weg ins Dritte Reich? Zu Genese und Wandel des Freikorps-Mythos* (Paderborn, 2008), 139. Sprenger shows how soldiers took women's participation in combat as evidence of the immorality, degeneracy, and inhumanity of the opponent. Few of the aforementioned stories, however, have actually proven true.
43. John Horne and Alan Kramer, *German Atrocities, 1914: A History of Denial* (New Haven, 2001), 110.
44. Callwell, *Small Wars*, 44.
45. Shay, *Achilles in Vietnam*, 35.
46. See Andreas Stucki, *Aufstand und Zwangsumsiedlung: Die kubanischen Unabhängigkeitskriege 1868–1898* (Hamburg, 2012); Andreas Stucki, "Streitpunkt Lager: Zwangsumsiedlung an der imperialen Peripherie," in *Die Welt der Lager: Zur 'Erfolgsgeschichte' einer Institution*, ed. Bettina Greiner and Alan Kramer (Hamburg, 2013), 62–86; Frank Schumacher, "'Niederbrennen, plündern und töten sollt ihr': Der Kolonialkrieg der USA auf den Philippinen (1899–1913)," in *Kolonialkriege: Militärische Gewalt im Zeichen des Imperialismus*, ed. Thoralf Klein and Frank Schumacher (Hamburg, 2006), 109–44; and Kreienbaum, *A Sad Fiasco*.
47. NAN ZBU 2369, p. 134.
48. NAN ZBU D.IV.L.3, vol. 1, p. 62.
49. Maercker, *Unsere Kriegsführung in Deutsch-Südwestafrika*, 11; and Belwe, *Gegen die Herero 1904/1905*, 79.
50. Heywood, *Warriors, Leaders, Sages, and Outcasts*, 143; and Kukuri, *Herero-Texte*, 125.
51. Leutwein, *Die Kämpfe der Kaiserlichen Schutztruppe*, 5 and 29.
52. Marchand-Volz, *Werner Freiherr Schenck v. Stauffenberg*, 137.
53. Brünneck, an adjutant in an artillery section, wrote that in this theater of war his unit was "superfluous" and "disruptive," an "abomination" to the "old Africans," who understood the importance of mobility and speed. See Brünneck letters, NAN, Private Accessions, A.583 (31 July 1904).
54. The profound effect of artillery on the morale of the indigenous opponent is almost a cliché of German war memoirs, but this may have reflected a one-sided view of black Africans more than actual wartime experience. The account of a February 1904 battle, for example, suggests that the Herero did not give up their well-fortified position

until they were surrounded by German troops; artillery fire was completely ineffective. See Admiralstab der Marine, *Das Marine-Expeditionskorps in Südwest-Afrika*, 22–23. The interrogations of captured Nama and Oorlam suggest that artillery had a minimal effect on the opponent's morale. See NAN ZBU D.IV.M.2, vol. 4.
55. Brünneck letters, NAN, Private Accessions, A.583 (31 July 1904).
56. See Wallach, *Das Dogma der Vernichtungsschlacht*.
57. See Viktor Franke, "Die Tätigkeit der 2. Feldkompanie vor und beim Ausbruch des Aufstandes in Süd-West-Afrika," BArch. N/1030, 21, pp.17, 34.
58. BArch. NL Viktor Franke, Nl. 30/3a, p. 357 (6 August 1904).
59. Ibid., p. 365 (16 August 1904).
60. Ibid., p. 362 (11 August 1904).
61. Marchand-Volz, *Werner Freiherr Schenck v. Stauffenberg*, 144.
62. These observations are based on the recollections of officer Rudolf von Hardenberg, who fought in the north and south of the colony. See "Kavalleristische Gedanken über den Hottentottenfeldzug 1904/05 (Kalkfontein, 24. Mai 1905)," NAN, Private Accessions, A.0151 v. Alten, no. 10, pp. 1–4.
63. Hardenberg diary, NAN, Private Accessions, A.0151 v. Alten, no. 2, vol. I, p. 48 (18 August 1904).
64. Admiralstab der Marine, *Das Marine-Expeditionskorps in Südwest-Afrika*, 17.
65. An anonymous diarist wrote that "feeding the horses and the unfamiliar way of caring for them make mobilization especially difficult. The horses are suffering, and we've lost a large proportion of them to the horse sickness. Many run away and can't be coaxed back. The Prussian horses in particular can't get used to the pasture." See "Kriegstagebuch," NAN, Sammlung Lemmer, L1032 (19 April 1904).
66. Within just a few days, the Seventh Company's horses ran away multiple times. It was a matter of luck that most were corralled after only one day. See "Kriegstagebuch," NAN, Sammlung Lemmer, L1032 (5 and 6 June 1904). On 6 May, the horses from another company and battery accidentally broke free. Catching them took days, and the units were "immobilized" in the meantime. See Eckl, *"S'ist ein übles Land hier,"* 243. The coarse grass hurt many of the animals' mouths; the cuts swelled and festered until the animals perished.
67. Eckl, *"S'ist ein übles Land hier,"* 230.
68. See NAN, Private Accessions, A.0151 v. Alten, no. 10, p. 2.
69. Admiralstab der Marine, *Das Marine-Expeditionskorps in Südwest-Afrika*, 36.
70. See, for example, "Die Tätigkeit der 2. Feldkompanie vor und beim Ausbruch des Aufstandes in Süd-West-Afrika," BArch. N/1030, 21, pp.17, 33.
71. See NAN, Private Accessions, A.0151 v. Alten, no. 10, pp. 2–3.
72. Admiralstab der Marine, *Das Marine-Expeditionskorps in Südwest-Afrika*, 19.
73. The consequences, according to Hardenberg, were grave: "How can a patrol leader (for example) ride properly, when his men are not masters of their own horses, when they constantly struggle not to fall down, when they can only ride alongside one another on a path, instead of fanning out on their own. In patrols that have had to retreat quickly, there have been riders who have ridden at a gallop for their first time in their lives." This sort of patrol had no "practical value." In these conditions, "riding en bloc as a company and in the various necessary formations was impossible." See NAN, Private Accessions, A.0151 v. Alten, no. 10, pp. 1–2.
74. Hardenberg explicitly noted that the "old" troops had developed their skills by fighting enemies like the Nama and Oorlam, who were capable and tough. See NAN, Private Accessions, A.0151 v. Alten, no. 10, pp. 2–3.
75. NAN, Private Accessions, A.0109, p. 90.
76. Warburg, *Das Militär und seine Subjekte*, 211–17.

77. Soldiers in the bush had to be prepared for close-range assaults at all times. When in doubt, riders had to act independently, without direct orders. Franke experienced situations where "the entire company was momentarily out of view of its leader," and so he understood that soldiers had to be trained so that "each one could take his designated place." Direction in battle was often "terribly complicated, almost impossible." The commander's voice was drowned out by gunfire, and sometimes he could not see most of his men. See "Die Tätigkeit der 2. Feldkompanie vor und beim Ausbruch des Aufstandes in Süd-West-Afrika," BArch. N/1030, 21, pp. 10, 19–20.
78. Stülpnagel, *Heiße Tage*, 110. Many soldiers may have glimpsed the face of modern warfare for the first time in Africa. Long-range breechloaders transformed the experience of combat in the twentieth century. Participants in the two world wars repeatedly described the battlefield as "cold," "empty," or the loneliest place in the world. See S. L. A. Marshall, *Men against Fire: The Problem of Battle Command* (Norman, 2000), 44. Carl Zuckmayer recalled the "tremendous loneliness" of the battles of World War I. "Whenever you faced the ultimate, you were alone. . . . Not a soul was in sight; everyone had crawled into a hole, hidden, buried himself. The loneliness was horrifying." See Carl Zuckmayer, *A Part of Myself: Portrait of an Epoch*, trans. Richard and Clara Winston (New York, 1970), 164. The soldiers felt as if they were fighting phantoms; they and their opponents fired from secure cover, across great distances. The soldiers in SWA had similar experiences fighting the Herero.
79. Horseback patrols could be risky, even when the enemy was not involved. In September 1904, Hardenberg found himself in a "desperate situation" when he could not find a watering hole. If he made the wrong assumptions about his location, his patrol would be "lost." See Hardenberg diary, NAN, Private Accessions, A.0151 v. Alten, no. 3, p. 11.
80. Stuhlmann diary, NAN, Private Accessions, A.0109, p. 125.
81. Warburg, *Das Militär und seine Subjekte*, 218.
82. NAN, Private Accessions, A.0109, p. 90.
83. Stuhlmann saw a connection between the newcomers' unreliability and their lack of self-sufficiency. Because they were used to obeying their superiors, they rarely did what was expected of them when not under supervision. They "always needed instructions." See NAN, Private Accessions, A.0109, p. 90.
84. "Aus Deutschland," *DSWAZ*, 6 September 1905, 2, insert.
85. Beckett, *Modern Insurgencies and Counter-Insurgencies*, 26.
86. See especially Daase, *Kleine Kriege*.
87. "Kriegstagebuch," NAN, Sammlung Lemmer, L1032, 19 April 1904.
88. Eckl, *"S'ist ein übles Land hier,"* 229–30.
89. Creveld, *Fighting Power*.
90. Eckl, *"S'ist ein übles Land hier,"* 246.
91. According to Martin van Creveld, fighting power "rests on mental, intellectual, and organizational foundations; its manifestations, in one combination or another, are discipline and cohesion, morale and initiative, courage and toughness, the willingness to fight and the readiness, if necessary, to die." See Creveld, *Fighting Power*, 3. See also Otto Busch, "Deutschlands Kleinkrieg," Cape Town, 27 January 1906 (no. 14), NAN, A.0529, p. 6.
92. Stuhlmann diary, NAN, Private Accessions, A.0109, p. 226. See also Heinz von Ortenberg, *Aus dem Tagebuch eines Arztes: Feldzugsskizzen aus Südwestafrika* (Berlin, 1908), 33.
93. Schwabe, *Der Krieg in Deutsch-Südwestafrika*, 219.
94. Stuhlmann diary, NAN, PA, A109, p. 185.
95. Shay, *Achilles in Vietnam*, 6.

96. Ibid., 5.
97. In the Vietnam War, doubts were raised by inferior munitions such as the small-caliber M16 rifle, which was considered unreliable. The Schutztruppe was outfitted by the Tippelskirch company, although its munitions were apparently inferior. In fact, the company had bribed the high command of the Schutztruppe in Berlin. See "Telegraphische Nachrichten," *DSWAZ*, 1 August 1904, 1–2.
98. This point is reached when the "rage of attack," a *"conditio sine qua non* for successful battle," is so deeply entrenched that soldiers can no longer distinguish between "civilians" and "combatants," or even between "comrades" and "enemies." See Jan Philipp Reemtsma, "Trauma und Moral: Einige Überlegungen zum Krieg als Zustand einer kriegführenden Gesellschaft und zum pazifistischen Affekt," in *Mord am Strand: Allianzen von Zivilisation und Barbarbei*, ed. Jan Philipp Reemtsma (Berlin, 2000), 357–58.
99. "The officers, you try to stay away from them, 'cause they're dangerous. They'll get you killed. 'Cause they don't know," one Vietnam War veteran stated. See Wallace Terry, *Bloods: Black Veterans of the Vietnam War: An Oral History* (New York, 2006), 123. Drawing on an earlier study by Shils and Janowitz, Savage and Gabriel have investigated the incompetence of officers in Vietnam. See Edward A. Shils and Morris Janowitz, "Cohesion and Disintegration in the Wehrmacht in World War II," *Public Opinion Quarterly* 12 (1948): 280–315; Paul L. Savage and Richard A. Gabriel, "Cohesion and Disintegration in the American Army: An Alternative Perspective," *Armed Forces and Society* 2, no. 3 (1976): 340–76; and Häussler, "Soldatische Hinterwäldler oder Avantgarde?" In SWA, soldiers mistrusted officers who had come to the colony only because of the war, and thus were unfamiliar with local conditions, but who nevertheless expected the same deference from soldiers and civilians that they had enjoyed in Germany. Settlers repeatedly complained about officers from Germany who knew nothing about local conditions; these officers stood out with their "incessant orders and complaints," which may have had to do with their training in Germany. See "Aus dem Schutzgebiet," *DSWAZ*, 1 March 1905, 1; and NAN, Private Accessions, A109, p. 90. "Fragging"—the murder of disliked superiors—drew attention in the Vietnam War, but it was not a new historical phenomenon. See Shay, *Achilles in Vietnam*, 125–27. Assaults against superiors did occur in SWA, although it is impossible to know how many officers may have been killed intentionally by their soldiers.
100. According to unconfirmed reports in the German newspapers *Vorwärts* and the *Norddeutsche Zeitung* (which were reprinted in the *DSWAZ*), there were "serious cases of mutiny" in the South-West African Schutztruppe. See "Aus Deutschland," *DSWAZ*, 28 July 1906, 2.
101. Because the Schutztruppe files no longer exist, we must rely on individual anecdotes. In one case, members of the Schutztruppe directed their anger against the white population. One soldier fired his rifle at bystanders and shouted, "You damned civilians, you fill your bellies and we have to go hungry; we haven't eaten since seven o'clock; you suck the land dry, you're worse than the Hereros; you should be shot like dogs." See "Eingesandt," *Windhuker Nachrichten*, 15 February 1905, 4.
102. On 24 April, Epp noted in his diary, "It appears more a[nd] more that neither the colonial administration here, nor the high command of the Sch[utz] Tr[uppe] at home, are up to the task. The organization will have to change fundamentally." See Epp, *"S'ist ein übles Land hier,"* 238.
103. NL Victor Franke, BArch. Nl. 30/3a, 17 July 1904, p. 351.
104. Anthony Ashworth, "The Sociology of Trench Warfare," *British Journal of Sociology* 19, no. 4 (1968): 420–21.

105. Shay, *Achilles in Vietnam*, 177. Shay notes that the opponent "is diligently stealing and studying training manuals, directives, standing orders, procedures, etc."; soldiers who cling to these can become predictable and give the opponent an advantage. His argument applies to the war in SWA in a more general way.
106. T. E. Lawrence wrote that "armies were like plants, immobile as a whole, firm rooted through long stems to the head." Quoted in Beckett, *Modern Insurgencies and Counter-Insurgencies*, 20.
107. Clausewitz, *Vom Kriege*, 278.
108. Franke noted in his diary on 27 August 1904, "These are the people who are sent to fight in our colonies. They are inferior to the natives in every way, so that—except in large numbers—they are irredeemably lost as soon as the enemy sees them." See NL Victor Franke, BArch. Nl. 30/3a, pp. 375–76.
109. Admiralstab der Marine, *Das Marine-Expeditionskorps in Südwest-Afrika*, 21.
110. Maercker, *Unsere Kriegsführung in Deutsch-Südwestafrika*, 44. See also Schwabe, *Der Krieg in Deutsch-Südwestafrika*, 161.
111. Eckl, *"S'ist ein übles Land hier,"* 223.
112. Erffa, *Reise- und Kriegsbilder von Deutsch-Südwest-Afrika*, 79.
113. Maercker, *Unsere Kriegsführung in Deutsch-Südwestafrika*, 44.
114. The artillery was not effective, for example, in the unsuccessful battle near Owikokorero on 13 March 1904. See Admiralstab der Marine, *Das Marine-Expeditionskorps in Südwest-Afrika*, 34.
115. NAN, Private Accessions, A.510, p. 25.
116. Eckl, *"S'ist ein übles Land hier,"* 225.
117. Häussler, "Zur Asymmetrie tribaler und staatlicher Kriegführung," 188.
118. Admiralstab der Marine, *Das Marine-Expeditionskorps in Südwest-Afrika*, 37.
119. Knoke diary, NAN, Private Accessions, A.0538, pp. 18–19 (6 July 1904).
120. Stülpnagel, *Heiße Tage*, 55.
121. Franke, *Die Tagebücher des Schutztruppenoffiziers Victor Franke*, 354.
122. Kroemer, *Für Kaiser und Reich*, 89.
123. Belwe, *Gegen die Herero 1904/1905*, 70.
124. See Shay, *Achilles in Vietnam*, 173ff.
125. NAN, Private Accessions, A.510, p. 20.
126. Eckl, *"S'ist ein übles Land hier,"* 235.
127. NL Victor Franke, BArch. Nl. 30/3a, p. 315 (13 April 1904).
128. Schwabe, *Der Krieg in Deutsch-Südwestafrika*, 284.
129. Bayer, *Mit dem Hauptquartier in Südwestafrika*, 61.
130. Brünneck letters, NAN, Private Accessions, A.583 (31 May 1904).
131. Malzahn diary, NAN, Private Accessions, A.510, p. 22.
132. Kroemer, *Für Kaiser und Reich*, 89.
133. James Belich, "Krieg und transkulturelles Lernen in Neuseeland im 19. Jahrhundert," in *Waffen—Wissen—Wandel: Anpassung und Lernen in transkulturellen Erstkonflikten*, ed. Dierk Walter and Birthe Kundrus (Hamburg, 2012), 254.
134. Tim O'Brien unites the two kinds of dehumanization, describing a magical fusion of the opponent and the natural world. This lends new meaning to Callwell's assertion that nature was the actual enemy in small warfare, recalling Franke's description of the "living bush." O'Brien writes, "We were fighting forces that did not obey the laws of twentieth-century science. Late at night, on guard, it seemed that all of Vietnam was alive and shimmering . . . . It was ghost country, and Charlie Cong was the main ghost. The way he came out at night. How you never really saw him, just thought you did. Almost magical—appearing, disappearing. He could blend with the land, changing form, becoming trees and grass. He could levitate. He could fly. He could pass

through barbed wire and melt away like ice and creep up on you without sound or footsteps. He was scary." See O'Brien, *The Things They Carried*, 202; and Callwell, *Small Wars*, 44.
135. See Leutwein's report to the Colonial Department (17 May 1904) BArch. R1001/2115, p. 62; and Auer, *In Südwestafrika gegen die Hereros*, 61.
136. Auer, *In Südwestafrika gegen die Hereros*, 59.
137. NAN, Private Accessions, A.0109, p. 206.
138. Frankenberg diary, NAN, AACRLS.070, p. 41.
139. Eckl, *"S'ist ein übles Land hier,"* 222.
140. NAN, AACRLS.070, p. 20.
141. NAN, Private Accessions, A.0109, p. 36.
142. Horne and Kramer, *German Atrocities*, 107–13.
143. Ibid., 74–86 and 113ff.
144. Franke, *Tagebücher*, 366.
145. BArch. N 1030 (Viktor Franke), 21: "Die Tätigkeit der 2. Feldkompanie vor und beim Ausbruch des Aufstandes in Süd-West-Afrika," 14.
146. Admiralstab der Marine, *Das Marine-Expeditionskorps in Südwest-Afrika*, 43.
147. Ibid., 18.
148. Eckl, *"S'ist ein übles Land hier,"* 252.
149. NAN, Private Accessions A.0109, p. 24.
150. Eckl, *"S'ist ein übles Land hier,"* 226.
151. Stülpnagel, *Heiße Tage*, 28.
152. Ibid., 21–23.
153. Bayer, *Mit dem Hauptquartier in Südwestafrika*, 51.
154. Regular armies fighting guerrillas suffer the most casualties "when they are caught off guard; when they actually catch up with the guerrillas, the disparity in arms usually makes for an easy victory." See Collins, *Violence*, 88. "Fairness" is relative.
155. NAN, ZBU, D.IV.M.1, p. 61.
156. Remarks made by German participants in the war repeatedly justified violence against women. Belwe wrote in his diary, "There, too, the Herero *women* had mutilated adolescent boys with knives, allowing them to lie there and bleed to death!— And should one still think about mercy, about compassion?" See Belwe, *Gegen die Herero 1904/1905*, 56.
157. Michel Wieviorka, *Violence: A New Approach*, trans. David Macey (London, 2009), 137.
158. According to Count Gleichen, the defeat at Owikokorero was an "unpleasant shock" and a "small catastrophe" for the Germans: "Secure in their belief that the German troops were the best in the world, so that any operations undertaken by them against natives must necessarily result in a 'walk-over' & an annihilation of their enemies, they find, to their immense disgust, that they have underrated the strength of their adversaries & the difficulties of the country, & that the ever victorious army has suffered a severe check at the hands of a small body of natives." See Lt. Colonel Count Gleichen to Sir Frank C. Lascelles, Ambassador Berlin (8 April 1904), PRO FO 64/1645, pp. 1, 3.
159. Bayer, *Mit dem Hauptquartier in Südwestafrika*, 130 (emphasis in original).
160. Hull, "Military Culture and the Production of 'Final Solutions,'" 154.
161. Hull, *Absolute Destruction*, 49ff.
162. NAN, Private Accessions A.0538, p. 30.
163. Executions of women and children had been common practice for some time, and are mentioned in diaries. On 12 August 1904, Franke reported from the command headquarters, "A Herero woman and child were shot at camp, the former took 2 shots, the latter, one. Vile mob!" See NL Viktor Franke, BArch. Nl. 30/3a, p. 362; and Frankenberg diary, NAN, AACRLS.070, p. 128.

164. Neitzel and Welzer, *Soldaten*, 16ff.
165. NL Victor Franke (12 August 1904), BArch. Nl. 30/3a, p. 362.
166. TA 122/17, 11 August 1904.
167. NAN, Private Accessions, A.151, no. 2, I, p. 49 (21 August 1904).
168. Marchand-Volz, *Werner Freiherr Schenck v. Stauffenberg*, 144.
169. NAN, Private Accessions A.0538, p. 29 (14 August 1904).
170. Hardenberg diary, NAN, Private Accessions, A.151 v. Alten, no. 2, vol. 1, pp. 47–48.
171. Ibid.
172. NL Viktor Franke (16 August 1904), BArch. Nl. 30/3a, p. 365.
173. Stuhlmann diary, NAN, Private Accessions, A.0109, p. 82.
174. Even before the battle, Deimling, a regiment commander, had not paid enough attention to watering the animals. Viktor Franke, a long-serving officer in the colony assigned to Deimling's staff, was appalled: "According to Deimling, animals can't drink anything before setting out . . . And we're still supposed to pursue the fleeing enemy. It's downright ludicrous." See NL Viktor Franke (9 August 1904), BArch. Nl. 30/3a, p. 360.
175. NL Viktor Franke (13 August 1904), BArch. Nl. 30/3a, p. 363.
176. Hardenberg diary, NAN, Private Accessions, A.151 v. Alten, no. 2, vol. 1, p. 48.
177. Epp provides an example. On 23 September, the troops received provisions for three-and-a-half days, but were instructed to make these last for seven. On 29 September, they learned that they would have to make due with these provisions until 4 October. Epp scornfully remarked, "The simplest solutions to problems are proposed so late! The provisions in this situation will never run out, like Christ feeding the five thousand." See Eckl, "S'ist ein übles Land hier," 284–85. The troops at this time rarely received more than half rations.
178. Wenstrup letters, NAN, Private Accessions, AACRLS.216 (15 November 1903).
179. Malzahn diary, NAN, Private Accessions, A.510, p. 26.
180. NAN, Private Accessions, A.151, no. 3, vol. 1, p. 14 (undated, late September or early October 1904).
181. NAN, Private Accessions, A.510, p. 26.
182. Stuhlmann diary, NAN, Private Accessions, A.0109, p. 115 (25 November 1904).
183. Hardenberg diary, NAN, Private Accessions, A.0151 v. Alten, no. 3, vol. 2, p. 14.
184. Trotha diary, TA 122/16, 28 September 1904.
185. Eckl, *"S'ist ein übles Land hier,"* 283.
186. NAN, Private Accessions, A.0109, p. 65.
187. Kroemer, *Für Kaiser und Reich*, 97.
188. NAN, Private Accessions, A.0109, p. 82.
189. BArch. N 1030, 21, p. 23.
190. NAN, Private Accessions, A.0109, p. 81.
191. Marchand-Volz, *Werner Freiherr Schenck v. Stauffenberg*, 143–44.
192. See the remarks by Rudolf von Hardenberg (NAN, Private Accessions v. Alten, A.151, no. 2, p. 48) and Stuhlmann (NAN, Private Accessions, A.0109, p. 79).
193. Bayer, *Mit dem Hauptquartier in Südwestafrika*, 74. See also Brünneck letters, NAN, Private Accessions, A.583 (17 July 1904). In May 1904, the lack of knowledge about comparatively well-explored areas was already a source of friction: "No one in the whole section knows the way to go from here." See Eckl, *"S'ist ein übles Land hier,"* 249.
194. Eckl, *"S'ist ein übles Land hier,"* 244.
195. Marchand-Volz, *Werner Freiherr Schenck v. Stauffenberg*, 144. In May, Epp had already reported on the dire conditions: "Every day some sick men leave; material is used up. Instead of the horses we requested, we got only a few cast-off nags that couldn't be used by other sections. The missing material that we requested weeks ago naturally hasn't arrived." See Eckl, *"S'ist ein übles Land hier,"* 245.

196. Stuhlmann diary, NAN, Private Accessions, A.0109, p. 261.
197. Eckl, *"S'ist ein übles Land hier,"* 279.
198. Ibid., 241.
199. NAN, Private Accessions, A.0109, pp. 253 and 271.
200. Stauffenberg to his mother (18 September 1904). See Marchand-Volz, *Werner Freiherr Schenck v. Stauffenberg*, 64. Brünneck did not think that any staff officers were needed in SWA. See NAN, Private Accessions, A.583. According to Stuhlmann, the General Staff had "no idea about local conditions," and "things would have gone at least as well without them." He raised similar concerns about the campaign's top commanders. See NAN, Private Accessions, A.0109, pp. 91, 93, 210, and 249–51.
201. Marshall, *Men against Fire*, 105.
202. Shils and Janowitz, "Cohesion and Disintegration in the Wehrmacht," 295–97.
203. Savage and Gabriel, "Cohesion and Disintegration," 362 and 366.
204. Marchand-Volz, *Werner Freiherr Schenck v. Stauffenberg*, 137 and 143–44. Stauffenberg wrote, "Is it unpatriotic if I hope for defeat, so we can return to more solid ground?"
205. Ibid., 135.
206. Ibid., 136–37.
207. Ibid., 136.
208. In World War I, enemy troops sometimes felt greater solidarity with one another than with their own leaders, or with anyone else who had not experienced the misery of the trenches. Carl Zuckmayer recalled how "hatred for the 'enemy' in the other trenches had long since faded. For all of us the enemy was the war, not the soldier in blue or khaki who had to endure what we were enduring." See Zuckmayer, *A Part of Myself*, 271. The original opposition between warring parties eroded, giving way to a new distinction: "We" encompassed fighters on both sides, while "they" referred to anyone "behind the frontlines." See Ashworth, "The Sociology of Trench Warfare," 421. There was no such solidarity among the fighters in South-West Africa. The German troops resented their leaders, but still felt immeasurably closer to them than to the opponent. The Herero fighters were not, and could never be, "comrades."
209. Friedrich Nietzsche, "Der Antichrist: Fluch auf das Christentum," in *Werke in drei Bänden*, vol. 2, ed. Karl Schlechta (Darmstadt, 1997), 1165–66. The English translations are from Friedrich Nietzsche, "The Anti-Christ," in *Twilight of the Idols and The Anti-Christ*, ed. and trans. R. J. Hollingdale (New York, 1979), 115–16. See also Schlettwein, "Zur augenblicklichen Lage," *DSWAZ*, 5 January 1904, 2.
210. The situation of the troops did not improve, even after they blocked the western edge of the Omaheke. The theater of operations was so remote that the needs of the troops could hardly be met. Sickness-related casualties remained high. Trotha's diaries indicate that Major von Mühlenfels, who was responsible for the cordoning measures, wired on 16 November 1904 that the troops had "no more provisions" and that everyone was "war-weary." On 7 December 1904, Trotha wrote that Mühlenfels had asked to be relieved, as "he could no longer assume responsibility for the troops because of provisions and sickness. Scurvy is taking a toll, and typhus won't stop." See Trotha diary, Sign. 122/16.
211. Omaruru mission chronicle, ELCRN V.23.1, pp. 305–8.
212. Montague, *Campaigning in Zululand*, 114.
213. "Aus meinen Kriegserlebnissen. Vortrag gehalten von P.A. Ziegenfuß," *Windhuker Nachrichten*, 1 June 1905, 1, insert.
214. Stuhlmann diary, NAN, Private Accessions, A.0109, p. 113.
215. Stauffenberg described a "battle" in a letter to his mother from 17 September 1904: "A good many dead, mostly women . . . . With artillery fire, that's just how it goes. It's

no pity, they're much rougher than the men." See Marchand-Volz, *Werner Freiherr Schenck v. Stauffenberg*, 106.
216. In contrast to the Herero, the German troops rarely suffered any more casualties in "battle." Of the various raids on villages that were reported on 15 February 1905, for example, sixty-seven Herero were killed, while only one German was lightly injured. See *Deutsch-Südwestafrikanische Zeitung*, 15 February 1905.
217. See v. Frankenberg diary, NAN, Private Accessions, AACRLS.070, p. 117; and Knoke diary, NAN, Private Accessions, A.0538, p. 33. See also the official reports under the heading "Der Aufstand" in the *Deutsch-Südwestafrikanische Zeitung* on 23 November 1904, 4 January 1905, 15 February 1904, and 2 August 1905. In a letter that appeared in the newspaper *Vorwärts* on 21 December 1904, a soldier described how he discovered a group of Herero: *"The guard slept*, I crept closer, *stole the weapons*, positioned myself behind a tree (like a *tiger*), and shot all 4 dead." See BArch. R1001/2089, p. 104.
218. Knoke diary, NAN, Private Accessions, A.0538, p. 33 (6 October 1904).
219. Ibid., 7 October 1904.
220. Ibid., 6 October 1904.
221. Greiner, *Krieg ohne Fronten*, 317.
222. "Der Aufstand," *DSWAZ*, 25 October 1905, 1.
223. Eckl, *"S'ist ein übles Land hier,"* 284. On 18 November 1904, in an article titled "German-South-West-Africa," the Cape Town newspaper *The Owl* reported on the last, failed battle: "General Von Trotha solaced himself for his futile pursuit of the Hereros by hanging a number of natives who had been brought in by patrols." Malzahn affirmed the connection between executions and failed operations: "Numerous Herero prisoners were sentenced to death here by hanging. And even later, I often saw a Herero on the bough of a tree, swinging back and forth." NAN, Private Accessions, A.510, p. 26.
224. See Greiner, *Krieg ohne Fronten*, 196.
225. Marchand-Volz, *Werner Freiherr Schenck v. Stauffenberg*, 136–37.

Chapter 5

From the Regime of the Camps to "Native Policy"

On 9 December 1904, Trotha received a telegram from the General Staff. The directive that, from now on, "mercy should be shown towards the Herero who voluntarily surrender," revoked substantial parts of Trotha's proclamation from 2 October.[1] Concentration camps were to solve the problem of what to do with the surrendering Herero.[2] The regime of the camps institutionalized the pardon that Trotha had previously refused to offer—a circumstance that says a great deal about how Germans imagined a "peaceful order" and further coexistence with the autochthonous population. Although the camps were not an instrument of exterminatory strategy, they were highly lethal.[3] Mortality was extreme among the interned Herero and Nama. According to Joachim Zeller, 7,682 (or 45.2 percent) of 17,000 internees died between October 1904 and March 1907.[4] On the infamous Shark Island near Lüderitzbucht, 1,032 of 1,795 internees were said to have died between September 1906 and March 1907 alone.[5] But even after the regime of the camps ended, Herero suffering continued under the auspices of "native policy." There was no "peacetime" recovery. Instead, the society of survivors continued to shrink, a phenomenon that some contemporaries attributed to an apparent "race suicide."[6] The process of violence entered a new phase, which was increasingly defined by a new group of actors: civil servants.[7] The authorities in Berlin hoped that replacing Trotha's military dictatorship with a civilian governor would at last "pacify" the

overseas colony, but things turned out differently.[8] This chapter investigates why the violence did not end under new circumstances, in the camps or thereafter.

The Change in Course

The order of 8 December 1904 represented a fundamental caesura, notwithstanding the concessions later made by Schlieffen, that allowed Trotha to save face and not immediately give up his command—if only to avoid a scandal.[9] The order was a caesura because it suspended the prevailing military logic of "pure war"—or, in Trotha's words, the "law of war"—although the opponent had not (yet) been annihilated.[10] The days of the military dictatorship were numbered, and Trotha announced his departure at the earliest possible opportunity.[11] Rumors soon circulated that Bülow had developed a new political program for the colony, which would replace the top military leaders with civilian counterparts.[12] Friedrich von Lindequist was quickly treated as the new "strong man" at the colony's helm, although almost a year passed before he formally took office.[13] While Trotha had assumed the top military command on the condition that he would not be subordinate to any civil authority, Lindequist made the opposite demand—that, as governor, the commander of the troops would be subordinate to him. Cooperation between Trotha and Lindequist was therefore out of the question. A civilian at the helm of the South-West African colonial administration was unprecedented.[14] Lindequist's appointment turned existing previous relations upside down, establishing the primacy of politics.

Many contemporaries, particularly in the colony itself, believed that this step was long overdue. On 14 December 1904, the *Deutsch-Südwestafrikanische Zeitung* complained that exclusively military perspectives had dominated the response to the uprising for far too long. Political and economic considerations could no longer be neglected, the newspaper argued, particularly given Trotha's poor record. His plan to encircle the Waterberg had not brought "the desired success," and little had been accomplished thereafter. The Herero were beyond the reach of the German troops, and it was feared that they were merely waiting out the rainy season to resume their fight. The remote parts of Hereroland had not yet been "pacified." Untold resources had been wasted and destroyed to achieve these meager results. Expulsion and annihilation robbed the colony of its "property"—that is, the indigenous residents and their cattle. The settlers' complaint that "the enemy had been weakened at our expense" was difficult to dismiss.[15] Given the undistinguished record of the "Trotha interregnum," it is hardly surprising that the residents of the colony welcomed the transfer of power to a "strong" civilian governor with local experience. The *Windhuker Nachrichten* reported that Lindequist was received with open arms,[16] while "no tear" was shed for Trotha.[17]

The change in course was driven primarily by the General Staff and its *military* assessment of the campaign. Neither the interests of the settlers, nor the future of the colony—and certainly not the fate of the Herero—played a significant role. Schlieffen endorsed Trotha's intentions, but he warned,

> He just doesn't have the power to carry it out. He has to stay put at the western edge of the Omaheke, so he can't compel the Hereros to leave it. But if they voluntarily leave the colony, not much is gained. From Bechuanaland, they would be a constant threat, in case the Cape government isn't willing and able to deal with them. Few options will remain, other than trying to compel the Herero to surrender.[18]

Trotha's strategy had come to an impasse. He had to "stay put," so he could no longer defeat the Herero militarily, or even "compel" them to leave the colony. At the same time, his proclamation—which represented the culmination of the logic of "pure war"—prevented the Herero from surrendering voluntarily. Given Mühlenfels's complaints from the "western edge of the Omaheke," the troops would probably not be able to "stay put" there much longer. This, too, was up in the air. Schlieffen was quite open with Bülow that Trotha's path was no longer militarily viable, leading Bülow to attempt to convince the Kaiser that it was time to change course.

Schlieffen's report, which drove this change, showed that "pacifist" considerations were hardly a concern. This can explain the General Staff's ambiguous position, and why not much changed on the ground thereafter. In contrast to Bülow, Schlieffen expressed no ethical reservations, and in fact he explicitly endorsed Trotha's extreme intentions. At the Imperial court, there was great dissatisfaction that the overseas war had become so costly, with so few successes to show for it. The Baroness Spitzemberg, who was one of the Kaiser's frequent guests, learned that the war in South-West Africa was "the most murderous one that Germany has ever waged, as every fifth man has perished."[19] It was incomprehensible that the well-trained German army could not defeat a few hundred, supposedly inferior, opponents.[20] The Kaiser responded with denial to the shameful discrepancy between expectations and reality. As previously mentioned, he forbade all discussion of affairs in South-West Africa, even when receiving guests from the colony. The wars apparently upset Wilhelm so greatly that they could not even be mentioned in his presence.[21] The General Staff and the Kaiser pushed for the change in course not because they doubted the militaristic premises of the existing approach, but much more because the ongoing setbacks wounded the grandiose self-image of Imperial Germany and its elites. The Germans chose a new path because they were tired of losing.[22]

Trotha bristled at the new orders. He immediately demanded that a governor be sent to implement the orders, as he declined all responsibility for them.[23] Until the current impasse, the war had been waged according to military interests alone. Now a civilian governor would have to be sent to wind down the hostilities, and to assume responsibility for what Trotha regarded as a false peace. Although Schlieffen had declared the military situation hopeless, and the Kaiser had the final word, Trotha was certain that the Imperial chancellor had instigated this new, detested course of action. Trotha even blamed the new course for Herero unrest behind the German lines.[24]

Although Trotha depicted the change in course in dire terms, it hardly pacified the colonial masters. His implementation of the unwelcome orders could be absurd; a telling example was his dispute with Bülow over holding the Herero in chains. If Trotha had to pardon the surrendering Herero, then he wanted to hold them in chains—a measure that Bülow rejected, as it seemed to undermine the very purpose of the new course, which was to encourage their voluntary surrender.[25] Indeed, the Germans continued to hunt down the Herero so brutally that the Herero trusted them even less than before. The chasm between the two sides only widened.[26] Word of the Germans' cruel treatment of their prisoners spread quickly, deterring many war-weary Herero from surrendering voluntarily. It was certainly no coincidence that thousands of Herero turned themselves in only after Trotha left the colony.[27]

Unclear signals from the metropole, particularly from the General Staff, weakened the change of course. In a telegram from 12 December 1904, Schlieffen reassured Trotha that the new orders in no way meant that "shooting at Hereros" was forbidden—"to the contrary." If the Herero showed no signs of seeking the "path of mercy," then they were to be handled as before, according to laws of war. And it was still expected that Trotha would resume "the intended offensive . . . after the start of the rainy season."[28]

For all of these reasons, few Herero surrendered, and so the face of the war hardly changed. Because Trotha made no secret of his contempt for the new orders, it seems unlikely that he made a serious effort to punish violations of these orders "from below."

In sum: as radical as the turnaround was in principle, the immediate circumstances of the campaign changed little. "Pacifist" motivations had not driven the turnaround to begin with, and it was further weakened by ambiguous signals from the metropole and local resistance. The transition was difficult for many officers—but they were not exclusively, or perhaps even primarily, responsible for the unending violence.

The Regime of the Camps

In the years that followed, military officers tended to limit the use of force, while civil servants, notably, tended to escalate it. The radicalism and intransigence of civil servants far surpassed that of the military.

The fighting that erupted in the south of the colony in the second half of 1904 brought many casualties, but no quick or spectacular victories. According to one regimental adjutant, German casualties were "3 to 4 times higher than those of the Hottentots," who proved to be tenacious and nimble opponents.[29] An end to their systematic guerrilla warfare was difficult to foresee. Some Nama groups retreated across the border to British territory, where they could hardly be stopped from obtaining weapons and munitions, despite the goodwill of British authorities toward the Germans. This led experienced colonial officers like Estorff—who had already advocated for moderation in the Herero campaign—to speak out in favor of a negotiated peace, in the hope that other groups in the field would be encouraged to lay down their arms. But the civilian administration bitterly resisted the officers' suggestions and initiatives. While the officers were content to accept more modest goals, Governor Lindequist insisted that the opponent be annihilated, and no concessions made to the rebels.

At the end of 1905, soon after Lindequist assumed his official duties, he became embroiled in a dispute with Estorff and Colonel Dame.[30] The source of disagreement was a peace treaty that Estorff had negotiated with the Witbooi-Oorlam against Lindequist's wishes. The governor immediately appealed to his superiors in Berlin. He denounced the officers' unauthorized actions and sought assurance that he, as governor, had the final word in political matters. Lindequist defended the primacy of politics, but he did not seek to restrict the exercise of violence.

Estorff had, in fact, disregarded the governor's stipulations. The governor's conditions for peace included compulsory labor, the execution of "murderers," restrictions on private property, and military supervision. The officers believed that these conditions were too severe; the rebels would not accept such "grave humiliation," and the "small war and banditry in Witbooi land" would continue.³¹ The officers had successfully encouraged the Witbooi to surrender, preparing the way for further peace settlements, only by disregarding Lindequist's conditions. He rejected their approach in no uncertain terms. Lindequist demanded that the war continue until the Witbooi were fully annihilated, so they would be compelled to accept his conditions. He was unwilling to make concessions.³²

The differences of opinion were not limited to major political questions and peace settlements, but extended to everyday matters such as the treatment of "prisoners of war." The new commander of the South-West African Schutztruppe, Berthold Deimling, arrived in the colony in 1906, having apparently been instructed by the Kaiser to end the war in SWA at any cost—including by negotiation.³³ Ironically, Deimling had once been a "saber rattler" who had ridiculed "humanitarian stupidity" at every opportunity, even before the Reichstag.³⁴ Now he argued on behalf of "considerations of humanity, insofar as they are permissible without endangering the security of the colony," although Lindequist remained unpersuaded.³⁵ The civilian administration resisted many measures that sought to improve the prisoners' conditions.

In a letter dated 30 August 1906, Deimling supported Estorff's proposal to send those still languishing in camps to reserves. The Colonial Department in Berlin expected the Schutztruppe to draw down quickly, but a large number of personnel were needed to guard the prisoners, bringing the camps to the commander's attention. Conditions for internees were so poor, especially on Shark Island, that its continued operation seemed out of the question. Since deporting the survivors to other colonies was no longer deemed feasible, Deimling saw the establishment of reserves as a viable alternative, especially since these might encourage groups still in the field to lay down their arms.³⁶ The fight against the Bondelswart-Nama had become so vexing that arguments for them to surrender were urgently needed.³⁷ Lindequist, however, was uninterested in Estorff's proposal, as he wrote in a letter on 12 September 1906.³⁸

On 19 February 1907, Deimling (following the advice of a missionary) suggested to the colonial government that at least all women and children be transferred from Shark Island to the mainland. The civil servant Oskar Hintrager did everything he could to stop this.³⁹ Once Estorff had succeeded Deimling as the commander of the Schutztruppe in SWA, he swiftly closed the camp on Shark Island and brought the prisoners to the mainland. On 8 April 1907, he wrote to the colonial government that he did not want to assume responsibility for the internees' continued detention on the island, which would have amounted to "leading them slowly but surely toward death." Once again, Estorff encountered bitter—but this time, unsuccessful—resistance from Hintrager.[40]

After the end of the military dictatorship, military officers—for various reasons, and to varying degrees—sought to limit the exercise of violence, while they consistently encountered resistance from the civilian administration. Officers sought to introduce "milder" conditions for peace instead of fighting to the bitter end, and they attempted to ease the threat of annihilation for women and children, or even for entire groups. Civil servants worked to thwart these efforts, and they succeeded in many cases. What drove the civil servants to act this way?

Lindequist rejected Deimling's proposal on 12 September 1906 because he saw the establishment of reserves as "politically dangerous." He emphasized that transferring the internees to a "freer way of living" had to occur gradually, "without harm to the colony," and thus could not be rushed. It was "absolutely essential" that every "Hottentot tribe" be imprisoned for a longer period, then "transplanted" from their homeland.[41]

Lindequist—like Hintrager and Tecklenburg—saw the regime of the camps as important in its own right, even an end in itself. The military approach to the camps was initially quite different. Trotha, notably, wanted to ensure that the prisoners would no longer pose a danger, and that their internment would not hinder operations.[42] He soon came to see that prisoners of war could contribute to the war effort by being forced to work. After October 1904, once the south of the colony had also descended into war and the Schutztruppe continued to grow, the camps provided a much-needed reservoir of forced labor.[43] The officers' approach to the camps remained comparatively pragmatic; the camps were merely the solution to a problem, which was itself a consequence of the strategy prescribed in Berlin. Trotha had no qualms whatsoever about exploiting indigenous labor, but as soon as internees could no longer work and no longer posed a danger, he saw no reason to keep them captive. In contrast to many civil servants, he did not hesitate to transfer prisoners who were unfit to work to the custody of the mission.[44]

Civilian officials thought more about long-term fundamental issues than their military counterparts. Because of their academic training, they tended to view problems through a theoretical and ideological lens. They bristled against the military's pragmatic solutions, even when these were expressly supported by the metropole. Officers like Trotha viewed the metropole and its elites as the actual clients of their military policies. Civil servants, on the other hand, promoted the interests of the colony and did not hesitate to express their disagreement with the metropole. The civil servants knew only too well that most officers would depart after the end of the war, with little concern for the colony's future. As experts in the use of force, the officers focused on the military aspects of counter-insurgency. Putting down the uprising was not enough for the civil servants; they wanted to make sure that it would never happen again.

The civil servants' tendency to escalate, rather than contain, the violence in South-West Africa can be explained by their role in the process of the violence, and the period of time when they became most involved.

Residents of the colony and Imperial Germany initially agreed that the rebels had to be taught a lesson "that they would not forget for generations."[45] Because Leutwein fell short of expectations, the responsibility fell to Trotha, but his campaign failed. Trotha's military successes were enough to break the opponent's will to resist—and might have even led to surrender, had the German leadership been willing to negotiate. Trotha's goals, however, were different, and this is where he fell short. His achievements lagged far behind initial expectations. Significantly, his operations were called off only because the German troops could go no further—a circumstance that vividly demonstrated how the Germans could not even control the territory that they formally claimed. They not only failed to show the desired strength and superiority; worse, the campaign could easily be taken as proof of their weakness and incompetence. Schlieffen himself feared that the Germans would expose themselves to ridicule when "the terrible threats of Trotha's proclamation from 2 October" proved to be empty, because "we cannot take even the smallest action against them [the Herero]."[46] The civil servants' task of overseeing the transition to a lasting peace became that much more difficult. They first had to make up for what the military had "bungled" (*verbumfiedelt*), to borrow an expression from Trotha.[47] The shame that had driven Trotha to proceed ever more ruthlessly persisted, leading civil servants to adopt an intransigent, hardline stance against the indigenous peoples, even as the metropole—tired of failures, casualties, and expenses—now sought pragmatic, comparatively moderate solutions instead.

The following remarks by Hans Tecklenburg are key to understanding how the camps were justified and how they functioned. Tecklenburg refused to slaughter cattle in order to alleviate the plight of the imprisoned Herero, explaining,

> The more the Herero people feel the consequences of the uprising on their own bodies, the less they will long for a repetition of the uprising for generations to come. Our actual successes in battle have made a lesser impression on them. I am convinced that the period of suffering they are now enduring will have a more lasting effect—which does not mean, incidentally, that I

want to stand up for the proclamation of Lieutenant General Trotha from 2 Oct. 1904. The death of so many natives will certainly be an economic loss. However, the powerful nature of the Herero people will soon restore what was lost, and the future generation, perhaps mixed with some Bergdamara blood, will have absorbed healthy subordination to the white race with their mothers' milk. Otherwise, we will do what is possible to alleviate the prisoners' plight.[48]

I would like to emphasize three points in this passage. First, in asserting that the "actual successes in battle have made a lesser impression" on the Herero, and that their "period of suffering" in the concentration camps will have "a more lasting effect," Tecklenburg underscored the significance of the camps.[49] Now that Trotha's actual campaign had failed, the camps had to make up for this loss. This implies, therefore, that Tecklenburg saw the camps as the continuation of war by other means. Finally, Tecklenburg himself suggested that there was something inherently excessive about the camps, which could not fully be explained by means-end calculations. For this reason, we ought to be wary of reducing the South-West African concentration camps to their officially stated functions.[50] It is hardly coincidental that Tecklenburg mentioned Trotha, and that he attempted to distance himself from Trotha's obviously autotelic strategy of extermination, as Tecklenburg's own interpretation of the camps had an autotelic quality itself. To adopt Sémelin's terminology, Tecklenburg sought to dominate and subjugate, not to eradicate, but he nevertheless espoused a cruelty that ignored all "petty misgivings" and any other signs of consideration toward the Herero.[51] He was willing to accept the "economic loss" that this cruelty would bring.

Hintrager adopted a similar line in rejecting Deimling's proposal to transfer at least women and children from Shark Island to the mainland:

> Given the dangers posed by this opponent [the Witbooi-Oorlam], and as long as the land is so sparsely settled by whites, I feel that only *full* measures can be useful to us, unless we are willing and able to maintain a larger number of forces in the land. I believe these considerations are, at the moment, more important than attending to the current shortage of native workers, and also [more important] than reasons of humanity. For the sake of its rule in South Africa, England considered the deaths of 20,000 women and children, during a very long period of detainment in the concentration camps, to be unavoidable.[52]

Hintrager knew as well as Tecklenburg how urgently the colonial economy needed indigenous labor. Nevertheless, the more aware both men became of the colony's dependence on the indigenous people, the more they were willing—even driven—to use force against the colonial subjects, placing these subjects' worthlessness and expendability on display. Although the colonial masters may have primarily sought to subjugate and dominate, we can nevertheless agree with Bley's assertion, made in a slightly different context, that "priority had to be given to the maintenance of German power."[53] If necessary, the autochthonous population could be sacrificed. Maintaining power, as Hintrager stated, was "more important than attending to the current shortage of native workers in the land, and also [more important] than reasons of humanity."

Blacks in the camps were at the mercy of whites—including former victims of Herero raids with scores to settle, and soldiers who had engaged in the fruitless pursuit. The camps became a space for the lower ranks of colonial society to act out their fantasies of submission and revenge.[54] Sexual violence was commonplace.[55] It was a massive problem even before the war, not least (although not primarily) for the German authorities, who were unable to rein in the violence from below. As we have seen, the decision of the Herero to take arms was closely related to the proliferation of sexual violence.[56] The problem intensified during the campaign, in part because it was rarely perceived as a problem. In this small war, it was more or less assumed that women were a legitimate target of violence. As Isabel Hull shows, the rates of infection for sexually transmitted diseases reached dizzying heights, characteristically highest for troops on the front lines.[57] Sexual violence was part of unlimited warfare, and this continued under the regime of the camps. The camps existed outside the formal legal system; internees were held in precarious circumstances, without consideration for basic rights. They found themselves in a "no man's land" without people or laws, only perpetrators and victims, compelled to play by the rules of a "deadly game" (to borrow the imagery of Olga Wormser-Migot).[58] The military leadership in South-West Africa had long been unable to enforce legal and soldierly norms; now the "undisciplined" soldiers were entrusted with the lives of internees. The situation of the autochthonous population had been precarious before the war, but in the camps they were utterly powerless and without rights. Guards and settlers found common cause, in some places organizing nightly "hunts" for female internees who were abducted and abused.[59] For this reason, whites were soon prohibited from entering the camps, at least at certain times of day.[60] Given the complicity between settlers and guards, it is doubtful whether this ban was consistently enforced.

The overall treatment of the internees was extraordinarily harsh. Women and children were not excepted from compulsory labor or corporal punishment.[61] Even before the uprisings, violence had defined relations between the white and autochthonous populations. The settlers claimed the right to do as they pleased with the "natives," if for no other reason than reinforcing their self-awareness as "masters." During the uprising, local authorities affirmed this legal superiority; in Swakopmund, for example, all whites were granted police authority over blacks. Impromptu or unofficial courts-martial were commonplace in the colony's interior; purported "murderers," "marauders," "plunderers," and "spies" were dealt with swiftly. Military leaders did attempt to contain the violence from below, but their half-hearted efforts were doomed to fail. The soldier who murdered James, the South African teamster, was sentenced to just seven weeks in prison—underscoring how little black lives were valued, and hardly serving as a meaningful deterrent.[62] With Trotha's proclamation, at the latest, all Herero were essentially declared "fair game," without any legal protection.[63] Even the end of the war did not "pacify" the whites. Leaders in Berlin pushed for the establishment of camps in order to signal a break with the previous military strategy, but the soldiers' behavior and attitudes hardly changed. Higher authorities wanted to discipline and exploit indigenous labor, but under the given circumstances, compulsory labor was unlikely to "educate" internees to become reliable workers. Instead, compulsory labor became merely another weapon of terror.

Beyond the Camps

As the need for indigenous labor grew, the Germans made sure that the "natives'" role in the development of the colony remained clearly subordinate.[64] Proceeding from a notion of radical, enduring inequality between colonizers and the colonized, colonial authorities worked to institutionalize and reinforce this inequality wherever they could. The less power the indigenous people had (and the less they represented an objective threat), the more relentless the colonial masters' racism became, and the more they worked to enshrine the new power relations on a permanent basis. The goal of "native policy" was to institutionalize racism.[65] A genocidal war of "pacification," followed by the institution of "native policy," turned German South-West Africa into an "overtly racist regime."[66]

The settlers mistrusted missionaries who sought to create new Christians overseas because this might encourage assimilation and bypass or undermine the inequality that was essential to colonial society.[67] The settlers feared that Christianization might awaken black Africans to concepts such as "equality and human dignity," which contradicted the colonial hierarchy,[68] and also that converts might become "arrogant, insolent, and refuse to obey."[69] This could hardly be in whites' interest.[70] If Christianization had to take place, then only "after centuries" of subjugation.[71] In the meantime, the settlers concluded, nothing should change.

Strict policies of racial segregation, including what later became known as apartheid, sought to ensure that dogmatically asserted differences and hierarchies would never blur again. These policies first emerged in the era of the camps; the last South-West African camp did not close until 1908. "Native policy," most simply stated, refers to all of the political measures in South-West Africa that sought to achieve this goal.[72]

Living conditions for the indigenous people remained oppressive, even outside the camps. Newcomers to the colony were sometimes disturbed that black Africans were treated like "cattle," expected to endure the "coarsest insults and forms of address, for no cause."[73] White children learned that it was acceptable to approach Africans with "reprehensible insults" and "uncalled-for acts of violence."[74]

Years after the uprising—long after the Herero were defeated and disenfranchised, and even as they faced the threat of extinction—South-West African newspapers did not tire of asserting whites' unlimited authority over "native" subjects.[75] White fantasies of power were boundless. Before the wars, these claims were usually linked to concrete military goals; armed and politically independent African groups posed at least a theoretical danger.[76] But the calls for dominion did not subside, even after military goals had long been achieved. Instead, white demands for "absolute," unlimited subjugation increased. This shows that "racial struggle" was permanent—insofar as it did not seek to exterminate, but to dominate and subjugate instead. The struggle intensified and expanded to more and more aspects of life, even (or especially) after open resistance had been extinguished. Insults and abuse were as much a part of this struggle as discriminatory laws.

For years, the colonial authorities did little to allay this abusive situation. Particularly outside the towns, on farms, settlers behaved like "little kings."[77] Only toward the end of German rule in South-West Africa did colonial authorities begin to assert state sovereignty beyond the towns by prosecuting farmers for crimes against indigenous workers.[78] It is hardly surprising that, even in "peacetime," the local people left a notably "downtrodden and unhappy impression" on the colonial secretary Wilhelm Solf.[79] The Herero did not recover after the war, and their society continued to shrink.

Estorff, a deeply religious man who had consistently lobbied for moderation, saw the handling of the autochthonous population as an outright "sin" that implicated "almost the entire colonial population." This is why, he believed, the colony was lost so quickly in World War I: "God's mills grind slow but sure."[80]

Notes

1. General Staff telegram to Trotha (8 December 1904), BArch. R1001/2089, p. 52. Bülow learned about the proclamation and its contributing circumstances from a report written by Schlieffen on 23 November 1904. Bülow appealed to the Kaiser the next day, requesting that General von Trotha be instructed by telegram to issue a new proclamation, in order to preserve the lives of "Herero who voluntarily surrender to our troops, with the exception of directly guilty parties and ringleaders." Notably, Bülow introduced and even prioritized ethical concerns, asserting that Trotha's direction of the war was "contrary to the principles of Christianity and humanity," and that he, Bülow, had a "moral obligation" to intervene. See BArch. R1001/2089, pp. 4–11. Once the responsible authorities in Berlin learned about the proclamation, they responded promptly. On 4 October 1904, Trotha sent Schlieffen a report that included the text of the proclamation. This report was in the mail for at least six weeks, as Jonas Kreienbaum has recently described. If Schlieffen "covered" for Trotha, then it was only for a few days; on 23 November he wrote to Bülow, who in turn appealed to the Kaiser the following day. According to Bülow, the Kaiser was initially outraged, but he came around "after a few hours" and agreed that Trotha should revoke the proclamation. See Kreienbaum, *A Sad Fiasco*, 47ff.; and Bülow, *Denkwürdigkeiten*, 21. A few more days passed before Schlieffen and Bülow agreed on the order's exact phrasing. (See Schlieffen's draft from 30 November 1904, R1001/2089, p. 14.)
2. Bülow clarified the Berlin authorities' intentions in a 11 December 1904 telegram to Trotha: "For now, the idea is not to create reserves, but rather concentration camps for the provisional feeding and sheltering of the remaining Herero people." See BArch. R1001/2089, pp. 54–55.
3. The following observations build upon the work of Jonas Kreienbaum, who argues against the conventional view that the concentration camps continued Trotha's strategy of extermination. The political circumstances of the camps' founding are key; the camps broke intentionally with previous military strategy, and Trotha understood this. Further, Kreienbaum shows that the camps fulfilled three functions that were incompatible with annihilation: punishment, "pacification," and "educating to work." Significantly, the responsible authorities did attempt to address the acute conditions in the camps, but the situation overwhelmed them. See Kreienbaum, "'Vernichtungslager' in Deutsch-Südwestafrika?," 1018ff.; and *A Sad Fiasco*, 91ff. and 166ff.
4. Joachim Zeller, "'Ombepera i koza—Die Kälte tötet mich': Zur Geschichte des Konzentrationslagers in Swakopmund 1904–1908," in *Völkermord in Deutsch-Südwestafrika: Der Kolonialkrieg (1904–1908) in Namibia und seine Folgen*, ed. Jürgen Zimmerer and Joachim Zeller, 2nd ed. (Berlin, 2004), 76. Kreienbaum shows that these figures, including the mortality rates, may well be incorrect, although exact numbers are impossible to determine. Mortality rates may have been significantly lower, although they also may have been higher (anywhere between 30 and 64 percent). See Kreienbaum, *A Sad Fiasco*, 90ff.
5. Fourteen camps were built, some of which were operated by private companies. Living conditions for internees also varied. See Claudia Siebrecht, "Formen von Unfrei-

heit und Extreme der Gewalt: Die Konzentrationslager in Deutsch-Südwestafrika, 1904–1908," in *Die Welt der Lager: Zur "Erfolgsgeschichte" einer Institution*, ed. Bettina Greiner and Alan Kramer (Hamburg, 2013), 97; and Kreienbaum, *A Sad Fiasco*, 176–77. I do not investigate such details here. Rather, my focus is on colonial power relations and the broader motivations of higher authorities, particularly after the war.
6. Krüger, *Kriegsbewältigung und Geschichtsbewusstsein*, 144–55.
7. Jürgen Zimmerer has shown that four civil servants—Lindequist, Golinelli, Tecklenburg, and Hintrager—were particularly influential in the formulation of "native policy." All were active in SWA before the wars, and all held key positions in the colonial administration or Imperial Colonial Office after 1905. Zimmerer rightly points to the three "Native Ordinances," issued by Lindequist in 1907, as essential to the coordination of "native policy" across the colony. The actors themselves were not new. After the war, however, their influence grew, as they distanced themselves from the military and sought to reorder colonial society according to their own vision. See Zimmerer, *Deutsche Herrschaft über Afrikaner*, 10 and 13. A key moment for the "new" protagonists was Trotha's refusal to assume responsibility for sheltering the prisoners, which led Bülow to task Deputy Governor Hans Tecklenburg with the "administrative details and . . . immediate accommodations for the surrendering Herero." See telegram from 11 December 1904, RK to Trotha, BArch. R1001/2089, p. 54.
8. Johannes Spiecker, an inspector with the Rhenish Missionary Society, learned—in part, from letters and newspaper reports—that mortality in the camps was "quite appalling," and he complained to the Berlin authorities. Oskar Stübel, director of the Colonial Department, assured him that a civilian governor would soon replace the "military dictatorship"—and that conditions would then improve. See Spiecker to Vedder (10 May 1905), ELCRN VII.31.1, p. 4.
9. The General Staff's telegram of 12 December 1904, which clarified and softened the order of 8 December, seems to have been decisive for Trotha's continued presence in the colony: "Above all, shooting at Hereros is not forbidden; to the contrary, the intended offensive should be executed after the start of the rainy season. Only the path of mercy, which was completely closed by the proclamation of 2 October, should be reopened for those who seek it and haven't gone too far. The means to disseminate the decree are the same as on 2 October . . . General Staff." See BArch. R1001/2089, p. 85. In any case, Trotha noted in his diary on 13 December 1904, "I've come to the conclusion, after all, that the new order is supposed to restore what the old one bungled. Very happy about this, otherwise I wouldn't have been able to stay."
10. Lothar von Trotha, "Politik und Kriegführung," 1.
11. Trotha's papers contain a copy of his 10 December 1904 letter to Dietrich von Hülsen-Haeseler, who was then chief of the military cabinet. In the letter, Trotha described how the Kaiser had promised him at a personal meeting in Strasbourg that he would not be subordinate to any civilian authority in SWA. This was Trotha's condition for accepting the post of commander-in-chief.
12. "Aus dem Schutzgebiet," *DSWAZ*, 14 December 1904.
13. On 18 January 1905, the *DSWAZ* relayed a report (dated 23 December 1904) from the German newspaper *Vorwärts*, which stated that Lindequist was prepared to take office.
14. Lindequist was, however, an officer in the reserves—like most of the male participants in "good society."
15. "Der Aufstand," *DSWAZ*, 14 December 1904, 2.
16. "Ein guter Anfang," *DSWAZ*, 29 November 1904, 1.
17. "Das Interregnum von Trotha—und sein Ende," *Windhuker Nachrichten*, 2 November 1905. The settlers' attitude toward the colony's leadership was erratic, to say the

least. They had done all they could to discredit Leutwein and accelerate his departure, so that Trotha, who promised to wage the kind of war they demanded, could take his place at the helm of the Schutztruppe. However, only a few weeks later they wanted Leutwein back, as he had apparently "always" enjoyed their "utmost trust." See "Der Aufstand," *DSWAZ*, 10 August 1904, 1. Once their initial enthusiasm for Lindequist waned, Trotha, too, was "rehabilitated." See Bley, *Kolonialherrschaft und Sozialstruktur*, 302.
18. Schlieffen's report from 23 November 1904, BArch. R1001/2089, p. 5.
19. Vierhaus, *Am Hof der Hohenzollern*, 221.
20. See, for example, Otto Busch, "Deutschlands Kleinkrieg," Cape Town, 27 January 1906 (no. 14), NAN, A.0529, pp. 6ff.
21. Stuhlmann diary, NAN, Private Accessions, A.0109, p. 271.
22. This recalls Bernd Greiner's thesis about the United States' withdrawal from Vietnam. Seventy percent of the US population wanted their country to withdraw from the Vietnam War, but Greiner shows that they were not necessarily motivated by pacifism. The United States' identity as a "victory culture" was unchanged; the majority of the population had simply grown tired of a war that could not be won. A familiar slogan was "Get out or win." The US withdrawal had less to do with a change of a heart, and more with a refusal to accept defeat any longer. See *Krieg ohne Fronten*, 545.
23. BArch. R1001/2089, p. 55. Telegram, 9 December 1904 (6:40 p.m.), Trotha to the General Staff in Berlin, copy to the Imperial Chancellor: "Most high command received. Request to be informed whether this decree will be made public. Have requested from the Imperial chancellor that a new governor be sent immediately, since only he can assume responsibility for future arrangements. Major v. Estorff directed to inform the Hereros that negotiations are to be tied to the surrender of weapons. Trotha" (p. 55).
24. "Ein Schritt näher zum Ziel," *Windhuker Nachrichten*, 1 January 1905, 2.
25. In a telegram dated 13 January 1905, Bülow more fully explained his intentions to Trotha: "I cannot endorse the command of your Excellency, that all surrendering Herero are to be put in chains, because this will hinder all voluntary surrender . . . . By contrast, I believe that the surrendering Herero should be placed in concentration camps at different sites in the colony, where they can be guarded and put to work" (BArch. R1001/2089, p. 116).
26. According to the Omaruru mission chronicle, the officers themselves conceded that the withdrawal of the proclamation was incompatible with how they conducted their patrols. By raiding settlements and shooting or hanging their inhabitants, the officers only confirmed Herero fears and discouraged them from surrendering to the German troops. In general, there was "little assent or approval" among the officers for pardoning the Herero (ELCRN, V.23.1, pp. 305–8).
27. Erichsen, *"The Angel of Death Has Descended Violently among Them,"* 40.
28. BArch. R1001/2089, p. 85.
29. Erich von Schauroth, *"Liebes Väterchen . . .": Briefe aus dem Namaaufstand 1905–1906*, ed. Bernd Kroemer (Windhoek, 2008), 126.
30. Colonel Dame became the interim commander of the South-West African Schutztruppe after Trotha's departure.
31. NAN ZBU 2369, pp. 17ff.
32. Estorff had given the Witbooi leaders his word as an officer, which neither Lindequist nor the authorities in Berlin could dismiss out of hand, although Lindequist did what he could to thwart the agreement. The Witbooi-Oorlam were ultimately sent to Shark Island, where they were almost entirely wiped out. Because Estorff felt bound to his word, he moved the survivors off the island once he had assumed the command of the Schutztruppe.

33. Kirsten Zirkel, "Vom Militaristen zum Pazifisten: Politisches Leben und Wirken des Generals Berthold von Deimling vor dem Hintergrund der Entwicklung Deutschlands vom Kaiserreich zum Dritten Reich," PhD diss., Heinrich Heine University Düsseldorf, 2006, 93.
34. Berthold von Deimling, *Südwestafrika: Land und Leute—unsere Kämpfe—Wert der Kolonie: Vortrag, gehalten in einer Anzahl deutscher Städte* (Berlin, 1906), 13.
35. NAN ZBU 2369, pp. 99–100.
36. Reserves had two different functions (see chapter 2, note 46). In the given circumstances (because the rebel groups' land would have otherwise been dispossessed), reserves offered autochthonous leaders a semblance of independence and intermediary rule. Because Trotha and Lindequist sought to eliminate all traces of "native" independence, they categorically rejected reserves. See Trotha's telegram to the Imperial Chancellor (9 December 1904), R1001/2089, pp. 53–54. This is why, after the uprisings, Tecklenburg and others replaced the existing reserves with "locations," which were indigenous settlements without traditional leadership structures, close to sites where workers were needed. See NAN ZBU, D.IV.l.2: Herero-Aufstand 1904. Feldzug; Politisches. Vol. 4: October 1904–December 1905, p. 34.
37. NAN ZBU 2369, pp. 93–94. Schauroth wrote to his father about this conflict: "Just between you and me—we must have peace." See Schauroth, *"Liebes Väterchen . . . ,"* 132.
38. NAN ZBU 2369, pp. 95–96.
39. See Hintrager's reply on 22 February 1907, NAN ZBU 2369, pp. 98–99.
40. NAN ZBU 2369, p. 105.
41. Ibid., pp. 95–96.
42. Trotha initially saw the concentration camps as a burdensome imposition. Guarding the prisoners tied up manpower, potentially weakening the frontline troops and hindering operations. See Trotha's telegram to the General Staff (24 January 1905), BArch. R1001/2089, pp. 128–29.
43. Because of the shortage of low-cost labor, private enterprise had come to a standstill in some places and relied on government subsidy. In Swakopmund alone, there was an unmet need for "300 natives who were fit for work" at the beginning of 1905. Trotha promised to help, but he emphasized that military needs came first. See NAN ZBU D.IV.L.3, vol. 1, pp. 29–30.
44. See Trotha's letter from 10 March 1905, NAN ZBU D.IV.L.3, vol. 1.
45. "Koloniales," *Tägliche Rundschau* (6 March 1904), BArch. R1001/2112, p. 169.
46. Chief of the Great General Staff to the Imperial Chancellor, Berlin (16 December 1904), BArch. R1001/2089, p. 108.
47. In a report from 15 October 1904, Hans Tecklenburg suggested that defeating the uprising would not be enough to secure the "life and property" of the settlers: "Our prestige with the natives, the prestige of the white man is beyond saving. Our enemies have too often had the opportunity to test their strength against our troops. Our native auxiliaries have too often been able to experience the helplessness of the white newcomer." Tecklenburg was concerned that "every white man" would no longer be approached with "respect and deference." See "Auszug aus jüngst zugegangenen Berichten über die Lage der Kriege in Südwestafrika," Berlin (24 December 1904), BArch. R1001/2089, pp. 105–6.
48. NAN ZBU D.IV.L.3, vol. 1, p. 61ff.
49. Tecklenburg's assumptions about the indigenous people reveal most about his own fears and projections, which were nevertheless real. See NAN ZBU D.IV.L.3, Bd. 1, p. 62.
50. See Kreienbaum, "'Vernichtungslager' in Deutsch-Südwestafrika?"; and *A Sad Fiasco*, 87–114.

51. Lothar von Trotha, "Politik und Kriegführung," 1.
52. NAN ZBU 2369, pp. 98–99 (emphasis in original).
53. Bley, *South-West Africa under German Rule*, 265.
54. See also Kreienbaum, *A Sad Fiasco*, 178–80.
55. Erichsen, *"The Angel of Death Has Descended Violently among Them,"* 46–47, 68, 86–87, and 122.
56. See also Wolfram Hartmann, "Sexual Encounters and Their Implications on an Open and Closing Frontier: Namibia from the 1840s to 1905," PhD diss., Columbia University, 2002; and Hartmann, "Urges in the Colony."
57. Hull, *Absolute Destruction*, 150–51.
58. Kotek and Rigoulot, *Das Jahrhundert der Lager*, 11–13.
59. See the mission report marked "strictly confidential" from 19 May 1906 (VEM, RMG 2.660 6/05, p. 28).
60. On 1 April 1904, the *Windhuker Nachrichten* published an order from 25 March, which stated that "until further notice, the white population was forbidden from entering local native werfts between 6 o'clock in the evening and 6 o'clock in the morning." Violators were threatened with fines or imprisonment.
61. See Martin Siefkes, *Sprache, Glaube und Macht: Die Aufzeichnungen des Johannes Spiecker in Deutsch-Südwestafrika zur Zeit des Herero-Nama-Aufstands* (Würzburg, 2013), 180.
62. A teamster named James fell ill during a convoy. Witnesses reported that he was summarily shot by a soldier after lagging behind. In a letter from 21 April 1906, the Foreign Office did not dispute the accusation and confirmed that the soldier had been sentenced on 16 December 1904—to seven weeks in prison (KAB GH 35/157: "Treatment of Natives in G.S.W.A. 1905," "Ill-Treatment of 3 Natives in G.S.W.A. 1905–1906"). A similar case occurred in the camp on Shark Island. An overseer named Benkesser shot a sick Herero woman multiple times and then let her bleed to death. Cases such as this may have upset the responsible officers, but usually had no consequences. See Kuhlmann's report about a trip to Lüderitzbucht, 10 August 1905, VEM, RMG 1.644a, pp. 33ff.
63. Kößler and Melber, "Der Genozid an den Herero und Nama," 49.
64. "Mutterland und Kolonie," *DSWAZ*, 1 August 1906, 1.
65. Zimmerer emphasizes the continuities in "native policy," arguing that its conceptional roots stretched back much earlier than the uprisings, as evidenced by the role of important protagonists such as Lindequist, Golinelli, Tecklenburg, and Hintrager. Nevertheless, the wars constituted a caesura by enabling more direct domination and the steady radicalization of policy. I concur with Zimmerer's assessment that wartime measures such as internment, deportation, and arbitrary execution represented an unprecedented escalation in the use of force, so that "the most radical white positions became decisive." The last remaining taboos surrounding Germans' treatment of the indigenous population broke down, and the enormous number of African casualties cleared the way for radical policy designs. See Zimmerer, *Deutsche Herrschaft über Afrikaner*, 32.
66. Frederickson, *Racism*, 1.
67. Settlers saw the purpose of colonization as enhancing their own economic wellbeing; any concern for "native" souls or other interests was secondary at best.
68. "Vortrag des Herrn Erdmann—Haris. Windhuk, 1.6.1905," *Windhuker Nachrichten*, 15 June 1905, 3, insert.
69. "Zur Missionsfrage," *DSWAZ*, 2 August 1905, 2.
70. "Vortrag des Herrn Erdmann—Haris. Windhuk, 1.6.1905," *Windhuker Nachrichten*, 15 June 1905, 3, insert.
71. Ibid.

72. The 1905 prohibition against mixed marriages was central to segregation; it was motivated less by demands of "racial hygiene" and more by the need to secure political domination. White men who were married to "colored" women were excluded from voluntary associations; "half-white" children were no longer allowed to attend school. Finally, all men who lived with indigenous women lost the right to vote for, or be elected to, the colony's organs of self-administration. The "one-drop" rule determined "native" identity. See Zimmerer, *Deutsche Herrschaft über Afrikaner*; Kundrus, *Moderne Imperialisten*, 222ff.; Häussler and Trotha, "Koloniale Zivilgesellschaft?," 300; and Jürgen Zimmerer, *Von Windhuk nach Auschwitz? Beiträge zum Verhältnis von Kolonialismus und Holocaust* (Münster, 2011), 104.
73. See the letter from Omaruru's district commissioner to the Governor (27 May 1913), quoted in Zollmann, *Koloniale Herrschaft und ihre Grenzen*, 282.
74. Letter from Governor Theodor Seitz to the public schools (5 June 1913), quoted in Zollmann, *Koloniale Herrschaft und ihre Grenzen*, 282–83.
75. "Mutterland und Kolonie," *DSWAZ*, 1 August 1906, 1.
76. "Zur augenblicklichen Lage," *DSWAZ*, 5 January 1904, 1.
77. Zollmann, *Koloniale Herrschaft und ihre Grenzen*, 275.
78. Bley, *Kolonialherrschaft und Sozialstruktur*, 295–96.
79. Zollmann, *Koloniale Herrschaft und ihre Grenzen*, 244.
80. Estorff, *Wanderungen und Kämpfe*, 118.

Conclusion

The "pacification" of South-West Africa ended in disaster, and the Herero genocide was its sad climax. The genocide was not planned in advance, but arose from the failure of German military leaders' original plans, and their subsequent attempts to bring the situation under control. The road to catastrophe was twisted, defined by the relationships and interactions between heterogeneous, sometimes antagonistic, forces. Each of these forces acted from a limited perspective, pursuing its own goals and pushing the course of events, vector-like, in a particular direction. The escalation of violence had no single cause, but many different authors.

The political situation was complex because the colony had no strong central authority. The colonial state was only one element in an order of violence that had quietly established itself before the uprising; I identify this as "despotism by the white colonizing class." War and the intervention of the metropole heightened the complexity of the colonial situation, increasing the number of actors who were involved and their mutual relations and conflicts.

In this study, I have devoted special attention to the role of the settlers. Although they held no formal political role, they nevertheless exerted considerable influence over political affairs because the colonial state allowed them room to maneuver. Their unsanctioned, increasingly aggressive behavior toward the Herero initially provoked the war, and they pushed for its escalation well beyond their direct involvement in the fighting.

The thrust of the first raids suggests that the Herero revolted primarily against the privatized violence they had endured in colonial society—and only secondarily against the colonial state, which either could not, or would not, protect them. Although the Germans frequently purported otherwise, the Herero were less opposed to political control in general, and more to individual settlers' claims to dominion. The Herero seemed to distinguish quite clearly between the state and private individuals. For good reason, the violence of the rebels was primarily directed against individual settlers, who undermined the state's monopoly on the exercise of violence and saw themselves as the vanguard of colonial conquest; thus, the settlers cannot be considered "civilians" in the traditional sense. Nevertheless, the actions of the Herero enraged observers in the metropole, who applied the standards of European state wars to the unfamiliar situation in the colony. In their eyes, the "barbaric" raids confirmed racist stereotypes about the "treacherous" and "beastly" Herero, justifying the subsequent behavior of the troops who were hastily sent to the colony to put down the uprising.

I began this study by depicting the living conditions in colonial society, devoting particular attention to the fear and mistrust that permeated the settlers' existence. The violence that cast its shadow over colonial society was a coping behavior, an attempt to reassert agency and cast off the humiliating stigma of economic and political dependency, to overcome the paternalism of state authority, and to restore solidarity among whites by affirming the superiority that they claimed.

A key structural condition of the wars, and the entire period of German rule, was that whites got away with almost everything, even in "peacetime"—despite the fact that everything was not actually permitted. Whites knew that they could count on the complicity of the colony's executive organs, indulgent superiors, and lenient judges. They rarely worried about legal sanctions. If a white was killed, multiple Africans were often sentenced and executed. If an African was killed, judges usually found a way to exonerate the white perpetrators altogether, or to issue token punishments. Deviance was the rule, which seemed acceptable to whites who saw themselves in a racial struggle that overrode all other considerations. The members of colonial society soon no longer saw anything monstrous in the day-to-day cruelty. Assaults on indigenous people went unpunished and were even applauded by other settlers, encouraging perpetrators to go to ever further extremes—until catastrophe struck and the Herero fought back. A long process of normalizing deviance led up to the war, which was ultimately triggered by the inherent dynamics of this process.

The dynamic character of racism informed the colony's violent conditions. Racism is tied to relations of power, reflecting and justifying how these change over time, as Norbert Elias and John L. Scotson show in their study of "established" and "outsider" relations.[1] As the balance of power in South-West Africa shifted in the settlers' favor, they became more aggressive and less interested in "fine distinctions." In the eyes of the settlers, the Herero were "no longer commoners or elites, respectable women or upright men . . . but equal representatives of a supposedly natural, unmediated state." The imbalances in power grew more extreme over the course of the war. The more miserable the Herero became, the more they seemed to earn the white settlers' contempt. The settlers no longer recognized "helpless children or dignified elders," but only "primitive, uncivilized beings," and they treated the Herero as such.[2]

The fate of James, the African teamster, bears witness to this observation. We know about him only because he was a British subject, and because British authorities investigated his sudden death.[3] His fate poignantly illustrates how little an African life was worth—even though there was an acute shortage of labor, and workers like James had to be recruited from abroad in order to fill the gaps. Commands "from above," which prohibited the mistreatment of transport workers, clashed with the accustomed behavior of rank-and-file soldiers. The commands did not, in any case, stop the guards from summarily shooting James; he had threatened to hold up the convoy because he was too sick to go on. The leaders' half-hearted efforts to rein in violence from below, and to uphold legal and soldierly norms, are underscored by the fact that the perpetrator was sentenced to just seven weeks in prison.

The colonial state was a weak state. Broadly accepted racism and the fragility of German claims to power gave civilian and military officials further reasons to turn a blind eye to the domineering behavior of their white subjects. This was true before the outbreak of war, but even more so thereafter. All wars are characterized by a reduction in norms and sanctions, but Trotha's campaign exceeded all usual boundaries, definitively shifting the standards of acceptable interactions with Africans. By the time that his proclamation declared the Herero "fair game," at the latest, the soldiers must have felt as if they could treat the Herero however they pleased. After the proclamation, privatized violence could no longer be contained. The war (further) brutalized colonial society and normalized cruelty, leading to asymmetric power relations with almost no limits on the exercise of violence. White fantasies of power were boundless. The regime of the camps and postwar "native policy" targeted the few, miserable survivors of a long defeated opponent. The "struggle between the races" was permanent, and it became more radical over time. This dynamic was heightened by the war and the even greater imbalance of power that followed. German South-West Africa became an "overtly racist regime."[4]

Because of the ongoing normalization of cruelty, orders to shoot women and children, or that led to the eradication of entire groups, were not only followed, but incited no great outrage. The campaign that was planned from above and privatized violence were mutually reinforcing.

This leads to a further observation. Elkins and Pederson argue that the settlement of South-West Africa is best understood as a state project that was initiated and directed from above—in contrast to older settler colonies in North America, for example, which were largely established by nonstate actors.[5] However, the example of South-West Africa clearly shows that this was not a privative opposition. Both types of settlement coexisted, and their destructive forces worked in tandem—with disastrous consequences for the autochthonous population.

With or without state intervention, settler violence throughout history has depopulated entire parts of the globe.[6] Modern states, however, possess particular destructive potential. They have the legitimacy, organizational strength, and material and human resources to enable large genocidal campaigns, as the history of the twentieth century shows.[7] In South-West Africa, settler and state violence were characteristically intertwined. The settlers acted as an independent motor of expansion within a weak colonial state. The brutality and anomie of the frontier situation provoked war, leading to the intervention of the metropolitan state, which unleashed its destructive force in order to protect white subjects and to assert its claim to power. The actual genocide occurred during this phase of the war.

An irony of history is that by pushing for radicalization, the settlers stirred up forces that they were no longer able to control. The settlers' loss of autonomy and self-determination perpetuated and intensified their sense of crisis, leading to coping behaviors that were typically violent. Metropolitan discourses overtook colonial politics and strategy, and the interests of the colony and its inhabitants became less and less important to the planning of the campaign. A crucial turning point was Leutwein's dismissal as commander of the South-West African Schutztruppe. Leutwein had always attended to the colony's broader development and worked to preserve its resources; these considerations were foreign to the metropole. The settlers weakened Leutwein's position with their polemics and protests because his approach seemed too "mild." Trotha initially seemed more accommodating of the settlers' strategic vision, but this impression was deceiving. Before long, it was clear that an unbridgeable chasm separated the vision of the homeland (military) from that of the colony. At the settlers' urging, the war acquired a dimension that threatened to consume the colony.

The influence of the imperial government fundamentally changed the character of the war. The metropole was less concerned about the future of the colony, and more about Germany's great power prestige. It saw only operational victories as essential; all other concerns were secondary.

Militarism drove the metropole's response. Immediately after the outbreak of the uprising, the General Staff assumed control over all operations. As the new man at the helm of the Schutztruppe, Trotha declared martial law even before he arrived in South-West Africa, which became a military dictatorship no later than the end of 1904, when Leutwein resigned as governor. Under Leutwein's command, military action had always been subject to strategic means-end calculations. His dismissal, however, ushered in a phase of almost exclusive attention to military and operational concerns, and questions about strategic viability were derided as "petty misgivings." The goal of the war became purely military. Political questions would be clarified only *after* total victory—although the Herero were clearly to be deprived of their last traces of sovereignty, and their political and social organization demolished. Berlin authorities demanded a war of annihilation, although their primary target was not Herero society and its members, but rather their political and social structures. I argue, therefore, that the conflict is best identified as a *political* war of annihilation. Even so, the influence of the metropole hastened the *strategic* escalation of the campaign, so that violence became an end in itself, no longer restrained by political concerns.

In contrast to Leutwein's approach, the Herero were now treated as "rebels," not as a legitimate warring party. Diplomatic relations were broken. For the authorities in Berlin, there was only one possible resolution to the conflict—the rebels' unconditional surrender. The metropolitan military officers overestimated their own abilities, believing that they could rely entirely on their own strength, without even considering the opponent. "Bimodal alienation," which had long characterized the local conflict, now extended to military strategy. Because the Germans broke off relations with the Herero and ruled out any compromise, the fronts continued to harden. In response to the Germans' intransigence, the Herero became less and less willing to surrender, and instead sought to save themselves by resisting or fleeing.

The devastating consequences of the campaign's militaristic turn were in no way foreordained. Conservative militarism still informed the spirit of the metropole's campaign against the Herero. Trotha's focus on the battle of annihilation intensified wartime violence in South-West Africa to an unprecedented degree, but battles of annihilation also harbored the opposite tendency—to contain violence instead. The campaign against the Herero was supposed to end in a great decisive battle. A short but intensive act of war that did not transgress the boundaries of "conventional" warfare might have ended the campaign, insofar as this was even possible in a colonial conflict. Had Trotha achieved the expected victory at the Waterberg, we might not be speaking of genocide today. Against the authorities' expectations and intentions, however, the tendency to escalate violence prevailed over the tendency to contain it. Certain conditions had to be in place for genocidal violence to occur. To this extent, genocidal escalation was contingent on outside forces.

The Herero themselves played an active role. Emphasizing Herero agency does not automatically relativize the excesses of German warfare, but rather helps to explain its escalation. The Germans were extremely reluctant to acknowledge Herero agency, which can explain Trotha's obsession with beating them. The exaggerated and arrogant expectations of the Germans—and Trotha, in particular—as they arrived in SWA are important to keep in mind. Against these expectations, the Herero were not decisively beaten at the Waterberg, and they did not surrender in the weeks thereafter. Finally, the Germans could no longer catch up to them and ultimately had to call off the pursuit. All of these events wounded the colonial masters' feelings of absolute superiority so deeply that they resorted to increasingly severe measures; in the end, they were prepared to do almost anything to make up for these deficiencies.

The metropole wanted the campaign to provide unambiguous proof of German superiority. However, it dramatically overestimated German capabilities while carelessly underestimating those of the Herero, thereby encouraging a certain path dependency. Once the path of proving superior strength was set, it was almost impossible to change without seeming weak. The pressure was especially great on Trotha, who adamantly refused to change course. As the responsible commander, he believed that his only option was to press ahead and turn the screws of violence tighter. His intransigence repelled the Herero and hardened the opposing fronts. The more Trotha worked in his one-dimensional way to bring the situation under control, the worse it became.

I have argued that the road from "conventional" to genocidal annihilation led through another strategy, which was described in the proclamation: the definitive expulsion of the Herero from the colony. This strategy was no mere "camouflage," as is sometimes assumed; Trotha considered this option early on. Thus, I situate the genocidal turn later than many other scholars. However, determining the "genocidal moment" is not so important, if it is even possible at all. I agree with Alexander Hinton's assertion that reconstructing the overall course of developments is ultimately more instructive than establishing the precise moment when the decision for genocide was made.[8] Two aspects of the process of escalation deserve particular attention: first, the (continued) failure of operations, and, second, the meaning of this unanticipated failure for the responsible authorities, who considered it unacceptable.

It is surprising how little attention has been paid to the effect of shame in colonial contexts. The colonial situation is characterized by colonizers' racist feelings of superiority, which are so exaggerated that disappointment is inevitable—but the nature of colonial power means that this disappointment cannot be acknowledged. Denied shame leads to rage and violence, as was evident in Trotha's proclamation. Issued after his troops could go no further and the pursuit had definitively failed, the proclamation marked a new stage of escalation, threatening every Herero with annihilation. Trotha experienced stinging incompetence, which he did not want to accept. Since revising his chosen path was out of the question, all that remained was doubling down.

Shame is generally painful and begets more shame. It also limits the subject's capacity for action. Certain factors predisposed Trotha to deny shame. Failure in a "small despicable Kaffir war" was unthinkable, and all the more so for Trotha, who had not only expended a great deal of time, but also "streams of money," to prepare for the campaign. He narrowed his options further by issuing grandiose pronouncements and treating the long-serving colonial officers with contempt.[9] The warrior ethos of "good society" abhorred any admission of weakness, such as shame. Trotha acted as an exponent of his milieu, although he was also a "hardliner" and embodied the warrior ethos in its purest form. His self-awareness as a soldier and "man of honor," more than any concern for the colony's future, kept him from changing course or backing down.

The constant setbacks went hand in hand with steadily growing rage, and the small war became a "campaign of disappointments." Unable to admit that his course had failed, Trotha insisted on forging ahead. His pursuit of the Herero became downright obsessive. The more illusory his goals became in light of the actual situation, the more stubbornly he clung to them. He fell out with numerous officers who advocated all too openly for changing course. He even wanted to challenge the Imperial chancellor to a duel in response to a minor slight—a sign of how extreme the situation had become. It was humiliating enough to have to stop at the edge of the Omaheke, kilometers away from the colony's border; all he could do was wait and react. For all of the troops' efforts and sacrifices, nothing of substance had been achieved. Whether or not the Herero would permanently stay away from the colony remained an open question. It was clear, however, that soldiers would need to be stationed at the edge of the Omaheke for some time—and that this already more than surpassed the capacity of the troops. As it became apparent that the Herero would not reach British territory, and that they also would not survive in the Omaheke, Trotha became that much more determined to uphold the cordoning measures. He was not only willing to take the extermination of the Herero in stride; he was also eager to facilitate it. Denied shame turned into rage and hatred. Trotha sought to extinguish the traces of his own military failure alongside the Herero themselves.

The German troops also suffered under the misguided strategy. Hunger, thirst, and disease took their toll. Many soldiers felt abandoned by their leaders, although their relationship did not break altogether, as occurred in the trenches ten years later—in no small part because solidarity with the Herero opponent was unthinkable. The chasm of racism was simply too wide; even the most detestable, slave-driving superior was much closer to the soldiers than their opponent. The soldiers often had no empathy, only contempt, for the miserable Herero survivors. They directed their aggression against the Herero, who were the actual victims of Trotha's strategy.

The soldiers were brutalized. Their experience during the advance was dominated by fear; they had been brought to the colony hastily and were often overwhelmed. After the Battle of Waterberg, fear gave way to embitterment, which gave the soldiers the motivation they needed to carry on. Brutalization was an unintended effect of the prolonged campaign, but it helped to keep the campaign going, even in its exterminatory phase.

As I have explained, the extreme violence against the Herero did not end when Trotha retracted his proclamation in December 1904—nor did it end when the war was formally declared over in 1907, nor when the last concentration camps were dissolved in 1908.

When Bülow intervened against the strategy of extermination, the Kaiser flew into a rage.[10] As the strategy's author, Trotha responded in like manner and immediately announced his departure. It was soon apparent, however, that the change in course was not nearly as radical as he had first assumed, and he ultimately remained in his command for almost one more year. Schlieffen's clarifications showed that things could mostly stay the same, except that voluntarily surrendering Herero were now to be pardoned. Since many Herero did not do so, Trotha's approach hardly changed. This heightened Herero suspicions and discouraged them from turning themselves in. The German troops gave up their old ways only haltingly, if at all. By softening the prescribed change in course, Schlieffen allowed Trotha to keep his command and save face. The objective discrepancies between the two officers were apparently not so wide. Schlieffen softened his orders, and the troops carried on as before.

Christian Gerlach has complained that genocide scholars are too concerned with distinguishing between forms of violence and limiting their attention to certain forms.[11] More important, however, is understanding the connections between the different forms—or, with respect to the present case—between successive phases. Genocides are an effect, and also a cause, of broader processes. They have a prehistory and aftereffects. In South-West Africa, the exterminatory phase of the campaign, at the latest, irrevocably shifted the horizon of how indigenous people might be treated. White fantasies of power lost all restraint—as witnessed not only by conditions in the concentration camps, but also during the "peace" that followed. Violence against "natives" was normalized to an extent that left some visitors from Germany speechless. Once the whites had become masters over life and death, they were reluctant to relinquish this power.[12]

Moreover, some settlers still had scores to settle with the rebels. The distant metropole had waged the war over the settlers' heads, and the settlers had experienced the war as a time of extreme foreign control. But their need for revenge persisted, as did their broader need to overcome powerlessness through violence, to reassert agency, and to assure their own superiority.

Broadly accepted racism devalued African life, which explains why concentration camps became the alternative to Trotha's strategy of extermination. The camps institutionalized the pardon that he had previously refused to extend to the Herero. Internment left the Herero defenseless, in the hands of settlers and soldiers who had pursued them. The ideologization of the regime of the camps, however, was the work of civil servants. They, too, were overwhelmed by anxiety and shame over Trotha's misbegotten campaign. Even though the Herero were thoroughly defeated, no demonstration of power had laid the groundwork for postwar rule. Thus, the regime of the camps was the continuation of (total) war by other means. Civil servants targeted the "enemy" society as a whole and worked to make up for Trotha's failings. The fatal consequences of shame continued.

Sarkin's recent attempt to trace the Herero genocide back to the uppermost leadership of Imperial Germany, the Kaiser himself, is not very persuasive. He underestimates the power of other historical actors by depicting them as "his"—that is, the Kaiser's—settlers and soldiers.[13] In fact, the situation was far more complex. Many different actors shaped the course of events in an active, independent way. The settlers had no formal political role, but they left their mark on colonial socialization. Their interactions with the indigenous people provoked the war, independent of the colonial state. The Herero reacted primarily against this privatized violence. By threatening apparent civilians, the Herero response incited outrage in the metropole and among officers and soldiers who were unfamiliar with colonial power relations. Embitterment shaped the further campaign. The settlers pushed for escalation, which quickly took on dimensions that they had neither anticipated nor wished for, and that spiraled entirely out of their control. The unfettered violence was defined by the interplay of different groups of historical actors. The logic behind their actions was informed by the time and place of their engagement, as well as by their interactions with rival actors. If we consider the broader course of events—including relations of violence that preceded, and later arose from, the actual genocidal phase—the lack of any coherent, centralized control is immediately apparent. To borrow the phrasing of Jean-Michel Chaumont, we can speak of a "competition" of perpetrators.[14] This does not, of course, alleviate responsibility or guilt. Imperial Germany and its legal successors bear responsibility for the atrocities that were committed in Germany's name by its representatives overseas. In order to establish this responsibility, we need not oversimplify the course of events. Differentiation is essential for *explaining* how this catastrophe arose—even if this appears to complicate the wish for a simple attribution of guilt.

Notes

1. Norbert Elias and John L. Scotson, *The Established and the Outsiders: A Sociological Enquiry into Community Problems*, 2nd ed. (London, 1994), xvff.; and Hund, *Rassismus*, 24.
2. Hund, *Rassismus*, 122.
3. KAB GH 35/157: "Treatment of Natives in G.S.W.A. 1905," "Ill-Treatment of 3 Natives in G.S.W.A. 1905–1906."
4. Frederickson, *Racism*, 1.
5. Elkins and Pederson, "Introduction."
6. See, for example, Mohamed Adhikari, "'We Are Determined To Exterminate Them': The Genocidal Impetus behind the Invasion of Commercial Stock Farmers of Hunter-Gatherers Territories," in *Genocide on Settler Frontiers: When Hunter-Gatherers and Commercial Stock Farmers Clash*, ed. Mohamed Adhikari (New York, 2015), 1ff.
7. Philip Zimbardo, *Der Luzifer-Effekt: Die Macht der Umstände und die Psychologie des Bösen* (Berlin, 2012), 214–15; Peter Fritzsche, "Genocide and Global Discourse," *German History* 23, no. 1 (2005): 105; and Eric J. Weitz, *A Century of Genocide: Utopias of Race and Nation* (Princeton, 2003), 6–7.
8. Alexander Laban Hinton, "Zündstoffe: Die Roten Khmer in Kambodscha," *Mittelweg 36* 15, no. 6 (2006): 70.
9. Marchand-Volz, *Werner Freiherr Schenck v. Stauffenberg*, 137.

10. Bülow, *Denkwürdigkeiten*, 21.
11. Gerlach, "Extremely Violent Societies," 464.
12. Wolfgang Sofsky, *Die Ordnung des Terrors: Das Konzentrationslager*, 4th ed. (Frankfurt, 1999), 196.
13. Sarkin, *Germany's Genocide of the Herero*.
14. Jean-Michel Chaumont, *Die Konkurrenz der Opfer: Genozid, Identität und Anerkennung*, trans. Thomas Laugstien (Lüneburg, 2001).

BIBLIOGRAPHY

Archival Sources

Archiv der Vereinten Evangelischen Mission (Wuppertal)
RMG 2.660: Deutsche Kolonialbehörden in Südwestafrika: u.a. Fürsorge für die Herero

Botswana National Archives and Records Services (GNARS)
RC 1/16: Native rising (of Herero) in German South West Africa (and Ngamiland precautions), 1904
RC 1/17: Secret and confidential correspondence relating to the Hottentot and Herero rebellions in German South West Africa, security measures on the Protectorate border, and measures to be adopted regarding fugitives seeking asylum in the Protectorate, January 1904 – November 1905
RC 2/41/1-3: Despatches, 1903–11, from High Commissioner to Resident Commissioner, Bechuanaland, on South West Affairs including Hottentot rising of 1903 and Herero unrest of 1909
RC 4/18: Memorandum by Ngamiland Magistrate on the native inhabitants of the German South West Africa Protectorate with special reference to the conditions affecting Ngamiland, 20th January, 1905
RC 10/18: Proposal to allow Hereros to settle in the Protectorate (following rebellion in German South West Africa); and 1914–15 papers on entry into Ngamiland of the Herero Chief Joseph and his followers, 1904–15
RC 11/1-2: Correspondence regarding Hereros (and flight to Ngamiland after rebellion in German South West Africa)
RC 12/12: Sub-Inspector Hodson: second visit to Kalahari (Patrols to Lehututu to intercept and disarm Damara refugees from South West Africa and investigate alleged violations of the Protectorate border by Hottentot rebels under Witbooi and Simon Kooper, 1905)
RC 13/6: Sub-Inspector H. V. Eason: Patrol to Lehututu (to preserve German South West Africa border from violation by belligerents in Hottentot rebellion); (Interception of armed Koranas and of Hottentots under Simon Kooper), 1905–1907

Bundesarchiv Koblenz
NL. 1030 (Nachlass Viktor Franke):
   Vol. 3a: Diary, 5 September 1903 – 29 December 1904
   Vol. 21: Der Aufstand in Deutsch-Südwestafrika und die nachfolgenden Jahre, 1903–1906
N/1783/1: Missionary Eich diary

Bundesarchiv Berlin-Lichterfelde
R1001 (Reichskolonialamt)
   2089: Differenzen zwischen Generalleutnant v. Trotha und Gouverneur Leutwein über das Verhältnis von militärischen und politischen Maßnahmen zur Beendigung des Krieges
   2111–2119: Aufstand der Herero 1904–1909

Cape Town Archives Repository (KAB)
CO (Colonial Office)
   4567: Correspondence on Campaigns against Natives in German South West Africa 1904–1907
GH (Government House)
   35/139: Correspondence: High Commissioner Re Rising of Natives in G.S.W.A., 1904–1906
   35/157: Treatment of Natives in G.S.W.A. 1905
PMO (Prime Minister's Office)
   199: Correspondence Files Nos. 211/05 – 286/05, Native Rising in German South West Africa, 1904–1906

Deutsches Tagebucharchiv Emmendingen (DTA)
Sign. 1704: Helene Gathmann diary

Evangelical Lutheran Church in the Republic of Namibia (ELCRN)
V.23.1: Gemeindechronik Omaruru

Trotha Family Archive (TA)
Sign. 315: Lothar von Trotha diary, May 1904 – December 1905; typescript (1a; with supplements: 2a and 3a), compiled by Lucy von Trotha, Bonn 1930
Handwritten diaries:
   122/15: 20 May 1904 – 5 July 1904
   122/16: 6 July 1904 – 8 July 1904; 24 October 1904 – 10 January 1905
   122/17: 10 July 1904 – 23 October 1904
   122/18: 11 January 1905 – 14 December 1905

The National Archive, Public Record Office (PRO), Kew, London
WO (War Office)
   106/265: "Herero-Rising 1904–7; Bondelswart Rising 1903"
   106/268: "Operations in German South West Africa" [Lt. Col. F. J. A. Trench to Secretary of the War Office]
FO (Foreign Office)
   64/1645: "Native Rising in German South West Africa"

National Archives of Namibia (NAN)
ZBU (Zentralbureau)
   D.IV.C.1: Feldzug gegen die Hereros und die Khauas-Hottentotten

D.IV.L.2: Herero-Aufstand 1904; Feldzug; Politisches; Vol. 3: August 1904 – September 1905
D.IV.L.2: Herero-Aufstand 1904; Feldzug; Politisches; Vol. 4: October 1904 – December 1905
D.IV.L.3: Hereroaufstand, Kriegsgefangene; Vol. 1: September 1904 – April 1906
D.IV.M.1: Erhebung über die Gründe des Witbooi-Aufstandes
D.IV.M.2: Vol. 1: Ausbruch der Witbooi-Unruhen
D.IV.M.2: Vol. 4: Verhörprotokolle
2369: Geheimakten Witboi-Hottentotten
BKE (Bezirksamt Keetmanshoop)
    No. 220
PA (Private Accessions)
    A.109: Stuhlmann, Tagebuch meiner Kriegserlebnisse in Süd-West-Afrika 1904 und 1905 als Oberleutnant der Schutztruppe
    A.151: v. Alten papers, Viktor v. Alten diary (no. 1), Rudolf v. Hardenberg diaries and writings (no. 2ff.)
    A.510: Emil Malzahn diary, 1901–1904
    A.529: Otto Busch, Berichte über Reisen nach Angola, in die Kapkolonie etc., 1900–1914
    A.538: H. F .R. Knoke diary, 20 April 1904 – 1 January 1905
    A.583: Gerhardt v. Brünneck letters
AACRLS (Archives on Anti-Colonial Resistance and Liberation Struggle in Namibia)
    No. 70: Kurt v. Frankenberg und Proschlitz diary, 1904–07
    L1032: Lemmer collection: Anonymous war diary

Published Sources

Pamphlets and Campaign Posters

GStA: Geheimes Staatsarchiv – Preußischer Kulturbesitz. XII: Hauptabteilung Druckschriften, VI: Flugblätter und Plakate. Nos. 48/ 48²/ 48³; 49 (SPD); No. 105 (Zentrum); No. 149, 151, 152 (Liberale); No. 154, 155 (Freisinnige); No. 156 (Deutsche Volkspartei); No. 172 (Konservative); Nr. 174 (Reichspartei)
StaBiB: Staatsbibliothek zu Berlin – Stiftung Preußischer Kulturbesitz. Reichstagswahlen 1903–1912: Gebundene Flugblätter in der Berliner Staatsbibliothek

Newspapers

Deutsch-Südwestafrikanische Zeitung (DSWAZ)
Windhuker Nachrichten (until 1904: *Nachrichten des Bezirks-Vereins Windhuk*) (WN)

Reichstag Proceedings

StBR: Stenographische Berichte über die Verhandlungen des Reichstags

Texts

Addington, Larry H. *The Patterns of War since the Eighteenth Century*. London: Croom Helm, 1984.
Adhikari, Mohamed. "'We Are Determined to Exterminate Them': The Genocidal Impetus behind the Invasion of Commercial Stock Farmers of Hunter-Gatherers Territories." In *Genocide on Settler Frontiers: When Hunter-Gatherers and Commercial Stock Farmers Clash*, edited by Mohamed Adhikari, 1–31. New York: Berghahn, 2015.
Admiralstab der Marine. *Das Marine-Expeditionskorps in Südwest-Afrika während des Herero-Aufstandes*. Berlin: Mittler, 1905.
———. *Die Tätigkeit des Landungskorps S.M.S. "Habicht" während des Herero-Aufstandes Januar/Februar 1904*. Berlin: Mittler, 1905.
Aron, Raymond. *Peace and War: A Theory of International Relations*. New York: Routledge, (1966) 2017.
Ashworth, Anthony. "The Sociology of Trench Warfare." *British Journal of Sociology* 19, no. 4 (1968): 407–23.
———. *Trench Warfare 1914–1918: The Live and Let Live System*. Basingstoke: Pan-Macmillan, 2000.
Auer, G. *In Südwestafrika gegen die Hereros: Nach den Kriegstagebüchern des Obermatrosen G. Auer*. Berlin: Ernst Hofmann, 1911.
Balandier, Georges. "The Colonial Situation: A Theoretical Approach." In *Social Change: The Colonial Situation*, edited by Immanuel Wallerstein, 34–61. New York: John Wiley, 1966.
Bart, Virginia. "En mémoire des Hereros et des Namas." *Le Monde*, 27 March 2015.
Barth, Boris. *Genozid – Völkermord im 20. Jahrhundert: Geschichte, Theorien, Kontroversen*. Munich: Beck, 2006.
Bayer, Maximilian. *Mit dem Hauptquartier in Südwestafrika*. Berlin: Wilhelm Weicher Marine- u. Kolonialverlag, 1909.
Beckett, Ian. "Another British Way in Warfare: Charles Callwell and Small Wars," In *Victorians at War: New Perspectives*, edited by Ian Beckett, 89–102. London: Society for Army Historical Research, 2007.
———. *Modern Insurgencies and Counter-Insurgencies: Guerrillas and Their Opponents since 1750*. London: Routledge, 2001.
Behr, H. F. von. *Kriegsbilder aus dem Araberaufstand in Deutsch-Ostafrika*. Leipzig: Brockhaus, 1891.
Belich, James. "Krieg und transkulturelles Lernen in Neuseeland im 19. Jahrhundert." In *Waffen – Wissen – Wandel: Anpassung und Lernen in transkulturellen Erstkonflikten*, edited by Dierk Walter and Birthe Kundrus, 239–57. Hamburg: Hamburger Edition, 2012.
———. *Replenishing the Earth: The Settler Revolution and the Rise of the Anglo-World, 1783–1939*. Oxford: Oxford University Press, 2010.
Belwe, Max. *Gegen die Herero 1904/1905: Tagebuchaufzeichnungen von Max Belwe: Mit einer Übersichtsskizze und achtzehn Abbildungen im Text*. Berlin: Mittler, 1906.
Benz, Wolfgang. "Kolonialpolitik als Genozid: Der 'Herero-Aufstand' in Deutsch-Südwestafrika." In *Ausgrenzung, Vertreibung, Völkermord: Genozid im 20. Jahrhundert*, 2nd ed., edited by Wolfgang Benz, 27–53. Munich: Deutscher Taschenbuchverlag, 2007.
Beyrau, Dietrich. "Totaler Krieg: Begriff und Erfahrung am sowjetischen Beispiel." In *Formen des Krieges: Von der Antike bis zur Gegenwart*, edited by Dietrich Beyrau et al., 327–54. Paderborn: Schöningh, 2007.

Bley, Helmut. "Gewaltverhältnisse in Siedlergesellschaften des südlichen Afrika." In *Siedler-Identität: Neun Fallstudien von der Antike bis zur Gegenwart*, edited by Christof Dipper, 141–65. Frankfurt: Lang, 1995.

———. *Kolonialherrschaft und Sozialstruktur in Deutsch-Südwestafrika 1894–1914*. Hamburg: Leibniz-Verlag, 1968.

———. *South-West Africa under German Rule 1894–1914*. Translated by Hugh Ridley. London: Heinemann, 1971.

Bodley, John H. *Victims of Progress*. 3rd ed. Mountain View, CA: Mayfield Publishing Company, 1990.

Böhlke-Itzen, Janntje. "Die bundesdeutsche Diskussion und die Reparationsfrage: Ein ganz normaler Kolonialkrieg?" In *Genozid und Gedenken: Namibisch-deutsche Geschichte und Gegenwart*, edited by Henning Melber, 103–19. Frankfurt: Brandes & Apsel, 2005.

Bourdieu, Pierre. *Distinction: A Social Critique of the Judgement of Taste*. Translated by Richard Nice. Cambridge: Harvard University Press, 1984.

———. *Outline of a Theory of Practice*. Translated by Richard Nice. Cambridge: Cambridge University Press, 1977.

Brändli, Sabina. "Von 'schneidigen Offizieren' und 'Militärcrinolinen': Aspekte symbolischer Männlichkeit am Beispiel preussischer und schweizerischer Uniformen des 19. Jahrhunderts." In *Militär und Gesellschaft im 19. und 20. Jahrhundert*, edited by Ute Frevert, 201–28. Stuttgart: Klett Cotta, 1997.

Brehl, Medardus. *Vernichtung der Herero: Diskurse der Gewalt in der deutschen Kolonialliteratur*. Munich: Fink, 2007.

Bridgman, Jon M. *The Revolt of the Hereros*. Berkeley: University of California Press, 1981.

Bridgman, Jon M., and Leslie J. Worley. "Genocide of the Hereros." In *Century of Genocide: Eyewitness Accounts and Critical Views*, edited by Samuel Totten et al., 3–40. New York: Garland Publishing, 1997.

Bröckling, Ulrich. *Disziplin: Soziologie und Geschichte militärischer Gehorsamsproduktion*. Munich: Wilhelm Fink, 1997.

Brogini-Künzi, Giulia. *Italien und der Abessinienkrieg 1935/36: Kolonialkrieg oder Totaler Krieg?* Paderborn: Schöningh, 2006.

Browning, Christopher R. *Ordinary Men: Reserve Police Battalion 101 and the Final Solution in Poland*. New York: HarperCollins, 1992.

Browning, Peter. *The Changing Nature of Warfare: The Development of Land Warfare from 1792 to 1945*. Cambridge: Cambridge University Press, 2006.

Buchheit, Gert. *Vernichtungs- oder Ermattungsstrategie? Vom strategischen Charakter der Kriege*. Berlin: Paul Neff, 1942.

Budack, Kuno F. R. H. "Kampf in den Oranjebergen 1897: Der 'Afrikaner-Aufstand' in Deutsch-Südwestafrika." In *Afrikanischer Heimatkalender 1980*, edited by Kirchenbundesrat des Deutschen Kirchenbundes Süd- und Südwestafrikas. Windhoek: Verlag Afrikanischer Heimatkalender, 1980.

Bühler, Andreas Heinrich. *Der Namaaufstand gegen die deutsche Kolonialherrschaft in Namibia von 1904–1913*. Frankfurt: IKO-Verlag für Interkulturelle Kommunikation, 2003.

Bührer, Tanja. *Die Kaiserliche Schutztruppe für Deutsch-Ostafrika: Koloniale Sicherheitspolitik und transkulturelle Kriegführung 1885 bis 1918*. Munich: Oldenbourg, 2011.

Bülow, Bernhard von. *Denkwürdigkeiten*. Vol. 2: *Von der Marokko-Krise bis zum Abschied*. Edited by Franz Stockhammern. Berlin: Ullstein, 1930.

Bülow, Franz von. *Deutsch-Südwestafrika: Drei Jahre im Lande Hendrik Witboois: Schilderungen von Land und Leuten*. Berlin: Mittler, 1896.

Bülow, H. von. *Deutsch-Südwestafrika seit der Besitzergreifung, die Züge und Kriege gegen die Eingeborenen.* Berlin: Wilhelm Süsserott, 1904.
Callwell, Charles Edward. *Small Wars: Their Principles and Practice.* Reprint of the 3rd ed. Lincoln: University of Nebraska Press, (1906) 1996.
Chatterjee, Partha. *The Nation and Its Fragments: Colonial and Postcolonial Histories.* Princeton: Princeton University Press, 1993.
Chaumont, Jean-Michel. *Die Konkurrenz der Opfer: Genozid, Identität und Anerkennung.* Translated by Thomas Laugstien. Lüneburg: zu Klampen, 2001.
Ciompi, Luc, and Elke Endert. *Gefühle machen Geschichte: Die Wirkung kollektiver Emotionen – von Hitler bis Obama.* Göttingen: Vandenhoeck & Ruprecht, 2011.
Clausewitz, Carl von. *On War.* Edited and translated by Michael Howard and Peter Paret. Princeton: Princeton University Press, 1976.
———. *Vom Kriege: Vollständige Ausgabe im Urtext.* 16th ed. Bonn: Dümmler, 1952.
Collins, Randall. "A Dynamic of Battle Victory and Defeat." *Cliodynamics* 1 (2010): 3–25.
———. *Violence: A Micro-Sociological Theory.* Princeton: Princeton University Press, 2008.
Conradt, Ludwig. *Erinnerungen aus zwanzigjährigem Händler- und Farmerleben in Deutsch-Südwestafrika.* Edited by Thomas Keil. Göttingen: Klaus Hess, 2006.
Coser, Lewis. *The Functions of Social Conflict.* New York: Free Press, 1956.
Creveld, Martin van. *Fighting Power: German and U.S. Army Performance, 1939–1945.* Westport: Greenwood Press, 1982.
———. *The Transformation of War.* New York: Free Press, 1991.
Crothers, George D. *The German Elections of 1907.* 2nd ed. New York: AMS Press, 1968.
Daase, Christopher. *Kleine Kriege – Große Wirkung: Wie unkonventionelle Kriegführung die internationale Politik verändert.* Baden-Baden: Nomos, 1999.
Damásio, Antonio R. *Descartes' Irrtum – Fühlen, Denken und das menschliche Gehirn.* 7th ed. Munich: List, 2012.
Dammann, Ernst. *Was Herero erzählten und sangen: Texte, Übersetzung, Kommentar.* Berlin: Reimer, 1987.
Dedering, Tilman. "A Certain Rigorous Treatment of All Parts of the Nation: The Annihilation of the Herero in German South West Africa 1904." In *The Massacre in History*, edited by Mark Levene and Penny Roberts, 205–22. New York: Berghahn, 1999.
———. "The German-Herero War of 1904: Revisionism of Genocide or Imaginary Historiography?" *Journal of Southern African Studies* 19, no. 1 (1993): 80–88.
Deimling, Berthold von. *Südwestafrika: Land und Leute – unsere Kämpfe – Wert der Kolonie: Vortrag, gehalten in einer Anzahl deutscher Städte.* Berlin: R. Eisenschmidt, 1906.
Deist, Wilhelm. "Voraussetzungen innenpolitischen Handelns des Militärs im Ersten Weltkrieg." In *Militär, Staat und Gesellschaft: Studien zur preußisch-deutschen Militärgeschichte*, edited by Wilhelm Deist, 103–52. Munich: Oldenbourg, 1991.
Dekker, Sidney. *Drift into Failure: From Hunting Broken Components to Understanding Complex Systems.* Farnham: Ashgate, 2011.
Delavignette, Robert. *Les vrais chefs de l'Empire.* Paris: Gallimard, 1939.
Delbrück, Hans. *Geschichte der Kriegskunst.* Vol. 2: *Die Neuzeit: Vom Kriegswesen der Renaissance bis zu Napoleon.* Berlin: Nikol, (1920) 2006.
———. *History of the Art of War.* Vol. 4: *The Modern Era.* Translated by Walter J. Renfroe, Jr. Westport: Greenwood Press, 1985.
Demeter, Karl. *Das deutsche Offizierkorps in Gesellschaft und Staat, 1650–1945.* Frankfurt: Bernard & Graefe, 1962.
Dincklage-Campe, Friedrich Freiherr von. *Deutsche Reiter in Südwest: Selbsterlebnisse aus den Kämpfen in Deutsch-Südwestafrika: Mit zahlreichen Porträts und Illustrationen nach Originalphotographien und Zeichnungen von E. Becker, B. Huen, O. Merte.* Berlin: Bong, 1908.

Docker, John. "Are Settler-Colonies Inherently Genocidal? Re-reading Lemkin." In *Empire, Colony, Genocide. Conquest, Occupation, and Subaltern Resistance in World History*, edited by A. Dirk Moses, 81–101. New York: Berghahn, 2008.
Drascher, Wahrhold. *Auslanddeutsche Charakterbilder*. Stuttgart: Strecker und Schröder, 1929.
Drechsler, Horst. *Südwestafrika unter deutscher Kolonialherrschaft: Der Kampf der Herero und Nama gegen den deutschen Imperialismus 1884–1915*. Berlin: Akademie, 1966.
———. *Südwestafrika unter deutscher Kolonialherrschaft: Der Kampf der Herero und Nama gegen den deutschen Imperialismus 1884–1915*. Berlin: Akademie, 1984.
Eck, Bernard. "Essai pour une typologie des massacres en Grèce classique." In *Le massacre, objet de l'histoire*, edited by David El Kenz, 72–120. Paris: Gallimard, 2005.
Eckart, Wolfgang U. "Medizin und kolonialer Krieg: Die Niederschlagung der Herero-Nama-Erhebung im Schutzgebiet Deutsch-Südwestafrika, 1904–1907." In *Studien zur Geschichte des deutschen Kolonialismus in Afrika: Festschrift zum 60. Geburtstag von Peter Sebald*, edited by Peter Heine and Ulrich van der Heyden, 220–35. Pfaffenweiler: Centaurus Verlagsgesellschaft, 1995.
———. "Medizin und kolonialer Rassenkrieg: Die Niederschlagung des Herero-Nama-Aufstandes im Schutzgebiet Deutsch-Südwestafrika (1904–1907)." In *Kriegsverbrechen im 20. Jahrhundert*, edited by Wolfgang Wette and Gerd Ueberschär, 59–71. Darmstadt: Wissenschaftliche Buchgesellschaft, 2001.
Eckenbrecher, Margarete von. *Was Afrika mir gab und nahm*. Berlin: Mittler, 1940.
Eckl, Andreas. *"S'ist ein übles Land hier": Zur Historiographie eines umstrittenen Kolonialkrieges: Tagebuchaufzeichnungen aus dem Herero-Krieg in Deutsch- Südwestafrika 1904 von Georg Hillebrecht und Franz Ritter von Epp*. Cologne: Köppe, 2005.
Eckl, Andreas, Matthias Häussler, and Jekura Kavari. "Oomambo wandje komuhoko wOvaherero: Lothar von Trotha's 'Words to the Ovaherero People.'" *Journal of Namibian Studies* 23 (2018): 125–33.
———. "Oomambo wandje komuhoko wOvaherero: Lothar von Trotha's 'Words to the Ovaherero People.'" In *Nuanced Considerations: Recent Voices in Namibian-German Colonial History*, edited by Wolfram Hartmann, 109–16. Windhoek: Orumbonde Press, 2019.
Elias, Norbert. *The Germans: Power Struggles and the Development of Habitus in the Nineteenth and Twentieth Centuries*. Translated by Eric Dunning and Stephen Mennell. New York: Columbia University Press, 1996.
———. *Studien über die Deutschen: Machtkämpfe und Habitusentwicklung im 19. und 20. Jahrhundert*. Frankfurt: Suhrkamp, 1992.
Elias, Norbert, and John L. Scotson. *The Established and the Outsiders: A Sociological Enquiry into Community Problems*. 2nd ed. London: SAGE, 1994.
Elkins, Caroline, and Susan Pedersen. "Introduction." In *Settler Colonialism in the Twentieth Century: Projects, Practices, Legacies*, edited by Caroline Elkins and Susan Pedersen, 1–20. New York: Routledge, 2005.
Endres, Franz Carl. "Soziologische Struktur und ihr entsprechende Ideologien des deutschen Offizierskorps vor dem Weltkriege." *Archiv für Sozialwissenschaft und Sozialpolitik* 58 (1927): 282–319.
Erdmann, Franz. *Die Ursachen des Herero-Aufstandes und die Entschädigungsansprüche der Siedler: Dargestellt von der Ansiedler-Abordnung*. Berlin: Verlag Wilhelm Baensch, 1904.
Erffa, Burkhart Freiherr von. *Reise- und Kriegsbilder von Deutsch-Südwest-Afrika: Aus Briefen des am 9. April bei Onganjira gefallenen Dr. jur. Burkhart Freiherrn von Erffa*. Halle: Verlag der Buchhandlung des Waisenhauses, 1905.
Erichsen, Caspar W. *"The Angel of Death Has Descended Violently among Them": Concentration Camps and Prisoners-of-War in Namibia 1904–1908*. Leiden: University of Leiden, 2005.

———. "Zwangsarbeit im Konzentrationslager auf der Haifischinsel." In *Völkermord in Deutsch-Südwestafrika: Der Kolonialkrieg (1904–1908) in Namibia und seine Folgen*, 2nd ed., edited by Jürgen Zimmerer and Joachim Zeller, 80–85. Berlin: Links, 2004.

Estorff, Ludwig von. *Wanderungen und Kämpfe in Südwestafrika, Ostafrika und Südafrika 1894–1910*. 2nd ed. Edited by Christoph-Friedrich Kutscher. Windhoek: von Goetz, 1979.

Evans, Raymond. "'Crime without a Name': Colonialism and the Case for 'Indigenocide.'" In *Empire, Colony, Genocide. Conquest, Occupation, and Subaltern Resistance in World History*, edited by A. Dirk Moses, 133–47. New York: Berghahn, 2008.

Fein, Helen. *Genocide: A Sociological Perspective*. London: Sage, 1993.

Fervers, Kurt. *Vernichtungskrieg*. Düsseldorf: Völkischer Verlag, 1941.

Fischer, Adolf. *Menschen und Tiere in Deutsch-Südwest*. 2nd ed. Stuttgart: Deutsche Verlags-Anstalt, 1914.

Förster, Larissa. *Erinnerungslandschaften im kolonialen und postkolonialen Namibia: Wie Deutsche und Herero in Namibia des Kriegs von 1904 gedenken*. Frankfurt: Campus, 2010.

Förster, Stig. *Der doppelte Militarismus: Die deutsche Heeresrüstungspolitik zwischen Status-quo-Sicherung und Aggression 1890–1913*. Stuttgart: Franz Steiner, 1985.

———. "Einleitung des Herausgebers." In *Moltke: Vom Kabinettskrieg zum Volkskrieg: Eine Werkauswahl*, edited by Stig Förster, 1–34. Bonn: Bouvier, 1992.

———. "Facing 'People's War': Moltke the Elder and Germany's Military Options after 1871." *Journal of Strategic Studies* 10, no. 2 (1987): 209–30.

———. "Krieg und Genozid: Überlegungen zum Problem extremer Gewalt in universalhistorischer Perspektive." *Mittelweg 36*, 5 (2009): 71–87.

———. "Optionen der Kriegführung im Zeitalter des 'Volkskrieges' – Zu Helmuth von Moltkes militärisch-politischen Überlegungen nach den Erfahrungen der Einigungskriege." In *Militärische Verantwortung in Staat und Gesellschaft: 175 Jahre Generalstabsausbildung in Deutschland*, edited by Detlef Bald, 83–107. Bonn: Bernard & Graefe, 1986.

François, Curt von. *Kriegführung in Südafrika*. Berlin: Reimer, 1900.

Franke, Victor. *Die Tagebücher des Schutztruppenoffiziers Victor Franke: Die Tagebuchaufzeichnungen vom 16.5.1896–27.5.1904*. 2 vols. Delmenhorst: Swalit, 2002.

Fredrickson, George M. *Racism: A Short History*. Princeton: Princeton University Press, 2002.

Freud, Sigmund. "Eine Schwierigkeit der Psychoanalyse." In *Gesammelte Werke, Bd. XII: Werke aus den Jahren 1917-1920*, 3–12. Frankfurt: S. Fischer, 1999.

———. "Über das Unbehagen in der Kultur." In *Gesammelte Werke*. Vol. 14: Werke aus den Jahren 1925-1931, 419–506. Frankfurt: S. Fischer, 1999.

Frevert, Ute. *Ehrenmänner: Das Duell in der bürgerlichen Gesellschaft*. Munich: Beck, 1991.

———. "Das jakobinische Modell: Allgemeine Wehrpflicht und Nationsbildung in Preußen-Deutschland." In *Militär und Gesellschaft im 19. und 20. Jahrhundert*, edited by Ute Frevert, 17–47. Stuttgart: Klett-Cotta, 1997.

———. *Die kasernierte Nation: Militärdienst und Zivilgesellschaft in Deutschland*. Munich: Beck, 2001.

———. "Das Militär als 'Schule der Männlichkeit': Erwartungen, Angebote, Erfahrungen im 19. Jahrhundert." In *Militär und Gesellschaft im 19. und 20. Jahrhundert*, edited by Ute Frevert, 145–73. Stuttgart: Klett-Cotta, 1997.

———. "Das Militär als Schule der Männlichkeiten." In *Männlichkeiten und Moderne: Geschlecht in den Wissenskulturen um 1900*, edited by Ulrike Brunotte and Rainer Herrn, 57–75. Bielefeld: Transcript, 2008.

Frijda, Nico H. *The Laws of Emotion*. New York: Routledge, 2013.
Fritzsche, Peter. "Genocide and Global Discourse." *German History* 23, no. 1 (2005): 96–111.
Geertz, Clifford. "Thick Description: Toward an Interpretive Theory of Culture." In *The Interpretation of Cultures*, 3–30. New York: Basic Books, 1973.
Gerlach, Christian. *Extrem gewalttätige Gesellschaften: Massengewalt im 20. Jahrhundert*. Munich: Deutsche Verlagsanstalt, 2011.
———. "Extremely Violent Societies: An Alternative to the Concept of Genocide." *Journal of Genocide Research* 8, no. 4 (2006): 455–71.
Gerwarth, Robert, and Stephan Malinowski. "Der Holocaust als 'kolonialer Genozid'? Europäische Kolonialgewalt und nationalsozialistischer Vernichtungskrieg." *Geschichte und Gesellschaft* 33 (2007): 439–66.
Geulen, Christian. *Geschichte des Rassismus*. Munich: Beck, 2007.
Gewald, Jan-Bart. *Herero Heroes: A Socio-political History of the Herero of Namibia 1890–1923*. Athens: Ohio University Press, 1999.
———. "Imperial Germany and the Herero of Southern Africa: Genocide and the Quest of Recompense." In *Genocide, War Crimes and the West: History and Complicity*, edited by Adam Jones, 59–77. London: Zed Books, 2004.
———. "Ovita ovia Zürn – Zürns Krieg." In: *Namibia – Deutschland, eine geteilte Geschichte: Widerstand, Gewalt, Erinnerung*, edited by Larissa Förster et al., 78–91. Cologne: Ethnologica, 2004.
Gibson, Gordon D. "The Social Organization of the Southwestern Bantu." PhD diss., University of Chicago, 1952.
Giesebrecht, Franz. *Die Behandlung der Eingeborenen in den deutschen Kolonien: Ein Sammelwerk*. Berlin, 1898.
———. "Die Behandlung der Neger: Ein Sammelwerk." *Neue Deutsche Rundschau* 8 (1897): 77–97.
———. "Kolonialgreuel: Eine kulturhistorische Studie." *Neue Deutsche Rundschau* (1895): 142–57.
Godendorff, Siegfried. "Späte Rechtfertigung zur Vorgehensweise der Abteilung von der Heyde bei den Gefechten am Waterberg durch den damaligen Abteilungsführer und späteren Generalleutnant a.D. Hermann von der Heyde." *Befunde und Berichte zur Deutschen Kolonialgeschichte* 6, no. 11 (2006): 49–56.
Godoy, Angelina. *Popular Injustice: Violence, Community, and Law in Latin America*. Stanford: Stanford University Press, 2006.
Graumann, Carl-Friedrich and Margret Wintermantel. "Diskriminierende Sprechakte: Ein funktionaler Ansatz." In *Verletzende Worte: Die Grammatik sprachlicher Missachtung*, edited by Steffen K. Herrmann et al., 147–77. Bielefeld: Transcript, 2007.
Gray, J. Glenn. *The Warriors: Reflections on Men in Battle*. Lincoln: University of Nebraska Press, 1998.
Greiner, Bernd. "Made in U.S.A.: Über politische Ängste und Paranoia." *Mittelweg 36* 24, no. 1/2 (2015): 137–55.
———. *Krieg ohne Fronten: Die USA in Vietnam*. Hamburg: Hamburger Edition, 2007.
Großer Generalstab. *Die Kämpfe der deutschen Truppen in Südwestafrika*. Vol. 1: Der Feldzug gegen die Hereros. Berlin: Mittler, 1906.
———. *Die Kämpfe der deutschen Truppen in Südwestafrika*. Vol. 2: Der Hottentottenkrieg. Berlin: Mittler, 1907.
———. *Kriegsbrauch im Landkriege*. Berlin: Mittler, 1902.
Gründer, Horst. *Geschichte der deutschen Kolonien*. 5th ed. Paderborn: Schöningh, 2004.
Guillaumin, Colette. "RASSE: Das Wort und die Vorstellung." In *Das Eigene und das Fremde: Neuer Rassismus in der Alten Welt*, edited by Ulrich Bielefeld, 159–71. Hamburg: Hamburger Edition, 1998.

Gumplowicz, Ludwig. *Der Rassenkampf*. Innsbruck: Wagner, 1928.
Häußermann, Hartmut, and Walter Siebel. *Stadtsoziologie: Eine Einführung*. Frankfurt: Campus, 2004.
Häussler, Matthias. "Between Annihilation and Clemency: Concentration Camp Rule in German South West Africa, 1904-1908." In *Nuanced Considerations. Recent Voices in Namibian-German Colonial History*, edited by Wolfram Hartmann, 187–204. Windhoek: Orumbonde Press, 2019.
———. "From Destruction to Extermination: Genocidal Escalation in Germany's War against the Herero, 1904." *Journal of Namibian Studies* 11 (2011): 55–81.
———. "Grausamkeit und Kolonialismus: Zur Dynamik von Grausamkeit." In *On Cruelty*, edited by Trutz von Trotha and Jakob Rösel, 511–37. Cologne: Köppe, 2011.
———. "'Die Kommandogewalt hat geredet, der Reichstag hat zu schweigen': How the 'Hottentottenwahlen' of 1907 Shaped the Relationship between Parliament and Military Policy in Imperial Germany." *Journal of Namibian Studies* 15 (2014): 7–24.
———. "'Kultur der Grausamkeit' und die Dynamik 'eradierender Praktiken': Ein Beitrag zur Erforschung extremer Gewalt." *Sociologus* 63 (2013): 147–69.
———. "On Asymmetric Warfare: The Case of OvaHerero in Precolonial and Early Colonial Times." In *Nuanced Considerations: Recent Voices in Namibian-German Colonial History*, edited by Wolfram Hartmann, 61–78. Windhoek: Orumbonde Press, 2019.
———. "Soldatische Hinterwäldler oder Avantgarde? Über die einsatzbezogenen Erfahrungen der Kaiserlichen Schutztruppe in 'Deutsch-Südwestafrika.'" *Militärgeschichtliche Zeitschrift* 71, no. 2 (2012): 309–27.
———. "Warum die Herero mit den Deutschen kooperierten: Zur 'Pazifizierung' einer akephalen Gesellschaft." *Mittelweg 36* 24, no. 4 (2015): 86–108.
———. "Why OvaHerero Accommodated the Germans? On the 'Pacification' of an Acephalous Society: Co-Operation and Violence." In *Nuanced Considerations: Recent Voices in Namibian-German Colonial History*, edited by Wolfram Hartmann, 41–60. Windhoek: Orumbonde Press, 2019.
———. "Windhoek 'apollinea' e 'dionisiaca': Stato e coloni nell'Africa Tedesca del Sud-Ovest." *Diacronie: Studi di Storia Contemporanea* 21, no. 1 (2015).
———. "Zwischen Vernichtung und Pardon: Die Konzentrationslager in 'Deutsch-Südwestafrika' (1904–08)." *Zeitschrift für Geschichtswissenschaft* 61, no. 7/8 (2013): 601–20.
———. "Zur Asymmetrie tribaler und staatlicher Kriegführung in Imperialkriegen: Die Logik der Kriegführung der Herero in vor- und frühkolonialer Zeit." In *Imperialkriege von 1500 bis heute: Strukturen – Akteure – Lernprozesse*, edited by Tanja Bührer et al., 177–95. Paderborn: Schönigh, 2011.
Häussler, Matthias, and Trutz von Trotha. "Brutalisierung 'von unten': Kleiner Krieg, Entgrenzung der Gewalt und Genozid im kolonialen Deutsch-Südwestafrika." *Mittelweg 36* 21, no. 3 (2012): 57–89.
———. "Koloniale Zivilgesellschaft? Von der 'kolonialen Gesellschaft' zur kolonialen Gewaltgemeinschaft in Deutsch-Südwestafrika." In *Zivilgesellschaft und Krieg*, edited by Dierk Spreen and Trutz von Trotha, 293–317. Berlin: Dunker & Humblot, 2012.
Hahlweg, Werner. *Guerilla: Krieg ohne Fronten*. Stuttgart: Kohlhammer, 1968.
Hansen, Dieter. *Stock und Peitsche im 19. Jahrhundert*. Dresden, 1902.
Hanson, Victor Davis. *The Western Way of War: Infantry Battle in Classical Greece*. Berkeley: University of California Press, 1989.
Hartmann, Georg. "Gedanken über die Eingeborenenfrage in Britisch-Südafrika und Deutsch-Südwestafrika." *Koloniale Rundschau* (1910): 26–43.
———. *Der Krieg in Südafrika und seine Lehren für Deutsch-Südwest-Afrika*. Berlin: Mittler, 1900.

―――. *Die Zukunft Deutsch-Südwestafrikas: Beitrag zur Besiedlungs- und Eingeborenenfrage*. Berlin: Mittler, 1904.
Hartmann, Wolfram. "Sexual Encounters and Their Implications on an Open and Closing Frontier: Namibia from the 1840s to 1905." PhD diss., Columbia University, 2002.
―――. "Urges in the Colony: Men and Women in Colonial Windhoek, 1890-1905." *Journal of Namibian Studies* 1, no. 1 (2007): 39–71.
Heer, Hannes. "Die Logik des Vernichtungskrieges: Wehrmacht und Partisanenkampf." *Vernichtungskrieg: Verbrechen der Wehrmacht 1941 bis 1944*, edited by Hannes Heer and Klaus Naumann, 104–38. Hamburg: Hamburger Edition, 1995.
Hegel, Georg Wilhelm Friedrich. *Ästhetik*, edited by Friedrich Bassenge. Vol. 1. Berlin: Verlag das Europäische Buch, 1985.
―――. *Phänomenologie des Geistes*. Edited by Wolfgang Bonsiepen and Reiner Heede. Hamburg: Meiner, (1807) 1968.
Helbling, Jürg. *Tribale Kriege: Konflikte in Gesellschaften ohne Zentralgewalt*. Frankfurt: Campus, 2006.
Heller, Agnes. *Theorie der Gefühle*. Hamburg: VSA-Verlag, 1980.
Henrichsen, Dag. *Herrschaft und Identifikation im vorkolonialen Zentralnamibia: Das Herero- und Damaraland im 19. Jahrhundert*. Basel: Basler Afrika Bibliographien, 2011.
Herrenkirchen, Helmuth Auer von. *Meine Erlebnisse während des Feldzuges gegen die Hereros und Witbois nach meinem Tagebuch*. Berlin: Eisenschmidt, 1907.
Heuser, Beatrice. "Small Wars in the Age of Clausewitz: The Watershed Between Partisan War and People's War." *The Journal of Strategic Studies* 33, no. 1 (2010): 139–62.
Heywood, Annemarie, ed. *Warriors, Leaders, Sages, and Outcasts in the Namibian Past: Narratives Collected from Herero Sources for the Michael Scott Oral Record Project (MSQRP) 1985-6*. Windhoek: MSORP, 1992.
Hillebrecht, Werner. "Die Nama und der Krieg im Süden." In *Völkermord in Deutsch-Südwestafrika: Der Kolonialkrieg (1904-1908) in Namibia und seine Folgen*, 2nd ed., edited by Jürgen Zimmerer und Joachim Zeller, 121–33. Berlin: Links, 2004.
Hinton, Alexander Laban. "Zündstoffe: Die Roten Khmer in Kambodscha." *Mittelweg 36*, 15, no. 6 (2006): 69–86.
Hintrager, Oskar. *Südwestafrika in der deutschen Zeit*. Munich: Oldenbourg, 1955.
Hochgeschwender, Michael. "Kolonialkriege als Experimentierstätten des Vernichtungskrieges?" In *Formen des Krieges: Von der Antike bis zur Gegenwart*, edited by Dietrich Beyrau et al., 269–90. Paderborn: Schöningh, 2007.
Holodynski, Manfred, and Wolfgang Friedlmeier. *Development of Emotions and Emotion Regulation*. Translated by Jonathan Harrow. Heidelberg: Springer, 2006.
―――. *Emotionen – Entwicklung und Regulation*. Heidelberg: Springer, 2006.
Horne, John, and Alan Kramer. *German Atrocities, 1914: A History of Denial*. New Haven: Yale University Press, 2001.
Howard, Michael. "Colonial Wars and European Wars." *Imperialism and War: Essays on Colonial Wars in Asia and Africa, 1870-1914*, edited by H. L. Wesseling and J. de Moor, 218–23. Leiden: Brill, 1989.
Hull, Isabel V. *Absolute Destruction: Military Culture and the Practices of War in Imperial Germany*. Ithaca: Cornell University Press, 2005.
―――. "Military Culture and the Production of 'Final Solutions' in the Colonies: The Example of Wilhelminian Germany." In *The Specter of Genocide: Mass Murder in Historical Perspective*, edited by Robert Gellately and Ben Kiernan, 141–62. Cambridge: Cambridge University Press, 2003.
Hund, Wulf D. *Rassismus*. Bielefeld: Transcript, 2007.
Huntington, Samuel P. *The Soldier and the State: The Theory and Politics of Civil-Military Relations*. Cambridge: Cambridge University Press, 1957.

Ioanide, Paula. *The Emotional Politics of Racism: How Feelings Trump Facts in an Era of Colorblindness*. Stanford: Stanford University Press, 2015.

Irle, Jakob. *Die Herero: Ein Beitrag zur Landes-, Volks- und Missionskunde*. Gütersloh: Bertelsmann, 1906.

———. *Was soll aus den Herero werden?* 2nd ed. Gütersloh: Bertelsmann, 1906.

James, Lawrence. *The Savage Wars: British Campaigns in Africa, 1870–1920*. London: Hale, 1985.

Jochmann, Werner. *Adolf Hitler: Monologe im Führer-Hauptquartier 1941–1944: Die Aufzeichnungen Heinrich Heims*. Frankfurt: S. Fischer, 1980.

Kaldor, Mary. *New and Old Wars: Organized Violence in a Global Era*. Oxford: Polity Press, 1998.

Kanya-Forstner, Alexander Sydney. *The Conquest of the Western Sudan: A Study in French Military Imperialism*. London: Cambridge University Press, 1969.

Katz, Jack. *How Emotions Work*. Chicago: University of Chicago Press, 1999.

Kaulich, Udo. *Die Geschichte der ehemaligen Kolonie Deutsch-Südwestafrika (1884–1914): Eine Gesamtdarstellung*. Frankfurt: Peter Lang, 2001.

Keegan, John. *The Face of Battle*. London: Penguin, 1978.

Keeley, Lawrence H. *War before Civilization: The Myth of the Peaceful Savage*. New York: Oxford University Press, 1996.

Kerremans, A. *Quelques observations sur la stratégie des Allemands dans leur guerre contre les Hereros*. Paris: Chapelot, 1913.

Klatetzki, Thomas. "Regeln, Emotion und Macht: Eine interaktionistische Skizze." In *Organisationen regeln: Die Wirkmacht korporativer Akteure*, edited by Stephan Duschek, et al., 93–109. Wiesbaden: VS-Verlag, 2012.

Koch, Hannsjoachim W. *Der Sozialdarwinismus: Seine Genese und sein Einfluss auf das imperialistische Denken*. Munich: Beck, 1973.

Kößler, Reinhart. "Im Schatten des Genozids: Erinnerungspolitik in einer extrem ungleichen Gesellschaft." In *Genozid und Gedenken: Namibisch-deutsche Geschichte und Gegenwart*, edited by Henning Melber, 49–77. Frankfurt: Brandes & Apsel, 2005.

Kößler, Reinhart, and Henning Melber. "Der Genozid an den Herero und Nama in Deutsch-Südwestafrika 1904-1908." In *Völkermord und Kriegsverbrechen in der ersten Hälfte des 20. Jahrhunderts*, edited by Irmtrud Wojak, 37–75. Frankfurt: Campus, 2004.

Kortüm, Hans-Henning. *Kriege und Krieger, 500–1500*. Stuttgart: Kohlhammer, 2010.

Kotek, Joël. "Le Génocide des Herero, Symptôme d'un Sonderweg Allemand?" *Revue d'histoire de la Shoah* 189 (2008): 177–97.

Kotek, Joël, and Pierre Rigoulot. *Das Jahrhundert der Lager: Gefangenschaft, Zwangsarbeit, Vernichtung*. Berlin: Propyläen, 2001.

Kreienbaum, Jonas. *"Ein trauriges Fiasko": Koloniale Konzentrationslager im südlichen Afrika 1900-1908*. Hamburg: Hamburger Edition, 2015.

———. *A Sad Fiasco: Colonial Concentration Camps in Southern Africa, 1900–1908*. Translated by Elizabeth Janik. New York: Berghahn, 2019.

———. "'Vernichtungslager' in Deutsch-Südwestafrika? Zur Funktion der Konzentrationslager im Herero- und Namakrieg (1904–1908)." *Zeitschrift für Geschichtswissenschaft* (2010): 1014–1026.

Krikler, Jeremy. "Social Neurosis and Hysterical Pre-Cognition in South Africa: A Case-Study and Reflections." *Journal of Social History* 28, no. 3 (1995): 491–520.

Kroemer, Bernd. *Für Kaiser und Reich: Kriegstage in China und Südwestafrika*. Windhoek: Glanz und Gloria Verlag, 2009.

Kroener, Bernhard R. "Antichrist, Archenemy, Disturber of the Peace: Forms and Means of Violent Conflict in the Early Modern Ages." *Transcultural Wars from the Middle*

Ages to the 21st century, edited by Hans-Henning Kortüm, 57–84. Berlin: Akademie Verlag, 2006.

Krüger, Gesine. "Koloniale Gewalt, Alltagserfahrungen und Überlebensstrategien." In *Namibia – Deutschland, eine geteilte Geschichte: Widerstand, Gewalt, Erinnerung*, edited by Larissa Förster et al., 92–105. Cologne: Ethnologica, 2004.

———. *Kriegsbewältigung und Geschichtsbewusstsein: Realität, Deutung und Verarbeitung des deutschen Kolonialkriegs in Namibia 1904 bis 1907*. Göttingen: Vandenhoeck & Ruprecht, 1999.

Kühl, Stefan. *Ganz normale Organisationen: Zur Soziologie des Holocaust*. Frankfurt: Suhrkamp, 2014.

Kühne, Thomas. *Kameradschaft: Die Soldaten des nationalsozialistischen Krieges und das 20. Jahrhundert*. Göttingen: Vandenhoeck & Ruprecht, 2006.

Külz, Ludwig. *Tropenarzt im afrikanischen Busch*. 3rd ed. Berlin: Süsseroth, 1943.

Kuhlmann, A. *Auf Adlers Flügeln*. Barmen: Verlag des Missionshauses, 1911.

Kukuri, Andreas. *Herero-Texte*. Edited and translated by Ernst Dammann. Berlin: Reimer, 1983.

Kundrus, Birthe. "Entscheidung für den Völkermord? Einleitende Überlegungen zu einem historiographischen Problem." *Mittelweg 36*, 15, no. 6 (2006): 4–17.

———. "Grenzen der Gleichsetzung: Kolonialverbrechen und Vernichtungspolitik." *izw* 27, no. 5 (2004): 30–33.

———. *Moderne Imperialisten: Das Kaiserreich im Spiegel seiner Kolonien*. Cologne: Böhlau, 2003.

Kunisch, Johannes. *Der kleine Krieg: Studien zum Heerwesen des Absolutismus*. Wiesbaden: Steiner, 1973.

Kuß, Susanne. "Deutsche Soldaten während des Boxeraufstandes in China: Elemente und Ursprünge des Vernichtungskrieges." In *Das Deutsche Reich und der Boxeraufstand*, edited by Susanne Kuß und Thoralf Klein, 165–81. Munich: Iudicium-Verlag, 2002.

———. *Deutsches Militär auf kolonialen Kriegsschauplätzen: Eskalation von Gewalt zu Beginn des 20. Jahrhunderts*. Berlin: Ch. Links, 2010.

———. "Der Herero-Deutsche Krieg und das deutsche Militär: Kriegsursachen und Kriegsverlauf." In *Namibia – Deutschland, eine geteilte Geschichte. Widerstand, Gewalt, Erinnerung*, edited by Larissa Förster, et al., 62–77. Cologne: Ethnologica, 2004.

———. "Kriegführung ohne hemmende Kulturschranke: Die deutschen Kolonialkriege in Südwestafrika 1904–1907 und Ostafrika 1905–1908." In *Kolonialkriege: Militärische Gewalt im Zeichen des Imperialismus*, edited by Thoralf Klein and Frank Schumacher, 208–47. Hamburg: Hamburger Edition, 2006.

———. "Von der Vernichtungsschlacht zum Vernichtungskrieg: Militärpublizisten in der Zwischenkriegszeit (1920-1939)." In *Der Zweite Weltkrieg und seine Folgen: Ereignisse – Auswirkungen – Reflexionen*, edited by Bernd Martin, 51–72. Freiburg: Rombach, 2006.

Kuzmics, Helmut, and Sabine A. Haring. *Emotion, Habitus und Erster Weltkrieg: Soziologische Studien zum militärischen Untergang der Habsburger Monarchie*. Göttingen: Vandenhoeck & Ruprecht, 2013.

Labanca, Nicola. *Oltremare: Storia dell'espansione coloniale italiana*. Bologna: Il Mulino, 2002.

Lammert, Norbert. "Deutsche ohne Gnade." *Die Zeit* (9 July 2015): 16.

Langewiesche, Dieter, and Nikolaus Buschmann. "'Dem Vertilgungskriege Grenzen setzen': Kriegstypen des 19. Jahrhunderts und der deutsch-französische Krieg 1870/71: Gehegter Krieg – Volks- und Nationalkrieg – Revolutionskrieg – Dschihad." In *Formen des Krieges: Von der Antike bis zur Gegenwart*, edited by Dietrich Beyrau et al., 17–50. Paderborn: Schöningh, 2007.

Laqueur, Walter. *Guerrilla Warfare: A Historical and Critical Study.* 7th ed. New Brunswick: Transaction Publishing, 2009.
Lau, Brigitte. "Uncertain Certainties." In *History and Historiography: 4 Essays in Reprint*, edited by Annemarie Heywood. Windhoek: MSORP, 1995.
———. "Ungewisse Gewissheiten." In *Der Wahrheit eine Gasse: Anmerkungen zum Kolonialkrieg in Deutsch-Südwestafrika 1904*, edited by H. R. Schneider-Waterberg, 141–58. Swakopmund: Gesellschaft für Wissenschaftliche Entwicklung, 2006.
Ledoux, Joseph. *Das Netz der Gefühle: Wie Emotionen entstehen.* 6th ed. Munich: Deutscher Taschenbuch Verlag, 2012.
Lettow-Vorbeck, Paul von. *Mein Leben.* Biberach: Koehlers Verlagsgesellschaft, 1957.
Leutwein, Paul. *Kampf und die Onjatiberge: Gouverneur Leutweins letzter Feldzug: Tatsachenbericht aus dem Hererokrieg.* Berlin: Steiniger Verlage, 1941.
Leutwein, Theodor. *Elf Jahre Gouverneur in Deutsch-Südwestafrika.* 4th ed. Windhoek: Namibiana Buchdepot, (1906) 1997.
———. *Die Kämpfe der Kaiserlichen Schutztruppe in Deutsch-Südwestafrika in den Jahren 1894–1896, sowie die sich hieraus für uns ergebenden Lehren.* Berlin: Mittler, 1899.
Lewis, Helen B. "Introduction: Shame – The 'Sleeper' in Psychopathology." In *The Role of Shame in Symptom Formation*, edited by Helen B. Lewis, 1–28. Hillsdale: Lawrence Erlbaum Associates, 1987.
———. *Shame and Guilt in Neurosis.* New York: International Universities Press, 1971.
Levene, Mark. *The Meaning of Genocide.* London: Tauris, 2005.
Lindholm, Karl-Johan. *Wells of Experience: A Pastoral Land-Use History of Omaheke, Namibia.* Uppsala: Uppsala University, 2006.
Lindner, Ulrike. *Koloniale Begegnungen: Deutschland und Großbritannien als Imperialmächte in Afrika 1880–1914.* Frankfurt: Campus, 2011.
Luhmann, Niklas. *Gesellschaftsstruktur und Semantik: Studien zur Wissenssoziologie der modernen Gesellschaft.* Vol. 1. Frankfurt: Suhrkamp, 2010.
Lundtofte, Hendrik. "'I believe that the nation as such must be annihilated...': The Radicalization of the German Suppression of the Herero Rising in 1904." In *Genocide: Cases, Comparisons and Contemporary Debates*, edited by Stephen B. Jensen, 15–53. Copenhagen: Danish Center for Holocaust and Genocide Studies, 2003.
Machiavelli, Niccolò. *The Prince.* Edited and translated by Peter Bondanella and Mark Musa. Oxford: Oxford University Press, (1532) 1998.
Madley, Benjamin. "From Africa to Auschwitz: How German South West Africa Incubated Ideas and Methods Adopted and Developed by the Nazis in Eastern Europe." *European History Quarterly* 35, no. 3 (2005): 429–64.
Maercker, Georg. *Unsere Kriegsführung in Deutsch-Südwestafrika.* Berlin: Paetel, 1908.
———. *Unsere Schutztruppe in Ostafrika.* Berlin: Siegismund, 1893.
Mainzer, Klaus. *Komplexität.* Munich: Wilhelm Fink. 2008.
Mann, Michael. *Die dunkle Seite der Demokratie: Eine Theorie der ethnischen Säuberung.* Hamburg: Hamburger Edition, 2007.
Marchand-Volz, Gertrud, ed. *Werner Freiherr Schenck v. Stauffenberg: Von München nach Deutsch-Südwestafrika.* 2nd ed. Göttingen: Klaus Hess, 1998.
Marshall, S. L. A. *Men against Fire: The Problem of Battle Command.* Norman: University of Oklahoma Press, 2000.
Marx, Christoph. "Entsorgen und Entseuchen: Zur Diskussionskultur in der derzeitigen namibischen Historiographie – eine Polemik." In *Genozid und Gedenken: Namibisch-deutsche Geschichte und Gegenwart*, edited by Henning Melber, 141–62. Frankfurt: Brandes & Apsel, 2005.
McCarthy, Thomas. *Race, Empire, and the Idea of Human Development.* New York: Cambridge University Press, 2009.

McNeill, William. "European Expansion: Power and Warfare since 1500." In *Imperialism and War: Essays on Colonial Wars in Asia and Africa, 1870-1914*, edited by H. L. Wesseling und J. de Moor, 12-21. Leiden: Brill, 1989.

———. *The Pursuit of Power: Technology, Armed Force, and Society since A.D. 1000*. Chicago: University of Chicago Press, 1982.

Melber, Henning. "Kontinuitäten totaler Herrschaft: Völkermord und Apartheid in 'Deutsch-Südwestafrika': Zur kolonialen Herrschaftspraxis im Deutschen Kaiserreich." In *Jahrbuch für Antisemitismusforschung*, edited by Zentrum für Antisemitismusforschung, 91-116. Berlin: Metropol, 1992.

Memmi, Albert. *Rassismus*. Frankfurt: Athenäum, 1987.

Menzel, Gustav. *"Widerstand und Gottesfurcht": Hendrik Witbooi – eine Biographie in zeitgenössischen Quellen*. Cologne: Rüdiger Köppe, 2000.

Messerschmidt, Manfred. "Ideologie und Befehlsgehorsam im Vernichtungskrieg." In *Militarismus – Vernichtungspolitik – Geschichtspolitik*, edited by Manfred Messerschmidt, 221-44. Paderborn: Schöningh, 2006.

———. "Völkerrecht und 'Kriegsnotwendigkeit' in der deutschen militärischen Tradition seit den Einigungskriegen." *German Studies Review*, 6, no. 2 (1983): 237-69.

Michels, Eckard. *"Der Held von Deutsch-Ostafrika": Paul von Lettow-Vorbeck: Ein preußischer Offizier*. Paderborn: Schöningh, 2008.

Michels, Stefanie. *Schwarze deutsche Kolonialsoldaten: Mehrdeutige Repräsentationsräume und früher Kosmopolitismus in Afrika*. Bielefeld: Transcript, 2009.

Miles, Robert. *Racism*. 2nd ed. London: Routledge, 2003.

Mitze, Katja. "'Seit der babylonischen Gefangenschaft hat die Welt nichts derart erlebt': Französische Kriegsgefangene und Franctireurs im Deutsch-Französischen Krieg 1870/71." In *In der Hand des Feindes: Kriegsgefangenschaft von der Antike bis zum Zweiten Weltkrieg*, edited by Rüdiger Overmans, 235-54. Cologne: Böhlau, 1999.

Möhlig, Wilhelm J. G., ed. *Die Witbooi in Südwestafrika während des 19. Jahrhunderts: Quellentexte von Johannes Olpp, Hendrik Witbooi jun. und Carl Berger*. Cologne: Rüdiger Köppe, 2007.

Moltke, Helmuth von. *Moltke on the Art of War: Selected Writings*, edited and translated by Daniel J. Hughes and Harry Bell. New York: Ballantine, 1993.

Mommsen, Wolfgang J. "Der Topos vom unvermeidlichen Krieg: Außenpolitik und öffentliche Meinung im Deutschen Reich im letzten Jahrzehnt vor 1914." In *Bereit zum Krieg: Kriegsmentalität im wilhelminischen Deutschland 1890-1914: Beiträge zur historischen Friedensforschung*, edited by Jost Dülffer and Karl Holl, 194-224. Göttingen: Vandenhoeck & Ruprecht, 1986.

Montague, W. E. *Campaigning in Zululand: Experiences on Campaign during the Zulu War of 1879 with the 94th Regiment*. LaVergne, TN: Leonaur Books, 2006.

Morgenstern, Christian. "Die unmögliche Tatsache." *Alle Galgenlieder*. Zurich: Diogenes, 1981.

Morillo, Stephen. "A General Typology of Transcultural Wars: The Early Middle Ages and Beyond." In *Transcultural Wars from the Middle Ages to the 21st Century*, edited by Hans-Henning Kortüm, 29-42. Berlin: Akademie Verlag, 2006.

Moritz, Walter. *Aus alten Tagen in Südwest*. Vol. 3: *Erlebnisse im Hereroaufstand 1904*. 4th ed. Werther: Selbstverlag, 1996.

Moses, A. Dirk. "Genocide and Settler Society in Australian History." In *Genocide and Settler Society: Frontier Violence and Stolen Indigenous Children in Australian History*, edited by A. Dirk Moses, 3-48. New York: Berghahn, 2004.

Mühlmann, Wilhelm E. "Der Ernstfall als ständige Erfahrung in den Primitiv-Kulturen: Über die Unwahrscheinlichkeit unserer modernen Existenz." In *Der Ernstfall*, edited by Rüdiger Altmann, 198-211. Berlin: Propyläen, 1979.

———. *Krieg und Frieden: Ein Leitfaden der politischen Ethnologie mit Berücksichtigung des völkerkundlichen und geschichtlichen Stoffes*. Heidelberg: Carl Winter, 1940.
Müller, Fritz Ferdinand. *Kolonien unter der Peitsche: Eine Dokumentation*. Berlin: Rütten & Loening, 1962.
Münkler, Herfried. *Die neuen Kriege*. Reinbek: Rowohlt, 2005.
———. *Über den Krieg: Stationen der Kriegsgeschichte im Spiegel ihrer theoretischen Reflexion*. Weilerswist: Velbrück, 2002.
———. *Der Wandel des Krieges: Von der Symmetrie zur Asymmetrie*. Weilerswist: Velbrück, 2006.
———. "Was ist neu an den neuen Kriegen? – Eine Erwiderung auf die Kritiker." In *Den Krieg überdenken: Kriegsbegriffe und Kriegstheorien in der Kontroverse*, edited by Anna Geis, 133–150. Baden-Baden: Nomos, 2006.
Naimark, Norman M. *Fires of Hatred: Ethnic Cleansing in Twentieth-Century Europe*. Cambridge: Harvard University Press, 2001.
Neckel, Sighard. *Status und Scham: Zur symbolischen Reproduktion sozialer Ungleichheit*. Frankfurt: Campus, 1991.
Nedelmann, Birgitta. "Dichte Beschreibungen absoluter Macht." *Kölner Zeitschrift für Soziologie und Sozialpsychologie* 46, no. 1 (1994): 130–34.
———. "Gewaltsoziologie am Scheideweg: Die Auseinandersetzungen in der gegenwärtigen und Wege der künftigen Gewaltforschung." In *Soziologie der Gewalt: Kölner Zeitschrift für Soziologie und Sozialpsychologie*, edited by Trutz von Trotha, 59–85. Opladen: Westdeutscher Verlag, 1997.
———. "Schwierigkeiten soziologischer Gewaltanalyse." *Mittelweg 36* 4, no. 3 (1995): 8–17.
Neitzel, Sönke, and Harald Welzer. *Soldaten: Protokolle vom Kämpfen, Töten und Sterben*. Frankfurt: S. Fischer, 2011.
Neumann, Michael. "Schwierigkeiten der Soziologie mit der Gewaltanalyse: Einige Bemerkungen zum Beitrag Birgitta Nedelmanns." *Mittelweg 36* 4, no. 5 (1995): 65–68.
Nietzsche, Friedrich. "The Anti-Christ." In *Twilight of the Idols and The Anti-Christ*, edited and translated by R. J. Hollingsdale, 113–87. New York: Penguin, 1979.
———. "Der Antichrist: Fluch auf das Christentum." In *Werke in drei Bänden*, edited by Karl Schlechta, vol. 2, 1161–235. Darmstadt: Wissenschaftliche Buchgesellschaft, 1997.
Nipperdey, Thomas. *Deutsche Geschichte 1866-1918*. Vol. 2: *Machtstaat vor der Demokratie*. Munich: Beck, 1992.
Nordbruch, Claus. *Völkermord an den Herero in Deutsch-Südwestafrika? Widerlegung einer Lüge*. Tübingen: Grabert, 2004.
Nuhn, Walter. *Feind überall: Guerillakrieg in Südwest: Der Große Nama-Aufstand 1904–1908*. Bonn: Bernard & Graefe, 2000.
———. *Sturm über Südwest: Der Hereroaufstand von 1904 – ein düsteres Kapitel der deutschen kolonialen Vergangenheit Namibias*. Bonn: Bernard & Graefe, 1989.
Oatley, Keith. *Emotions: A Brief History*. Malden: Blackwell Publishing, 2004.
O'Brien, Tim. *The Things They Carried*. New York: Broadway Books, 1998.
Olusoga, David, and Casper W. Erichsen. *The Kaiser's Holocaust: Germany's Forgotten Genocide*. London: Faber and Faber, 2010.
Ortenberg, Heinz von. *Aus dem Tagebuch eines Arztes: Feldzugsskizzen aus Südwestafrika*. Berlin: Schwetschke und Sohn, 1908.
Palmer, Alison. *Colonial Genocide*. London: C. Hurst, 2000.
Pape, Günther A. *Lorang: Ich, die Seefahrt, der Krieg am Waterberg, meine Farm in Südwestafrika*. Göttingen: Klaus Hess, 2003.
Paul, Gerhard, and Klaus-Michael Mallmann. "Sozialisation, Milieu und Gewalt: Fortschritte und Probleme der neueren Täterforschung." In *Karrieren der Gewalt:*

Nationalsozialistische Täterbiographien, 2nd ed., edited by Gerhard Paul and Klaus-Michael Mallmann, 1–32. Darmstadt: Wissenschaftliche Buchgesellschaft, 2011.
Piers, Gerhart, and Milton B. Singer. *Shame and Guilt: A Psychoanalytic and a Cultural Study*. New York: Norton, 1971.
Plümecke, Tino. *Rasse in der Ära der Genetik: Die Ordnung des Menschen in den Lebenswissenschaften*. Bielefeld: Transcript, 2013.
Poewe, Karla. *The Namibian Herero: A History of Their Psychological Disintegration and Survival*. New York: Lewiston, 1985.
Pool, Gerhard. *Samuel Maharero*. Windhoek: Gamsberg Macmillan, 1991.
Popitz, Heinrich. *Phänomene der Macht*. 2nd ed. Tübingen: Mohr, 1992.
Reckwitz, Andreas. "Praktiken und ihre Affekte." *Mittelweg 36* 24, no. 1/2 (2015): 27–45.
———. "Warum Affekte?" *Mittelweg 36* 24, no. 1/2 (2015): 15–26.
Reemtsma, Jan Philipp. "Die Idee des Vernichtungskrieges: Clausewitz – Ludendorff – Hitler." In *Vernichtungskrieg: Verbrechen der Wehrmacht 1941 bis 1944*, edited by Hannes Heer und Klaus Naumann, 377–401. Hamburg: Hamburger Edition, 1995.
———. "Trauma und Moral: Einige Überlegungen zum Krieg als Zustand einer kriegführenden Gesellschaft und zum pazifistischen Affekt." In *Mord am Strand: Allianzen von Zivilisation und Barbarei*, edited by Jan Philipp Reemtsma, 347–68. Berlin: Siedler, 2000.
———. *Vertrauen und Gewalt: Versuch über eine besondere Konstellation der Moderne*. Hamburg: Hamburger Edition, 2008.
Retzinger, Suzanne M. "Resentment and Laughter: Video Studies of the Shame-Rage Spiral." In *The Role of Shame in Symptom Formation*, edited by Helen B. Lewis, 151–81. Hillsdale: Lawrence Erlbaum, 1987.
Rink, Martin. "Die Verwandlung: Die Figur des Partisanen vom freien Kriegsunternehmer zum Freiheitshelden." In *Rückkehr der Condottieri? Krieg und Militär zwischen staatlichem Monopol und Privatisierung: Von der Antike bis zur Gegenwart*, edited by Stig Förster, 153–70. Paderborn: Schöningh, 2010.
Ritter, Gerhard. *Der Schlieffenplan: Kritik eines Mythos*. Munich: Oldenbourg, 1956.
Rohrbach, Paul. *Aus Südwest-Afrikas schweren Tagen: Blätter von Arbeit und Abschied*. Berlin: Wilhelm Weicher, 1909.
———. *Deutsche Kolonialwirtschaft*. Vol. 1: *Südwest-Afrika*. Berlin: Buchverlag der Hilfe, 1907.
Roth, Gerhard. *Fühlen, Denken, Handeln: Wie das Gehirn unser Verhalten steuert*. Frankfurt: Suhrkamp, 2001.
Ruch, Floyd L., and Philip G. Zimbardo. *Lehrbuch der Psychologie*. Berlin: Springer, 1974.
Russell, Penny. *Savage or Civilised? Manners in Colonial Australia*. Sydney: University of New South Wales Press, 2010.
Rust, Conrad. *Krieg und Frieden im Hereroland: Aufzeichnungen aus dem Kriegsjahre 1904*. Leipzig: L. A. Kittler, 1905.
Salzmann, Erich von. *Im Kampfe gegen die Herero*. Berlin: Mittler, 1905.
Sarkin, Jeremy. *Germany's Genocide of the Herero: Kaiser Wilhelm II, His General, His Settlers, His Soldiers*. Cape Town: UCT Press, 2011.
Savage, Paul L., and Richard A. Gabriel. "Cohesion and Disintegration in the American Army: An Alternative Perspective." *Armed Forces and Society* 2, no. 3 (1976): 340–76.
Schaller, Dominik J. "Am Rande des Krieges: Das Ovambo-Königreich Ondonga." In *Völkermord in Deutsch-Südwestafrika. Der Kolonialkrieg (1904–1908) in Namibia und seine Folgen*, 2nd ed., edited by Jürgen Zimmerer und Joachim Zeller, 134–41. Berlin: Links, 2004.
———. "Kolonialkrieg, Völkermord und Zwangsarbeit in 'Deutsch-Südwestafrika.'" In *Enteignet – Vertrieben – Ermordet: Beiträge zur Genozidforschung*, edited by Dominik J. Schaller, 147–232. Zurich: Chronos-Verlag, 2004.

Schauroth, Erich von. *"Liebes Väterchen . . .": Briefe aus dem Namaaufstand 1905–1906.* Edited by Bernd Kroemer. Windhoek: Glanz & Gloria, 2008.
Scheff, Thomas J. *Bloody Revenge. Emotions, Nationalism and War.* Lincoln, NE: iUniverse, 2000.
Scheff, Thomas J., and Suzanne M. Retzinger. *Emotions and Violence: Shame and Rage in Destructive Conflicts.* Lincoln, NE: iUniverse, 2001.
Schmidl, Erwin A. "Kolonialkriege: Zwischen großem Krieg und kleinem Frieden." In *Formen des Krieges: Vom Mittelalter zum "Low Intensity Conflict,"* edited by Manfred Rauchensteiner et al., 111–38. Graz: Styria, 1991.
Schmidt, Max. *Aus unserem Kriegsleben in Südwest-Afrika: Erlebnisse und Erfahrungen.* Berlin: Edwin Runge, 1907.
Schmidt-Lauber, Brigitta. *Die abhängigen Herren: Deutsche Identität in Namibia.* Münster: LIT-Verlag, 1993.
———. "Die ehemaligen Kolonialherren: Zum Selbstverständnis deutscher Namibier." In *Namibia – Deutschland, eine geteilte Geschichte: Widerstand, Gewalt, Erinnerung*, edited by Larissa Förster et al., 226–43. Cologne: Ethnologica, 2004.
———. *"Die verkehrte Hautfarbe": Ethnizität deutscher Namibier als Alltagspraxis.* Berlin: Reimer, 1998.
Schmitt, Carl. *Theorie des Partisanen: Zwischenbemerkung zum Begriff des Politischen.* 6th ed. Berlin: Duncker & Humblot, 1962.
Schneider-Waterberg, H. R., ed. *Der Wahrheit eine Gasse: Anmerkungen zum Kolonialkrieg in Deutsch-Südwestafrika 1904.* Swakopmund: Gesellschaft für Wissenschaftliche Entwicklung, 2006.
Schumacher, Frank. "'Niederbrennen, plündern und töten sollt ihr': Der Kolonialkrieg der USA auf den Philippinen (1899–1913)." In *Kolonialkriege: Militärische Gewalt im Zeichen des Imperialismus*, edited by Thoralf Klein and Frank Schumacher, 109–144. Hamburg: Hamburger Edition, 2006.
Schwabe, Kurd. *Dienst und Kriegführung in den Kolonien und auf überseeischen Expeditionen.* Berlin: Mittler, 1902.
———. *Der Krieg in Deutsch-Südwestafrika 1904–1906.* Berlin: Weller, 1907.
Selous, Frederick Courteney. *Sunshine and Storm in Rhodesia.* London: Ward & Co., 1896.
Sémelin, Jacques. "Elemente einer Grammatik des Massakers." *Mittelweg 36* 15, no. 6 (2006): 18–40.
———. *Purify and Destroy: The Political Uses of Massacre and Genocide.* Translated by Cynthia Schoch. New York: Columbia University Press, 2007.
Shaw, Martin. *War and Genocide: Organized Killing in Modern Society.* Cambridge: Polity, 2003.
———. *What is Genocide?* Cambridge: Polity, 2007.
Shay, Jonathan. *Achilles in Vietnam: Combat Trauma and the Undoing of Character.* New York: Athaneum, 1994.
Shils, Edward A., and Morris Janowitz. "Cohesion and Disintegration in the Wehrmacht in World War II." *Public Opinion Quarterly* 12 (1948): 280–315.
Shooman, Yasemin . ". . . *weil ihre Kultur so ist": Narrative des antimuslimischen Rassismus.* Bielefeld: Transcript, 2014.
Siebrecht, Claudia. "Formen von Unfreiheit und Extreme der Gewalt: Die Konzentrationslager in Deutsch-Südwestafrika, 1904–1908." In *Die Welt der Lager: Zur "Erfolgsgeschichte" einer Institution*, edited by Bettina Greiner and Alan Kramer, 87–109. Hamburg: Hamburger Edition, 2013.
Siefkes, Martin. *Sprache, Glaube und Macht: Die Aufzeichnungen des Johannes Spiecker in Deutsch-Südwestafrika zur Zeit des Herero-Nama-Aufstands.* Würzburg: Königshausen & Neumann, 2013.

Sigrist, Christian. *Regulierte Anarchie: Untersuchungen zum Fehlen und zur Entstehung politischer Herrschaft in segmentären Gesellschaften Afrikas*. 3rd ed. Hamburg: Europäische Verlagsanstalt, 1994.
Silvester, Jeremy, and Jan-Bart Gewald, eds. *Words Cannot Be Found: German Colonial Rule in Namibia; An Annotated Reprint of the 1918 Blue Book*. Leiden: Brill, 2003.
Simmel, Georg. *Die Großstädte und das Geistesleben*. Frankfurt: Suhrkamp, (1903) 2006.
———. *Soziologie: Untersuchungen über die Formen der Vergesellschaftung*. Edited by Otthein Rammstedt. Frankfurt: Suhrkamp, (1908) 1992.
———. "Zur Psychologie der Scham." In *Georg Simmel: Schriften zur Soziologie: Eine Auswahl*, 2nd ed., edited by Heinz-Jürgen Dahme and Otthein Rammstedt, 140–50. Frankfurt: Suhrkamp, (1901) 1995.
Simplex Africanus, Leutnant Laasch, and Hauptmann Leue. *Mit der Schutztruppe durch Deutsch-Afrika*. Minden: Köhler. 1905.
Sobich, Frank Oliver. *"Schwarze Bestien, rote Gefahr": Rassismus und Antisemitismus im deutschen Kaiserreich*. Frankfurt: Campus, 2006.
Sofsky, Wolfgang. *Die Ordnung des Terrors: Das Konzentrationslager*. 4th ed. Frankfurt: S. Fischer, 1999.
———. *Traktat über die Gewalt*. Frankfurt: S. Fischer, 1996.
———. *Zeiten des Schreckens: Amok, Terror, Krieg*. Frankfurt: S. Fischer, 2002.
Sombart, Nicolaus. "Männerbund und Politische Kultur in Deutschland." In *Männergeschichte – Geschlechtergeschichte: Männlichkeit im Wandel der Moderne*, edited by Thomas Kühne, 136–55. Frankfurt: Campus, 1996.
Sonnenberg, Else. *Wie es am Waterberg zuging: Ein Originalbericht von 1904 zur Geschichte des Herero-Aufstandes in Deutsch-Südwestafrika*. Wendeburg: Uwe Krebs, 2004.
Spraul, Gunter. "Der Völkermord an den Herero: Untersuchungen zu einer neuen Kontinuitätsthese." *Geschichte in Wissenschaft und Unterricht* 12, no. 12 (1988): 713–39.
Sprenger, Matthias. *Landsknechte auf dem Weg ins Dritte Reich? Zu Genese und Wandel des Freikorps-Mythos*. Paderborn: Schöningh, 2008.
Steinmetz, George. *The Devil's Handwriting: Precoloniality and the German Colonial State in Qingdao, Samoa, and Southwest Africa*. Chicago: University of Chicago Press, 2007.
———. "Von der 'Eingeborenenpolitik' zur Vernichtungsstrategie: Deutsch-Südwestafrika 1904." *Peripherie* 25 (2005): 97–98.
Stone, John. *Military Strategy: The Politics and Technique of War*. London: Bloomsbury, 2013.
Straus, Scott. *The Order of Genocide: Race, Power, and War in Rwanda*. Ithaca: Cornell University Press, 2008.
Streit, Christian. *Keine Kameraden: Die Wehrmacht und die sowjetischen Kriegsgefangenen, 1941–1945*. Bonn: Dietz, 1991.
Stucki, Andreas. *Aufstand und Zwangsumsiedlung: Die kubanischen Unabhängigkeitskriege 1868–1898*. Hamburg: Hamburger Edition, 2012.
———. "Die spanische Anti-Guerilla-Kriegführung auf Kuba 1868-1898: Radikalisierung – Entgrenzung – Genozid?" *Zeitschrift für Geschichtswissenschaft* 56, no. 2 (2008): 123–38.
———. "Streitpunkt Lager: Zwangsumsiedlung an der imperialen Peripherie." In *Die Welt der Lager: Zur 'Erfolgsgeschichte' einer Institution*, edited by Bettina Greiner and Alan Kramer, 62–86. Hamburg: Hamburger Edition, 2013.
Stülpnagel, Conrad von. *Heiße Tage: Meine Erlebnisse im Kampf gegen die Hereros*. Berlin: Richard Eckstein, 1905.

Taguieff, Pierre-André. "Die Metamorphosen des Rassismus und die Krise des Antirassismus." In *Das Eigene und das Fremde: Neuer Rassismus in der Alten Welt*, edited by Ulrich Bielefeld, 221–59. Hamburg: Hamburger Edition, 1998.
———. "The New Cultural Racism in France." In *Racism*, edited by Martin Bulmer and John Solomos, 206–213. Oxford: Oxford University Press, 2009.
Terry, Wallace. *Bloods: Black Veterans of the Vietnam War: An Oral History*. New York: Ballantine, 2006.
Tilly, Charles. "War Making and State Making as Organized Crime." In *Bringing the State Back In*, edited by Peter Evans et al., 169–91. Cambridge: Cambridge University Press, 1985.
Trotha, Lothar von. "Politik und Kriegführung." *Berliner Neueste Nachrichten*, 3 February 1909, 1–2.
Trotha, Trutz von. "Das 'deutsche Nizza an Afrikas Westküste': Zur politischen Soziologie der kolonialen Hauptstadt am Beispiel Lomés der Jahre 1897–1914." *Sociologus* 49 (1999): 98–118.
———. "Einleitung: Zur Soziologie der Gewalt." In *Soziologie der Gewalt: Kölner Zeitschrift für Soziologie und Sozialpsychologie*, edited by Trutz von Trotha, 9–56. Opladen: Westdeutscher Verlag, 1997.
———. "Formen des Krieges: Zur Typologie kriegerischer Aktionsmacht." In *Ordnungen der Gewalt: Beiträge zu einer politischen Soziologie der Gewalt und des Krieges*, edited by Sighard Neckel and Michael Schwab-Trapp, 71–95. Opladen: Leske + Budrich, 1999.
———. "Genozidaler Pazifizierungskrieg: Soziologische Anmerkungen zum Konzept des Genozids am Beispiel des Kolonialkriegs in Deutsch-Südwestafrika, 1904–1907." *Zeitschrift für Genozidforschung* 4, no. 2 (2003): 30–57.
———. *Koloniale Herrschaft: Zur soziologischen Theorie der Staatsentstehung am Beispiel des Schutzgebietes Togo*. Tübingen: Mohr, 1994.
———. "'One for Kaiser': Beobachtungen zur politischen Soziologie der Prügelstrafe am Beispiel des 'Schutzgebietes Togo.'" In *Studien zur Geschichte des deutschen Kolonialismus in Afrika: Festschrift zum 60. Geburtstag von Peter Sebald*, edited by Peter Heine and Ulrich van der Heyden, 521–51. Pfaffenweiler: Centaurus Verlagsgesellschaft, 1995.
———. "Über den Erfolg und die Brüchigkeit der Utopie staatlicher Herrschaft: Herrschaftssoziologische Beobachtungen über den kolonialen und nachkolonialen Staat in Westafrika." In *Verstaatlichung der Welt? Europäische Staatsmodelle und außereuropäische Machtprozesse*, edited by Wolfgang Reinhard, 223–51. Munich: Oldenbourg, 1999.
———. "Was war Kolonialismus? Zu Soziologie und Geschichte des Kolonialismus und der Kolonialherrschaft." *Saeculum* 55, no. 1 (2004): 49–95.
Trotha, Trutz von, and Michael Schwab-Trapp. "Logiken der Gewalt." *Mittelweg 36* 5, no. 6 (1996): 56–64.
Turner, Jonathan H. *Human Emotions: A Sociological Theory*. London: Routledge, 2007.
Turner, Jonathan H., and Jan E. Stets. *The Sociology of Emotions*. Cambridge: Cambridge University Press, 2005.
Turney-High, Harry Holbert. *Primitive War: Its Practice and Concepts*. 2nd ed. Columbia: University of South Carolina Press, (1949) 1991.
Vierhaus, Rudolf. *Am Hof der Hohenzollern: Aus dem Tagebuch der Baronin Spitzemberg 1865–1914*. Munich: Deutscher Taschenbuchverlag, 1979.
Veracini, Lorenzo. *Settler Colonialism: A Theoretical Overview*. Basingstoke: Palgrave Macmillan, 2010.
Vivelo, Frank Robert. *The Herero of Western Botswana: Aspects of Change in a Group of Bantu-Speaking Cattle Herders*. St. Paul: West Publishing. 1977.

Vogel, Jakob. "Stramme Gardisten, temperamentvolle Tirailleurs und anmutige Damen: Geschlechterbilder im deutschen und französischen Kult der 'Nation in Waffen.'" In *Militär und Gesellschaft im 19. und 20. Jahrhundert*, edited by Ute Frevert, 245–62. Stuttgart: Klett Cotta, 1997.

Vogt, Ludgera. *Zur Logik der Ehre in der Gegenwartsgesellschaft: Differenzierung, Macht, Integration*. Frankfurt: Suhrkamp, 1997.

Waldmann, Peter. "Rache ohne Regeln: Zur Renaissance eines archaischen Gewaltmotivs." In *Terrorismus und Bürgerkrieg: Der Staat in Bedrängnis*, edited by Peter Waldmann, 168–93. Munich: Gerling Akademie Verlag, 2003.

Wallach, Jehuda L. *Das Dogma der Vernichtungsschlacht: Die Lehren von Clausewitz und Schlieffen und ihre Wirkungen in zwei Weltkriegen*. Munich: Deutscher Taschenbuch Verlag, 1970.

Walter, Dierk. "Imperialkriege: Begriff, Erkenntnisinteresse, Aktualität." In *Imperialkriege von 1500 bis heute: Strukturen – Akteure – Lernprozesse*, edited by Tanja Bührer et al., 1-29. Paderborn: Schönigh, 2011.

———. *Organisierte Gewalt in der europäischen Expansion: Gestalt und Logik des Imperialkrieges*. Hamburg: Hamburger Edition, 2014.

———. "Warum Kolonialkrieg?" In *Kolonialkriege: Militärische Gewalt im Zeichen des Imperialismus*, edited by Thoralf Klein and Frank Schumacher, 14–43. Hamburg: Hamburger Edition, 2006.

Warburg, Jens. *Das Militär und seine Subjekte: Zur Soziologie des Krieges*. Bielefeld: Transcript, 2009.

Weber, Max. *Economy and Society: An Outline of Interpretive Sociology*. Edited by Guenther Roth and Claus Wittich. Translated by Ephraim Fischoff et al. Berkeley: University of California Press, 1978.

———. *Wirtschaft und Gesellschaft: Grundriß der verstehenden Soziologie*. Edited by Johannes Winckelmann. 5th ed. Tübingen: Mohr, (1921) 1990.

Weikart, Richard. *From Darwin to Hitler: Evolutionary Ethics, Eugenics, and Racism in Germany*. New York: Palgrave Macmillan, 2004.

Weitz, Eric J. *A Century of Genocide: Utopias of Race and Nation*. Princeton: Princeton University Press, 2003.

Wesseling, H. L. "Colonial Wars: An Introduction." In *Imperialism and War: Essays on Colonial Wars in Asia and Africa, 1870–1914*, edited by H. L. Wesseling and J. A. de Moor, 1–11. Leiden: Brill Academic Publishers, 1989.

———. "Colonial Wars and Armed Peace, 1870–1914." *Itinerario* 2 (1981): 53–73.

Welzer, Harald. *Täter: Wie aus ganz normalen Menschen Massenmörder werden*. 2nd ed. Frankfurt: S. Fischer, 2008.

Wieviorka, Michel. *Violence: A New Approach*. Translated by David Macey. London: SAGE, 2009.

Wissmann, Hermann von. *Afrika: Schilderungen und Rathschläge zur Vorbereitung für den Aufenthalt und den Dienst in den deutschen Schutzgebieten*. Berlin: Süsserott, 1895.

Wohlfeil, Rainer. "Der Volkskrieg im Zeitalter Napoleons." In *Napoleon und Europa*, edited by Heinz-Otto Sieburg, 318–32. Cologne: Kiepenheuer & Witsch, 1971.

Wünsche, Dietlind. *Feldpostbriefe aus China: Wahrnehmungs- und Deutungsmuster deutscher Soldaten zur Zeit des Boxeraufstandes 1900/1901*. Berlin: C. H. Links, 2008.

Wurmser, Leon. *Die Maske der Scham: Die Psychoanalyse von Schameffekten und Schamkonflikten*. 5th ed. Eschborn: Dietmar Klotz Verlag, 2007.

Zajonc, Robert. "Feeling and Thinking: Preferences Need No Inferences." *American Psychologist* 35, no. 2 (1980): 151–75.

Zeller, Joachim. "'Ombepera i koza – Die Kälte tötet mich': Zur Geschichte des Konzentrationslagers in Swakopmund 1904–1908." In *Völkermord in Deutsch-Südwestafrika:*

Der Kolonialkrieg (1904–1908) in Namibia und seine Folgen, 2nd ed., edited by Jürgen Zimmerer and Joachim Zeller, 64–79. Berlin: Ch. Links, 2004.

Zimbardo, Philip. *Der Luzifer-Effekt: Die Macht der Umstände und die Psychologie des Bösen*. Berlin: Springer, 2012.

Zimmerer, Jürgen. "Annihilation in Africa: The 'Race-War' in German Southwest Africa (1904–1908) and Its Significance for a Global History of Genocide." *GHI Bulletin* 37 (2005): 51–57.

———. *Deutsche Herrschaft über Afrikaner: Staatlicher Machtanspruch und Wirklichkeit im kolonialen Namibia*. 3rd ed. Münster: Lit, 2004.

———. "Das Deutsche Reich und der Genozid: Überlegungen zum historischen Ort des Völkermordes an den Herero und Nama." In *Namibia – Deutschland, eine geteilte Geschichte: Widerstand, Gewalt, Erinnerung*, edited by Larissa Förster et al., 106–21. Cologne: Ethnologica, 2004.

———. "The First Genocide of the Twentieth Century: The German War of Destruction in Southwest Africa (1904–1908) and the Global History of Genocide." In *Lessons and Legacies VIII: From Generation to Generation*, edited by Doris Bergen, 34–64. Evanston: Northwestern University Press, 2008.

———. "Krieg, KZ und Völkermord in Südwestafrika: Der erste deutsche Genozid." In *Völkermord in Deutsch-Südwestafrika: Der Kolonialkrieg (1904–1908) in Namibia und seine Folgen*, 2nd ed., edited by Jürgen Zimmerer and Joachim Zeller, 45–63. Berlin: Links, 2004.

———. "Rassenkrieg und Völkermord: Der Kolonialkrieg in Deutsch-Südwestafrika und die Globalgeschichte des Genozids." In *Genozid und Gedenken: Namibisch-deutsche Geschichte und Gegenwart*, edited by Henning Melber, 23–48. Frankfurt: Brandes & Apsel, 2005.

———. *Von Windhuk nach Auschwitz? Beiträge zum Verhältnis von Kolonialismus und Holocaust*. Münster: Lit, 2011.

Zimmermann, Martin. "Antike Kriege zwischen privaten Kriegsherren und staatlichem Monopol auf Kriegführung." In *Formen des Krieges: Von der Antike bis zur Gegenwart*, edited by Dietrich Beyrau et al., 51–70. Paderborn: Schöningh, 2007.

Zirkel, Kirsten. "Vom Militaristen zum Pazifisten: Politisches Leben und Wirken des Generals Berthold von Deimling vor dem Hintergrund der Entwicklung Deutschlands vom Kaiserreich zum Dritten Reich." PhD diss., Heinrich Heine University Düsseldorf, 2006.

Zollmann, Jakob. *Koloniale Herrschaft und ihre Grenzen: Die Kolonialpolizei in Deutsch-Südwestafrika 1894–1915*. Göttingen: Vandenhoeck & Ruprecht, 2011.

Zuckmayer, Carl. *Als wär's ein Stück von mir: Horen der Freundschaft*. 32nd ed. Frankfurt: S. Fischer, 2005.

———. *A Part of Myself: Portrait of an Epoch*. Translated by Richard and Clara Winston. New York: Harcourt Brace Jovanovich, 1970.

Index

Afrikaner—Oorlam (ǀAixaǀaen), 80
annihilation, viii, 16, 17, 77, 84, 90n82,
  91, 91n92, 92, 92n97, 94n115, 98n135,
  99nn149–50, 101, 103, 116–17, 125, 126,
  131, 134–141, 144, 146, 149–52, 166,
  168, 170, 131n102, 134n139, 140n179,
  147n213, 170n361, 207–8, 221,
  221n158, 240n3, 241, 246, 263–64
    battle of annihilation, 116, 129,
      135–45, 262
    struggle of annihilation, 80
    war of annihilation, 16, 76, 77,
      90–93, 102, 136, 137, 144n197,
      228, 262
antagonism, 31–36, 38–39, 40, 51, 97, 100
attrition, 98n135, 136, 141, 208, 221

Beaulieu, Martin Chales de, 95, 131,
  145n205, 153n255, 164, 164n324,
  165n333, 208
bimodal alienation, 55, 59, 86, 102, 262
Bismarck, Otto von, 140
Bley, Helmuth, 5n33, 33, 36, 51, 51n139,
  98n143, 199
brutalization, 16–17, 18, 19, 199–239, 265
Bülow, Bernhard von, 101, 101n167,
  145n205, 150, 154, 164n326, 165,
  165n334, 172–73, 173n383

Callwell, Charles Edward, 143n189, 203–4,
  206–7, 214, 217n134
Caprivi, Leo von, 77n5

Chatterjee, Partha, 38, 40
Chaumont, Jean-Michel, 267
Clausewitz, Carl von, 83, 91, 93, 100,
  101n163, 130n98, 136, 138
colonial situation, 14–15, 31–32, 38, 40, 54,
  59n187, 97, 98n135, 201, 258, 264
communal terror, 55, 59
complexity, 3, 4–9, 5n33, 9n60, 13, 258,
  266
concentration camps, 1, 1n7, 21, 33, 63,
  80–81, 207, 240–57, 265, 266
cruelty, 2, 9, 14, 16, 17, 37, 46, 61,
  87, 88n70, 115, 134, 144, 166, 170,
  170n361, 199, 202, 248, 259–261
cult of ruthlessness, 14, 157

dependent masters, 36–38, 36n50
despotism, 32, 199
    despotism by the white colonizing
      class, 8, 40, 258
divide and rule, 81, 98, 127
Drechsler, Horst, 5–7, 5n31, 5nn33–34,
  8n53, 30, 131, 133–34
dueling, 88, 157, 157n285, 163, 165,
  170n361, 171, 171n369, 173, 173n383,
  264

Eckl, Andreas, 1n2, 21
Eich, Wilhelm, 50, 59n183
Elger, August, 59
embitterment, 14, 17, 55n162, 103, 203,
  221–29, 265, 267

emotion, 3, 12–15, 17–19, 32–33, 46, 49, 62–63, 154–56, 158–59, 161, 163, 170, 222
Estorff, Ludwig von, 49n129, 77n6, 78, 122n47, 123, 127n77, 127n79, 128n84, 133n132, 147, 152n249, 153nn251–52, 162, 164, 164n322, 170, 172, 243n23, 244–46, 245n32, 251
expulsion, 30, 81, 92, 95, 115, 115n4, 117, 152, 152n246, 166, 168–69, 241, 263
extermination, viii, 2, 6, 11, 30, 60, 81, 90, 90n81, 92, 94–95, 117, 134–35, 145–6, 152, 154, 169–70, 207, 227, 229, 240n3, 248, 265–66

fear, 13–15, 17, 31–34, 35n34, 38n59, 44, 46–49, 54–55, 55n165, 96, 98, 131n104, 134, 142, 143, 155, 155n270, 157n281, 158, 161, 203, 206–7, 206n42, 213, 214–221, 222, 224, 228–29, 259, 265
Franke, Victor, 19, 51, 59, 59n183, 79n15, 120, 131, 133, 133n131, 146n210, 160, 201, 208–210, 210n77, 214n108, 216, 218, 222n163, 223, 223n174
frustration, 14, 203, 220, 221–22, 225, 227, 229

Gewald, Jan Bart, 21, 34, 51–52, 163n318
Gerlach, Christian, 4, 9n60, 200, 266
Glasenapp, Franz Georg von, 121–24, 128n84

Hamakari, 116n7, 131, 131n104, 131n108, 134n136, 223
Hartmann, Georg, 36, 77, 95–97, 115
Hartmann, Wolfram, 43
Heyde, Hermann von der, 131n100, 131n104, 131n108, 164, 164n322, 170n362
Heydebreck, Joachim von, 163n318
Hintrager, Oskar, 45n106, 240n7, 245–46, 248–49, 250n65
honor, 44, 77n6, 86–90, 99, 157, 157n281, 157nn287–88, 159, 163, 165n335, 169, 170n362, 171–72, 171n363, 171n369, 227–28, 264
Hull, Isabel V., 14n89, 19, 101, 101n163, 146n208, 150, 151n243, 153–54, 170, 170n361, 249
Hülsen-Haeseler, Dietrich von, 165nn334–35, 241n11

Irle, Jakob, 1n7, 46n117, 49n129, 58n179

Kambazembi, Salatiel, 127, 152n249
Khauas-Oorlam (Kailkhauan), 78n8, 80–81, 98n143
Kreienbaum, Jonas, 1n7, 8n53, 240n1, 240nn3–4
Kuhlmann, August, 1n7, 48, 51n138, 54n157, 54n159, 56n172, 57n174

Leutwein, Theodor, 2, 2n11, 10, 16, 41, 43–46, 44n98, 48–49, 49n129, 59n186, 60, 63, 76, 77–85, 77nn5–6, 78n8, 78n12, 81n27, 85n45, 85n47, 85nn51–52, 86, 89–90, 89n78, 92–98, 96n125, 98n135, 98nn142–43, 100n54, 101–3, 115–129, 115n4, 122n47, 123n50, 126n67, 127n72, 127n74, 127n77, 127n80, 128nn82–84, 133, 133n119, 133n124, 143–44, 143nn192–93, 146n211, 157, 159, 164–65, 164nn325–26, 165n334, 168–173, 173n383, 206, 220, 222, 242n17, 247, 261–62
Levene, Mark, 4, 6n38
Lewis, Helen B., 14, 117, 154–56, 161
limited warfare, 12, 76, 77–85, 95, 97, 101–2, 141
Lindequist, Friedrich von, 36, 41, 100, 164n326, 240n7, 241–42, 241nn13–14, 242n17, 244–46, 245n32, 245n36, 250n65

Machiavelli, Niccolò, 96
Maharero, Samuel, 1n1, 46, 46n110, 50, 52, 52n141, 53, 54, 54n157, 54n159, 55n165, 56–57, 56n169, 57nn174–75, 82, 123n50, 125, 147–8, 150n231
Mann, Michael, 4, 95n118
metropolitanization, 16, 129n87, 130, 135, 143
militarism
    bourgeois militarism, 140
    conservative militarism, 116, 135–45, 262
Moltke, Helmuth von, 90n85, 133, 139–41, 140n174, 202
Morenga, Jakob, 2, 158
Moses, A. Dirk, 153
Mühlenfels, Karl Ludwig von, 153, 164, 164n323, 167, 167n355, 227n210

native policy, 1, 17, 33, 63, 240–56, 240n7, 250n65, 260
Neckel, Sighard, 13, 14n91, 154–55

Okahandja, 1n1, 52, 55, 58n179, 82, 117–20, 123, 125, 128n84
Okaharui, 122, 125, 219
Omaheke, 131, 131n102, 147–48, 150, 153, 153n253, 158, 160, 163–64, 167–68, 203, 224, 226, 227n210, 242, 264–65
Omaruru, 38n64, 53, 79n15, 117–18, 120, 123–25, 243n26
Oviumbo (battle of), 125–26, 215–16
Owikokorero, 90n83, 122, 215n114, 221, 221n158

Popitz, Heinrich, 98
Post-traumatic stress disorder, 202
process of violence, 4, 7n49, 9, 14n89, 17, 51, 95n118, 101, 150, 151n243, 152, 201, 240
proclamation, 101n167, 128, 128n82, 144–46, 144n197, 149, 150–54, 150n231, 151nn242–43, 163, 167, 170, 226, 240, 240n1, 241n9, 242, 243n26, 247, 248, 250, 260, 263–65
pursuit, 117, 125, 132, 145–150, 146n208, 148n221, 153, 160–63, 166, 168, 203, 208, 221, 223–26, 228, 228n223, 249, 263–64

racism, 3, 10–12, 10n67, 12n80, 15, 17, 31, 43–44, 46, 49, 51, 60, 88, 94–95, 94n115, 101–3, 129, 154, 159, 166, 169, 203, 227, 229, 250, 259–60, 265–66
Retzinger, Suzanne M., 117, 154–56
revenge, 16, 58–63, 202, 219, 225, 229, 249, 266
rule
  direct rule, 79
  indirect rule, 80n23, 84, 96, 128
  See also divide and rule

Sarkin, Jeremy, 6nn39–41, 8n54, 266
Scheff, Thomas J., 14, 117, 154–57
Schlieffen, Alfred von, 88, 88n73, 94n108, 99n150, 101n167, 140–41, 140n174, 145n205, 148, 150–54, 153n255, 162–63, 165, 165nn332–34, 168, 173, 173n383, 240n1, 241–43, 247, 265–66
Schmidt-Lauber, Brigitta, 35n34, 36, 36n50
Sémelin, Jacques, 4, 7, 97, 102, 151
shame, 13–15, 14n91, 16–17, 154–58, 155n270, 157n281, 161–62, 164, 220, 247, 264, 266

bypassed shame, 14, 155–56, 158, 168, 170
unidentified shame, 155, 161
shame-rage mechanism, 14, 117, 154–56, 163, 168, 170, 221, 264–65
Social Darwinism, 2, 6, 10, 94, 94n112, 97, 103
Steinmetz, George, 14n89, 102n168, 154, 173, 173n383
settler colonialism, 34, 40n79
struggle between races, 48, 94, 94n112, 97, 98n135, 128, 163n319, 226, 228, 260
Stübel, Oskar, 48–49, 60, 86, 89, 143n193, 202, 241n8
Stuhlmann, First Lieutenant, 40, 60, 129n89, 131, 144, 146n210, 147, 166–67, 201, 210–12, 211n82, 217, 219, 224, 225n200
Swakopmund, 35n37, 53, 53n150, 56, 56n172, 58–59, 61–62, 85, 119, 119n23, 122, 123n49, 128n84, 246n43, 250

Tecklenburg, Hans, 60n193, 207, 240n7, 245n36, 246–48, 274n47, 250n65
teleology, 4, 9, 11, 13, 131, 134
Tilly, Charles, 98
Trotha, Lothar von, 39, 41, 49, 61, 63, 33n12, 76–77, 78n12, 79, 81–82, 86–87, 89, 93, 94–103, 95n17, 98nn135–36, 98n145, 99n149, 100n154, 101n167, 102n168, 115–16, 122, 127, 127n72, 127nn79–80, 128–173, 128n82, 128n84, 129n87, 130n95, 131n102, 131n104, 131n108, 133n118, 134n136, 143n192, 145n205, 146n210, 148n219, 148n221, 149nn225–26, 152n246, 152n249, 153n252, 153n255, 158n290, 163nn318–19, 164n322, 164nn324–228, 164n331, 165nn332–335, 167n355, 170nn361–62, 173n381, 173n383, 206, 208, 221, 223–24, 227n210, 228n223, 240–43, 240n1, 240n2, 240n3, 241n9, 241n11, 242n17, 243n23, 243n25, 245n36, 246–48, 246nn42–43, 261–66
Trotha, Trutz von, 13–14, 17, 40n81, 43, 98

unconditional surrender, 59n186, 85–86, 88, 88n73, 93, 133, 152, 152n249, 167n355, 262

Veracini, Lorenzo, 34–35

violence from below, 18, 61, 200–2, 222, 249–50, 260

war
   great war, 142, 204–5, 210, 214
   race war, 8, 39, 94n112
   small war, 19, 129, 138, 141–43, 143n189, 168, 203–7, 211, 214, 221, 244–45, 249, 264
Waterberg, 56–57, 82, 82n39, 99–100, 116–118, 123–25, 144, 156, 159–60, 162, 164–65, 168, 127n79, 128n84, 131n103, 152n250, 164n322, 209, 219, 221–23, 225, 263
   Battle of Waterberg, 57n175, 93, 98n135, 99–100, 127, 128–135, 144–46, 145n205, 148–49, 150, 158, 160, 170n362, 202–3, 208, 221–22, 265
   battle plan, 116, 116nn6–7, 130n98, 143n192, 241

Weber, Max, 34, 44
(Kaiser) Wilhelm II, 3, 5, 6nn40–42, 38–39, 63, 85, 85n52, 89, 89n80, 94, 98n135, 101, 101n167, 119, 121, 121n36, 123n49, 128n82, 140–41, 150n231, 164–65, 165nn334–35, 172–73, 213, 242–43, 245, 240n1, 241n11, 265–66
Windhuk, 37n58, 53, 53n150, 59, 59n186, 76, 78–79, 78n12, 81, 86, 117–20, 122n47
Witbooi (|Khowesin), 2, 2n11, 15, 46, 53, 56, 77, 115n4, 123, 158, 212, 244–45, 245n32, 248
Witbooi, Hendrik, 53
Wyk, Hermanus van, 53

Zeller, Joachim, 240
Zeraua, Zacharias, 55, 120, 167n355
Zimmerer, Jürgen, 144n197, 240n7, 250n65
Zollmann, Jakob, 8n53

www.ingramcontent.com/pod-product-compliance
Lightning Source LLC
Chambersburg PA
CBHW071334080526
44587CB00017B/2831